FOUNDATIONS OF OBJECT RELATIONS FAMILY THERAPY

COMMENTARY

"As family therapists are beginning to rediscover the self in the system, they are also beginning to recognize the need for a psychology of depth to better understand the individuals in the families they work with. Families, we are beginning to realize, function on two levels. At one level, family interactions represent realistic and appropriate responses to developmental issues and tasks; at another level, the behavior of family members is determined by shared unconscious fantasies and unconscious assumptions, generated by instinctual needs and defensive requirements. Unfortunately, much of the writing about what goes on beneath the surface of family interactions is simplistic ('unmet needs,' 'emotional reactivity,' 'distorted perceptions') or impractically theoretical. Jill Savege Scharff's splendid book, *Foundations of Object Relations Family Therapy*, is a happy exception. Neither simplistic nor impractical, this extraordinarily useful book on object relations family therapy is a gold mine of useful information.

"The writing is uniformly excellent. The authors draw on their extensive psychoanalytic understanding of the individual to illuminate the shadowy underside of complex marital and family interactions. Family therapists who shy away from the arcane abstractions they find in psychoanalytic journals will be delighted to find explanations of the unconscious life of families that are pithy and concise without sacrificing depth or significance. Unconscious expectations are often as obscure as they are potent. Here, however, depth psychology is made very clear and then made eminently practical. Among the topics illuminated by the papers in this volume are:

- the interaction between family dynamics and borderline pathology
- the development of narcissism in the family context
- the inner and outer struggle of adolescents in the process of individuation
- the reverberations between boundary issues at various levels
- the psychodynamics of incest

"These chapters are so richly illustrated with fascinating clinical material that readers will get a disturbing look into the dramas of disturbed families. They will also be given a privileged look at what goes on inside the psychoanalytic consulting room when gifted clinicians combine and integrate individual family therapy."

—Michael P. Nichols, Ph.D.

FOUNDATIONS OF OBJECT RELATIONS FAMILY THERAPY

David Berkowitz, M.D.
Justin Frank, M.D.
Juliana Day Franz, M.D.
Irving Ryckoff, M.D.
David Scharff, M.D.

Jill Savege Scharff, M.D.
Edward Shapiro, M.D.
Roger Shapiro, M.D.
Robert Winer, M.D.
Lyman Wynne, M.D.

John Zinner, M.D.

Edited by

JILL SAVEGE SCHARFF, M.D.

JASON ARONSON INC.
Northvale, New Jersey
London

New Printing 1991

Library of Congress Cataloging-in-Publication Data

Foundations of object relations family therapy / edited by Jill Savege
    Scharff.
        p.   cm.
    Includes bibliographies and index.
    ISBN 0-87668-946-2
    1. Family psychotherapy.   2. Object relations (Psychoanalysis)
I. Scharff, Jill Savege.
    [DNLM: 1. Family Therapy -methods.   2. Object Attachment.   WM
430.5.F2 F771]
RC488.5.F68 1989
616.89' 156—dc19
DNLM/DLC   89-19472
for Library of Congress

Manufactured in the United States of America.
Jason Aronson Inc. offers books and cassettes.
For information and catalog write to
Jason Aronson Inc.
230 Livingston Street
Northvale, NJ 07647

*Dedicated to the faculty, students, and staff of
the Washington School of Psychiatry
Psychoanalytic Family Therapy Training Program*

Contents

PART II
ADOLESCENT DEVELOPMENT
IN THE FAMILY CONTEXT

PART III
SHARED UNCONSCIOUS FANTASY
AND PROJECTIVE IDENTIFICATION

PART IV
THE ANALYTIC,
GROUP-INTERPRETIVE APPROACH

PART VI
AN OBJECT RELATIONS APPROACH
TO SEXUALITY IN FAMILY LIFE

PART VII
OBJECT RELATIONS FAMILY THERAPY

Acknowledgments

I am grateful to Justin Frank, Irving Ryckoff, David Scharff, Roger Shapiro, Robert Winer, and John Zinner of the faculty of the Psychoanalytic Family Therapy Training Program of the Washington School of Psychiatry for contributing their papers to our collaborative venture. I want also to thank their junior and senior co-authors from earlier years—Juliana Day, David Berkowitz, Edward Shapiro, and Lyman Wynne—and their publishers for giving permission to reprint. Most of all, I appreciate the authors' support and the authority they have given me as editor, letting me make minor revisions to minimize repetition of shared ideas and to conform to contemporary American publishing house style.

On behalf of the authors, I want to thank all the families that have worked with us in therapy, in research, in clinical observation seminars, and in television studios. Their case material has been prepared for publication by eliminating or altering identifying details so that we can illustrate our concepts without betraying confidentiality. There are many families whose material has not been used in this volume, but we are just as grateful to them for contributing to the development of theory and technique.

Tricia Tomsko calmly and efficiently converted our various handwritten and typed drafts to a consistently readable print-out and also took care of my editorial correspondence. At Jason Aronson Inc., I had the pleasure of working with an attentive editor, Ms. Elena LePera, and with Ms. Anne Patota, who handled the promotional material. Jason Aronson has been wonderfully encouraging and patient while waiting for the book to come together.

Lastly I want to thank the people at home, including my housekeeper, Pearl Green, who managed the house while I was in the office. My husband, David, now preoccupied with program building and management since his appointment as Director of the Washington School of Psychiatry, has, in the meantime, generously yielded to me the privilege of writing. I am grateful to my children for rescinding their injunction against my having my nose in a book ever again, and I am glad and sometimes amazed that we still find time and energy to be a loving family.

Jill Savege Scharff, M.D.
Chevy Chase, Maryland, 1988

Preface

As family therapists, psychiatrists, and psychoanalysts, we have devoted ourselves to the application of general psychoanalytic principles to family therapy. Of course, there are differences among us, depending on our backgrounds and current interests. Yet our commitment to an in-depth approach that offers both individual and family psychodynamic understanding has united those of us who have been teaching family therapy together at the Washington School of Psychiatry. That postgraduate psychotherapy teaching institution, founded by trustees gathered around Harry Stack Sullivan in 1936, has always represented interpersonal psychiatry and the application of psychoanalysis to psychotherapy, the humanities, and the arts. Instrumental in the school's logical extension of analytic principles to family therapy was its dean of faculty and later director, Irving Ryckoff, and his volunteer faculty colleagues, Roger Shapiro and John Zinner, all of them analysts and clinical family research scientists.

They were soon joined by Robert Winer, Jill Scharff, David Scharff, and Justin Frank, clinicians whose work built upon the research of Ryckoff, Shapiro, and Zinner. Together we shared ideas and developed new concepts and directions. Our final common pathway is object relations family therapy.

The aim of this volume is to reveal the development of object relations family therapy from its roots in object relations theory and to indicate its current directions. There are three major phases to be represented:

- The early years of clinical research, before and after the family was selected as the unit for study;

- The development of the analytic, group-interpretive approach to families (R. Shapiro 1979), deriving from the application of Klein's concept of projective identification and Bion's theory of small-group process;

- The recent emergence of object relations family therapy (Scharff and Scharff 1987), deriving mainly from Fairbairn and Winnicott and from the group-interpretive approach.

These phases are covered more fully in the opening chapters and are evident in the chronological order of the papers in each section.

The main inspiration for this book are the writings of Roger Shapiro and John Zinner, based on research carried out with their collaborators at the National Institute of Mental Health in the 1960s. Shapiro and Zinner readily admit their nostalgia for those days of adequate congressional funding for research into the nature of disturbed human relationships. But they have always resisted publishing a retrospective collection of their research-group papers; they do not want their work petrified, as though it ceased back then. Of course, the detailed full-time research enjoyed at that time has not since been funded in the current biologically oriented climate. But their thinking still applies to and informs our technique, and it continues to generate new theory. So Shapiro and Zinner have generously agreed for the first time to the collection of their previously published articles and research-group papers. Papers by Frank, J. Scharff, D. Scharff, Winer, and Zinner, and Ryckoff's classic paper represent the work now being produced by the Psychoanalytic Family Therapy Training Program at the Washington School of Psychiatry.

As editor, I demonstrate how object relations family therapy developed from earlier thinking. In Part I, a history of the accumulated experience with and ideas about family dynamics is presented, followed by a review of basic object relations theory as we have variously applied it to develop object relations family therapy.

Part II, which traces the origins of the present approach based on research on adolescent development in the family context, begins with a chapter by Ryckoff. This chapter describes the families of more dysfunctional patients and gives a vivid clinical example of "role stereotyping," which we can now see is a clear antecedent of the concept of projective identification. Shapiro's chapter focuses mainly on individual adolescent development and its family determinants. The next chapter, also by Shapiro, introduces the concept of the family's "defensive delineation" of disturbed qualities seen to reside in its index patient.

In Part III, Shapiro and Zinner present their critical discovery of object relations theory, which took psychodynamic family theory to a new level of development. In the first chapter of Part III, they describe Bion's concept of unconscious fantasy and defense in small-group process and apply it to the family as a group. In the next chapter, they take Klein's (1946) concept of projective identification and Dick's (1967) use of this concept in marital interaction and extend these ideas to family dynamics. A later paper by the Shapiro research group shows how projective identification in family experience affects borderline personality development. The concept of projective identification is next applied to marital relationships by Zinner. Frank elaborates on Kleinian understanding of unconscious fantasy in marriage.

The family as a group is the focus of Part IV. Shapiro and Zinner develop their ideas about the adolescent and the family group. This work, culminating in the development of their method of treatment called "the analytic, group-interpretive approach to families," is summarized in Chapter 13 by Shapiro and further illustrated by Zinner's chapter on the effects of shared unconscious fantasy on family communication.

Part V, the integration of individual and family therapy, begins with chapters by Shapiro's group, who studied concurrent individual and family therapies. Included in this part is a chapter by Zinner on the technical arrangements for concurrent treatments. Another of Zinner's chapters covers the continuum from health to pathology as he describes the effects of parental self-esteem—expressed through parent–child interactions—on adolescent individuation. Together with Winer's description of the integration within the therapist of individual and family development models, these chapters on integration reflect a major current in our shared work.

Our interest in sexuality in family life was spurred by D. Scharff's (1982) development of an object relations theory of sexuality, published as *The Sexual Relationship: An Object Relations View of Sex and the Family*. Part VI deals with sexuality and family life. Winer contributes to his area of special interest, the incestuous family, in which the family's space for transitional relatedness is lacking and therefore cannot sustain the transitional phenomena that Winnicott described as necessary for separation and individuation. Zinner uses a case history to highlight aspects of adolescent sexuality. In conclusion, D. Scharff condenses and illustrates anew his object relations view of sexuality in family life.

Just as his book led to the later publication of *Object Relations Family Therapy* (1987), co-authored with J. S. Scharff, David Scharff's chapter offers a bridge to Part VII, in which a sample of object relations family therapy shows how it is distinguished from generic psychodynamic or group analytic family therapy. His contribution is concerned with the focus on transference and countertransference in object relations family therapy technique, while J. S. Scharff's chapter on play emphasizes the approach's sensitivity to the interlocking threads of family and child development. Thus the book concludes with the current direction of ideas in object relations family therapy.

The ideas put forth in this book are of interest both to individual therapists and family therapists who, like the authors, have had to struggle with the limitations of existing theory and the requirements of new treatment settings. Psychodynamically trained individual therapists uncomfortable with family systems methods have tried unsuccessfully to apply classical psychoanalytic theory and then have retreated from family work. Systems family therapists, on the other hand, are now looking for a way to include the individual again. Object relations family therapy offers both groups of therapists a theory that allows individual therapy to extend to family treatment and enables family therapy to reach greater depths and understanding.

In the last year, I have had the pleasure of discovering a proliferation of interest among family therapists who are studying or working with object relations theory, from private practice in New York to the Langley Porter in California, from Jewish Child and Family Services in Atlanta, Georgia, to Warm Springs Clinic in Boise, Idaho. Such widespread interest has encouraged the compilation of the present volume, which traces the foundations and present practice of object relations family therapy.

Jill Savege Scharff, M.D.

Contributors

David A. Berkowitz, M.D.
Associate Clinical Professor of Psychiatry, Tufts University School of Medicine. Faculty Member, Boston Psychoanalytic Society and Institute, Boston, MA.

Justin A. Frank, M.D.
Associate Clinical Professor of Psychiatry, George Washington University Medical Center. Faculty, Washington Psychoanalytic Institute. Faculty and Coordinator of Couples Section, Psychoanalytic Family Therapy Training Program, Washington School of Psychiatry, Washington, DC.

Juliana Day Franz, M.D.
Staff Psychiatrist, Montgomery County Government, Colesville Health Center, Silver Spring, MD.

Irving Ryckoff, M.D.
Faculty, Psychoanalytic Family Therapy Training Program, Washington School of Psychiatry. Medical Director, Meyer Treatment Center, Washington School of Psychiatry. Member Washington Psychoanalytic Society, Washington, DC.

David E. Scharff, M.D.

Director, Washington School of Psychiatry. Associate Clinical Professor of Psychiatry, Georgetown University. President, American Association of Sex Educators, Counselors, and Therapists. Faculty, Washington Psychoanalytic Institute. Faculty, Psychoanalytic Family Therapy Training Program, Washington School of Psychiatry. Associate Clinical Professor of Psychiatry, Uniformed Services University of the Health Sciences, Washington, DC.

Jill Savege Scharff, M.D.

Associate Clinical Professor of Psychiatry, Georgetown University. Washington Psychoanalytic Institute. Faculty and Coordinator of Child Section, Psychoanalytic Family Therapy Training Program, Washington School of Psychiatry, Washington, DC.

Edward Shapiro, M.A., M.D.

Associate Clinical Professor of Psychiatry, Harvard Medical School. Director, Adolescent and Family Treatment and Study Center, McLean Hospital. Faculty Member, Boston Psychoanalytic Institute. Board of Directors, A.K. Rice Institute and Boston Center for the Study of Groups and Social Systems, Boston, MA.

Roger L. Shapiro, M.D.

Clinical Professor of Psychiatry and Behavioral Sciences, George Washington University School of Medicine. Teaching Analyst, Washington Psychoanalytic Institute. Consultant, Adolescent and Family Treatment, Chestnut Lodge. Faculty, Psychoanalytic Family Therapy Training Program, Washington School of Psychiatry, Washington, DC.

Robert Winer, M.D.

Chair, Psychoanalytic Family Therapy Training Program, Washington School of Psychiatry. Chair, Psychoanalytic Psychotherapy Program, Washington Psychoanalytic Society. Faculty, Washington Psychoanalytic Institute, Washington, DC.

Lyman C. Wynne, M.D., Ph.D.

Professor of Psychiatry, University of Rochester School of Medicine and Dentistry, Rochester, NY. Member, American Psychoanalytic Association. Past President, Western New York Psychoanalytic Society.

John Zinner, M.D.

Clinical Professor of Psychiatry and Behavioral Sciences, George Washington University School of Medicine. Member, Washington Psychoanalytic Society. Faculty, Psychoanalytic Family Therapy Training Program, Washington School of Psychiatry, Washington, DC.

PART I

THE FOUNDATIONS
OF OBJECT RELATIONS
FAMILY THERAPY

1

The Development
of Object Relations
Family Therapy Ideas

JILL SAVEGE SCHARFF, M.D.

To understand the development of object relations family
therapy, a brand of psychodynamic family therapy based
on object relations theory, we have to go back three
decades—before Roger Shapiro and John Zinner's application of object relations theory to family therapy, and
long before they and Irving Ryckoff were associated with
the Washington School of Psychiatry.

In the 1950s and 1960s, American psychoanalysis was
dominated by ego psychology. It dealt with conflict
between internal structures and their defenses in the
individual psyche and therefore did not lend itself to
interpersonal situations. Object relations theory was flour-
ishing in Britain at that time, and was even diversified,
encompassing at least Kleinian and Fairbairnian schools
of thought. But strict adherence to ego psychology in
American psychiatric culture ensured that object relations

3

theory remained an ocean away for most mental health professionals. Later, the American psychoanalytic environment changed in response to the writing of Jacobsen (1954), Kohut (1971, 1977), and Kernberg (1975, 1976), so that now there is much more openness to diverse points of view. But when Ryckoff and Shapiro began their family research studies, they were restricted by the limitations of their training in ego psychology. Ryckoff broadened his vision through the hospital psychiatry of Stanton and Schwartz (1954) and the interpersonal psychiatry of Sullivan (1953), but Shapiro was still looking for a theory with more explanatory power in the area of family dynamics, but one that could still apply to individual depth psychology. Thus they struggled to integrate previous training in intrapsychic dynamics with the family process they observed. The papers reprinted in this book chronicle that struggle in the 1960s and its resolution by the 1970s. I have chosen to demonstrate this process because many of us have had similar integrative tasks to master. It is my hope that this book will convince the reader who is competent in individual psychotherapy that this skill can apply to family therapy.

Ryckoff had been working with chronic schizophrenic patients at Chestnut Lodge in the 1950s. Those were the days when the Lodge patients were independently wealthy people who came from out of town. Their families were not around, and so the family interactive patterns could not be observed directly. Ryckoff, who had read the fine study of the subculture of the hospital ward by Stanton and Schwartz (1954), confirmed that patients tended to recreate their family dynamics in the ward group and found that family interaction could thus be inferred.

In 1953, when the National Institute of Mental Health (NIMH) opened, Ryckoff jumped at the chance to move away from inference to direct observation by developing a research project on families of schizophrenics under the leadership of Robert Cohen. But the family was hardly the unit for study. Schizophrenic inpatients were seen in individual therapy, and each of their parents was seen individually. Further influenced by their analytic training, Ryckoff and Cohen agreed that the therapists should not communicate with one another. Laughing, Ryckoff today admits, "We were far away from the concept of family therapy. How the hell were we to coordinate the separate therapies? We hadn't figured it out. I guess we were going to do it at the end of the case or something." To the 1980's reader the answer is obvious. But in the mid-1950s, Ryckoff and Juliana Day, joined by Lyman Wynne, worked together in the analytic tradition for three years, quite successfully writing about families even before they hit on the idea of seeing the family as a unit of study. Then they saw the family as a whole, the index patient in individual therapy, and later the parents in couple therapy as well.

This fruitful collaboration led to the publication of a series of well-known papers, including the widely reprinted "Pseudomutuality in the Family Relations of Schizophrenics" (Wynne et al. 1958). Ryckoff's research is represented in this volume by "Maintenance of Role Stereotypes in Families of Schizophrenics," written before the family as a whole had been discovered as a unit for study (Ryckoff et al. 1959). The scientific search for contributants to mental illness had the unfortunate effect of appearing to blame the families for causing terrible suffering. Now the pendulum is swinging the other way, with the patient seen as the one who can confuse and fragment the family unless the family strength is recognized and supported (Hatfield 1987). Family researchers were studying family phenomena such as role stereotyping (Ryckoff et al. 1959), trading of dissociations (Wynne 1965), and delineation (R. Shapiro 1968). The emphasis of their research was on the family determinants of individual illness. At the time, including the family at all was a new step, but looking back we can see that in keeping with the tenets of ego psychology, they were pursuing the issue of identity and integrity of the individual, not yet of the family. Although it was not yet sophisticated enough to do so, the theory at that time was reaching toward describing a multiple determination of family difficulty arising in both the parents' and the children's generations. Such a description would not be possible until Shapiro and Zinner brought into play the concept of projective identification and described repressed unconscious object relations affecting both parents' and children's generations.

Like Ryckoff, Shapiro joined the staff at NIMH from his position at Chestnut Lodge, where he had been working with disturbed adolescents to try to determine the factors contributing to their faulty development. His research project and supporting treatment program for hospitalized adolescents began in 1959. There, well-trained, bright young clinical associates treated the individual adolescents while a gifted, clinical psychiatric social worker (Carmen Cabrera) saw the parents. Again, this was not a family research project at first. But the ideas of Murrary Bowen, who had just left NIMH, were still in the air. A more direct influence was that of Wynne, who had begun treating families of schizophrenics on another unit and attending the same clinical conferences. Wynne had to hospitalize one of his schizophrenic adolescents on Shapiro's adolescent unit and came to the ward to do the family treatment, which Shapiro observed.

Shapiro was also intrigued by Wynne and co-workers' (1958) concept of pseudomutuality, a property in families of schizophrenics whereby apparent calm barely conceals a series of tightly stereotyped roles. Shapiro began to wonder about the dynamics of the coercive stereotyping. Then he discovered on his unit that the social worker was bringing in to conferences very different views of the parents and the adolescent than those of the individual adolescent therapist. Shapiro surmised that parental views of the adolescent and adolescent views of the parents were dynamic distortions determined by

transferences (that is, distortions of relationships determined by early developmental experiences) and that these
distortions by each family member might account for
these phenomena. Then he thought of seeing the whole
family together. At first, family interviews were merely a
research tool, but Shapiro soon became convinced of their
therapeutic value.

Shapiro's research design was to record and review
transcripts of concurrent interviews of (1) the individual
adolescent with the individual therapist three times
weekly, (2) the parents with the social worker weekly,
and (3) the whole family with both therapists weekly.
From these various and not always congruent data bases,
Shapiro and colleagues were able to observe transference
distortions and to speculate about their role in determining illness patterns. Shapiro called these distortions
defensive delineations. Ronald D. Laing consulted with the
project and was enthusiastic about the concept of defensive delineation, likening it to his concept of attribution,
but he did not impress upon Shapiro the explanatory
power of object relations theory.

Shapiro acknowledges that Laing may well have
talked about object relations theory, but in the grip of the
ego psychology mind set, Shapiro would not have seen its
relevance. At any rate, he remained unaware of the
importance of the dynamics of projective identification
until he experienced them in a practical setting in two
group relations working conferences designed to demonstrate among the participants the group theory of Bion, a
Kleinian analyst who had applied Kleinian theory to
group process. The first, in 1964, was a Tavistock Conference in Leicester, England. The second was at Mount
Holyoke in 1965, the first A. K. Rice conference in the
United States, co-sponsored by the Washington School of
Psychiatry and Yale and led by Pierre Turquet and Ken
Rice, who later also consulted on group process to the
staff on Shapiro's unit. From the personal experience of
projective identifications (his own and others') in group

interaction—a learning process so intense that it cut through the bonds of previous theory—Shapiro began to appreciate the potential of Kleinian theory to illuminate interpersonal dynamics and brought that knowledge to family therapy.

About this time he was joined by John Zinner as his associate director. Having read more about Kleinian concepts, together they developed their framework for understanding defensive delineation by applying the Kleinian concept of projective identification. From observed transference distortions, they could now infer the inner object relations in the family. Their landmark work was presented at a meeting of the American Psychoanalytic Association in 1971 and gave rise to the twin papers "Family Organization and Adolescent Development" (R. Shapiro and Zinner 1971) and "Projective Identification as a Mode of Perception and Behaviour in Families of Adolescents" (Zinner and R. Shapiro 1972). When Zinner joined the project, concurrent couple therapy for the parents was added and generated material from which he wrote "Projective Identification in Marital Interaction" (1976). Clinical associates Edward Shapiro and David Berkowitz also contributed to the idea pool and were co-authors or senior authors of papers included in this book.

In the 1960s, Ryckoff and Wynne introduced a one-semester course in family dynamics at the Washington School of Psychiatry. Ryckoff then got the idea for a family therapy program with psychodynamically oriented live family interviews and necessarily eclectic didactic seminars reviewing the meager psychodynamic family therapy literature. In 1973, Ryckoff asked for help with teaching from R. Shapiro and Zinner, whose work he had known at NIMH and whose research papers were on his reading list. Now full-time academic clinicians at George Washington University (GW), they agreed to form a small volunteer psychodynamic family therapy faculty with him at the Washington School of Psychiatry; they were joined by Robert Winer, who had formerly been a clinical associate with Shapiro at NIMH.

They found other colleagues with compatible but different backgrounds in object relations theory. In 1975, they recruited me, Jill Savege (later Scharff), because I was working in family therapy with Shapiro and Zinner at GW and had trained close to the source of object relations theory in London at the Tavistock Clinic and in Edinburgh with John D. Sutherland, an expositor of Fairbairn. In 1976, Ryckoff handed over leadership to Winer, who expanded the group by adding David Scharff and Justin Frank, both of whom had studied object relations theory during a year of postgraduate training in the adolescent department of the Tavistock Clinic in London, a hotbed of Kleinian thinking and family therapy experimentation. Frank, D. Scharff, and J. Scharff had participated in the family therapy workshop there when Sally Box and Hyatt Williams were members contributing to the development of transference and countertransference interpretation in family therapy (Box et al. 1981, Williams 1981), while Shapiro and D. Scharff shared an interest in A. K. Rice group relations conferences. The Scharffs also brought child psychiatry experience, so the group became interested in families with younger children as well as adolescents.

In sharp contrast to the systems approaches that dominate family therapy, our approach has always been psychodynamic and, more recently, frankly psychoanalytic. Not that we ignore systems, we work with conscious and unconscious systems of relationships within individuals and families. This has been possible because our approach derives from object relations theory, an individual psychology developed from observation of relationships and one that therefore readily applies to marriages and families. Since object relations theory consists of the overlapping contributions of a number of theorists whose work we apply, there is room for variation among our approaches without loss of consistency. We found our different emphases, which will be apparent in the chapters that follow, stimulating rather than divisive. For instance, the work of Shapiro and Zinner, which referred at first to the theories of Kernberg and Jacobsen, later relied on Bion, Dicks, and Klein for development of the group-interpretive approach, while the Scharff's object relations family therapy approach derived mainly from Fairbairn (on whose work Dicks's application to marriage was largely based) and Winnicott, although also referring to Bion, Dicks, Klein, Shapiro, and Zinner.

Despite such theoretical differences, our ideas were unified into a coherent whole by our shared commitment to psychodynamic understanding of individual and family development, based on object relations theory. We built our clinical work on the foundation of concepts from the research of Ryckoff, Shapiro, and Zinner and further enriched them with ideas from our various backgrounds in Kleinian or Fairbairnian theory, in group or child psychotherapy or psychoanalysis. This cross-fertilization of ideas led to further development, from the group-interpretive approach to families to the present theory and practice of object relations family therapy.

2

Object Relations Theory and Its Application to Family Therapy

JILL SAVEGE SCHARFF, M.D.

Object relations family therapy uses nondirective listening and deeply personal communication with unconscious processes to achieve full understanding. When the family unconscious is personally experienced, rather than merely perceived consciously and intellectually, the resulting interpretation is likely to be more effective because the family will feel more thoroughly related to and understood. Thus we create an environment for tolerance of pain, ambiguity, and loss—a necessary condition for the development of insight. Unlike systems family therapists, we hold that insight is essential to change. Early in treatment, we analyze the family's resistance to being helped and our own resistances against involving ourselves in painful family experience. Continued work on resistance at each point of progress paves the way for further development and working through.

So far, these techniques clearly derive from Freud (1912). But to find a theory that lends itself to the interpersonal field we have had to move beyond Freud to the object relations theorists. Object relations theory was developed from the study of the experience of the early mother–infant relationship as it emerged in the transference in psychoanalysis. In keeping with this, object relations theory holds that the infant's primary need is for attachment to a caring person, whereas Freud viewed the infant as struggling to come to terms with instincts of libido and aggression aimed at acquiring gratification from the parent. In comparison to the more purely intrapsychic, drive-oriented Freudian theory, object relations theory offers us a way of conceptualizing the vagaries of the primary human relationship between infant and parent. The transferences resulting from this period persist as potential or actual distortions of the present relationships among family members. Thus object relations theory is an individual psychology that is apt in the family context and provides the basis for our object relations family therapy approach.

For the reader who is unfamiliar with object relations theory, here is a brief review of the major theorists and their contributions as applied to our theory of family functioning.

FAIRBAIRN

Unlike Freud, Fairbairn held that the infant is not motivated by instincts, but by the need for a relationship with the caretaker. Compared to the experience of uterine bliss, the infant's experience is now one of need and impending frustration because of its helpless dependency. After all, even a good empathic mother cannot meet all her infant's needs at every moment. To the extent that the organismic distress is intolerable, the infant deals with the psychic pain induced by the experience with the caretaker by introjecting the experience and repressing parts of it (Fairbairn 1952, 1954).

The external object is experienced in one of three ways:

1. as the ideal object that is just right, which leads to feelings of satisfaction,
2. as the rejecting object that frustrates needs, which leads to anger, or
3. as the exciting object that excites needs, which leads to longing.

The external object is now internalized in the ego. The ideal object remains in consciousness, but the rejecting and exciting objects are split off from it and repressed into unconsciousness.

The ego that related to the object is then also split by the relative trauma of life after birth into a conscious and two unconscious parts, each in relation to ideal, rejecting, and exciting internalized objects characterized by their respective affects. The resulting endopsychic situation (Fairbairn 1963) is now as follows:

1. a central ego, conscious, adaptable, satisfied with its ideal object,
2. a rejecting ego, unconscious, inflexible, frustrated by its rejecting object, or
3. an exciting ego, unconscious, inflexible, in a state of longing for a tempting but unsatisfying object.

This endopsychic situation of the infant in relation to mother is represented diagrammatically in Figure 2-1 on p. 14.

After myriad interactions with the external object, endopsychic structure forms according to this basic pattern, but with individual variation. To put it simply, the infant has a conscious, capable central ego that relates to others, adapts to its environment, thinks, feels, and

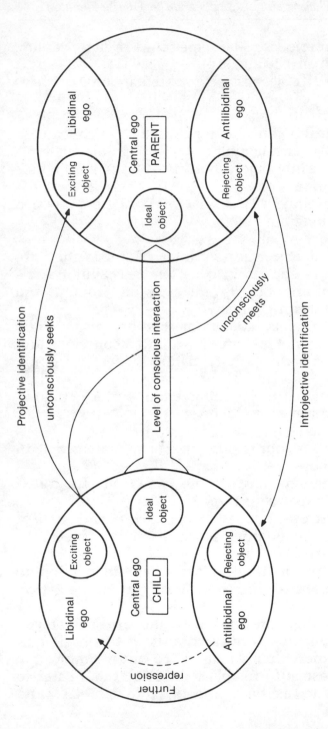

Figure 2-1. The mechanism here is the interaction of the child's projective and introjective identifications with the parent as the child meets frustration, unrequited yearning, or trauma. The diagram depicts the child longing to have his needs met and identifying with similar trends in the parent via projective identification. If he meets with rejection, he identifies with the frustration of the parent's own antilibidinal system via introjective identification. In an internal reaction to the frustration, the libidinal system is further repressed by the renewed force of the child's antilibidinal system.

learns from experience. This ego is capable of experiencing its main object and future objects as ideal. The more satisfied by its experience with its caretaker, the more the infant can develop this central ego. But it is always diminished to some extent by the need to repress painful experience. Thus in unconsciousness the infant has a rejecting ego in relation to its rejecting object and an exciting ego in relation to its need-exciting object. These two systems, being repressed, are not available to learn from experience (Sutherland 1963). With these unconscious parts of itself, the infant thus tends to perceive its main object and new objects as rejecting or exciting and by its behavior may actually evoke these qualities in its objects. The repressed systems cannot be modified until they return from repression. This happens in breakdown, in therapy, and during the psychological flux of developmental crises, such as pregnancy or marriage.

DICKS

Dicks (1967) was particularly interested in marriage. He subscribed to Fairbairn's view of individual psychic structure and was fascinated to note a certain correspondence regarding the conscious and unconscious parts of their personalities among marital partners that he had studied in parallel individual therapies. Whereas marital choice was based on compatibility at a conscious level, there was also an unconscious fit. Thus the repressed rejecting system of the wife might fit with a similarly rejecting system of the husband in a shared style of defending against neediness, or the rejecting ego of the wife might pair with the husband's already repressed exciting object and squash it into oblivion—a consequence both desired and hated, since the repressed objects always seek expression, however dangerous this may be. Alternatively, the wife may be experienced as the exciting object that the husband's ego longs to relate to and yet finds painfully elusive. Dicks showed that the individual spouses dealt with the inevitable frustrations of marriage (compared to the bliss of romance) in the ways Fairbairn had described for the infant, except that Dicks recognized that this was a mutual process, understandable by applying to it Klein's concept of projective identification.

KLEIN

Klein (1946) described projective identification as a primitive defensive process that enables the infant to cope in fantasy with the anxiety inherent in the early infant–mother relationship. Like Fairbairn, she was most concerned with this process from the individual infant's point of view. Unlike Fairbairn, she thought that infantile anxiety derived not from helpless dependency, but from the death instinct. Klein (1935, 1946) described two main developmental stages in the infant's mastery of anxiety, namely the paranoid-schizoid and the depressive positions. These remain within the adult personality as constellations of object relations that can be activated in anxiety-evoking situations.

THE PARANOID-SCHIZOID POSITION

To deflect the death instinct, which could otherwise hurt baby or mother, the infant *projects* the resulting aggressive part of itself into parts of its object—such as the mother's breast, face, or imagined penis—to protect itself from its destructive power. Projective identification occurs when the object is then perceived as having the characteristics of the projected part of the self (Segal 1964). The infant then perceives that part of its mother as aggressive. Williams (1981) pointed out that *projective identification* is a term that ought to refer to the result when the object receives the projection and then identifies with it. In other words, the projected part of the self actually evokes in the object feeling and behavior appropriate to a repressed part of the self.

Let us take the example of the breast, since it is the most commonly referred to part-object. The infant's ego has to deal with the imagined or somewhat real threat from the aggressively perceived breast. It does so by disarming the breast through *introjecting* its persecutory image. The ego then identifies with the introjected persecutor in the process of *introjective identification*.

At the same time, in the early months of life, under the influence of the life instinct, the infant perceives parts of its mother as ideally good. Then the infant feels secure, comforted, and loving toward a breast that seems endlessly wonderful. The infant also introjects this ideally good part-object and identifies with it. From this ideal, the infant splits off the bad—for instance, when the infant hates the source for disappearing or, envious of its power to satisfy, greedily tries to devour it. Thus the breast, standing for the experience with the mother, is split into quite separate wonderfully good and awfully bad part-objects, which nevertheless operate in relationship to each other, attacking and mollifying the ego, taking from, assaulting, and making primitive reparation to the object.

THE DEPRESSIVE POSITION

Gradually, as the infantile ego grows in cognitive development, the split cannot be maintained because differing impressions can now be recalled. The mother is perceived as a whole object, with both comforting and frustrating aspects, about whom the infant feels both love and hate. This capacity for ambivalence about the object is achieved by the age of approximately 8 months. The "good breast" at this stage is a more mature concept than the earlier "ideally good breast" object, which was good only because the bad was split off. The infant now realizes that this good breast is vulnerable when the infant is angry with it. The infant feels concern for its object, mourns its loss when it disappears, and feels guilt for having temporarily destroyed it. There is still the possibility of regression to more primitive operations of splitting and projection, or there may be manic flight from the depression. But in the normal course of development, the infant becomes able to tolerate its depression and guilt through its capacity for concern and mourning. Projective identification at this stage is used in the service of empathy and reparation rather than for self and object protection.

MUTUAL PROJECTIVE IDENTIFICATION IN MARRIAGE

Dicks (1967) was the first to note that in marriage one's self was the other's object, and thus projective identification was a mutual process. Zinner (1976), working with couples in marital therapy, elaborated on Dicks's finding. Looking back on it now, we find it obvious that the mother–infant relationship is also a mutual projective identification system. This is represented diagrammatically on p. 14 in Figure 2-1. The good mother receives the infant's projections without being compelled to identify with them. Thus she contains the infant's anxiety that led to the projections. At the same time, she also has some anxiety and projects into the baby as her object.

Similarly, in marriage, processes of introjective and projective identification characterize the unconscious communication between the spouses. Marriage, being a relationship of commitment, of physical intimacy, of meeting each other's needs, and of giving each other identity, is in these respects similar to the mother–infant relationship. It generates unconscious communication about primitive, repressed parts of each self that originated in the earliest relationships.

When a couple has children, unmetabolized ego and object aspects of the repressed object relationship system of the marriage are now projected into the various children in order to preserve the marriage and therefore the family. The child is then seen as the hated or longed for part of the self or spouse and resembles a hated or elusive part of a grandparent. Hate or uncomfortable longing is then felt inside the parent to or from the child, depending on whether it is the repressed ego or object that has been projected (Scharff and Scharff 1987).

WINNICOTT

Winnicott (1956) felt that the mother had to provide a good-enough experience so that the infant could be satisfied and could feel loved and understood. She could do this through her psychological state of "primary maternal preoccupation," her devotion to understanding and satisfying her infant's needs, her daily holding and handling of her baby, and through the rhythm of vocal and gaze conversations she has with her child. Mother and infant exist together in "a psychosomatic partnership" (1960), cuing each other, responding to and gradually confirming each other's trustworthiness and identity. This aspect of Winnicott's theory is particularly helpful in understanding the sexual relationship, as D. Scharff points out in Chapter 22.

When the relationship reaches a certain stage, the infant is ready for experience that is more separate from the mother. There is a gradual transition from staying engaged with her to relating to other things and people. A way station is provided by "the transitional object"—a stuffed animal or a favorite toy associated with, yet separate from, the mother. A less tangible form of this object might be a light in a window, a crack on a ceiling, a tune, or a smell (1951). These transitional phenomena and objects are enjoyed by the infant in the "transitional space" between mother and child. Both partners contribute to this space as one where they can relate creatively and playfully at a degree of distance that allows for exploration of self and otherness (1971). Thus the infant and mother playing in the gap between them relate as separate beings who can enjoy intimacy with a good balance between contact and personal autonomy and without invading each other's boundaries or regressing to earlier states of physical and psychological fusion. In Chapter 20, Winer applies this concept to families; he shows how incestuous families are unable to create and benefit from "a transitional space" within the family.

BION

Bion (1961) used the Kleinian concept of projective identification to help him understand the processes he observed in small groups. He viewed the small group as a work group with a task to do in relation to its leader. Quite often, he found, group processes impeded the group's work. Bion categorized three main types of basic assumption functions or subgroup formations crystallizing from three typical ways of defending against anxiety about the task in relation to the leader—namely, by helpless dependency on the leader, by fight against or flight from the leader, or by pairing with the leader or his representative to create a savior. These subgroups express the defensive behavior on behalf of the group. Bion hypothesized that they form as a result of the clustering of projection processes around those individuals with valences for receiving the projections. In Parts III and IV of this book, Shapiro and Zinner describe Bion's theory more fully and show how they applied it (R. Shapiro 1979, R. Shapiro and Zinner 1971).

SHAPIRO AND ZINNER

Like Bion's groups, families are small groups doing their work of facing a series of developmental challenges that raise anxiety. This anxiety is defended against by mutual projective identification processes that give rise to various subgroup formations. Shapiro and Zinner found that these defenses can be identified and that the underlying anxiety can eventually be named and faced in family therapy. One common defense is that of delineation of an individual as sick (R. Shapiro 1966, Zinner and R. Shapiro 1972). They hypothesized that this occurs by projection of bad, unwanted parts of the self into one unconsciously designated recipient in order to keep the family good. Shapiro and Zinner extended the work of Dicks and Bion to apply to families. They found that every present relationship within a family is subject to two-way transference distortion. Thus in every family there is a network of multiple projection processes that result in a family unconscious object relations set through which the family as a "single psychic entity" deals with others at its boundary (R. Shapiro and Zinner 1979, Zinner and R. Shapiro 1974). All relationships in the family develop within and contribute to the unconscious object relations. These are the focus of the group-interpretive approach to family therapy, elaborated upon by Shapiro (1979) in Part IV.

SCHARFF AND SCHARFF

Scharff and Scharff (1987), interested in interaction at the family boundary as the family enters treatment and relates to the therapist over time, focused less on the transference distortions within the family and more on the family's transference to the therapist. They noted that this transference takes two forms. First, the contextual transference occurs in relation to the therapist as the external object providing a holding environment in which focused, intimate exchanges can take place. Second, the focused transference results from experiencing the therapist as the external object for intense, unconscious, mutual projection of internal object relations. The Scharffs showed how the therapist could use countertransference extensively to understand the family's projection into the therapist of its unconscious object relations set expressed through expectations about the provision of the holding environment and the occurrence of focused, intimate exchanges. In addition, having worked with families of young children, they emphasized the developmental aspects of the group interpretive approach, expressed in practice through their use of play in family therapy. Described fully in their book *Object Relations Family Therapy* (1987), the Scharffs' approach is represented in this book by chapters on transference, countertransference, and play in family therapy.

PART II

ADOLESCENT DEVELOPMENT IN THE FAMILY CONTEXT

3

Maintenance of Stereotyped Roles in the Families of Schizophrenics

Irving Ryckoff, M.D.
Juliana Day, M.D.
Lyman C. Wynne, M.D., Ph.D.

Schizophrenia has been considered by those concerned with environmental factors to have etiological roots in various aspects of environmental pathology, including symbiotic mother–child relationships, trauma, and empathically communicated anxiety. Although this approach has been fruitful, it has seemed to us to emphasize selectively one or another single factor; we have felt that it would be helpful to begin to develop a larger frame of reference which would make possible the inclusion of the environment as a whole in our formulations. The family, comprising almost all of the child's environment, seems to be a natural object of study in an attempt to arrive at formulations based not on any one relationship or event but on dynamic elements that permeate all relationships and events in the child's life.

THE FAMILY AS A UNIT

Our approach, then, is based on the view of the family as an integrated unit, a social subsystem, the character of whose operations can be greatly illuminated but not defined only in terms of knowledge of the separate, individual family members. The reciprocal expectations of the family members, translated into role behavior, become organized into a conception of the family shared by the family members. This familial conception may become experienced as a force in its own right by the family members, and, in effect, may reflexly act upon the individuals to reaffirm and fix their roles. In this sense, there may develop a family identity that generates self-perpetuating forces and in pathological cases seriously constricts, or even entirely displaces, individual identity.

This paper is a product of a long-term study begun at the NIMH in 1954 on the nature of family relationships in mental illness. During the first phase of this program, the research plan called for intensive study of family units, with the hospitalized schizophrenic patient seen in intensive psychotherapy and the parents seen twice weekly on an outpatient basis. Data from other family members, friends, nursing staff, and the ward administrator were included in the reconstruction of the family patterns.[1] The prime object of this phase of the research was preliminary delineation of qualities and patterns of relationships in the families of schizophrenics, and the formulation of hypotheses regarding their effect on ego development and identity. A general statement of our hypotheses has been previously published (Wynne et al. 1958). The present paper will focus more especially upon the quality of *schizophrenic family*[2] role organization and role behavior in relation to the development of a sense of personal identity. Some of the relevant issues will be illustrated by clinical material from a particular family.

Our clinical observations of the families of schizophrenics[3] have led us to hypothesize that a family pattern of seemingly significant occurrence includes the following main elements:

1. Family roles are grossly condensed and stereotyped; complex expectations and experience are reduced to a series of simplified formulas.

2. There is a rigid organization to the family's conception of itself, from which no deviation is permitted, even though in some families exchange of roles is possible.

3. Each family member collaborates in enforcing adherence to the roles defined by the shared conception of the family.

4. Any attempt to modify or amplify these rigidly defined roles has to contend with the powerful, repressive forces against drives, such as aggression, in the family members.

These factors lead to the establishment of a family legend or myth, in which each family member makes an anxious investment. In ways we will specify, the investment in the maintenance of a family concept of itself, a family myth, can seriously interfere with the individual's identity, and can lead in adolescence to an "identity crisis," to use Erikson's (1956) term, of psychotic proportions.

FAMILY ROLES AND IDENTITY FORMATION

The crucial area, in which the success or failure of the attempted achievement of identity lies, is the relation of the individual to the role. The taking of a variety of roles is a form of experimental learning of what can or cannot be done, of what does or does not fit with others' expectations. Roles provide individuals with techniques of getting along, of a continuing consciousness of themselves in relation to others, of the position they occupy in the social situation; but, somewhat paradoxically, the ultimate value of these achievements depends on a movement that carries individuals beyond role learning. This movement is the separation of the individual from his roles, the capacity to gain a critical distance—the separation of the observing ego from roles—which makes possible the selection, rejection, and modification of roles, and their integration into a unique identity. This selective, critical integration of roles involves the qualities of flexibility, resourcefulness, and imagination, which make possible the adaptation along original lines of what has been learned to the new situation. Its opposite, the mechanical capacity to take certain roles, is most apparent in the as-if quality of schizophrenics who have made a social recovery.

The family, then, must provide a context that is larger than that established in the learning of particular roles, a context in which the individual can imaginatively and actually have a distinct identity and feel safe with this identity. This includes not the mere tolerance of not fitting into the expected roles completely and automatically, but a positive valuation of such noncomplementarity as an evidence of individuation. Parents, as objects of identification, must also demonstrate the capacity to alter and rework their roles in original ways that suit them. The context under discussion permits the individual to consider all possibilities within himself, so that his resultant conformity to societal expectations becomes a matter of choice, and not as captive to his failure to imagine alternatives.

The point at issue is the distinction between roles and identity. Erikson (1956), in discussing identifications in an analogous way, says: "Identity formation, finally, begins where the usefulness of identification ends. It arises from the selective repudiation and mutual assimilation of childhood identifications, and their absorption in a new configuration." He goes on to point out that identifications, being made only with aspects of people, do not, when added together, result in a functioning personality. Similarly, the sum of roles does not yield a functioning personality. It is precisely this big jump, from roles and identifications to identity, that the schizophrenic fails to make. The breakdown at adolescence, when childhood identifications and roles are no longer the only materials needed to live, is the stage at which inner drives and societal expectations require an original being who brings a unique self to relationships in work, sex, and so on.

It should be added that there is an element of the future in the matter of identity; that is, identity brings with it a sense of what one is becoming, as well as what one is. Buber (1957) points out that it is possible to imagine another—that is, understand his identity—only if it is possible to imagine what he is becoming. Erikson states:

> From a genetic point of view, then, the process of identity formation emerges as an evolving configuration—a configuration which is gradually established by successive ego syntheses and resyntheses, throughout childhood; it is a configuration gradually integrating constitutional givens, idiosyncratic libidinal needs, favored capacities, significant identifications, effective defenses, successful sublimations, and consistent roles. [1956, p. 71]

This future-directed aspect of identity marks identity as a process, and not as a static achievement. The fixed, "finished" quality of schizophrenics seems related to this failure of the forward-directed process in identity.

It is our impression that in his prepsychotic living the potential schizophrenic, because of his participation in intrafamily operations,[4] can neither articulate his emerging personal identity with nor differentiate it from the roles available to him in the shared ideology of family life. In addition, new roles and role modification in the future do not seem possible within the framework of this familial ideology. The shared mechanisms or operations by which such a familial ideology is enforced and role modification is blocked have been described in a previous paper (Wynne et al. 1958). In any event, the result is a diffusion and confusion of experience and identity that can no longer be matched with the only varieties of role behavior that seem available.

It should be noted in passing, if it is not obvious, that both "native" individual characteristics[5] and the family characteristics may contribute to such difficulty. When the family role structure and ideology is highly amorphous, vague, or inconsistent, and yet all-encompassing, it is relatively easy to see how such a setting for psychological development may contribute to identity diffusion. When the family roles are unusually distinct, however, the implications for identity development are less manifest. Therefore, we wish to exemplify such a family ideology and structure to note how stereotyped family roles may provide a setting for an identity crisis of the kind found in acute schizophrenic episodes.

In the F. family there was remarkably complete agreement about the character of each member and about the nature of his relationships with the rest of the family. The family consisted of two parents, in their 40s, and two daughters—Jean, who was 20, and Nancy, aged 17, the hospitalized one. Some quotations from interviews may convey the flavor of this striking unanimity.

Jean, describing herself and her sister, stated: "We're so entirely different. Nancy was always the quiet one, and I was always the heller, always in trouble. . . . I was a great chore to my family . . . . I'm a lot like my father. I have a very quick temper. I was always my father's favorite, and he never really paid much attention to Nancy. . . . Nancy was always the one who had the good marks. I never had good marks in school. I was always very boy-crazy. I used to do horrid things. I used to sneak out about midnight, open the garage door, and just take the car and be out until 3:00 in the morning. I don't think anything like that would ever dawn on Nancy. . . . Nancy was always a good girl. She really was. Nobody ever had any trouble with her. She never told a lie. I was getting to be a pathological liar. Every word that came out of my mouth was a lie."

The father, in speaking of this elder daughter, said: "She was the one who gave us the trouble. She had a disposition much like mine. Volatile . . . Jean was a very determined person. I would spank her with feeling. Never so with Nancy. Nancy's conduct was always beyond reproach. At least she was smart enough to know when to stop or cover up. . . . She was so well poised, so apparently placid, although very determined."

The mother said: "Jean was always difficult. You could talk Nancy into anything. Jean and her father are alike. They blow their tops. Nancy and I keep things quiet. Jean and her father were at one another's throats in two seconds. They understand each other. Jean defies him. Nancy never got into conflict with him and never required a reprimand."

Nancy, the one who was hospitalized, said: "Daddy and Jean are alike in their tempers, and mother and I. Mother and I have greater poise, and we say what we mean. Daddy and Jean have identical personalities. When they get angry, they say things that make no sense. They have no poise."

Both these girls struggled to gain a clearer view of their behavior, which troubled them, but the sources of which were out of their awareness and beyond their capacity to evaluate. Jean's rebellious adolescent behavior was extreme, to the point of endangering her future. She was frightened, felt she did not know what drove her on, and was relieved when her family happened to move to another city, thus removing her from the disturbing situation. She had been going with a boy who on occasion beat her and threatened her with a gun. She said: "I was getting more mixed up, was getting to be a pathological liar. I hope my children never have to go through that." This behavior reached its height near the end of high school, when she, without premeditation, decided to go to nursing school; this decision meant a separation from her family. She did surprisingly well, and rather quickly stopped the delinquent behavior. Toward the end of her nursing training, she met, and subsequently married, a quiet, serious young man who runs a hardware store. She has since become a settled young housewife and mother, with no outward sign of the previous behavior. She regards it as a serious crisis through which she safely passed, saying, with relief, "I survived," thus indicating the vital nature of this struggle to alter her legendary role in her family.

Nancy, at 17, had a psychotic episode, the onset of which was characterized by difficulty in concentrating, feeling lost, and not knowing what to do. She was completing her last year of high school, at a boarding school. By this time Jean was getting ready to graduate from nursing school, was engaged, and had completely stopped the behavior that had so worried the mother particularly. The onset occurred when the mother was away to visit Jean for several weeks. Here is her description, a year later, of her complete diffusion of identity during this psychotic crisis, and of her agonizing attempts to find new roles out of which her identity might be reintegrated.

When it all began, it was like, well, it was like losing everything and beginning all over, starting right from scratch, trying everything out. I felt that everything I had ever done was wrong. So then I tried to throw out everything I ever felt or did before to do the exact opposite. That didn't work, and just constantly pushing things away and starting again. And when I'd get on the wrong track and it wouldn't work, I'd feel worse than not trying at all, and try something else.

After the affair was mainly when I felt the very worst. I didn't want to see another boy, to be with people, to go to another party. I wouldn't wear lipstick; I wouldn't wash my hair; I didn't care how I looked, which was unlike me.

That went along for awhile. It didn't work. I still felt terrible;

so I threw all that away and then I threw all my studies away, put my lipstick back on, washed my hair again, started smoking again and went overboard; went to more parties, was too gay, and too familiar with people.

Then that fell through, that wasn't what I wanted, either. Then I went into a slump. I didn't know what I wanted; I didn't know what to do; I didn't know where to start, and it got so that even getting up in the morning and getting dressed was a very big problem. I'd just do what anyone would tell me, just do what anyone said; I didn't trust my own judgment. I felt that if I did what everyone told me I would be all right, that that was my answer.

Then I was going to be defiant and stand on my own two feet and knock everyone away. I was going to do it all by myself. So then I was outspoken, demanding. Then that didn't work either.

I'd go from one extreme to another, back and forth. Then I thought that all that was worth living for was to sit down and eat a meal. Then all that was worth living for was to work, just working myself to death. Then all that was worth doing was being nice and sweet and having nothing in mind, being very indifferent toward everything; all that was important was that I got out of the hospital and went along with everything, and was a good girl and was nice to people and helped around the house.

Nancy became increasingly frightened and confused during these weeks. She reported some of this to her father, including her concern about her sexual experimentation, and her father minimized this as nothing to worry about. She had some manic periods, and finally became extremely excited, delusional, and assaultive. On being hospitalized, she continued to be violently hostile, especially toward her parents, and ran away from one hospital. Her family felt she was not the same person at all.[6]

The amazement of the family at the breakdown of the accepted role arrangements in the family was evident in the reactions of the parents, Jean, other relatives, and Nancy herself.

Jean says: "I can remember when Nancy was in the first hospital, and she lost her temper about something, and she was saying,

'Why do I have to stay here?' and my mother said; 'Now Nancy, stop hollering. You don't have to holler.' And I remember she turned around to me and said, 'I don't belong here. Jean and Daddy belong here. They're the ones that do all the hollering.' She said: 'If anybody hollers, if that's what you're here for, hollering, then Jean and Daddy belong here.' And I can remember thinking, 'Oh Lord! How right she is!,' because my father and I used to have the worst battles."

She points out, in effect, that Daddy and Jean, behaving this way all the time, are regarded as normal, while she gets put into the hospital because she has changed from her usual behavior. It is the *change* in roles that has led to her being treated as sick. The universal response was one of disbelief, accompanied by a remark along the lines of "Oh no! Not Nancy! I could understand this happening to Jean, but not to Nancy!" This was, of course, as much an expression of their disbelief of Jean's conformity as it was of Nancy's rebellion, and this incredulity is a measure of the rigidity in the view commonly held about the girls.

Both the content of the roles ascribed to various individuals and their rigid, stereotyped form are psychodynamically determined. Let us examine some of the data regarding the parents, which throw some light on at least the major determinants of the role pattern in the family. The mother had been rebellious toward her parents until early adolescence, at which time she changed radically and developed a guilty anxiety about the effect on the parents of defiance from her or her siblings. Earlier she can recall being beaten by father and thinking, "No one is going to make me do what I don't want to—I will not give in, no matter how he beats me." She never cried when beaten. Her siblings were extremely rebellious; her brother was jailed for smashing up cars and driving recklessly, and was expelled from several schools. Her sister consistently lied to the parents, climaxing this by concealing from her parents that she was failing in high school, and leading them to believe, by altering records and destroying letters sent by the school, that she was going to graduate. Not until graduation night, with the family seated in the auditorium, did she reveal the situation.

After her own reformation, Mrs. F. (the mother of our patient, Nancy) observed her brothers' and sisters' behavior with amazement and envy. Her frequent thought was: "How do they get away with it?" She became increasingly "satisfied" with what she had, and very proud of this capacity to be satisfied, so that when she and her sisters bought similar items of clothing, she would be contented but they would seem dissatisfied and wish they had gotten something else. She feels that her sisters, and now her husband, envy her capacity to be satisfied. Along with this she developed the ability to "play it safe" in her relationships, by maintaining a distance, by "not getting too involved" with others. She feels generally that she can elevate herself above what is happening around her and keep herself apart from it.

Mr. F. had been an undisciplined, overindulged youngster, never having to account to an authority, whose resulting anxiety took the form of uncertainty, feeling vaguely dissatisfied with what he was doing, and wanting to change careers frequently. His defenses have taken the form of being intensely "practical," getting things done, and ruling out subjective considerations. In the familial conception, he is notorious for his impatience, irritability, and temper outbursts, although it is striking that his work calls for a high degree of diplomacy and tact.

In both parents, then, we find resources for the roles subsequently assumed by the children. The mother's hostility and rebelliousness is represented but is unconsciously valued; the father's inability to conform to authority and his infantile omnipotence have been similarly repressed, but with inconsistency and frequent breakthroughs. Jean became the representative of these drives toward rebellion and toward infantile indulgence of whims regardless of consequences. Nancy's role seemed fashioned out of what the parents more consciously valued—quiet conformity, being satisfied, compliance. There is much striking evidence of the parents' reenforcement of these roles by their failure to become aware of the destructive connotations in the restricted development of their daughters. The father, for example, never felt that Jean's behavior was a matter of serious concern and felt that she would be all right if left alone. He saw no need for concern about her escapades, although the girl herself was badly frightened. The mother made continual but ineffectual efforts to stop the delinquent behavior. Neither parent had any concern about Nancy's extreme compliance and docility, although she did poorly in the first few grades in school, was left back twice, and was daydreaming a great deal, according to teachers.

An inevitable corollary to the rigid maintenance of stereotyped roles is the violence that must accompany any change. In this instance a psychotic episode, a period of turmoil and crisis, and, it should be added, periods of depression in the parents accompanied the change within the family and the achievement of a new equilibrium. It is our feeling that the upheaval within the family is not in itself therapeutic, since it may lead to an exchange of roles but not necessarily a greater integration of those roles within the individual. In this family, for example, Jean has successfully shifted from the role of self-destructive rebellion and is now married, "settled down," and outwardly easygoing and jovial. She is still anxious, has occasional marked outbursts of temper at her children, and suffers from persistent hypertension. She identified herself with a maternal aunt who was also rebellious when younger and who died of hypertension recently. Nancy, too, seemingly made a good recovery from the psychotic episode and is now happily married, but has tended to overemphasize her new-found assertiveness, which appeared to contain in it a denial of anxiety. In other families, the new equilibrium has been attended by a greater distance among the family members and a less intense involvement with one another.

Summary

In presenting an approach to the family as a unit, we have attempted to describe schizophrenic family[2] dynamics in terms of role patterns and to formulate some implications for identity development. In the clinical material cited, we have described one particular role pattern, in which rigid, oversimplified, and stereotyped roles constricted identity development and contributed to serious crises, including psychosis. We have further tried to trace some of the dynamic, unconscious determinants of those roles.

NOTES

To orient the reader in the 1980s to this article from the 1950s, co-author Wynne has provided the following footnotes:

[1] The concepts in the case material reported in this paper were derived from the earliest phase of the family research program at NIMH, from 1954 to 1957, prior to the use of *conjoint* family therapy. That is, the data were derived from interviews with the individual patient and the parents; sometimes the parents were seen together, but the whole family did not meet together. Thus, the material represents retrospective reconstructions of the family patterns rather than direct observations of their interaction together.

[2] The term *schizophrenic family*, both here and in the "Summary" section of the paper, was used in a shorthand way and was never intended to mean that all the family members were regarded as schizophrenic. The phrase *families of schizophrenics*, as used in the next paragraph, is more precise.

[3] The reader of the 1980s should be aware that in the 1950s, clinical observations were commonly reported without giving data about the number of patients included in the

sample. When the material in this paper was formulated in 1957, about six families were seen intensively, with others seen more briefly and incompletely. It is important to recognize, as stated in the text, that the intent of this paper was to present hypotheses rather than definitive research conclusions. It is noteworthy that the hypotheses under consideration include nothing that would suggest that these ideas would be exlusive to the families of schizophrenics or specific for such families. Rather, the intent was to present observations that had been made in certain selected families in which a member had been diagnosed as schizophrenic by the criteria used in the 1950s. Many later observations have suggested that the family pattern in which roles are stereotyped and inflexible is highly interesting and important for family theory and family therapy, whether or not these phenomena occur with any special frequency in the families of schizophrenics.

[4] The clause "because of his participation in intrafamily operations" suggests an etiologic or causative effect of the intrafamilial operations leading to schizophrenia. At the time of this report, there were no prospective, direct observations of family relationships in the prepsychotic phase. Prospective, longitudinal observations of children and adolescents at risk for later schizophrenia were begun more than a decade after the publication of this paper. Thus the statement here suggesting an etiologic interpretation must be regarded strictly as a working hypothesis,, not as an established finding either then or now.

[5] The recognition here of the potential contribution of "native" individual characteristics clearly indicates that even at this early period, the authors accepted the concept of *joint* effects of biological and environmental contributions to these serious psychiatric difficulties.

[6] According to DSM-III (1980) criteria, this patient probably would not now be diagnosed as schizophrenic, but more likely as bipolar psychotic. Psychotic identity diffusion, of course, is no longer a basis for a diagnosis of schizophrenia, and the description of the patient's "manic periods" and

"extremely excited delusional and assaultive behavior" is not at all distinctive for schizophrenia. With more diagnostic detail available, it is conceivable that a diagnosis of schizophreniform disorder or schizoaffective disorder could be considered, but the data presented in the paper do not suggest these diagnoses. Certainly, the course of illness described in the paper is inconsistent with even a subchronic form of schizophrenia. The patient is described as having a personality of "extreme compliance and docility," which could have contributed to her vulnerability to a psychotic breakdown, but this is not highly predictive of a characteristic schizophrenic illness. The observations of family dynamics still are noteworthy, regardless of the diagnosis of the hospitalized daughter.

4

Identity and Ego Autonomy in Adolescence

ROGER L. SHAPIRO, M.D.

Maturation in the ego and the id at puberty leads to developments in the adolescent personality designated by Erikson (1950, 1956, 1962) as the crisis of identity. The core of Erikson's discussion of identity is a specification of the psychosocial character of identity formation. He describes the relation of self-definition to social definition as fundamental to the identity of the individual in every psychosocial phase. In Erikson's view, it is in adolescence that identity formation becomes an ascendant task of the ego, because of the characteristics of the maturation in the ego and in the drives in this phase.

EGO AUTONOMY

Current theories (Hartmann 1939, 1950, Jacobson 1964, Rapaport 1958) regarding autonomous ego development are highly relevant to the personality theory of adolescence. Descriptively, adolescence is characterized by striking alterations of patterns of dependency characteristic of childhood, with the achievement in adolescence of a new degree of relatively independent behavior. Autonomy concepts of ego psychology concern aspects of ego development and functioning that may be considered to have a relative independence from the control of forces outside of the ego—that is, the forces of the external environment and the forces of the drives. One autonomy concept is that of independence of development and the other a concept of independence of function.

Adolescence has for years been characterized in terms of the drive development of puberty (A. Freud 1936, S. Freud 1905). From the side of the ego there has been less agreement about what occurs in adolescent development. I have previously proposed the hypothesis that a primary autonomous development in the cognitive ego functions occurs in early adolescence (R. Shapiro 1963). I would postulate that this is one basis for the increase in the relative autonomy of the ego characteristic of this phase. This has not been generally assumed in psychoanalytic personality theory. It has usually been assumed that the developments in the functions of the ego seen in adolescence were secondary to, dependent upon, and in response to the drive development of puberty (A. Freud 1936, 1958), or were due to an increase for unspecified reasons in the degree of secondary autonomy of the ego or superego (Jacobson 1964). Interesting evidence in favor of the hypothesis that a primarily autonomous development in the cognitive ego functions occurs at puberty exists in the studies of characteristics of adolescent thinking reported by Inhelder and Piaget (1958). These authors have described a consistent change in the ability to conceptualize and to generalize between ages 11 and 14, with a progression from characteristic concrete operations in the thinking of the child to new characteristics of abstract thought in the adolescent. A new capacity for hypothesis formation develops, with the use of hypothetico-deductive reasoning and experimental proof. The consistency of this finding in early adolescence suggests an extension of Hartmann's (1939) assumptions about autonomous ego development in childhood to the period of early adolescence, to account for the maturational events of this phase. Intellectualization as a mechanism of defense in adolescence would then be an example of an autonomous ego capacity being drawn into conflict and used as a defense.

In his paper "The Theory of Ego Autonomy," Rapaport (1958) states that the ego's relative autonomy from the id is guaranteed by ego apparatuses of primary and secondary autonomy. Following Hartmann, he considers the apparatuses of primary autonomy to be derived from evolutionary givens in the organism, while the apparatuses of secondary autonomy are not innate, but represent structure formation determined by drives and experience. He also points to Erikson's (1950) formulation that ego development, though co-determined by drives and environmental stimulus nutriment, follows a lawful sequence of its own. This facet of ego autonomy—that is, its maturational course—is, according to Rapaport, crucial. He states:

> If ego development were not autonomous, only secondary ego autonomy (derived either from drives or from environmental influences or from ad hoc combinations of the two) would be conceivable. Autonomous ego development (its sequence and regulative principles) is a primary guarantee of ego autonomy: it links the apparatus of secondary autonomy to those of primary autonomy and regulates both the environmental and drive contributions to ego structure formation. [pp. 27–28]

The cognitive development described by Inhelder and Piaget is further evidence of autonomous ego development in striking personality growth in adolescence. This has been conceptualized in various ways by different investigators, with Erikson (1956) emphasizing psychosocial considerations in his discussion of identity formation; Jacobson (1964), the remodeling of psychic structure in adolescence in terms of an increased secondary autonomy of the ego and superego; and Blos (1962), integrative and synthetic ego functions in the consolidation of the sense of self.

The origins of the identity of individuals in every psychosocial phase derive from the relation of their self-definitions to social definitions of them. Thus, the essential experience from which adolescent ego identity grows is the concept of the adolescent implicit in the behavior of meaningful others toward him and his integration of this with a changing concept of himself. The process of self-definition is an activity of the ego, as is the comprehension of social definitions of the self. In adolescence, the new ego capacities for abstract thinking allow these processes of definition to reach a new level of generalization, complexity, and independence. Ego identity, furthermore, is a particular and selective integration of experience defining the self. Identity formation can consequently be seen to be dependent upon an enhanced autonomy of the adolescent ego, which is essential in order to accomplish a new synthesis of social definitions of the self. Identity diffusion can be conceptualized as a consequence of failure of this integrative process in the ego and a failure in the achievement of an effective relative autonomy of the ego in the adolescent. Clarifying the determinants of ego autonomy in adolescence will consequently contribute to an understanding of identity diffusion.

THE RELEVANCE OF FAMILY EXPERIENCE

The manifestations of autonomous maturation of the ego are co-determined by the reality experience, which fosters the new capacities. Through experience, ego potentials that mature autonomously are supported or inhibited, are patterned, and are molded in particular ways. A central locus determining ego formation is experience within the family. In our study of families of disturbed adolescents, we developed a method that isolates aspects of the parent–adolescent relationship in order to assess the relevance of the family experience to the outcome of impaired ego autonomy in the adolescent. We attempt to define characteristic parental behavior toward the adolescent and to infer its relevance for adolescent disturbance. Our data consist of regular observations of the family group in interaction and psychological assessments of the parents and the adolescent through research interviews, psychological tests, and behavior in psychotherapy.

We have studied a series of 30 late adolescents (between the ages of 17 and 19) and their families. These are cases in which the adolescents have had a severe emotional disturbance during the first prolonged separation from their families, requiring them to withdraw from college. The adolescents have had a variety of diagnoses: acute psychoses, borderline states, severe symptom neuroses, and character disorders of the acting-out or inhibited varieties. In all these cases we have combined individual two- or three-hour-per-week psychotherapy of the adolescent and weekly sessions with the parents as a marital couple, with weekly family therapy. We are able to make a series of precise observations from which inferences can be made about the specific intrapsychic organization that is expressed in particular behaviors within a family group. We also are able to observe the consequences of these behaviors.

Our observations of the family make available a range of data relevant to the broad area of identification processes. We are interested in specifying the experiences that determine the similarities between adolescent and parent. Identification processes represent broad areas of learning in the context of those significant object relationships of childhood and adolescence that have crucial importance in personality development. The learning may be an imitative behavior in which the child or adolescent observes the thinking or the action of a parent (or other significant person) in innumerable specific situations and through this learns to organize experience as the parent does. The appearance of identification may be more complex than this, however; parents and other significant persons may actively impose their view of the world and, more specifically, their view of the child or adolescent upon him. We believe that these interactions represent a class of behavior relevant to the broader area of identification processes. In these interactions, the adolescent's view of himself and of what is possible in a given situation may be limited in a specific way by the parents' views of him and of the situation. This may be one basis of establishing in the adolescent over time a particular view of himself with a systematic relationship to the parents' view of him. It may also lead to the appearance of similarity between adolescent and parent in specific areas of functioning, which might lead to an inference of identification.

FAMILY DELINEATION OF THE INDIVIDUAL

A central hypothesis of our study has been that there is a significant relationship between parental delineation of the adolescent and adolescent identity formation, and that in families in which there is serious psychological disturbance in the adolescent there will be evidence of striking constraints, distortions, inconsistencies, and contradictions in parental delineation of the adolescent. More specifically, in families in which there is significant impairment of ego autonomy in the adolescent, parental delineation will be detrimental to the development of autonomous behavior in the adolescent. By *delineation*, we mean the view or image one person has of the other person as it is revealed explicitly or implicitly in the behavior of the one person with the other person. In the language of ego psychology, it is behavior that contains the expression of an object representation and the ego organization mobilized in relation to this object representation and behavior with an object.

A highly important subgroup of delineations consists of those which we call defensive delineations. When behavior of an individual with an object contains evidence of distortion of the object related to the individual's defensive organization, then defensive delineation exists. The concept of defensive delineation thus represents an integration of two structural concepts in ego psychology. It includes behavioral referents of the concepts of object representation and defensive organization. Defensive delineation is a conceptualization of those situations in which defense alters the behavioral referents of object representation. It is a response to behavior of the other person that stimulates anxiety in the one person and gives rise to defensive operations that are revealed in the nature and style of his delineation of the other person.

Examination of examples of family interaction allows specific discussion of the proposition that in families in which adolescent ego autonomy is impaired, parental delineation will be detrimental to the development of autonomous behavior in the adolescent. These examples come from observations of content and style of parental delineation, in families in which the identity problem of the adolescent is a manifestation of impairment of ego autonomy. The content of delineations in many of these families, in excerpts in which discussion centers upon issues of adolescent independence, communicates a view of the adolescent that challenges his right and his ability to be independent. In these families, the parents delineate the adolescent as subject to their control and evaluation and as incapable of caring properly for himself. Their delineation of the adolescent suggests that he has not only internalized his parents' wishes but also must be controlled by them. We postulate a relationship between these parental delineations and the fact that the identity crisis of the adolescent himself is frequently manifested in great anxiety over his capacity to exist separately from his parents. In the adolescents in our series, we find evidence of profound doubt about their own ability to function independently. This is an aspect of their disturbance in identity that appears to reflect characteristic parental delineation of them. This problem in identity is generalized in their view of themselves as highly vulnerable to the control of others. Here clinical pictures of defective ego autonomy, specifically of an impairment in the ego's autonomy from objects in reality, are found in families in which the content of parental delineation of the adolescent does not contain within it the potential for the adolescent to become autonomous. Family experience thus does not reinforce the maturing cognitive capacities of the adolescent's ego to promote independent development. On the contrary, cognitive development crystallizes an identity in accord with the parents' view of the adolescent, in which he sees himself as weak, helpless, and highly vulnerable to outside control. In these adolescents, one sees submission to parental delineation despite superficial manifestations of rebelliousness. Efforts to achieve greater autonomy through overt behavior in defiance of parental requirements are accompanied by guilt and disorganizing anxiety. The parental delineations of the adolescents frequently evidence striking characteristics of containment and imperviousness to adolescent potential for effective independence.

In cases in which impairment in ego autonomy leads to identity diffusion in the adolescent, we see a great diversity of manifestations of parental interference with efforts of the adolescent to achieve increased independence from them. These may be explicit delineations of the adolescent as dependent, helpless, and vulnerable to control, as has been described. They may also be implicit delineations, which can be inferred from parental behavior with the adolescent and which may be contradictory to their explicit verbalized delineations. It should be emphasized that from the side of the adolescent we also see resistance to moving in the direction of greater independence. In some cases this is complementary to the parents' need to maintain the adolescent in a dependent position. In other cases we have seen the adolescent retreat from a new position of independence when such a position seemed to provide a license for an immature parent to depend upon him. In these cases the maturation of the adolescent allows the immature parent to find a new justification for relating to the adolescent in a dependent way, looking to the adolescent to provide support, satisfy sexual and affectional needs, and contribute tangible evidence of care. At the same time, these parents react sensitively and antagonistically to the adolescent's own dependency needs, seeing him then as a depleting agent draining the parent of supplies. We see in these instances a frequent shifting of delineation of the adolescent as the parents express their expectation that the adolescent nurture them and also express antagonism and drastic rejection when the adolescent's own need is expressed.

The role of delineation as a determinant in such adolescent disturbances must be weighed against other possible determinants, such as identification. Evidence of impaired ego autonomy in the parents themselves suggests a basis for the adolescent failures in identification with them. It is possible to define, clinically and in projective tests, areas of ego impairment in parents and in adolescents that appear to be similar and may be presumed to be evidence of identification, and areas of ego impairment that appear to be related but not congruent, and may better be explained as the consequence of delineation. Singer and Wynne (1965), in their discussion of prediction and matching from projective tests of parents and their adolescent or young adult, emotionally disturbed offspring, distinguish parental behaviors that seem to serve as models for identification from those that elicit or provoke complementary behavior in offspring. Complementary behavior may be an expression of adolescent ego identity that grows from and reflects parental delineation, or it may be manifested in adolescent behavior that is a reaction against parental delineation.

To understand the relationship of identification and delineation to adolescent ego autonomy, genetic determinants must also be considered. Observation of the parent –adolescent relationship allows us to make inferences about the nature of the parent–child relationship over issues of autonomy that are helpful in the reconstruction of the childhood history. This relationship of childhood experiences to adolescent development provides a necessary longitudinal dimension to an assessment of the determinants of adolescent ego autonomy and identity formation.

Murphy and colleagues (1963) described families in which the development of autonomy in competent adolescents was accompanied by the maintenance of a feeling of positive relatedness to the parents. Our findings regarding the families of disturbed adolescents are in sharp contrast to this, in that the development of autonomy in the disturbed adolescent seems regularly to carry with it a pronounced threat of alienation from the parents. When autonomous behavior results in alienating the parents, the alienation constitutes a severe inhibition to the development of ego autonomy in the adolescent.

Summary

I have discussed evidence in studies of adolescent cognitive development in support of a formulation of autonomous ego development in adolescence. Highly important co-determinants of the development of relative ego autonomy in the adolescent are found in his family experience. This increase in autonomy of the adolescent ego is a precondition for identity formation, whereas the family experience determining impairment in ego autonomy results in adolescent identity diffusion.

5

The Origin of Adolescent Disturbances in the Family: Some Considerations in Theory and Implications for Therapy

ROGER L. SHAPIRO, M.D.

Contemporary personality theory of adolescence looks both to determinants in the current experience of the adolescent and to determinants in the developmental experience to understand adolescent disturbance (R. Shapiro 1963). The study of the current family relationships of the adolescent helps to identify the nature of these determinants. It provides data about current highly important object relationships of the adolescent and their roles in inhibiting or distorting phase-appropriate development. It also provides a basis for inference about what the quality of these relationships was in the infantile period and during childhood, making possible a more discriminating and reliable formulation of the genetic determinants of the disturbance than could be obtained from history alone. The formulation of the importance of current family relations to the personality development of

the adolescent comes from considerations regarding the
drive and ego epigenesis of that developmental phase and
the altered relation to reality that this epigenesis makes
possible.

DRIVE AND EGO DEVELOPMENT
IN ADOLESCENCE

Consideration of the drive epigenesis of puberty centers
around the transition from a pregenital to a genital drive
organization and the altered relation to libidinal objects
demanded by this transition. A. Freud (1958) has pointed
out that the relationship to the parents is in the center of
these alterations, with drive development reviving old
patterns of oedipal anxiety and stimulating defenses that
have a new characteristic. This characteristic is the predominance of defenses against the existence of the oedipal objects themselves and the attempt at solution of
this problem by the finding of new objects. Pathological
outcome in adolescence is regularly associated with difficulty in the alteration of object relations, which the drive
development demands. Withdrawal of libidinal investment from parents and reinvestment of libido in new
objects is one of the complex tasks of adolescence, a task
that has many vicissitudes and much potential for pathological outcome. The characteristics of the parent–adolescent relationship in cases of pathological outcome provide
data of great relevance for an understanding of the
libidinal meaning of the parents to the adolescent and the
structure of the libidinal problem in the adolescent.
   Consideration of the ego epigenesis of puberty derives from formulations of Inhelder and Piaget (1958)
regarding new cognitive capacities in the sphere of logical
thinking that develop in early adolescence, and from
formulations of Hartmann (1950) and Jacobson (1961)
regarding the increasing ego autonomy that characterizes
this phase. I have previously suggested (R. Shapiro 1963)
that the consistent finding of a change in the nature of

abstract thought in early adolescence, with the development of hypothesis formation and the use of hypothetico-deductive reasoning and experimental proof, justifies the assumption that autonomous ego development occurs in this phase. This assumption defines the basis in ego epigenesis for the observations of personality growth conceptualized by Jacobson (1961) as remodeling of psychic structure and increasing secondary autonomy of the ego, and by Erikson (1956) as the establishment of the sense of ego identity. These new capacities are another foundation of the alteration in the nature of adolescents' relationships to their parents specifically, and in their object relations generally. Pathological outcome in adolescence has, as another determinant, relationship characteristics within the family that work against the evolving capacity for autonomous functioning in the ego of the adolescent and may draw this capacity into conflict. The new order of abstract thinking in adolescence allows them a new freedom in the conceptualization of themselves in relation to their parents and to society. It provides the adolescent with a new potential for assessing the positions taken by his parents and relating these to the rest of what he sees in reality. It provides him with a new basis for differentiating himself from his parents and aligning himself with new objects and institutions. Parental reaction to this new potential in the adolescent has great effect upon the nature of the development of ego autonomy in the adolescent. Parent–adolescent interaction over issues of autonomy then becomes another phase-specific area that may illuminate some aspects of disturbances of adolescence.

PSYCHOSOCIAL ASPECTS OF EGO IDENTITY

Formulation of the altered relation to reality, made possible by the drive and the ego epigenesis of puberty, has derived from conceptualizations of Erikson (1950, 1956, 1958) relating to the establishment of ego identity as the psychosocial crisis of adolescence. The relation of the adolescent's concept of himself to the concept of him implicit in the behavior of meaningful others toward him constitutes the essential experience from which ego identity grows. This relation of self-definition to social definition is the essence of the core of the individual's identity in every psychosocial phase. However, identity consolidation becomes an ascendent task of the ego in adolescence and arises from the new drive and ego capacities of this developmental phase. The altered self-definition demanded by the drive development of puberty, coupled with the new conceptual capacities of the ego, allows the adolescent to integrate complex internal changes with a changing social recognition of his growth. At the same time, the adolescent's ability to conceptualize external reality is altering. His new capacities in the realm of logical thinking, and his abilities for hypothesis formation and generalization, allow him a new perspective of his family, of society, of the past and of the future, as well as a new view of himself in the context of this perspective. The psychosocial task of adolescence—the establishment of ego identity—is incomplete and lacking in integration in cases of pathological outcome conceptualized by Erikson as cases of identity diffusion. The relevance of parent–adolescent interaction to identity diffusion and of parental delineation of the adolescent to the adolescent self-definition is a central issue in the diffusion of identity of the adolescent. The relationships within the family then become psychosocial events contributing to identity consolidation or diffusion, and these events can be observed with the hypothesis that they constitute important determinants of adolescent disturbance.

STUDIES OF FAMILY RELATIONSHIPS AND INTRAPSYCHIC ORGANIZATION

Studies of the family relationships of adolescents have been conducted by various research groups, with some differences in methodology. I will presently discuss the research of my group at the NIMH, in which attention has been directed to behavior within the family, and where the disturbed adolescent and his parents are observed in interaction. In other family studies, the adolescent and one or both parents have generally been studied and treated individually, and the interrelations between parental personality disorders and adolescent personality disorders have been formulated from the material of the individual therapy. This was true of the Johnson–Szurek group at the Institute for Juvenile Research in Chicago in the 1930s and 1940s (see the papers by Johnson 1949, and by Szurek et al. 1942). This group arrived at the important formulation that parents may find gratification of their own poorly integrated, forbidden impulses in the acting out of the adolescent through their conscious, or more often unconscious, permissiveness or inconsistency toward the adolescent in these spheres of behavior. Their study of antisocial adolescents was done through collaboration with the therapists doing individual psychoanalytic psychotherapy with the adolescent and the parent most involved in the acting out.

The current research project on adolescence of the Hampstead Child-Therapy Clinic goes beyond the emphasis on the antisocial adolescent and employs the technique of simultaneous analysis of adolescents and their mothers to highlight, in a variety of cases, the points of interaction between the abnormalities of mother and child. In a discussion of this research, A. Freud (1960) emphasizes the importance of replacing the vague generalization derived from child guidance work to the effect that most mental disturbances of children can be traced back to the disturbances of their parents, by precise analytic findings that detail the complexities of the influence of the mother's actions, her manifest attitude, and her conscious and unconscious fantasies—influences that are neither straightforward nor uniform. A. Freud makes the observation that the disturbances of the children can be similar to those of the mother or can be of a completely

different nature. They may or may not show the characteristic consequences of identification, of the overlapping
of fantasy activity, or of *folie à deux* phenomena that
characterize the cases from the Hampstead series reported
by Burlingham (1955), Hellman (1960), and Levy (1960).
The children may show indirect consequences of an
illness in the mother that interferes with her capacity for
effective mothering, rather than direct reactions to the
mother's symptoms. A. Freud goes on to state that the
understanding of the interaction between parents and
their children is of the highest importance, and not only
where the first foundations of the personality or the roots
of mental illness are concerned. As children move forward on the developmental scale, each step demands the
giving up of former positions and gains, not only from the
children themselves, but also from the parent. She states
that it is only in the most healthy and normal cases that
both sides—parents and child—wholly welcome the progressive move and enjoy the child's increasing maturity
and gradually increasing libidinal and moral independence. More often, it is one or the other partner who lags
behind, the child being unable to free himself from
fixations or the parent clinging to attitudes of protective-
ness or mothering that have become unjustified. In the
worst cases, mother and child may join forces in a
regressive move. Such interlocking, she states, becomes
particularly fateful with the onset of puberty. Here the
simultaneous analysis of mothers and their children have
proved helpful in specifying the various manners in
which individual adolescents strive to free themselves
from the infantile object ties to their parents. Finally, A.
Freud makes the important observation that no more than
a dim impression of the parent's responses is received in
those cases in which the adolescent alone is in treatment;
however, simultaneous analyses make it possible to trace
the contribution made by both sides to the sources of
failure of this particular developmental task.

My group at the NIMH, working from these considerations in theory, has added two aspects to the study of the family of the disturbed adolescent. First, we have required the participation of both parents and any adolescent siblings in our study, thus providing the possibility for evaluation of the contribution of each family member to the personality difficulties of any other. Second, we have made regular and systematic observations of the family group in interaction, as well as making assessments of the individual psychology of the parents and the adolescent, and considering the interrelationship of the individual psychological systems.

We have studied a series of twenty-five late adolescents (between the ages of 17 and 19) and their families. These are cases in which the adolescents have had a severe emotional disturbance as a result of the first prolonged separation from their parents in the first year of residence at a university, resulting in their being required to withdraw from school. The adolescents have had a variety of diagnoses, from acute psychoses to borderline states, with severe symptom neuroses and character disorders of the acting-out or inhibited varieties. In all of these cases, we have combined individual two- or three-hour weekly psychotherapy sessions with the adolescents with weekly sessions for the parents as a marital couple and weekly family therapy.

Our research focus has been on the family sessions. Our method makes it possible to directly observe behavior within the family group, which contains in action the expression of the individual psychodynamics of the family members. This allows a new order of specification and documentation of the psychological operations of the parents with the adolescent. These behaviors can be detailed, and their impact directly assessed. Instead of stopping at a formulation of the intrapsychic organization of the parents and the adolescent, with hypotheses about how the one affects the other, we are able to go a step further and to observe these systems in interaction. This allows us to formulate, from observations of actual behavior, mechanisms that have been derived in other ways in other personality development research. It enables us to make a series of precise observations about the manner in which specific intrapsychic organization is expressed in behavior within a particular family.

THE CONCEPT OF PARENTAL DELINEATION

In our study of adolescent personality development, we are attempting to clarify the impact of characteristic parental behavior with the adolescent upon adolescent personality formation. We organize our observations of behavior through the use of the concept of delineation, which I shall presently define. A central hypothesis of our study has been that there is a significant relationship between parental delineation of the adolescent and adolescent identity formation. Our hypothesis further states that in families in which there is serious psychological disturbance in the adolescent, there will be evidence of striking distortions, inconsistencies, and contradictions in parental delineation of the adolescent. Our study of the parent–adolescent relationship includes questions about the kinds of parents who are particularly vulnerable to various manifestations of adolescent development, the manner in which these vulnerabilities are expressed—and here we use the language of delineation—and the effects of these modes of parental behavior on the personality functioning of the adolescent.

By *delineation*, we mean the view or image one person has of the other person, as revealed explicitly or implicitly in the behavior of the one person with the other person. In the language of ego psychology, it is behavior that contains the expression of an object representation and the ego organization mobilized in relation to this object representation. Various ego functions are mobilized in relation to object representation and behavior with an object. For example, the characteristics of autonomous ego functioning or state of ego regression effect the behavior of delineation. A highly important subgroup of delineations consists of those we call defensive delineations. When behavior of an individual with an object contains evidence of distortion of the object related to the individual's defensive organization, then defensive delineation exists. The concept of defensive delineation thus represents an integration of two structural concepts in ego psychology. It includes behavioral referents both of the concept of object representation and of defensive organization. Defensive delineation is a conceptualization of those situations in which defense alters the behavioral referents of object representation. It is a response to the behavior of the other person that stimulates anxiety in the one person and gives rise to defensive operations, which are revealed in the nature and style of his delineation of the other person.

The concept of delineation provides a bridge between the intrapsychic and the interpersonal spheres, with similarities to that bridge provided by the theory of transference in the conceptualization of the psychoanalytic relationship. Transference is a conceptualization of the effect of earlier object relationships and related defensive organization upon a current regressive object relationship. This effect is manifested in characteristic idiosyncratic distortions of behavior in the current object relationship. This is also the way we conceptualize the structure of defensive delineation.

ASSESSMENT OF DELINEATION

We employ the following method in the analysis of family interaction for delineation. We isolate excerpts of interaction during family sessions that are characteristic of the parent–adolescent relationships. In the analysis of these samples we ask the following questions:

1. What is the situation in reality in which these interactions occur? What is the nature of the actual events and issues with which the family members are dealing? What is the adolescent's behavior in the reality context under discussion?

2. What delineations of the adolescent by each parent can be inferred from this particular interaction?

3. Is there an apparent distortion in the parent's view of the adolescent? This may be a clear and obvious disjunction between the view of the adolescent expressed by the parent and that seen by the observer. It may become evident only when the delineation is viewed in the context of a particular reality situation and of the specific behavior in reality of the adolescent. It may become evident from contradiction or bias expressed in delineation. The parent's inappropriate, biased, exaggerated, or idiosyncratic view of the adolescent can be defined by an observer. If the delineations contain evidence of distortion, then the inference of defensive delineation is made.

4. What hypotheses about the determinants and structure of defensive delineations can be formulated? These inferences are made clinically from the material of the family session. They are compared to formulations from research interviews and psychological tests of the parents, which define areas of conflict and need as well as organization of defenses. If there is good correspondence between the dynamics of defensive delineation and evidence from the individual assessment about individual psychodynamics, then we can assume that the delineation is a manifestation of relatively enduring parental character structure. This supports the argument that defensive delineation is not simply a reflection of the

adolescent's actual characteristics, but represents an expression of the parent's needs and defensive organization. These lead to characteristic emphases and to distortions of delineations of the adolescent.

ILLUSTRATION OF DELINEATION IN FAMILY INTERACTION DURING DISCUSSION OF ISSUES AND EVENTS

Our use of the concept of delineation will be clarified by two examples of interaction from one of our family groups. This is the family of a deeply anxious and inhibited, highly narcissistic, passively aggressive boy of 19 with symptoms of depression, exhibitionism, and school failure. The first excerpt, taken from a family session that occurred about six months after treatment began, indicates an aspect of the father's delineation of the adolescent.

This family session was conducted just before David was to resume a full academic program, having successfully completed a part-time academic program during the summer. He is to leave the hospital to live in the college dormitory but will continue in therapy as an outpatient. In the previous family session David had, in a provocative way, expressed ambivalence about leaving the hospital and returning to school.

EXCERPT 1:

Father: Do you like school or you don't like school? Do you like to go now to school?
Mother: You ended last session by saying you don't know if you really want to go to school.
Father: You have to make up your mind and it's not just. . . .
David: But it's not school that's the issue, the way I see it. It's

my negative way of doing anything—like going to camp—if you have to force me to go to camp then obviously you have to force me to work, you have to force me to play, you have to force me to eat; you have to force me to do anything.

Father:　You see, if I give you this food in the basket—then I better not give you—the cleaning up afterwards.

David:　So you do it yourself.

Father:　So if you want to go to school and not to make the grade and not to study, better not start it.

David:　I remember I did that in the kitchen and Sarah would say; "If you are that hungry, make something yourself instead of always coming and begging for a sandwich or something." So I would make a mess of the kitchen and between the two of you, you would just realize somebody's got to take care of the poor kid or else he'll starve to death.

Father:　You lost a year, your whole year now was a big struggle. This summer I was against your study and according to the doctors, you were okay. Now I am again questioning, I am questioning although you have a dormitory and have a schedule again, like with the German, I think he is not qualified to study. If he can come up with remarks like this after he did well during the summer, in German, and that a dry subject completely, just words—it is something—and I'm questioning now, not because I want to bring out all this negative that you should fight me, but I am really thinking that maybe you are not qualified to go to college.

David:　Well, I don't know. . . .

Father:　[interrupting] It seems to me, Doctor. . . .

David:　[interrupting] It seems to me this is an example. . . .

Father:　If he could at the last minute turn over the whole—you know the cow what gives beautiful, the whole time, good milk and then the last minute she turns it over, the whole business—the pail—so the same thing is with David. After we talked, and after we paid in, and after everything is prepared, then he just says maybe he doesn't want it, so—so now I am questioning that he needs it altogether.

Delineations of David by the Father

Excerpt 1

1. David can't decide whether he does or does not want to return to school.

2. David is unwilling to exert effort and unable to persevere if any demand is made on him.

3. David is prone to start things and not to finish them, and should not start school if he isn't going to make the grade.

4. David is lazy and likely to spoil whatever he attempts, and after a big struggle lost an entire year in school.

5. David was not ready to go to summer school, although the doctors said he was ready. Now he again is not ready.

6. David did well during the summer, but if he can come up with doubts now about school after succeeding, he is not qualified for college.

7. David is like the cow that gives beautiful milk and then kicks over the pail. He promises to produce and to give and then he frustrates and destroys.

Apparent Distortions Suggesting Defensive Delineation in Excerpt 1

1. The father's pessimism about David's capacity to succeed seems exaggerated in light of his recent success in summer school.

2. The father seems to be reacting with great anxiety to David's provocative expression of ambivalence about returning to school. This reaction seems excessive. The imagery of milk produced by David to feed his father and the expectation that David will kick over the pail to frustrate his father implies a great need on the part of the father to be fed by David's success. His anger at David for chronically frustrating him is evident in this interaction.

3. Contradictory delineations with regard to success are seen, in this interaction, in the predominance of delineations that ignore the success of the summer and define David as not qualified for college.

4. The imagery of the cow and the milk implies a feminine definition of David.

Hypotheses About the Determinants and Structure of Defensive Delineation in Excerpt 1

1. The father seems to have both a great wish to be fed by his son's success and great apprehensiveness that his son will not nurture him with success but will frustrate him by his failure. The hypersensitivity to frustration by his son suggests that the father's need to be gratified by him is great and implies an inordinate degree of dependency on the part of the father as well as great anxiety when his sources of dependent gratification are threatened.

2. The father is clearly ambivalent about his son's success of the summer. This may be determined by competitive feeling toward the son, which may also result in his feminine definition of him.

3. The father may see David's departure from the

protection of the hospital as an event that will lead to David's making increased demands upon him.

Projective tests and research interviews with the father provide detailed substantiation and further elaboration of the dynamics of defensive delineations inferred from these interactions.

Another excerpt will illustrate an aspect of the mother's delineation of the adolescent. It is taken from a family session that occurred approximately one year after the beginning of family therapy.

In the previous family session, one co-therapist (the adolescent's individual therapist) had announced that he would be leaving NIMH in four months. During the evening after that family session, David had been at home, had been depressed, and had made statements to the effect that life was meaningless and the whole world should be destroyed. Two days after that, while driving family members home from the airport, David abruptly changed lanes and entered the right of way of another car, angering the driver.

Excerpt 2

Mother: Last week at home he came up with a glorious statement of, uh—that the whole world should be destroyed. Uh, he had made this remark—I could think that maybe it had to do with Dr. Crown's leaving; that maybe he's not all well; that he's still sick and needs attention. But he made such a remark about a year ago. And I didn't like it then, but I just thought he was being very flippant and smart.

David: So, so, so!

Mother: But this last week when he mentioned it, it did upset me.

David:	Did it really! You didn't seem very upset then. You must have, uh, gotten upset since then. At the time, both you and Daddy thought it very amusing (brief laugh). And Daddy was ready to send me off to, uh. . . .
Mother:	Amusing? And Daddy thought it was so amusing he was ready to send you off to St. Elizabeth's?
David:	But *you* certainly weren't upset. I mean, I. . . .
Mother:	Okay. We *try* to rationalize such talk, and so on, and not to get into a huff and a puff. But the fact still remains.
Therapist:	That's a rather characteristic David-sort-of response, though, it seems to me—when your mother brings up an issue of something that's going on in the group, you often minimize it or say that you don't feel it's important or worth discussing or. . . .
David:	Well, I. . . .
Mother:	Well, I think a person has a right to differ.
Therapist:	Yes—we get a lot of that.
Mother:	But—this is *so* different [slight pause] that it just sounds too destructive—to let it go.
Therapist:	This is so different? You mean David's attitude on Sunday?
Mother:	Yeah!
David:	Actually, it was on Friday evening.
Mother:	Well, whenever it was. It probably was Friday because Sunday, when you went to the airport I was worried about just how they would get back.
Father:	Hmmm.
Mother:	[tearfully] And haven't mentioned it—I was worried about them. And the fact that he cut across and there could have been an accident . . . (David snickers). The idea is, "What is life—we all die, and so what? Sooner or later. Might as well push the button and all go together." So I think he made it clear then that if he really has feelings. . . . If he feels that way, I can't change him.
David:	I've been making remarks like that for years. I mean, how . . . ?
Father:	I have my. . . . [voice becomes inaudible]
Mother:	Well, I'm not finished yet.

David: That's the way I think. Okay.

Mother: I think—I don't know, I may be wrong—I'm just gonna make up a—theory. I think—that maybe possibly, I think everyone fears death to a degree [David laughs]; I'm inclined to think that David fears death. I think we have apprehension all over the world—I mean, it's just such an age. And I think especially the youngsters. So why don't we just push the button and get rid of it! But I don't see *why*—why *he* should think of pushing the button—in such terms. When the button will be pushed, then you'll be eliminated. We'll be eliminated. Fine. All right? [David mumbles, "Yes, yes."] Then I'm not so sure how easily we're eliminated. Plenty remain sick, maimed for the rest of their lives. [David interjects, "Well . . ."] They just don't die conveniently for you. Uh—(slight pause, then sighs) I think he's so afraid of death that he's afraid to live. That's what *I* think. And would like everyone else to go with him. Now, this again may have no connection with my father, but I want to register it for what it's worth. My father at one time was thinking of committing suicide. And wanted my mother to go with him. And she didn't want to go.

Delineations of David by the Mother in Excerpt 2

1. David is potentially explosively destructive.

2. David is prone to act sick and disturbed to enlist the parents' care and gain their sympathy.

3. David requires care and becomes irresponsible and destructive when he is denied care.

4. David's destructiveness is threatening and upsetting to his mother.

5. David is only being flippant and smart with his threats of world destruction.

6. David's instability and poor control warrant sending him to a mental hospital.

7. David has a right to differ with his mother unless the difference is too different and too destructive to let it go.

8. David is so destructive he almost destroyed his family in an automobile accident.

9. David is very depressed and is potentially self-destructive.

10. David is despondent and his mother can't change him.

11. David is too fearful and inhibited to take any action in life (so afraid of death he's afraid to live).

12. David intends to eliminate himself and everyone, but plenty remain sick, maimed for the rest of their lives, and don't die conveniently for him.

13. David is like her father, who at one time wanted to commit suicide and take her mother with him.

Apparent Distortions Suggesting Defensive Delineation in Excerpt 2

1. The mother's striking and persistent definition of David as dangerously and unpredictably destructive and self-destructive in much of this excerpt does not seem warranted by his actual behavior in the events discussed.

2. An alternative quality of delineation of David as manipulative, flippant, pretending to be disturbed, and too fearful and inhibited to take any action in life provides a confusing and contradictory theme of attributions of impotence in counterpoint to the theme of destructiveness throughout this excerpt.

Hypotheses about the Determinants and Structure of Defensive Delineations in Excerpt 2

1. A marked inconsistency is seen between the predominant, apparently exaggerated definition of the adolescent as destructive and self-destructive, and a definition of him as weak, manipulative, and too fearful to act. This suggests a marked ambivalence in the mother about aggression in her son.

2. The apparent exaggeration in the view of her son as aggressive and as anxious seems to result from the mother's tendency to project her own aggression and anxiety onto him.

3. The delineation of her son as destructive and self-destructive is also the consequence of the mother's tendency to project aspects of her depressed father onto her son and to attribute to her son the suicidal actions her father carried out in reality.

Without going into more detail, evaluation of the mother through research interviews and projective tests provided substantiating evidence of a characteristic tendency to project; of readily mobilizable anger, depression, and anxiety; and of great vulnerability to the anger, depression, and anxiety of others.

DISCUSSION

These examples suggest the nature of the view obtained in the family sessions of the manner in which the parents delineate the adolescent. In families in which the adolescent is severely disturbed, we have repeatedly seen evidence of anxiety in the parents over the adolescent's expression of his new developmental potentials. Two areas of adolescent maturation repeatedly give rise to defensive and contradictory parental delineations of the adolescents in our series: (1) the new potential for individuation and separation from the parents, determined in part by the cognitive development of the adolescent, and (2) the manifestations and new expressions of the adolescent's libidinal development. These general findings are not surprising in themselves. What is of great interest, however, is the detailed study of pattern and styles of parental response to evidence of maturation in the adolescent, the relationship of characteristic delineation to defensive need in the parent, and its relationship to particular dimensions of disturbance in the adolescent. In our series we find a range of parental behavior. On the one hand there may be evidence of defensive delineation in a particular area, such as sexuality, reflecting a specific parental personality difficulty over adolescent development in that area, with nondefensive and phase-appropriate definition of the adolescent in other areas of functioning. The impact of parental defensive delineations upon the adolescent's functioning can be inferred both from the area of difficulty the adolescent presents and from his defensive style in the management of anxiety. These are cases that would be diagnosed as severe neuroses, where there is no evidence of thought disorder or generalized ego defect but where the disturbance is circumscribed and dealt with in a characteristic way, and where this can be related to circumscribed difficulty in the parent. At the other end of the continuum are families such as those described by Wynne and Singer

(1963) at the NIMH, in which erratic and autistic parental delineations of the adolescent are a reflection of pervasive thought disorder and an autistic interpretation of reality in the parents. Here the adolescents themselves frequently manifest borderline or psychotic disturbances apparently related to the thought disorder of the parents.

OBSERVATION AND INTERPRETATION
IN FAMILY THERAPY

I should like finally to discuss the family session as a therapeutic instrument that we believe to have a phase-specific usefulness in the treatment of middle and late adolescents. We use the concept of delineation both to organize our understanding of the situation and as an important focus for interpretation.

In our therapeutic design, the weekly parent–adolescent group session supplements two or three hours per week of individual psychotherapy for the adolescent. In our program, the individual therapist of the adolescent is also one of the therapists of the family group. The psychiatric social worker is co-therapist of the family group session, and she also sees the parents as a marital couple in a weekly session outside of the family session.

This structured encounter between adolescents and parents is a highly useful situation in which to clarify and interpret the interrelation between characteristic parental delineation of the adolescent and disturbance in the adolescent. This situation enlists and uses the new capacities of the adolescent in the conceptual sphere—the new psychological potentials for abstraction that bring him for the first time within the range of his parents' level of psychological functioning. The family session is an excellent situation in which to establish the actuality (Erikson 1962) of the adolescent's maturation and the idiosyncratic and defensive aspects of the parents' response to it.

In the family session as we use it, therapists orient

themselves toward the observation of interactions between the parents and the adolescent that illuminate the concept or image each has of the other. In our terminology, the therapist focuses particularly upon the delineations of the adolescent implicit in the behavior of the parents with the adolescent. This is the data upon which the therapist bases his comments. His interpretations are conceptualizations of the evidence about distortions of delineation determined by parental defense and parental need. By making explicit those attitudes of parents toward the adolescent that have been implicit and often unconscious, these interpretations lead to the gradual illumination of various dimensions of relationship of which the participants have been unaware, or about which they have been unclear. The conceptual abilities of the adolescent are enlisted in examining the nature of his parents' image of him and the ways in which this has defined and limited him. His conceptual capacities are also directed toward self-reflection and toward an examination of his behavior toward his parents and the ways in which this provokes particular directions of response in them.

By interpreting evidence of defensive delineation, we are intervening in a way that has many structural parallels to the basis of transference interpretation in individual therapy. We are commenting on the idiosyncratic nature of a relationship in which the patient and the parents become involved and which is a reflection of the view or image each has of the other. The similarity in the two situations is in the focus of both on idiosyncratic behavior that reflects distortions of attitude in relationship, and is identified and called into question by being isolated for comment. In the family, the behavior is an aspect of the actual relationships being studied, containing attributions determined by internal need of one member about the other member. In individual therapy, the behavior interpreted reflects attributions on the part of the patient toward his therapist, which in turn reflect indirectly the internal images of the parents or other transference figures.

Interpretation of defensive delineation leads to an implicit question about the determinants of distortion. The asking of such a question implies the existence of alternative possibilities of attitude and feeling in the parent. It calls into question the consequences of the parental delineation for the personality functioning of the adolescent. This is a step toward the adolescent's achieving the freedom to explore other possibilities of behavior free of the parents' constricting view of him. The capacity of the adolescent to conceptualize and to abstract is capitalized upon in this process. The conceptual clarity of the therapists in formulating the implications of behavioral interaction between the patient and his parents provides evidence used by the adolescent for a new understanding of himself. The family session then becomes an arena for new action of the adolescent in relation to his parents. Correspondingly, the parents are able to understand implications for the adolescent of their behavior and feeling in relation to him. They are able to recognize the elements in their reaction to the adolescent determined by their individual vulnerabilities, although perhaps aggravated by specific aspects of the adolescent's behavior toward them. As this recognition proceeds, the parents, too, are able to experiment with new possibilities of feeling and response, which grow out of a new clarity about the determinants and implications of their characteristic behavior and can mobilize their capacity for change within the setting of therapy.

What I am describing is obviously a complex process. A parent–adolescent relationship that has given rise to pathological outcome is invariably resistant to change. The resistance to change is seen clearly in stereotyped dimensions of behavior in the family session, and where it is perceived it is interpreted. This interpretation has as its ally the new developmental capacities of the adolescent and what ability the parents have for reflection, experimentation, and change. The neutrality and conceptual clarity of the therapists support the family members in this effort and provide a model for it. The individual therapy of the adolescent and the therapy of the parents with the social worker further explore the genetics and implications of these resistances and facilitate new dimensions of freedom in the adolescent and the parents, as well as new dimensions of behavior in the family group session. The therapists support these directions of new response in both the adolescent and the parents, which then can be continued and built upon in other contacts and in other places.

This effort to define and alter defensive delineation of adolescent by parents and of parents by adolescent is given specific impetus in the family session and is the focus of therapeutic attention in these sessions. Marked shifts in the quality of the adolescent–parent relationship are a characteristic of this developmental phase. This technique of therapy derives its effectiveness from its capacity to mobilize the energies and capacities that accomplish these shifts and characterize this phase. The family session is a setting that can catalyze a developmental trend for both adolescent and parents by focusing on interactions that represent resistances to this trend. It is an aspect of the adolescent's actuality, where new action with figures of great emotional relevance can begin new directions of development.

PART III

SHARED UNCONSCIOUS FANTASY AND PROJECTIVE IDENTIFICATION

6

Family Organization and Adolescent Development

ROGER L. SHAPIRO, M.D.
JOHN ZINNER, M.D.

INTRODUCTION

This chapter is concerned with the experience comprising the boundary between the individual adolescent and his family. Exploration of transactions across this boundary area entails two levels of observation: that of individual behavior and that of family group behavior. The goal of such exploration is to clarify the relationship of adolescent personality functioning to family functioning and the consequences of family functioning for the individual adolescent.

The understanding of adolescence is enhanced by study of the adolescent in the context of his family (R. Shapiro 1967). During adolescence, a marked alteration occurs in the individual's relationship to his family, to his peer group, and to other groups in society (Erikson 1956, 1962, R. Shapiro 1963). This alteration is in part determined by maturation in the ego and the id during puberty, resulting in important changes in cognitive and affective capacities (A. Freud 1936, 1958, Inhelder and Piaget 1958). It is co-determined by the nature of the internalizations of family relationships that have occurred through infancy and childhood (Jacobson 1964, Schafer 1968). Adolescent development brings about a reorganization of these internalizations in relation to ego–id maturation and new experience (Blos 1962, Erikson 1956). One consequence of this reorganization is an increase in the relative autonomy of the ego of the adolescent, which leads to the establishment of ego identity (R. Shapiro 1966, 1969) described more fully in Chapter 4.

The adolescent's relationship to his family is his central experience of continuity in relationships from earliest childhood through late adolescence. Family experience establishes a core of internalizations derived not only from characteristics of the parents as persons, but also from the quality of their perceptions of and attitudes toward the child and adolescent (Loewald 1960). These perceptions and attitudes may be ascertained through direct observation of family interaction.

Our study of the family is facilitated through application of Rice's concept of primary task to the family (Rice 1969). From the point of view of adolescent development, we consider the primary task of the family to be the promotion of relative ego autonomy and identity formation in its adolescent members, leading to their individuation and eventual separation. This task may be interfered with by unconscious assumptions in the family that militate against the development of ego autonomy and individuation in the adolescent. In this paper we will consider evidence in family interaction from which we infer the existence of such unconscious assumptions within the family, and discuss the consequences of these assumptions for the accomplishment of the task we have defined.

In order to study the family as a group distinguished from the individual members comprised by it, our research with forty-five disturbed adolescents and their families includes weekly sessions of conjoint family therapy, as well as weekly marital therapy for the parents, and three sessions per week of individual psychotherapy for the adolescent. The weekly conjoint family therapy sessions are the source of the research observations of family interaction.

LEVELS OF INFERENCE REGARDING DELINEATION

A central concept in our study of family interaction is delineation, a concept closely linked to observable behavior (R. Shapiro 1967, 1968). *Delineations* are behaviors through which one family member communicates explicitly or implicitly his perceptions and attitudes—in fact, his mental representation of another family member—to that other person. Through use of the concept of delineation we make formulations involving three levels of inference from observations of family interaction.

A first level of inference is that specified behaviors in one person imply a particular delineation of the other person.

A second level of inference is about the determinants of delineation. Delineations may communicate a view of the other person that appears to be predominantly determined by his reality characteristics. Or delineations may communicate a view of the other person that appears to be predominantly determined by the mobilization of dynamic conflict and defense in the delineator. We call the latter category *defensive delineations*. We pay particular attention to parental defensive delineations of the adolescent. When parental delineations are observed to be distorted, stereotyped, overspecific, contradictory, or otherwise incongruent with the range of behavior manifested by the adolescent, we make the inference that these delineations serve defensive aspects of parental personality functioning. That is, they are not simply realistic responses to the current characteristics of the adolescent. Also, we further hypothesize that the parents, through their defensive delineations, seek to hold the child and adolescent in relatively fixed roles throughout development.

A third level of inference involves the characteristics of the family group as a whole. From excerpts of family interaction containing defensive delineations, we accrue evidence of shared or complementary characteristics of the family as a group and of the unconscious determinants of these characteristics. We conclude that this evidence of coordinated, shared, complementary behavior in the family relates to a level of unconscious fantasy and defense in the family group analogous to Bion's (1961) concept of small-group behavior organized around particular unconscious assumptions. Bion's group theory derives from psychoanalysis and is a way of conceptualizing conscious and unconscious systems of motivation and defense in the group as a whole. Bion's small-group theory characterizes the basic-assumption group as one in which, for defensive reasons, the group appears to be dominated and often united by covert assumptions based on unconscious fantasies. The work of the group—its functioning and task performance—is impaired, with deterioration of the ego functioning of the members. The realities of the situation and the task are lost sight of, reality testing is poor, secondary-process thinking deteriorates, and more primitive forms of thinking emerge. The new organization of behavior seems to be determined by fantasies and assumptions that are unrealistic and represent a failed struggle to cope with the current reality situation. The group thus survives as such, though its essential functioning and primary task are now altered in the service of a different task (Turquet 1971).

When the family is in a situation of anxiety leading to predominance of defensive delineations, there are interesting analogies to small-group basic-assumption behavior. When defensive delineations predominate in family interaction, conflicting motivations, anxiety, and defense are seen, with accompanying ego regression and behavior determined more by fantasy than by reality. Work failure is evident in the family situation, similar to basic-assumption functioning: There is emergence of confused, distorted thinking; failure of understanding and adequate communication; and breakdown in the ability of the family to work cooperatively or creatively on a task, to maintain a progressive discussion in which family members understand one another, or to deal realistically with the problems under discussion. In short, the family is in a situation in which unconscious assumptions and associated anxiety are mobilized, and various defensive behaviors are seen. The family's reality functioning is disturbed. In contrast, in the absence of anxiety related to unconscious assumptions, the family does not manifest predominantly defensive behavior, is clearly reality oriented, and is well related to the family primary task.

We now turn to consideration of the individual child and adolescent maturing within the framework of family group assumptions. We consider identification processes to be internalizations that are central determinants of structure formation in the child (Schafer 1968). In addition, we believe that the child internalizes aspects of family relationships in which the parents attribute particular characteristics to him and communicate attitudes toward him. These delineations also modify the child's self-representation and are determinants of structure formation. Delineations of the child and adolescent that serve a defensive function for the parent are particularly coercive in that behavior in the child that counters these parental delineations leads to anxiety in the parent. The child is then motivated to behave so as to mitigate this parental anxiety. The child's internalization of the parent's defensive delineations of him moves the developing child and adolescent into a role that is complementary to parental defensive requirements (Singer and Wynne 1965, Wynne and Singer 1963). Consequently, defensive delineations are dynamic determinants of role allocation in the family. The role allocated is necessary to maintain parental defense and mitigate parental anxiety. The dynamics of role allocation operate in a broader framework of unconscious assumptions of the family as a group and modify the internalizations of the self-representation. These influences are important in the reorganization of internalizations that leads to increased ego autonomy and identity formation in adolescence.

EXAMPLE OF A FAMILY'S INTERACTION

We will now present material from one of the families we have studied to exemplify the methods of observation and inference we have discussed. First the identity crisis of the adolescent is described and then observations of family interactions containing defensive delineations are reported in the form of excerpts from tape recordings of conjoint family therapy sessions. First-level inferences from family interactions are formulations of the delineations they contain. Second-level inferences concern evidence that the delineations are defensive and are statements of the dynamics of delineations in these interactions. Finally, we make formulations about the unconscious assumptions of the family as a group, a third level of inference from these observations. The excerpts are selected as examples of defensive delineations in which unconscious assumptions of the family are central dynamics of interaction. Shifts are seen over time in the roles played by the various family members in relation to shared assumptions. These assumptions are clearly operative in all members of the family group. We will consider in particular the importance of the family's unconscious assumptions for the identity crisis of the adolescent.

In this family, a dramatic personality change occurred in the adolescent, a boy of 18, during his first two years of college. This change reached a crisis, with feelings of confusion and of merging with and being controlled by others, withdrawal, extreme shifts in mood, and rage episodes, which finally resulted in his hospitalization. In the patient's freshman year at college, he followed the pattern he had established in high school of compliance, obsessive studying, and constricted social relationships. He initially dealt with the transition from living at home to living in a large university in another city by attempting to maintain continuity with the pattern of life he had previously known. He did well academically, wrote frequent, long letters to his parents, and established no close new relationships with boys or girls. His identity as compliant student and relative social isolate was familiar but ungratifying. He became more aware of other choices and other possibilities in observing the lives of other students. He envied their greater freedom to enjoy life and wanted to emulate them, but he could not, and he felt inadequacy and confusion in any other than his familiar pattern of living. His old equilibrium was disturbed, however, and when he returned home for the summer, he felt estranged there as well. In the presence of his parents, particularly his mother, he felt pressures against change. He felt the dilemma that in order to remain related to his parents as a son, he could not be the person he wanted to be in college. He felt ashamed of his family and felt alienated from them because of wishes to grow beyond the identity he had established with them. During the summer he was solitary and spent much time reading, particularly in the areas of Zen, Yoga, and psychoanalysis. Upon his return to college, he determined to follow a new direction to avoid the identity of a "grind" and to dedicate himself to some cause larger than himself, to develop his human relationships, and to relate his mind to "real life." He became active in a campus political organization, became involved in a Yoga study group, and neglected his academic work. He pursued this course with a clear feeling that he had found the life of a grind unrewarding and with a determination to find something more gratifying. Within a few weeks he was feeling agitated and confused. He felt overinvolved in extracurricular activity, concerned about his academic commitments, and unsure about the choices he had made. Intense feelings of unworthiness and guilt tormented him, and he sought refuge in Yoga exercises and meditation. He wrote to his parents about his new interests, hoping to obtain his mother's approval and understanding. His mood shifted frequently from feelings of unworthiness and despair to periods of euphoria and excitement. The latter feelings eventuated on several occasions in mystical experiences characterized by feelings that there was a central unity in the universe, that all consciousness was identical to his individual consciousness, and that his individual identity was only a temporary and artificial separation from a larger identity. He attended few classes, and after several months his adviser recommended that he see a student health psychiatrist. Because of preoccupation and withdrawal, as well as unusual behavior such as long periods of meditation and poor academic performance, it was finally determined that he should leave college and return home.

Throughout this period of turmoil, the patient felt an agonizing diffusion in self-definition. This was manifested in personal relationships in disturbing feelings of merging, of being controlled by and becoming the other person. The loss of a sense of himself was confusing and frightening, and resulted in feelings of great weakness and vulnerability. He originally felt a danger of loss of himself in relation to his parents, and his original repudiation of the identity of student grind was a reaction against this. His actual separation from his parents facilitated this reaction. Similar feelings of vulnerability at college led to wariness in new relationships and defensive isolation. His attraction to Eastern philosophy and particularly to meditation techniques was part of an effort to augment his independence in new relationships. However, the shift in identity from grind to mystic resulted in disorganization of obsessional defenses. Ego regression ensued, in which Yoga exercises and meditation seemed to have dynamic consequences analogous to sensory deprivation experiences. They did promote a new degree of ego autonomy from the environment, but they left the ego's autonomy from the id impaired. This led to further withdrawal, to mystical experiences, to bizarre affective states, and to rage episodes, which eventually resulted in the patient's hospitalization.

DISCUSSION OF THE EXAMPLE

In conceptualizing the identity crisis described, ego regression is assumed to be a consequence of preexisting impairment in adolescent ego development. Instead of an adolescent development characterized by gradual achievement of relative ego autonomy, a disturbance in the ego's autonomy from objects in reality is manifested by persisting feelings of vulnerability in relationships. In the investigation of determinants of this ego disturbance, we turn to examples of family interaction for analysis of content and dynamics of parental delineations of the adolescent.

Since it is in the area of independent functioning that the adolescent manifests his greatest disturbance, we select for investigation characteristics of delineations in family interactions in which concrete independent behaviors of family members are discussed. In this family, a striking and characteristic pattern of behavior is seen when issues of independent functioning are discussed. These behaviors are initially most apparent in delineations of the adolescent. Later they are seen to be present in reaction to independent behavior and thinking in other family members also.

An aspect of delineation of particular importance to independent functioning is the response of family members to differences and disagreements. In family observations we focus upon the degree of tolerance of family members for differences—for separate, distinct, and disparate ideas and feelings within the family group. In this family, the adolescent's feeling of being controlled by his parents' disapproval is clearly illustrated in the first two excerpts. In the third and fourth excerpts, a similar sensitivity and similar feeling of being controlled is expressed by the mother in response to disagreement and disapproval from the adolescent, and it is clear that it is not only the adolescent who feels controlled by differences and disagreements. This is further exemplified in the fifth and sixth excerpts, in which the father's response to criticism and feeling of vulnerability to control by the adolescent and by the mother is seen. It is apparent that intolerance of disagreement and the feeling that disagreement is equivalent to the exercise of control is a shared feeling in this family. This is important with respect to the models for identification available to the adolescent and the relation of these models to the identity problems he manifests.

It is assumed that in the adolescent, identification with important aspects of the personality functioning of each parent is found. In this case, the adolescent's striking intolerance to criticism and disagreement is a characteristic shared with his parents, which is evidence of identification. However, these parents appear to reinforce identification through their delineations of the adolescent. They are impaired in their capacity to differentiate themselves from the adolescent and tend to project their own characteristics onto him. Under these circumstances we find identification and delineation to be related in a specific way: The bridge between them is *projection* (Zinner and R. Shapiro 1972). Through identification, the adolescent internalizes parental images, which determine characteristics of his personality functioning. Through delineation, projection onto the adolescent of aspects of the parents' personality characteristics results in an active definition of him by the parents systematically related to what the parents are themselves. Thus certain characteristics that have been learned by the adolescent in identifications are also actively imposed by the parents in defensive delineations.

In the following excerpts of family interaction, we will attempt to elucidate the interplay of adolescent identification and parental delineations determined by projective identification.

The first excerpt is taken from a family session which occurred ten months after the patient's admission to the hospital. The patient has been talking in recent family sessions about returning to college in several months. He has been working successfully for two months in the community at a part-time job. He raises the issue of college again in this session, but this time it is coupled with a new and more immediate project. He states that he wants to leave the hospital as soon as possible, but to move into an apartment of his own rather than live again with his parents.

Excerpt 1

Allen: I'm thinking of leaving here and getting an apartment on the outside . . . and I think I've found that . . . for my *own* good, the approval I want is the absence of disapproval.

Father: That I don't understand. I don't know what the absence of disapproval means.

Mother: Either you approve or you disapprove.

Allen: Well, you don't disapprove or don't approve. You can. . . .

Mother: In other words, you're going to do this regardless of how we feel? Is that it?

Father: No, no, no, no—that is not what he is trying to say. . . .

Mother: The absence of disapproval . . . .

Allen: That's probably true, though, anyway. But that's not what I said. It's your interpretation.

Mother: Well, I'm interested in hearing what your plans are.

Therapist: I wonder how you arrived at that conclusion, though. . . .

Mother: At *what*?

Therapist: . . . from what Allen said.

Mother: That it means whether we approve or disapprove, he's going to go ahead anyway—with his own plans? Is that what you're referring to?

Therapist: Well, what Allen said originally, I thought, was that he—merely hoped for the absence of disapproval. That it meant something to him, more than approval. I wonder how you made the move—from *that*—which to me, at least, implied he was very sensitive to disapproval—to your statement, which was that he's going to do what he wants to do whether you approve or not.

Mother: Well, that's what I got from the fact of . . . [short laugh] from the absence of approval. Of *dis*approval . . . I mean, if we don't say anything about . . . not wanting to, not approving of the fact of his going into the apartment—he's going to do it *anyway*. That's the way it sounded to *me*.

Father: I mean getting to the point of absence of disapproval—I mean I just don't . . . get it! He . . . even if we sat and didn't say a word about it, you would *know* whether we approved or disapproved.

Allen: How? . . . How?

Father: I think you lived with us long enough and know our thoughts and our ways and . . .

Allen: [Quickly] And you . . . you haven't changed any of them.

Father: Huh? Basically, I don't think so.

Allen: I was afraid of that.

Father: I don't think you've changed any eith—. . . basically either.

Mother: [Brief silence] But in order to give you our approval

> Therapist: or disapproval, we have to know what it is you're planning.
>
> Therapist: It doesn't matter . . . that he doesn't want it . . . he'll get it anyway?
>
> Mother: You mean he doesn't want our disapproval? If I disapprove I'll let him know anyway! If I approve I'll . . . I'll also let him know.

This interaction exemplifies the mother's delineation of Allen as someone she has the unquestioned right to control. She defends her definition of him with great energy, insisting that she know Allen's plans in order to register her approval or disapproval. It is clear that she fears and disapproves his independent actions. A related and characteristic delineation is the mother's view that unless she exerts great force, her son may not acquiesce to her wishes. Her need to operate as a constraint upon him appears automatic and unyielding, and the inference of defensive delineation is based upon this and upon evidence of anxiety and great need for control in her response to him.

The interaction further exemplifies the father's delineation of Allen as someone who knows what his parents think without asking and who must be controlled by this. He communicates an extremely pessimistic attitude about the possibility for increased independence and for change. The formulation of defensive delineation is based upon the inference of projection in this interaction. The father attributes to Allen his own feelings of the inevitability of compliance, at a time when Allen is actively attempting a different kind of behavior.

EXCERPT 2

Mother: If you go into an apartment. . . .
Allen: . . . it's a way of defending myself.
Therapist: Against what?
Father: What are you defending against?

Allen: Against both of you.

Mother: [Rather vehemently] I want to know that if you go into an apartment, that you're going to live like a human being.

Therapist: Which is . . . ?

Mother: Which is—knowing that he's going to have three meals a day, because I know how negligent he has been about his meals, even being here. . . .

Allen: [Low voice] I don't get three meals a day here either.

Mother: Well, that's your own fault! I know that he gets up late and he hasn't been eating breakfast—and he has his lunch, maybe 3 o'clock, maybe not. Then he has no supper! . . . and *that's* under proper supervision. Now what's he going to do if he's in an apartment by himself?

Therapist: He'll need a supervisor, won't he?

Mother: [Brief pause] Well, that's what I mean! Those things concern me. He's . . . unless he realizes that these things are important . . . to his health, and his maintenance . . . he has to know that he's . . . that he has to sleep on time, if he doesn't get enough sleep, which he feels isn't important, at least he didn't . . . and I had hoped already that he had thought that eating was important. (This speech spoken with much feeling.)

Allen: I'm surprised you haven't brought this up earlier. It's the first time you've mentioned this since. . . .

Mother: And if he goes into an apartment . . . I mean, when you say "apartment" you can get a one-room apartment, you can get a two-room, three-room apartment . . . I want to know that he's with somebody!

The mother's delineation of Allen as unable to care for even his basic physical needs, as well as her insistence that he needs supervision, is contradicted by current evidence known to the mother that he can in many ways care for himself. This evidence is ignored in her delineations of him, and the inference of defense is made because of the incomplete and strikingly limited view of Allen she communicates. The view is derogatory of his ability to maintain himself independently and, in its emphasis upon his need for supervision, supports the view that he is still in fact very much in need of her. Her repeated expressions of mistrust of Allen and insistence upon his need for supervision do not reflect his current demonstrated ability to work and to behave appropriately in the community. These attitudes seem to be determined more by the mother's need to remain necessary to Allen than by realistic evaluation of him.

Underlying these delineations of Allen was a continuing struggle for control within the family. This struggle became more explicit following Allen's discharge from the hospital as he, with increasing clarity, questioned the basis of his parents' authority. His attacks upon them were similar to attacks he had experienced from them. He repeatedly questioned their competence.

The following excerpt is a discussion of the argument that ensued. It is taken from a family treatment session three months after Allen's discharge from the hospital.

EXCERPT 3

Mother: [Very accusing voice] And you feel that I'm so—ignorant—that I'm so *moronic*—and he told me last night . . . he informed me that I should go to *college*.
Allen: [Quickly] I didn't say that.
Mother: Well, that I should educate myself more. . . .
Allen: You're not getting along with me very well either. You don't know how to get along with *me* . . . your knowledge. . . .
Mother: No, I don't know how to get along with you at all—you're the only person I can't get along with! Evidently. [pause] And I'd like to know the reason *why!* Because no matter . . . how much education I would get, if I told you, you would still be . . . education-wise, you would be above my level anyway. And I have no intentions of . . . uh getting more education just for your sake!

Allen: [Starts to speak but Father intervenes.]

Father: This, I think, is a basic. . . .

Mother: [Louder] I don't know *what* it is. . . .

Father: I think your . . . I think your basic thing is . . . to understand each other better . . . and to try . . . try to make a point of understanding each other better and do it different ways. Not *one* way.

Mother: Well, I think I *try* to understand Allen and I . . . I know that I . . . what he expects of me and what he doesn't want me to say and. . . . when I ask him something and if he feels I'm trespassing on his privacy, well, he's very wrong. [Hurt tone]

Allen: Perhaps I feel you should get more education for your *own* sake. [10-second silence]

Father: Now see, when I mentioned the point of trying to understand each other better . . . uh . . . you gave me, you came up with the answer that you were trying to understand. Allen is . . . did *not* come up with an answer; but *he* . . . is trying to understand *you*. And it's not a . . . one-way track. Things have to work both ways.

Mother: [sounds offended] But I'm not a mind-reader and I can't, uh, react in the way he expects me to react, on the spur of the moment. Uh . . . he thinks I should give him a serious answer possibly—the answer—not particularly just *an* answer or . . . uh . . . if I want to act in a spontaneous way. . . .

Father: Well, here I can't understand . . . is . . . I don't talk the same language that Allen does . . . uh . . . possibly I am as far off course as you are . . . in the . . . when we talk to Allen, who is a brilliant person, has a vast knowledge in his head. And when I talk I try to talk understandably in *my* own fashion . . . he has learned to accept . . . *my* way, but why he is trying to fight to accept *your* way, I don't know. Maybe *you* can come up with an answer. [Brief omission]

Father: But I don't condemn mother's way of thinking. I don't think she's. . . . as far as her . . . her herself . . . this is the way she thinks, this is the way she feels . . . this is the way she thinks and feels, then this is her way of living her life. . . .

Mother: And not only that, but when I say something, I don't sit and think, Well, am I hurting somebody or I'm not hurting someone. I say what I want to say at the time.

Allen: Not caring whether you hurt someone or not.

Mother: Have you seen or heard me hurt someone intentionally?

Allen: No, you do it *unintentionally*.

Therapist: Apparently Allen has hurt *you* quite a bit.

Mother: Yes, he has! . . . because . . . uh . . . for the greater part of the day I mean he's . . . just like his old self. [*Allen*: Old] but then it seemed as though all of a sudden a screw turns — and it's the other side of the record!

The delineations in this excerpt reflect the mother's view of Allen as controlling her or attempting to control her through his hostility and criticism. They communicate a view of Allen as a persecutor and an accuser when he is critical of and hostile to her. The issue of control is central. The mother sees her son's anger and criticism as implying a demand that she should change. She describes two views of Allen in this excerpt: one in which he is his old self (presumably compliant and nonattacking) and another in which he is angry, critical, and controlling. It is clear in this interaction that Allen also experiences his mother as hurtful and, by implication, coercive and controlling. Although there has in fact been an unpleasant argument in the family and Allen has been angry at his mother, it is less evident that he has as a central motivation the wish to control his mother. His argument with her seems rather an effort to defend against her attempts to control him. His interest seems more to preserve the new increment of independence he has attained than to change his parents.

In her delineation of Allen, his mother emphasizes a view of Allen as attempting to change her. She attributes to her son a wish to tell her what to do, which is characteristic of her behavior with him. Her view of the angry, critical Allen as a persecutor who is trying to control her seems to refer more to the mother's mode of operating than to Allen's behavior as it has been described and as it is seen in the interaction. Thus, projection appears to be an important determinant of the mother's view of Allen as attempting to control her. It is significant that Allen's view of her in this excerpt is clearly that she is trying to invade and control him. His reactions to feelings of being criticized, pried into, and trespassed upon are to fight and to insult his mother. Her view of this behavior is that it is unjustified and motivated by a wish to change her, and she denies any basis in her own actions that might have caused Allen to be angry.

The father expresses a view of Allen as superior to him intellectually, defining Allen as a brilliant person with vast knowledge. The father claims that Allen is tolerant of him despite the fact that they think differently. Here the father does not see Allen as critical and controlling as the mother does, but seems more identified with Allen in his struggle with the mother.

The dilemma that there are not identifiable bases for negotiation in the relationship other than submission and control continues to be the dominant dynamic in the family. These issues are further exemplified in the following interaction.

EXCERPT 4

Mother: Disagreement is one thing. Disagreements I can understand. It's . . . after all . . . uh . . . nobody agrees with *me* or I don't agree with Daddy all the time or with you or with anyone. Disagreement is one thing, but the way you vented your anger—or whatever you want to call it—on *me* . . . I mean, for no reason at all!

Allen: Perhaps I was angry at you!

Mother: Well, *why?*

Allen: Because you weren't trying hard enough. . . .

Mother: [Sounds very puzzled] Trying hard enough to do what. What do I have to try, uh, so hard to do? I was being myself, that's all! I accept *you* for what you are. Can't you accept me for what I am? For what I say?

Allen: You *don't* accept me for what I am. You know you don't accept me for what I am. Do we have to go through that again?

Mother: I think I accept you . . . uh . . . the same way that *daddy* does. . . . No—Just as much. But you don't . . . you don't . . . feel the same way. *You* don't perceive it in the same way. Perhaps.

Allen: I don't think you accept me . . . uh . . . looks like I'm going to mention the dirty word again . . . [slight laugh] Yoga—you don't accept me as a Yogi. Or as a student of Yoga.

Mother: [Louder] I don't accept Yoga. *No*. But that doesn't mean that I don't accept *you* for what you are. I don't like the idea of your getting so involved in Yoga . . . I thought that was something of the past. But I was surprised. . . .

Allen: You surely didn't accept me as a chela.

Mother: A *what?*

Allen: Chela. Means student—a Yoga student.

Mother: If I showed surprise . . . when you told me how involved you are in Yoga, yes, I was surprised.

Allen: No—but you don't accept me for that . . . .

Mother: That wasn't something that you have to get so angry about. . . .

Allen: We're not getting anywhere with this . . . along this line. . . . I'm just pointing out disagreements.

Mother: [louder] But that's what makes you *angry*—when I disagree with *you* you get . . . completely off . . . and you really let me have it!

Therapist: [Brief pause] How did Allen "let you have it"?

Mother: [As if the therapist should know] Well, I mean, he becomes so insulting—as though I was the most stupid person in the world . . . and I don't understand him and I'm prying, and uh . . . I'm not, uh, if I don't ask him questions then I'm not interested. If I ask him questions I'm spying—I'm being critical. And, uh, I don't know, he was just very insulting and very obnoxious toward me.

Allen: I guess I was.

This excerpt contains further delineations of Allen by his mother as someone who becomes enraged and insulting any time she disagrees with him. She insists that there is no reason for his anger. However, when the discussion focuses upon an interest of Allen's of which the mother explicitly disapproves—his interest in Yoga—there is contradiction in her delineation of Allen as someone she accepts. It is apparent that her acceptance is conditional upon her control of Allen and her approval of his behavior, although she denies this. It further appears that his anger at her reflects a continuing feeling of vulnerability to her. She is unable to see this and continues to define him as someone who is rude and who tries to control her with his insults. She does not perceive his attachment to her and his sensitivity to her disapproval.

The issue of Allen's involvement in Yoga, which is unacceptable to the mother, becomes the focus of this discussion. Allen's definition of himself as a chela arouses anxiety in the mother, who considers Yoga not only an unconventional interest that she does not understand, but also a symptom of his illness. She criticizes her son while insisting that the problem is his attempt to change her. She does not see his anger at her as an evidence of his vulnerability to her, although this is interpreted frequently in this phase of therapy. She insists upon her right to criticize Allen but remains indignant when he becomes angry with her.

The struggle over issues of controlling and being controlled continued to be the focus of discussion in the family sessions. The mother was generally the protagonist for the parents in these discussions, with the father tacitly agreeing with her. If he presented a view other than the mother's, it was with such unclarity as to render it ineffective. When the struggle between Allen and his mother was overt, the father retreated to an alliance with her. When Allen was critical of both parents, the father reacted defensively.

Excerpt 5

Allen: When I said I was embarrassed by you [omission] this was an indication of my feelings—and my feelings about *you*. Uh . . . I wish you would appreciate it more as something that's going on within me rather than something which is about you. And . . . I don't mean to say when I'm embarrassed by I . . . I don't mean to say your, you lack as a human being . . . or that uh . . . there are things that cause me embarrassment or the standard against which, in comparison, you embarrass me. That those standards are right rather than you are right. I don't mean that at all. When I said I was embarrassed, that was a feeling I had in me. And it had to do with *me*. As well as with you. And to some extent I feel that even though I am embarrassed, what this means to me is not so much that I have to throw *you* over and take up—whatever it is, the great intellectual standard . . . but, uh, to some extent I have to find out what it is about *you* that's good, and there *are* good things about you.

[Omission]

Father: Let's look at it from *this* point. It's not every student that can say their father is a genius!

Allen: [Brief pause, then thoughtfully] No . . . but . . . .

Father: Then how can you uh . . . your mother be inadequate if she married a genius?

Allen: Are you saying you're a genius?

Father: I *am*.

Mother: [facetiously] Oh, and am I a genius too?

Father: I didn't say that. [laughs]

Allen: [sounds amused] This . . . this . . . this . . . .

Mother: You said uh if . . . if I married you I have to be a genius too. . . .

Father: No. I said, uh, How can you be inadequate if you, uh . . . if you married a genius.

Allen: I'm rather reluctant to . . . using such superlatives. But . . .

Father: I'm not. I feel that I *am*. In *my* field, I think I am.

Therapist: That's the first time you've told Allen.

Father: No.

Therapist: You reacted, I thought, as if it were the first time you had ever heard your father tell you that.

Allen: In public. Where other people could . . . gets embarrassing! For you to say that.

[Omission]

Father: What, does it embarrass you?

Allen: It sounds vain.

Father: I don't think so. I think if a person develops himself . . . or is at that point where . . . they feel that they surpass other people in a certain field . . . that they can take credit of being . . . a genius.

The delineations of Allen in this excerpt grow from his assertion that he is embarrassed by his parents because of their lack of sophistication and education. His father reacts defensively to this discussion and proceeds to define himself as a genius, which embarrasses Allen further. Allen has stated that his feeling embarrassed by his parents is his own problem. His parents do not understand or accept this. His father is clearly extremely hurt, despite Allen's contention that his feelings about his parents are a problem for him, not for them.

The parents are extremely vulnerable to Allen's criticism. Differences between family members and critical attitudes continue to stimulate anxiety and defensive responses. The father is moved to define himself as a genius, a definition mobilized by his son's criticism. This is a striking interaction because it contains the overt expression of a fantasy of superiority, which the father uses here defensively in self-definition. In a previous excerpt, delineation of Allen as brilliant contained elements of the father's fantasy of superiority projected into his son. In this session he takes these qualities back into himself and defines himself as a genius. The argument over where the superiority and genius resides continues to be related in this family to a right to criticize and control others. In other discussions, authority was seen to require a fantasy of absolute morality and knowledge, which was a burden both to the parents and to the adolescent. Many of the struggles in the family were over this issue. Freedom to act independently in a state of uncertainty was sharply inhibited in all family members.

In ensuing family sessions and in relation to discussion of these issues in therapy, the father revealed more of his own thinking. This resulted in a clear differentiation between the father and the mother for the first time. A shift ensued away from the old alignment of the father joining the mother in argument against the adolescent. Now a new alignment between the father and the adolescent against the authority of the mother was seen. An excerpt from a family session two months later exemplifies this change. Early in this session the father says that he missed Allen when he did not visit home last week. He goes on to amplify his reasons for this.

Excerpt 6

Father: I actually think it was uh—probably I use him for somebody to lean on.

Therapist: How do you mean?

Father: Well, maybe as somebody that can understand me . . . a lot of times we get into . . . discussions . . . and . . . reasoning and things. He hears me . . . I think this is important. [low voice, slight laugh] Nobody understands me anymore!

Therapist: "Nobody" being. . . .

Father: [low voice] Well, in our family . . . people in our family . . . that I'm more, so intimate with—you know, the family group. [*Therapist*: Like?] . . like my wife, like my sister-in-law, like my brother-in-law . . . I guess that's part of it.

Therapist: Mrs. N. isn't looking very understanding at this moment. [slight laugh]

Mother: [irritated voice] So I suppose that every time you disagree with *me*, I'm supposed to say that you don't understand *me*! Is this the idea?

Father: Well, if I disagree with you, I don't *understand*
          you. . . .
Mother: Well . . . .
Therapist: So you've been having disagreements all week?
Father: I guess we've been having them, but I guess this
          past week was the . . . uh . . . no more than usual,
          but the fact that . . . uh—I feel I'm . . . sort of lost.
          [short laugh]

Here we find delineation of Allen by the father as similar
to him and as the only one in the family who understands
some aspects of what he says and thinks. The father
makes it explicit that he feels lost without the support and
agreement of the mother, a feeling which has been
expressed most frequently by Allen. As the discussion
continues, both parents describe how the father is different from the mother and her family. The similarity
between the father and Allen is implicitly in their opposition to the mother. The father seems to equate the
mother's ideas with the standards of society. However, he
really has many ideas contrary to hers. Allen is seen as
similar to the father in this.

The discussion continues with the father asserting
that the mother wants him to change his views. It is
similar to discussions the mother and Allen have in which
Allen protests that the mother wants him to change and
the mother insists he wants her to change. Allen is
important in this struggle in that, being antisociety himself, he is seen by the father as someone who can
understand his ideas and sympathize with them, which
the mother and her family will not do.

EXCERPT 6 (*continued*)

Father: . . . and don't you say . . . haven't you said that,
          "You're talking just like Allen!" . . . doesn't *this* in-
          volve him?
Mother: Well, the fact that people don't agree with you, or they

give their *own* point of view, doesn't mean that you're not accepted. If you don't agree with them, does that show that *we're* not accepted?

Father: I would like people, to whom I'm closer, to . . .

Mother: [louder, interrupting] Well, you can't change other people!

Father: [continuing] . . . accept my point of view as my point of view. I'm not asking *any*body to change their way of thinking and change their way of thinking to think the way I think . . . . I don't ask anybody to do that. What . . . if somebody wants me to express my point of view, I express it. [In background, *Mother*: Well, nobody asked you to change your point of view either.] When I ask somebody else to express their point of view, I accept it. But whether they *change* me or not, that's up to *me*. But I accept their point of view.

Mother: Nobody's trying to change you! Because you know they think a great deal of you! Even though you *think* that they don't! [pause] Well, *elaborate*.

There is great tension over the father's disagreement with the mother. Her assertion of acceptance of disagreement is no more believed by the father than it was believed by Allen when she told him she accepted him in a previous excerpt. It is as difficult for the parents to agree to disagree as it is for them to allow disagreement in Allen; in a disagreement it seems one family member or the other must change.

It is not clear from what has been discussed in the family session that the father's definition of Allen as like him in his deviant thinking is accurate. He assumes Allen's support, saying that Allen understands him and implying that he and Allen think the same way about things. In fact, they seem to share primarily their opposition to the mother. The father seems more to use Allen in fantasy for support in a struggle with his wife than to share with him a common point of view. This delineation of Allen seems to be a defensive projection into him by the father of qualities similar to his which have little to do with any agreement with Allen about what he actually feels about the matters that have been under discussion.

To recapitulate for a moment, these excerpts have been selected to illustrate aspects of parent–adolescent interaction relevant to independent functioning. Delineations of the adolescent by both parents contain no clear or consistent view of the adolescent as capable of effective independent actions. Independence in thinking is almost as great a problem. Here arguments about differences in values or beliefs are experienced as struggles for dominance and control. Differences are not tolerated within the family and when they emerge they are accompanied by the imperative that someone must change. This is true not only for differences between adolescent and parents, but also for differences between the parents themselves. The parents are initially able to maintain a facade of unity when they are joined in an effort to control the adolescent. In these arguments the father characteristically follows the mother's lead.

The adolescent is perceived as a persecutor by both parents when he is critical of them. The mother insists that he wants to change her when he criticizes and disagrees with her. Projection seems to be an important determinant of the delineation. The father takes back into himself the qualities of brilliance and genius he has projected into his son, to defend against the threat he feels from the adolescent's critical attitudes. Authority in this family is closely tied to fantasies of omniscience and perfection, and any criticism or argument threatens this illusion. The consequent threat to authority results in extreme defensive behavior. The feeling of being bereft of authority results in great uncertainty in the conduct of independent behavior.

As treatment progresses and the adolescent is in fact functioning independently, differences between the parents themselves become increasingly overt. These differences are accompanied by the same quality of anxiety and struggle which characterized the differences with the adolescent. The father is now regarded as the deviant by the mother, and in their arguments both feel attacked and controlled. Here the adolescent is delineated as being like his father in his deviance. In both, difference constitutes an attack upon the mother. The model for identification provided by the father has been one of submission to the mother, with characteristic suppression of differences. Identification is reinforced by explicit delineation of the adolescent as similar to his father when the father's thinking is revealed to deviate significantly from the mother's. This carries with it a built-in expectation that the adolescent will eventually give in to the mother as the father has.

The adolescent identity crisis is rooted in identifications that do not support the adolescent's new struggle for independent functioning. The father has accepted the mother's definition of difference as an attack and has characteristically acquiesced to the mother. The adolescent is in a crisis of redefinition of the consequences of differences and the basis of authority for independent behavior. He must define whether relationships can be maintained despite differences, whether authority exists without omniscience, and whether control must be the central issue between people.

Conclusion

Evidence of struggle over independent functioning in this family has been elucidated through analysis of excerpts of family interaction. Analysis of content and dynamics of delineations allow inferences to be made about the unconscious assumptions of the family as a group and the consequences of these for adolescent development.

In the conjoint family sessions, delineations having the aim of containment and control are regularly seen when thinking or action of one family member is perceived as independent of the control of other family members. Differences are interpreted within the family as attacks and imply a serious threat of loss and alienation. This is particularly true when differences and disagreements are expressed by the adolescent. His parents' delineations of him communicate their expectation of conformity and their intense antagonism to behavior independent of their supervision. Similar reactions are seen within the family to disagreements between the parents.

This family group is characterized by disturbance over independent functioning of individual members. Anxiety over authority and control, sensitivity over disagreements, and provocation of disagreements are all configurations that have been seen in family interactions. The consequences of these characteristics of family functioning for adolescent personality formation are particularly marked. The maturation of cognitive ego capacities allowing independent functioning makes the adolescent particularly vulnerable to the presence or absence of nutriment for these capacities in the family environment. The quality of such nutriment in the family system may be considered with reference to delineations and their dynamic determinants, and the unconscious assumptions of the family as a group.

Parental delineations of the adolescent in this family do not contain a reliable view of him as capable of effective independent action or thinking. We propose a relationship between these parental delineations and the fact that the identity crisis of the adolescent himself is manifested in great anxiety over his capacity to exist independently from his parents. His profound doubt of his own ability to function independently is an aspect of his disturbance in identity. It is a reflection of parental delineations of him. This problem in identity is generalized in his view of himself as highly vulnerable to the control of others. The clinical picture he presents—that of a defect in ego autonomy, specifically of an impairment in the ego's autonomy from objects in reality—is found in a family in which parental delineations do not contain within them the potential for the adolescent to become independent. Family experience thus does not integrate with the maturing cognitive capacities of the adolescent's ego, to promote a self-definition of independent functioning. On the contrary, cognitive development crystallizes an identity in accord with the parents' view of him, so that the adolescent sees himself as helpless, dependent, and vulnerable to outside control. Efforts to achieve greater independence through overt behavior in defiance of parental requirements are accompanied by guilt and disorganizing anxiety.

Unconscious assumptions of this family as inferred from these excerpts can be summarized as follows:

1. Independent thinking and action are threatening and must be discouraged;
2. Control over possible deviance must be exercised constantly;
3. Differences between members constitute attacks;
4. Attributes of authority are closely tied to fantasies of omniscience and may not be questioned;
5. Independent behavior contains a grave threat of separation and alienation;
6. The anxiety inherent in this threat may lead to personality dissolution or physical disorder; any family member seeking independence will be in a dilemma, facing, on the one hand, loss of individuation and differentiation through suppression of independent functioning or, on the other hand, anxiety and alienation through independent behavior and separation. These unconscious assumptions are internalized in the adolescent and impair his development of increased ego autonomy and individuation.

The internalizations under discussion represent more than delineations. Internalizations based upon identifications are also shown in behavior from which unconscious assumptions are inferred. We assume that through identification, images of the parents are internalized during development. These images shape important characteristics of adolescent personality functioning. We have presented evidence that through delineation, projection into the adolescent of particular characteristics of the parents results in an active definition of him related to qualities of the parents themselves. Thus certain characteristics that have been learned by the adolescent in identifications are also actively imposed and dynamically reinforced in defensive delineations. We consider the interplay between identification processes and delineations determined by family dynamics to be of great importance in the final determination of ego identity in adolescence, and to be crucial in determining differences in personality characteristics between siblings related to the dynamics of role allocation in the family.

Although the family group differs in important ways from the small groups studied by Bion, his conceptualization of the group as a whole and of the unconscious assumptions that frequently determine the behavior of group members facilitates an organization of observations of family interaction that elucidates unconscious assumptions and dynamics of role allocation. Unconscious assumptions and defensive delineations seek to hold the child and adolescent in relatively fixed roles throughout development. In this way, they interfere with the primary task of the family with regard to adolescent development. They militate against increased ego autonomy and the establishment of an identity that allows the adolescent to individuate and separate from the parents.

7

Projective Identification as a Mode of Perception and Behavior in Families of Adolescents

JOHN ZINNER, M.D.
ROGER L. SHAPIRO, M.D.

Projective identification is an activity of the ego that, among its effects, modifies perception of the object and, in a reciprocal fashion, alters the image of the self. These conjoined changes in perception influence and may in fact govern behavior of the self toward the object. Thus projective identification provides an important conceptual bridge between an individual and interpersonal psychology, since our awareness of the mechanism permits us to understand specific interactions *among* persons in terms of specific dynamic conflicts occurring *within* individuals.

The interpersonal ramifications of projective identification have been studied most carefully in transference and countertransference phenomena and in the therapeutic process (Malin and Grotstein 1966, Racker 1957, Searles 1963). While the counteridentifications of the analyst generated by the patient's projections are transitory, there are other interpersonal events in which projective identification leads to authentic and lasting structural change in the *recipient* of the projections. A prime example of this phenomenon is the effect of family interaction on the developing personality of the child. In our discussion we will describe the operation of projective identification within the family. We wish to show how the adolescent identifies with parental images of him and how these images may be distorted by the effect of parental projective identification.

Previously, we (R. Shapiro and Zinner 1971) have conceptualized characteristics of the family group *as a whole*, drawing upon, as an analogue, Bion's (1961) theory of small-group behavior. In Bion's formulation, which is based on psychoanalytic principles, small-group behavior is determined by both shared unconscious fantasies and more reality-oriented secondary-process thinking directed toward the fulfillment of particular tasks.

We view the family as such a small group, and, more metaphorically, as the cast of a drama, the themes of which are some combination of adaptive and functional family "work" tasks and a variety of generally unconscious fantasies, or covert assumptions, often conceived of as if they were a "hidden agenda."

Families with adolescent children have as a primary task to facilitate the development of ego autonomy and individuation in the offspring (R. Shapiro and Zinner 1971). This task, whose successful outcome implies a significant restructuring of the family group, is endangered by demands placed upon the child to collude with the unconscious assumptions of family life that are implicitly striving to maintain the status quo ante in family relationships. From the very formation of a new family, unconscious assumptions exert an important influence on behavior. Marital choice is motivated by a desire to find an object who will complement and reinforce unconscious fantasies (Dicks 1963). Prior to their birth, children are introduced into the covert assumptions of family life in their parents' fantasies, and from birth onward, a variety of parental coercions interact with the child's own instinctual requirements to fix him as a collusive participant in the family's hidden agenda.

Given the family drama, its fabric of conscious and unconscious themes, and an actively engaged but often unwitting cast, we wish to focus on the way in which roles are created and maintained. Our setting will be the nodal point of adolescence, during which the task of individuation is particularly vulnerable to contrary forces requiring conformity with family role expectations.

Forty-five emotionally disturbed adolescents and their families have been studied at the Clinical Center of the NIMH in an inpatient program that combines long-term conjoint family therapy, psychoanalytically oriented psychotherapy for the adolescent, and conjoint marital therapy for the parents. Because we have been interested in the way in which parents may influence the process of adolescent identity formation, our observations centered upon parental perceptions of and behavior toward their children. Included within the realm of parental behavior are acts and statements that communicate to the adolescent his parents' image of him. We have referred to these behaviors as *delineations*. As observers of the family, we make inferences, based upon an accumulation of delineating statements, about the composite object representation of the adolescent residing within the parental psychic structure.

Among parental delineations are those which are more determined by their service on behalf of parental defensive needs than by their capacity to appraise or perceive the realistic attributes of the adolescent. These *defensive delineations* are an expression of parental defensive organization and, as such, the parent is strongly motivated to sustain these perceptions of the adolescent, regardless of the adolescent's behavior that might otherwise alter the parental image. Defensive delineations are the expression at an individual level of family group behavior that is determined more by shared unconscious fantasies than by reality considerations.

As an illustration, in Chapter 6 we have described (R. Shapiro and Zinner 1971) a family in which the group shared this unconscious assumption, among others: that independent thinking and differences of opinion constitute an attack and a threat of separation and alienation.

Parental delineating communications are of immense significance to the developing child. They are part and parcel of parental behavior and, as with any other parental characteristic, constitute the raw material for adolescent internalization and subsequent identification. The adolescent does identify with defensively distorted parental images of him, and in this fashion, his own subjective self-experience is likely to be affected by his parents' efforts to diminish their own anxiety.

THE MECHANISM OF PROJECTIVE IDENTIFICATION

The translation of unconscious assumptions of family life into more concrete modes of perceiving and behaving in family interaction is accomplished by the mechanism of projective identification at the level of the individual member.

Jaffe (1968) has provided a careful review of the evolution of the concept of projective identification, including recognition of the clinical phenomenon prior to its naming in 1946 by Klein. At that time she defined projective identification as "a combination of splitting off parts of the self and projecting them on to another person" (1946, p. 108), later adding "the feeling of identification with other people because one has attributed qualities or attributes of one's own to them" (1955, p. 58). Klein saw this as a defensive mode evolving from an early infantile developmental stage characterized by splitting of the ego and objects as a defense against anxiety. In this connection it is important to recall A. Freud's (1936) earlier elaboration on Bibring's concept of "altruistic surrender" in terms of projection and identification. Here the self finds in others a "proxy in the outside world to serve as a repository" (p. 136) for the self's own wishes. A. Freud views this defensive mode as providing vicarious gratification of the projected impulse. Implicit in her formulation is the willingness, unconscious or not, of the recipient of the projections to collude in providing vicarious gratification on behalf of the other. In the absence of this collusive process the defense fails, or the projection is "lost," an extrapolation of the view of Malin and Grotstein (1966) made from a somewhat different perspective:

> What is projected would be lost like a satellite rocketed out of the gravitational pull of the earth. . . . A projection, of itself, seems meaningless unless this individual can retain some contact with what is projected. That contact is a type of internalization, or, loosely, an identification. [p. 27]

To what extent has this phenomenon of projective identification been encountered by those concerned with formulating an interpersonal psychology?

In the literature, a wide variety of terms have been employed to describe, qualitatively, relationships in which a participant interacts with others *as if* they were not themselves but someone else. The phenomenon has been repeatedly observed in family relations, brought to our attention by diverse investigators with disparate theoretical perspectives. It does appear that such relationships, whether they are called "scapegoating" (Vogel and Bell 1960), "trading of dissociations" (Wynne 1965), "merging" (Boszormenyi-Nagy 1967), "irrational role assignments" (Framo 1970), "symbiotic" (Mahler 1952), "evocation of a proxy" (Wangh 1962), "narcissistic" (Brodey 1965), or "family projection processes" (Bowen 1965), have sufficient common threads that we believe it useful to consider the possibility that they may be variants of a rather broadly defined concept of projective identification. The common threads are:

1. The subject perceives the object *as if* the object contained elements of the subject's personality,
2. The subject can evoke behaviors or feelings in the objects that conform with the subject's perceptions,
3. The subject can experience vicariously the activity and feelings of the object,
4. The participants in close relationships are often in collusion with one another to sustain mutual projections — that is, to support one another's defensive operations and to provide experiences through which the other can participate vicariously.

The meaning of the word *identification* used in this context has generated considerable discussion (see Jaffe 1968, p. 666 ff). In general, the term *projection* alone has not been considered sufficient to describe the entire defensive operation. As previously noted (Malin and Grotstein 1966, p. 27), the individual who is projecting must "retain some contact with what is projected" or the "projection, of itself, seems meaningless." In our conceptualization, *identification* (as in *projective identification*) refers to the *relationship* between a subject and his projected part as he experiences it within the object. The subject's behavior in this relationship is directed by two principles. The first is that the subject interacts with, or relates to, that projected part of himself in the object as he would interact with the self-part were it internalized. Freud (1921) has given us an example in characterizing the "falsification of judgment" that accompanies the idealization of loved objects:

> The tendency which falsifies judgment in this respect is that of *idealization* but now it is easier for us to find

our bearings. We see that the object is being treated in the same way as our own ego, so that when we are in love a considerable amount of narcissistic libido overflows on to the object. It is even obvious, in many forms of love choice, that the object serves as a substitute for some unattained ego ideal of our own. We love it on account of the perfections which we have striven to reach for our own ego, and which we should now like to procure in this roundabout way as a means of satisfying our narcissism. [p. 112]

The second principle governing behavior of the projecting subject toward the recipient object is that efforts must be made to involve the latter as a collusive partner in conforming with the way in which he is perceived. From an existential point of view, Laing (1962) notes:

We are denoting something other than the psychoanalytic term "projection." The one person does not wish merely to have the other as a hook on which to lay his projections. He strives to find in the other, or to induce the other to become, the very embodiment of that other, whose cooperation is required as "complement" of the particular identity he feels . . . impelled to sustain. [p. 101]

Wangh (1962) likewise has emphasized the active incitement process associated with the projection in the case of "altruistic surrender."

For projective identification to function effectively as a defense, the true nature of the relationship between the self and its projected part must remain unconscious, although the individual may feel an ill-defined bond or kinship with the recipient of his projections. The disinheriting of the projected part is not so complete that the subject loses his capacity to experience vicariously a wide range of the object's feelings, including those which the subject has himself evoked. These vicarious experiences contain features associated not only with gratification, but also with punishment and deprivation.

Within a family, then, a parent may be free both to experience the vicarious gratification of his own impulse through his adolescent and to repudiate and punish the adolescent for expressing those same impulses. Had this gratification–punishment axis remained internalized, one might imagine the parent to be bound by a corresponding neurotic turmoil. With one aspect of a previously internalized conflict now projected onto an interpersonal relationship, one can envisage a diminution of parental anxiety with, for example, the parent speaking for the superego, and the adolescent, as the parent sees him, speaking for the instinctual demand. This will be recognized as a modification of Johnson's (1949) formulation of the psychology of the individual delinquent.

We turn now to the matter of what "parts of the self" are in fact projected. We believe that the clinically observed variants of projective identification may have as some of their discriminating features these very differences in the content of the projections. Thus, whole objects, part-objects, drive representations, ego ideal, and superego elements all have been identified in one phenomenon or another as the projected elements of the personality. Our own conclusion is that the nature of the projected material, insofar as the relationships of parents to adolescents are concerned, contain highly conflicted elements of an object relationship with the parents' own families of origin. In these situations, the parent's projection of elements of his own previously internalized relationships serve not only a defensive function but also a restorative one to bring back to life in the form of the offspring the parent's own lost objects, both good and bad. Jaffe (1968) has similarly commented on the dual function of projective identification. This reenactment of the parent's own early object relations within the context of the family in which he himself is a parent may assume the form of highly fluid role attributions in which the adolescent may be perceived at one time as the parent's parent, and at other times as the child who his parent once was. Thus in the same family a child can be both parentified and infantilized. In our ongoing studies of families, we are attempting to relate the contents of parental projective identifications to the specific psychopathology of the disturbed adolescent.

The latter statement illustrates our belief that projective identification is a dimensional concept that is operative in both "healthy" and "disturbed" families. The variables relevant to the development of psychopathology in the offspring seem to involve the content of the projected material, the capacity of the parent to differentiate himself from the child, and the intensity of the parental defensive requirements. Depending upon the nature of the interaction of these factors, projective identification can endow a relationship with salutary empathic qualities or, to the contrary, generate binding attributions in which the child remains a creature of parental defensive economy.

How do we account for the extent to which adolescents may collude in this activity, with the result that parental defensive delineations become a self-fulfilling prophecy? Our view is that there are a variety of motivations and coercions for the adolescent's collusion with a parental projective identification. Among these are the opportunity for impulse gratification (as in the case of Johnson's delinquents), actualization of omnipotent fantasies supported by the child's power to determine his parent's self-experience, tacit parental compliance with the adolescent's defensive needs, and selective parental reinforcement of attributes of the adolescent that conform to parental projections. We believe, however, that the motivation that may need to be most reckoned with is the adolescent's fear of object loss which might ensue were he not to act on behalf of the parent's defensive organization. If we view our disturbed adolescents as walking a fine line between fulfillment of their own strivings for an autonomous identity and conformity with a parental delineation serving parental defense, we are deeply impressed with the power that parental anxiety holds in tipping the balance. This notion helps to explain a phenomenon not infrequently seen in family therapy wherein a previously asymptomatic parent becomes emotionally disturbed following independent activity and improvement in the clinical status of the adolescent.

Throughout this discussion we have focused on parents' defensive delineations of their children. Reciprocally, for the adolescent, projective identification with his parents represents to a similar extent the utilization of the family small group for defensive purposes. In one of its most familiar manifestations, many parents experience themselves as misperceived by their adolescent children by being delineated as far more authoritarian and unsympathetic than they feel themselves to be. In fact, the renewed experimentation with sources of drive gratification, which is characteristic of adolescence, may require partial reprojection of adolescent superego onto parents to alleviate the inhibition of action that might ensue were the harshest aspects of adolescent superego persistently internalized.

CLINICAL MATERIAL

Excerpts from conjoint sessions of the B. family will serve to demonstrate some of the vicissitudes of projective identification and particularly the dynamic alterations between projective and internalizing modes and their impact on family members.

We frequently observe that parents delineate their adolescent offspring in comparison with themselves. On occasion, the distinction between the parent's perception of himself and of the adolescent becomes quite blurred, with the result that the parent appears to introject or reinherit an attribute that was previously assigned to the adolescent and eschewed by himself. This seems to initiate parental anxiety and motivates a repetition of the projective defense. In the first example, mother's final defensive delineation of her son Tom, our index patient, as "not liking people" defuses a potential marital conflict that threatens to erupt as a consequence of her internalizing her own conflicted feelings regarding social relationships with other individuals.

EXAMPLE 1

During a family therapy session, Mrs. B. was commenting on Tom's isolation and reluctance to participate in family activities. She noted that this quality was in distinction to her own feelings about being with people and continued:

I think maybe the difference is I find I can get along with almost anybody but I don't always enjoy it . . . uh . . . [rather long pause] for instance, in the Army where much . . . lunch parties, tea parties, and things are almost obligatory are terribly boring to me [shallow laugh]. Uhhh, I must say I did as little of that sort of thing as I could help, but I'm quite aware that I have a tendency to uh push people off when I don't think they're particularly attractive and yet no doubt a lot of the fault lies in the beginning with me not finding them particularly worth seeing or knowing and this may well be why I didn't [sounds awkward], why Tom was in so much trouble. You know, to say "Well, Tom doesn't like people; well, not everybody but lots of people or people of all kinds."

Once this delineation has been firmly reprojected onto her son, she is then shortly afterward able to respond with enthusiasm—"oh gosh yes,"—to her husband when he insists, "But we have enjoyed and I thought you had enjoyed the social life."

EXAMPLE 2

In the B. family, a shared unconscious assumption is that the variety and intensity of sexual interests are "irrepressible" and impossible to control. Mother has repeatedly delineated herself as unaffected by this problem while insistently regarding her son Tom as being unable to contain his impulses. She tells him that his efforts to "suppress" them will be in vain because "you can't turn your back on it." In this family session, Tom consistently denies and refutes this delineation and, in response, Mrs. B., who has previously spoken of impulse control as entirely Tom's problem, begins to talk of her own experience:

[T]hat I was uh constantly trying to avoid thinking about sex because it was on my mind so much [anxious laugh]. So I wouldn't say I suppressed it, I repressed. I had not . . . no intention of having any serious sexual experiences before I got married and I . . . didn't! But I . . . and I think the older you get up to a certain point, the stronger your feelings are. Something I don't think Tom's considered looking ahead two or three years. Now if this can be true of me, I've always understood, it wouldn't be necessarily . . . feelings wouldn't necessarily be stronger or as strong as mine but that's no reason I'm a freak. I don't *think* I am.

Coupled with the apparent internalization of her previously projected conflict is a rising titer of anxiety in the mother as she develops concern about the possibility of her being a "freak." It is as if she has been saying, "if Tom is a freak, then I am not; but if he is not a freak, as he says he is not, then I must be." In this situation, her defensive delineation, a projective identification, has met an unaccepting recipient, and the defensive economy is no longer served. She has failed to evoke in her son a complementary identification. The adolescent in this process has tenaciously refused to modify his own perception of himself, but clearly at his mother's expense.

EXAMPLE 3

In the following interaction, the therapist's efforts to encourage internalization by father of his projective delineation of Tom met with collusive resistance from Tom as well as father. The eventual yielding of defense is accompanied by a shift from Tom to father as the family member perceived as troubled.

With his father, Tom seems to be more reluctant to assert a separate and distinct self-image. Mr. B. had been consistently aloof, frequently absent from his family while he was active in a military career. He is chillingly remote in his interpersonal relationships. Yet Mr. B. has frequently assailed Tom for Tom's isolation, withdrawal, and preoccupation with fantasy, denying that quality in himself:

I realize you are not interested in anything outside of your dream world, that you were sort of closed off from any engagement, any interest, any awareness of things going on outside.

Tom mildly repudiates this view as he argues:

But you said that I wasn't aware of the outside world and I feel I was.

Here the therapist intervenes with an observation of Mr. B.:

You referred to the feeling that Tom described about wanting to turn your invitations down and not wanting to have to but not wanting to do things with you. This kind of pushing people away—I think it's reflected in you to some extent.

Mr. B. responds to the therapist's attempts to encourage internalization by creating a new distinction between Tom and himself:

I feel personally an intense interest in everything. Very often I prefer uh solitary activity. I've always enjoyed uh fishing by myself, walking on the beach by myself, things like that. Well, I feel in my mind, I like solitary activity, but . . . which brings me into contact with the environment, and I see Tom as withdrawing from his environment in his solitude. In other words, I can be content walking for hours around the streets of New York by myself without talking to anybody but enjoying shop . . . windowshopping and seeing people and . . . enjoying uh . . . seeing the activity. He wants to . . . solitude truly, alone truly. Well, I enjoy travel and I've had a lot more opportunity for travel than any other members of my family. To me to travel in a big city is a tremendous form of recreation in the literal sense and I can get this recreation without having to talk to anybody, without having associates with me. Then I can enjoy new sights and new sounds by myself and my only recreation here really is on weekends when I take one afternoon off from my family and I walk. I walk ten miles, sometimes longer. Walk from here to Georgetown or walk from here to uh . . . not as far as the Capitol yet but I feel that I need exercise and walking to me is a solitary form of exercise which I do enjoy.

Tom very much seems to collude with his father in affirming this rather elusive distinction between Mr. B.'s view of himself and of Tom. Tom says:

Well, yeah, I would say it in different words, though. I see my father as being interested in the outside really and content with life and uh wanting to be alone. But with me it's I feel bored with life and I should say bored with the outside world and discontent with life. Wanting things that I don't have. And so uh . . . so looking inward on an inward world and being content with that.

With further encouragement by the therapist, Mr. B. elaborates on his own active fantasy life but continues to rely heavily on a distinction between himself and his troubled son:

Sometimes I'm thinking. I could be out in the middle of a lake and thinking about some place else uh at the same time I'm engaged in from time to time in admiring the fact that I'm out in the middle of the lake, I sort of daydream. I don't know whether I daydream more than average or not. It's only gonna—tell me what the average is. I play the Harvard–Yale game over in my mind and I'm the star and hell, I'm a gay man with the ladies and everything else, so I have daydreams. I dream of power and wealth and success and love.

Although now the delineations of Tom and of himself have become blurred, Mr. B. adds "But I'm concerned that the removing of (Tom's) self too completely from his environment, that uh I think there's a place in everybody's consciousness for daydreams."

Now the therapist deals more directly with Mr. B.'s projection:

I think you may be concerned because you understand it very well, actually, and it may even be that it concerns you about yourself. You see some things in Tom that remind you of yourself and maybe they are things that you've fought in yourself.

On the heels of this interpretation, Mr. B. appears to internalize a previously projected aspect of himself that he had apparently viewed as "sick" and as attributable only to Tom:

Well, I feel, Dr. S., well adjusted and I feel that I'm probably happier than the average man is; I don't know. Because I don't know what the average is. I uh have uh never felt the requirement for psychiatric treatment. Uh this fact is pertinent because I have been worried about high blood pressure and uh other symptoms and my doctor at the Army Hospital has said, "Well, maybe you need" well, he hasn't suggested it exactly, he said uh, "Would you like to see a psychiatrist?" and I told him I didn't feel I needed a psychiatrist. I thought my symptoms were organic [lowers voice]. I still do. This came up today. I felt very tense this fall and sleepless and a ringing in the ears. I felt perhaps blood pressure might be a factor. I had my blood pressure taken and it was high but not abnormally so. The ear ringing has been persistent. Now the doctor feels that perhaps this is—I think that perhaps the doctor doesn't believe I have ringing in the ears but uh for several months now my ears have been—is this psychosomatic? I don't think so. Or is it a symptom of high blood pressure? I don't know. I have another appointment next week with an ear specialist, maybe, so I. . . .

In this interaction there is a rather vivid demonstration of the defensive nature of the father's delineation of his son. As this defense is encountered openly by the therapist, considerable resistance appears in the form of new delineations. Furthermore, the son, by identifying with the percept of the only "sick family member" acts in a collusive manner to maintain the father's new delineation of him. Finally, the projection disintegrates and the father is left with the "sick" part of himself internalized. Mournfully, he begins to elaborate his own symptoms.

We recognize that attempts to describe family interaction with the sort of reductive analysis we have applied here may highlight the phenomenon under our immediate scrutiny while obscuring from view a rich variety of contemporaneous family events. Family interaction consists of an intricately coordinated flow (both simultaneous and serial) of shared and complementary behaviors and perceptions, the sequencing of which resists characterization by discursive prose. For example, we have intentionally focused upon parental perceptions of their adolescents although we are cognizant that simultaneous reciprocal delineations of parent by adolescent are equally present and important. Nor, for clarity's sake, have we stressed the existence of a hierarchy of delineations of the object by the subject, or "metaperspectives" (Laing, Phillipson, and Lee 1966)—that is, A's view of B, A's view of B's view of A, and so forth.

Implicit, but not yet emphasized, in our analysis is the role of social context—that is, the presence or absence of significant others in the determination of the defensive delineations. As illustration, the mother's delineation of Tom (Example 1) as "not lik(ing) people" was influenced by the presence in the room of father, who needed, for his *own* defensive purpose, to delineate mother as having "enjoyed the social life." Were the father absent, the mother may not have felt compelled to comply with his perception of her, which would, in turn, modify her image on that occasion of Tom and of herself.

Our observations are drawn from long-term therapeutic experiences but are essentially cross-sectional when viewed from a total developmental perspective. The dynamic processes that we are describing operate throughout childhood development as they do throughout the entire history of the family. What we see during adolescence is certainly the product of years of family functioning according to covert assumptions, some of which are unvarying, while others are subject to modification. New unconscious assumptions into family life may certainly be introduced by the entry of the child into a new developmental phase—by puberty, for example, which revitalizes oedipal conflicts within the family as a group as it does in the individual adolescent (Rangell 1955).

We have made no mention thus far of different psychological outcomes in siblings. Except in the most superficial sense, there exists no single milieu within a family. Insofar as each child holds a different meaning for his family and may provide different opportunities for the playing out of parental defensive requirements, his experiential grasp of family environment will differ significantly from that of his sibling. Thus in examining the quality of child rearing within families, we cannot regard parental behaviors as representative of relatively unvarying parental "traits" but must take into account the nature of parental delineations of each particular child as a primary source for understanding the influence of the family on the personality development of that child.

Summary

In summary, we have been examining from a psychoanalytic perspective family dynamics in relation to psychological outcome of the adolescent. Family behavior and subjective experience are determined to varying degrees by shared unconscious fantasies or unconscious assumptions. Role allocations for the collusive playing out of these fantasies are communicated and evoked in family members by the mechanism of projective identification. The threat of parental anxiety and object loss is an important factor in determining the collusion of the adolescent with parental projections.

Projective identification occurs in all families, but the adolescent outcome is determined, among other factors, by the contents of parental projection, intensity of parental defensive needs, and the parent's own ability to experience himself as separate from his offspring.

The fact of differing adolescent outcomes within the same family can be accounted for by the relationship-specific quality of parental projective identifications, that is, by the different meanings each child has for his parents.

8

The Influence of Family Experience on Borderline Personality Development

EDWARD R. SHAPIRO, M.A., M.D.
JOHN ZINNER, M.D.
ROGER L. SHAPIRO, M.D.
DAVID A. BERKOWITZ, M.D.

There is general agreement in the recent psychoanalytic literature that the characteristic personality features of the borderline patient derive from a developmental impasse that initially occurs during the early childhood separation–individuation stage (Kernberg 1967, 1972, Mahler 1968, 1971). This impasse—due to pathological factors in the interplay of inborn drive, ego disposition, and experience—results in a partial failure to move beyond the symbiotic relationship with the mother to a position of relative separateness. Theoretically, the difficulty occurs after self–object differentiation, but prior to the development of object constancy. It is clinically manifest by a persistent use of splitting as a defense—that is, a dissociation between self and object images that are libidinally tinged and those that are colored by aggressive tones (Kernberg 1966, 1967, 1972).

Previous investigations of the possible experiential components of early developmental difficulties have pointed to a failure in the "holding environment" (Winnicott 1954, 1969) characterized both by an anxious maternal response to the infant's aggressive expression (Greenacre 1960, Kernberg 1972, Winnicott 1969, 1970), and by failure of the infant to evoke good-enough mothering (Benedek 1970, Escalona 1963, Ritvo and Solnit 1958). Although several studies have documented through psychoanalytic observation the child's responsiveness to unconscious needs of the mother (Burlingham 1955, Levy 1960, Sperling 1950), none of this work has taken into account the quality of relationships to both parents, which can be ascertained through observations of the entire family in interaction.

In this chapter we explore certain specific contributions of the family to the development of this ego impairment in the borderline child. In our study of borderline adolescents and their families, we find that certain characteristics of the adolescent's internalizations, as manifested in the individual transference (Loewald 1962), are also observable in regressive family interactions (Zinner and E. Shapiro 1975) that occur during this "second separation–individuation period" (Blos 1967). This observation has allowed us to discern consistent patterns of family reaction to dependent and autonomous behavior, which appear both to serve complementary defensive needs in the parents and to function as a developmental interference for their child.

In his epigenetic view of ego development, Erikson (1959) proposes an inborn sequence of developmental tasks which requires a crucial, mutual coordination between developing individuals and their human environment. In Erikson's view, caretaking persons are coordinated to the developing individual by their specific inborn responsiveness to his needs and by phase-specific needs of their own (Rapaport 1959). In this chapter, we will present a detailed case study of a borderline adolescent and her family—transference, retrospective history, and current interaction—in an attempt to delineate more specifically genetic and dynamic aspects of a particular failure in this coordination during separation–individuation. We will illustrate how this failure, the derivatives of which reappear during the child's adolescence, contributes to an impairment in the formation of the adolescent's ego identity.

We will focus our observations on three levels. First, we will outline the development of the parents' personalities in their families of origin. Second, we will review the development of relationships in the current family and their reflexions in the individual transference. Finally, in the context of both transference and reconstructed history, we will examine current family interaction to illustrate the reenactment of earlier patterns of behavior in which the designated child's need for nurture and support mobilized aggression in the family.

THEORETICAL BACKGROUND

Kernberg (1966, 1972) describes the borderline outcome as a specific failure in ego development characterized by a fixation at an early stage in the development of internalized object relations, during which there is an active defensive splitting of "all good" (organized around pleasureable mother–child interactions) and "all bad" (derived from painful and frustrating interactions) self-images, object-images, and their affective links. Failure to achieve the normal coalescence of these two polar constellations is seen by Kernberg (1966) as a consequence of a quantitative predominance of negative introjections. The intensity of these negative internalized relationships requires that they be split off and projected onto the outside in order to allow a consolidation and protection of the positive relationship with mother in the face of frustration. Fixation at this point leads to the splitting of contradictory ego states characteristic of borderline patients (Kernberg 1966, 1967, 1972).

What creates this intensity? Either constitutional or environmental sources of increased aggression and frustration may contribute. In either case, however, it is the family's task to facilitate the integration of positive and negative internalized relationships in their developing child. Kernberg states (1972) that the mother's role is crucial:

> [H]er tolerance of [the child's] anger and her continuing provision of love may crucially strengthen the infant's conviction in the strength of the good self and the good object, and decrease his fear over his own aggressive tendencies. [p. 241]

This comment parallels Winnicott's (1954, 1960, 1969) description of a "holding environment" in which the mother "survives" her child's instinctual assaults without retaliation or withdrawal. By this capacity to survive, the mother demonstrates to the infant her own autonomy and independent existence, thus enabling him to develop a relationship with her as a real object rather than as a projective entity.

According to this formulation, if the mother retaliates for the infant's aggression or withdraws from his demands, she confirms his fear of the power of his aggressively tinged self and object representations, making it increasingly difficult for him subsequently to integrate them because of the increased threat to the now fragile sense of the positive relationship with mother. Responding to the mother's retaliation and withdrawal, the infant generates increased rage and greater demands, thus contributing to a spiralling crisis in their interaction and intensifying his need for defensive splitting and projection.

Although the initial and determining interactions occur primarily in the dyadic relationships of the first two years, resurgence of instinctual pressures and maturation of the ego between ages 2 and 3 and in adolescence, during attempts at separation–individuation (Blos 1962, 1967, Mahler 1971), confront the child with the task of further integrating positive and negative aspects of self and object into an integrated self-concept and an integrated conception of others in his development of an ego identity (Erikson 1956). Achievement of this integration is essential in order to overcome residual symbiotic ties to original objects and to develop flexible relationships with objects that can then, in Winnicott's (1969) word, be "used" according to their own changing properties. This development takes place within and is affected by the family group, who must provide, then, a "holding environment."

BORDERLINE ADOLESCENTS AND THEIR FAMILIES

Work with families of borderline adolescents (Berkowitz et al. 1974b, R. Shapiro 1968, Zinner and E. Shapiro 1975) reveals that the adolescence of the borderline child becomes a period of family regression as well. During separation–individuation periods (ages 2 to 3 and adolescence) of the borderline child, family behavior becomes dominated by unconscious fantasy that requires defensive operations.

ADOLESCENT AUTONOMY AND DEPENDENCY AS THREATS

Previously we (Zinner and E. Shapiro 1975) presented clinical evidence from a series of families with borderline adolescents to demonstrate the defensive use of splitting as a regressive group phenomenon in response to behaviors that herald autonomy and separation on the part of these designated adolescents. We characterized various forms of family splitting in which attributes of "goodness" (loving, gratifying, and providing) and "badness" (hating, punishing, depriving) were dissociated from each other and reinvested either in different family members or in the family and the outside world. In the families presented, the predominant parental solution to conflicts over autonomy involved a denial of *autonomous* wishes and a projection of these wishes into the borderline adolescent. The parents were then observed to behave intolerantly toward the child's autonomous strivings. We inferred a shared unconscious fantasy in these families that the child's autonomous wishes represent a hostile condemnation of the family which would destroy the loved ("good") anaclitic object. This shared assumption, we suggested, created the defensive imperative for family members to split off and project these hostile self and object representations in order to preserve the paramount positive libidinal ties. During the adolescence of their borderline child, family members appeared unable to provide a holding environment in which the adolescent could safely attempt autonomous behavior without threatening the existence of his loving and sustaining family ties.

Further study has revealed that the foregoing dynamic is but one side of a larger problem. There is a second group of borderline adolescents whose families respond intolerantly to their phase-appropriate needs for nurture and support. These *dependent* needs are unconsciously perceived by the parents as hostile, draining demands, from which they withdraw. Intensive study of these cases reveals that the source of this perception resides in denied dependency needs in each of the parents.

We see, then, two types of families. In one, the parents complain that their borderline child is too independent and that he is more interested in his friends than in the family. In the second, the parents worry that their child is too dependent on them, and not sufficiently involved with the outside world. Although the superficial presentation is strikingly different in these two groups, the underlying developmental impairment is the same.

In both types of families, the parents remain symbiotically bound to their families of origin (Mahler 1952, Masterson 1972), having failed to achieve a stable integration of their positive and negative internalized relationships. Critical experiences with their own parents during separation–individuation have contributed to an unconscious association of either autonomous or dependent behaviors with either libidinally or aggressively tinged self and object representations (that is, autonomy is associated with a "good" experience and dependency with a "bad" one, or vice versa). These positive and negative self-perceptions are unintegrated and in conflict with each other. In an attempt to deal with this conflict, each parent identifies with the positively toned self-perception (that is, each sees himself as "lovingly dependent" or "strong and autonomous") and disavows and projects the other.

The marital relationship in these families is characterized by a complementarity of defenses (Dicks 1963, Lidz et al. 1957, Wynne et al. 1958) and the shared use of primitive forms of projective identification in their relationship with their children. Projective identification (Zinner 1976, Zinner and R. Shapiro 1972) is the mechanism described in Chapter 7 by which unconscious assumptions are translated into more concrete forms of behavior and response. It comprises a projection of unaccepted parts of the parents' own personalities, responsive behavior in the child, and an identification with and vicarious experiencing of the child's behavior by the parent.

In the families studied, the borderline child is unconsciously chosen by the parents to participate with them in a relationship that embodies their denied, aggressively tinged self–object representations. On the one hand, if each parent perceives himself in his own way as "lovingly dependent," then the borderline child is unconsciously perceived as ruthlessly independent. On the other hand, if each parent views himself as "strong and autonomous," without dependent needs, then the designated child is perceived as ravenously demanding and aggressively dependent. These perceptions have particular impact during periods of separation–individuation when, depending on their own self-perception, the parents unconsciously view the child's independent moves as hostile rejections or his needs for nurturance and support as draining demands. Early interactions between parent and child that are dominated by these unconscious assumptions become one important basis for the child's internalizations (R. Shapiro and Zinner 1971) and may contribute developmentally to an impairment in his ego formation. Motivated by his inability to tolerate either parental anxiety or his own anxiety over the possible loss of parental love, the borderline child unconsciously attempts to modify his subjective experience in accordance with defensive parental projections (Zinner and R. Shapiro 1972).

In both types of families the effect on the borderline child is the same: He is inhibited by the shared parental perception of his attitudes as hostile. In response to this misperception and to his own intensified autonomous strivings or dependent longings, he oscillates in anxiety and uncertainty between a complete repudiation of family ties and a total, age-inappropriate dependency. This oscillation is the behavioral manifestation of the borderline child's defensive split in internalized relationships. It is in marked contrast to the normal developmental transition, which combines gradually emerging autonomy with gradually attenuating dependency.

THE DEVELOPMENT OF REGRESSIVE
FAMILY INTERACTIONS

In the following case report, we will attempt to demonstrate the *development* of this deficient holding environment and its relationship to the intrapsychic structure of the borderline adolescent. We have chosen for discussion a family in which both parents have denied their dependent wishes, projecting them on to their borderline child. We will illustrate how the unconscious parental equation of dependent longings with hostile, draining demand appears to be a repetition of a similar response to dependent needs in the borderline child's infancy, as well as a regressive reenactment of similar conflicts experienced by the parents in their respective families of origin. It is our thesis that these unconscious family assumptions and delineations constitute a developmental interference. In interaction with the borderline child's inborn drive and ego disposition, this interference leads to an intensification of negative self and object images and a resultant pathological continuance of defensive splitting of positive and negative internalized relationships.

In the following, we will describe a borderline adolescent girl, whose transference relationship to the therapist alternates between two extremes. On the one hand, she perceives herself as helpless, bereft, and longing in relation to a therapist perceived as warm, nurturant, and providing. On the other hand, she perceives herself as angry, repudiating, and autonomous in relation to a therapist (more frequently) perceived as cold, ruthless, and depriving. These two perceptions of the therapist are dissociated, and although they may both occur within the same session, they are effectively split from each other.

The origin of these transference dispositions can be understood through observation and reconstruction of the nature of her family interactions. Through the use of retrospective history (from both parents and adolescent), representative excerpts from current family interaction, and transference observations, we will demonstrate how the parents' defensive denial of their own dependent longings leads, at each crucial stage of this adolescent's development, to a deficient familial "holding environment" and a severe impairment in the formation of her ego identity. We will illustrate how expression of dependent longings during the three critical periods (early infancy, ages 2 to 3, and adolescence) by this designated child confronts the parents with disavowed parts of themselves, thus threatening their own tenuous sense of autonomy and evoking from them a powerful response.

CLINICAL OBSERVATIONS

The case to be described is representative of a subgroup among over fifty adolescent inpatients and their families treated by our group on a residential unit at the NIMH. Therapeutic modalities include intensive psychoanalytically oriented individual psychotherapy for the adolescent, weekly conjoint family therapy, and conjoint marital therapy for the parents. All of these sessions were audiotaped and observed. In the following case, one of us (E.R.S.) treated the patient and family (the latter with a co-therapist) and observed the marital therapy. Further material about this family will be presented in Chapter 16.

Sarah Blackwell is a 19-year-old female who was admitted to the hospital after a three-year history of running away; promiscuity; amphetamine, barbiturate, and hallucinogen abuse; and, most seriously, repetitive alcohol intoxication almost nightly to the point of unconsciousness. Her main complaint was that she found herself increasingly "spaced out," an experience she described as being overwhelmingly alone, unable to talk or think clearly, and totally devoid of feeling. Her alcohol use was related to an attempt to medicate herself for this isolation. She related, in a bland tone, how alcohol allowed her to change from being isolated and inhibited to being aggressive and outgoing. She had been able to have sex only when drunk, often punching and biting her partner.

The dissociated nature of these experiences is one

aspect of the widespread splitting characteristic of this patient. Of particular note in this admission history is Sarah's inability to experience her needfulness without entering a dissociated state facilitated by the use of alcohol. The pathological split in internalized object relationships represented by these contradictory ego states can be understood, in part, as a product of transactions occurring in Sarah's relationships with her parents. Reconstruction of these relationships through the three generations reveals consistent difficulty in responding to dependent needs, which are seen, with varying intensity, as hostile, draining demands.

THE PARENTS

It is important to note that reconstruction of the Blackwell parental history, without the confirmation of either additional witness or current observation, is colored by the nature of parental splitting. What we are interested in is the current *perceptions* each parent has of his family of origin. These perceptions reflect the nature of internalized self–object images. The monochromatic pictures that emerge reflect the internalized split in each of the parents, particularly in relationship to dependency and autonomy.

Mrs. Blackwell was the last child of a poor, strict, Midwestern Catholic farming couple. She remembers often being told by her "cold, withdrawn mother" that she had been an unwanted child and that there "was not enough food." Emotional supplies, as she recalls, were also sparse: She remembers following her mother around, wishing for her to smile and wondering what she had done wrong. Her older brother was favored by mother and was, as she saw it, kept at home too much. He became psychotic in adolescence and, at age 40, is still at home with mother. Mrs. Blackwell sees this as a consequence of prolonged intimacy and says, "[my mother] wanted to keep him a little boy—a *sick* little boy."

Mrs. Blackwell sees herself as having become very independent in relation to her family. Critical, frustrating interactions with her parents about her expression of dependent longings led to a denial of her dependency and an unconscious association of dependent needs with feelings of "badness." Her reconstruction of her early life presents an unrelieved picture of deprivation, a picture that provides defensive justification for her subsequent repudiation of her family.

She left home early in high school in order to "earn money" and insisted on paying her own college bills. She refused her parents' allowance because "they wanted to control me"; angry at the frustration of her dependent longings, she projected her anger, thus enabling herself to leave these "hostile" parents. Independent moves, for Mrs. Blackwell, required a disavowal of all family values: She moved to a biracial dormitory, indulged in premarital sex, and married a man of a different religion and nationality. Since her marriage, she has felt extremely guilty for what she "did to [her] parents," a statement that reflects her guilt over her hostile rejection of them, as well as over her now denied oral cravings.

In order to achieve autonomy, then, Mrs. Blackwell had to defensively repudiate her parents, as well as her painful and frustrating dependent relationships, which constituted her "bad" self–object relationship with them. Guilt and self-hatred are, for Mrs. Blackwell, the consequences of expression of need, and motivate her agonizing struggle for autonomy.

Although Mr. Blackwell recalls predominantly *positive* images of his relationship with his family, he also was unable to obtain the necessary emotional supplies. The youngest son of wealthy, elderly South Americans, Mr. Blackwell was the "baby" in the family—overprotected, pampered, and praised as long as he entertained but severely punished when he transgressed. Throughout his childhood he was allowed to run up large accounts at local stores ("Money was always available," he says). He seldom discussed anything with his "distant" parents, however.

In his early adolescence, Mr. Blackwell was abruptly sent off to boarding school for six months without any discussion with his parents, after he and a friend were caught pinching the family maid. He saw this as typical of the many austere punishments he received at home and says, "The retribution was always much heavier than the sins." In relation to his family, Mr. Blackwell saw himself as "compliant" but independent, recognizing no anger or needfulness in response to them. Angry outbursts were not tolerated by his parents, whose marginal involvement was reserved for his "best behavior." The fragility of his proclaimed independence and the enormity of his denied unmet dependency needs are manifest in his description of himself as an adolescent (a description that is still highly accurate):

My ideal of behavior was a crystal sphere. That is . . . perfect . . . doesn't matter what's inside. And, uh, there is no . . . nothing can touch it. Nothing to grab, nothing to break it. Well, I suppose crystal can be broken . . . the whole thing goes to pieces at once. There's no little chink.

At age 16, Mr. Blackwell abruptly left home for good, without a word to his parents or to his older sister, Sarah (after whom his daughter is named), who had cared for him and with whom he had spent much of his adolescence. His departure coincided with her marriage and he recalls, "I considered [her marriage] a rejection of me."

In Mr. Blackwell's family of origin, negative self–object images were related to the display of affection and the associated wish for affective supplies. Although he considered his sister's marriage a "rejection," he was unaware of any affective response. His apparent autonomy was achieved at the price of a rigid defense against his own sense of need and depletion, which he projected onto others. After leaving his home, Mr. Blackwell became an active worker for liberal causes, supporting the rights of underprivileged groups. Following his marriage, he insisted on sending money to his parents and he sees himself as a thoughtful, generous man.

The Blackwell marriage provided for each partner a convenient collaborator for maintaining his particular split-off ego state. Mr. Blackwell is able to maintain his self-perception as "good" (warm, generous, and strong) in relation to his children because of his wife's willingness to accept his delineation of her as "bad" (cold, depriving, and fragile). She accepts, out of her own guilt and her need to see herself in a depriving relationship with her children, to protect herself (and them) from her disavowed, aggressively tinged symbtiotic wishes. In addition, by her denial of her own bad wishes for oral gratification, she protects her husband's fragile generosity by not making any real demands on him.

The following two excerpts demonstrate the nature of the parental interaction. In Excerpt 1, the illusion of the marriage is illustrated by Mr. Blackwell's defensive delineation of his wife as fragile and unable to provide, a projection necessitated by his own insecurity when he leaves the family for business trips.

Excerpt 1

Sarah: Well I know, Dad, whenever you go on trips and stuff like that, you sort of said, "Well, be nice to your mother, and, ah, make sure . . . help her out and everything" and . . . I used to . . . I don't know, Mom, I just don't think you're going to be able to handle things . . . if I uh . . . something was to happen to Dad, you'd just go crazy. You couldn't handle the whole family, I've always had that feeling, the feeling that you'd just sort of fall apart

	or something . . . and like, when Dad found out I was pregnant, he said, "Well, be extra nice at home because of Mom, because she's . . . all upset."
Mother:	I . . . you know . . . I don't know where that comes from, I thought I was always. . . .
Father:	I probably am responsible as anybody for that.
Mother:	You really think I'm not going to, you know. . . .
Father:	Well, ah . . . it's not that I don't think that you'll make it. I am just worried that . . . ah that the strains and stresses will get too much.
Mother:	What's going to happen?
Father:	I don't know [laughs] but I've never wanted to find out.
Mother:	Well, what do you imagine . . . what do you imagine?
Father:	Well, you know . . . sometimes you do just . . . get very irrational. Just . . . so that it's almost impossible to. . . .
Therapist:	What's your fear? How frightening is it that you can't say it?
Father:	Nervous breakdown or whatever you want . . . to call it.
Mother:	I don't really think you need to worry about it.
Father:	Well, but it is something that I . . . have . . . been uneasy about.

Mr. Blackwell experiences his wife as someone who cannot "make it" without him, someone who will fall apart if she is left alone. In his view of their relationship, *he* is the autonomous adult while she is the helpless child. In addition, the delineation informs his children that this bad (fragile, "irrational") mother cannot provide for them and that they should worry and care for *her*. This illusion persists despite Mrs. Blackwell's disclaimer ("I don't really think you need to worry about it") and the reality of her competence in managing the family without him. As will be demonstrated in Excerpt 2, this delineation represents an inability to survive without a mothering figure.

On the rare occasions when Mrs. Blackwell leaves the

home and her husband is forced to confront genuine demands, his tenuous "crystalline perfection" fails, and the source of the projection becomes clear:

EXCERPT 2

Therapist: If you got up to make the kids breakfast, what would that be like for you? How would you imagine that?

Father: There would be all kinds of small crises to deal with and, ah, I guess, yeah, I would find them . . . I would find that very taxing.

Therapist: How do you mean?

Father: [Very softly] To be arguing with somebody about something and telling somebody else to do something, and a third person would find that the eggs were cooked wrong, and that would irk me as much as it does her.

Mother: But you're always giving me advice on how to handle things like that, Robert. [*Sarah*: Dad . . . .] I really am amazed . . . to hear you say that kind of thing.

Father: Why?

Mother: [Loudly] Because you're always giving me advice on how to handle that kind of thing . . . should not bother me . . . I should do it this and this way to handle it.

Father: Well, the fact that I give you advice doesn't mean that I'd be any more competent to handle it.

Sarah: Dad, Dad what I think about is that time Mom went out of town and you freaked out and smashed the glass against the wall. You just couldn't handle things without Mom here, but when Mom goes away you flip out, you don't know what to do.

Father: What?

Sarah: [Excitedly] You just took it up and smashed it, you know, and then started . . . throwing stools down the stairs and breaking them. You flipped out when Mom wasn't there, you know. . . .

Father: I'm not denying it.

It is *Mr.* Blackwell who becomes "irrational" in the face of demands. His detached position as the warm, giving, good parent can be sustained only in the presence of a complementary perception of his wife. The stability of the Blackwell marital illusion (Excerpt 1) depends on the willingness of all members of the family to sustain these perceptions. In the absence of the bad mother, and in the face of genuine demands, the illusion fails, and the shared parental impoverishment is revealed.

The foregoing description of the Blackwell parents puts the nature of the setting into which Sarah was born into some perspective. Both parents rely on splitting to protect themselves from symbiotic wishes, which are seen, in a shared way, as aggressive, draining demands. Both can provide *some* gratification—father to a projected dependent self, mother to the point at which her own sense of impoverishment is evoked. Sarah's "excessive" infantile needfulness evokes previously split-off rage in father and rejection and disavowal from mother.

THE BORDERLINE CHILD

In their first year of marriage, Mrs. Blackwell became "unintentionally" pregnant with Sarah, at a time when she had been planning, with mixed feelings, to begin a full-time job. Angry about the unwanted pregnancy, she concealed it with bulky dresses for the first seven months. She now had within her a recipient for her split-off (bad) dependency and a guaranteed way to avoid continuing with her conflicted independent plans. (She subsequently had three other "unintentional" pregnancies.) Guilty about her anger and recognizing her own sense of deprivation as an unwanted child, she consciously resolved to show Sarah extra love, telling herself that "Sarah must never want for anything" (unconsciously recognizing that Sarah would *want* too much).

As an infant, Sarah could not respond to her father's

wish to be the "good" parent. When her mother would leave her alone with him, she would scream inconsolably. Mr. Blackwell remembers, "I guess I was mad because I didn't feel like I was enough for her." He saw in this infant his own denied angry needs and found himself jealous. He says, "Everything revolved around her and I felt like I didn't matter."

Sarah was born, then, into a family whose members perceived her in a shared unconscious manner as exploitative, unpleasant, and demanding. On her first day home, she screamed for "six straight hours" until the pediatrician came by and burped her. She had colic in her first few days, and Mrs. Blackwell gave her drops of whisky to stop her screaming. At night Mrs. Blackwell would get up at Sarah's slightest whimper. She remembers, "What I put myself through at night—at a whimper I would get up and nurse her for hours until my nipples got sore."

Both parents found Sarah's screaming intolerable. Her frequent tantrums turned into breath-holding and syncopal episodes, which terrified them. Sarah was 2 when her sister Margaret was born. For several years they shared a room. Mr. Blackwell remembers hearing Margaret cry at night and "smothering her with a pillow" so that she would not wake Sarah. He says, "From the day she was born, you wouldn't cross Sarah." These words demonstrate Mr. Blackwell's attempts to project his denied rage onto Sarah; however, it is really *he* who cannot be crossed (Excerpt 2). Sarah, for instance, remembers her father holding her head under water to stop her screaming. The interactions demonstrate the failure of the projection (he smothers Margaret and holds Sarah under water while he dissociates his own rage).

Both parents felt unable to provide adequately for the infant's needs; their response was an attempt to decrease or eliminate her needfulness with alcohol, avoidance, or retaliation. Terrified by the confrontation with their own disavowed projections, they responded to Sarah's age-appropriate needs for nurturing with anxiety, anger, and frantic attempts to constrain her. In this crucial stage of splitting, the Blackwells were unable, in Winnicott's term, to "survive" the infant's instinctual assaults. Sarah's projected negative self–object representations were intensified by their retaliation and withdrawal, threatening the increasingly tenuous positive relationship and necessitating continued splitting. In response to their rejection, Sarah's rage increased and the cycle was begun. The following excerpt illustrates a contemporary derivative of this interaction which, in a remarkable manner, relives this early phase:

Excerpt 3

Sarah: It's just so . . . you know why I get so mad? It's just like the same reaction, I call home and I, you get so flustrated [*sic*] like you're scared to death of me or something. You don't know how to . . . you can't do *anything*, you know. [Deep sigh]

Father: Well, you're the same way.

Mother: [Pause] What do you want from me, Sarah?

Sarah: *Nothing*! That's what I'm just begin . . . I don't want a *fucking thing* from you!

Mother: Well, I think you must though. You call and you don't get what you want.

Sarah: [Raising voice] I asked you . . . and I just want to hang up. I mean, I think maybe there'll be more of it, and then I just want to get off the phone. Because you have nothing to say to me . . . *at all* . . . never do!

Therapist: But you run from her question as to what you want when you say "nothing."

Sarah: I wish she could talk to me like a person and not be scared of me.

Mother: I wish that too.

Sarah: Why are you scared of me?

Mother: Obviously I am afraid of . . . what you do to me. Uh. . . .

Sarah: What do I do to you?
Mother: [Pause] Well, you make me feel helpless.

This excerpt is a clear derivative of the early conflict in the Blackwell family during the stage of splitting. Sarah makes a demand, which mother interprets as frightening. Her mother feels threatened by the confrontation with her disavowed and projected dependency (*"You make me* feel helpless") and, with the perception that she cannot provide for this child (You don't get what you want"), responds with a defensive withdrawal and self-criticism for not giving (in Sarah's word, she gets "flustrated"). The father rushes to his wife's defense in order to help maintain her equilibrium ("Well, you're the same way"). At this point mother's withdrawal and father's lack of support evoke a reactive rage in Sarah and she repudiates the family ("I don't want a *fucking thing* from you!").

In this interaction we see evidence of Sarah's two polarized ego states (the dependent infant and the repudiating adult), so adaptive to the dynamics of parental defense. As the demanding, dependent "infant," she represents denied aspects of both parents. As the angry, repudiating "adult," she is representing her father's dissociated rage as well as her mother's "autonomous" solution (Mrs. Blackwell angrily "hung up" on her own family).

SEPARATION-INDIVIDUATION STAGES

When Sarah was 2½ years old (shortly before Margaret's birth), Mrs. Blackwell became anxious about their mutual attachment and decided to send Sarah to nursery school. She remembers experiencing an enormous urgency about this decision and describes her memory of it as follows:

I wasn't able to do it gradually. I suddenly got, I got panicky. Then I could see that Sarah . . . I thought would be better off playing with other kids, and not so much, so, uh . . . such a strong attachment with, you know uh . . . um . . . and she resisted, you know, literally we had to put her in the car. You know, it was a car pool and she would go off crying.

Sarah was inconsolable at nursery school. Her separation anxiety was made manifest by a need to urinate every few minutes while at school. At their pediatrician's suggestion, the Blackwells gave her phenobarbital to calm her down. Mrs. Blackwell says,

This whole thing was more intense with Sarah—probably because there was a more intense relationship between Sarah and myself, partially. This became a big thing for Sarah—asking for the medicine, so she wouldn't have to go pee-pee, or something like that.

This sequence demonstrates the nature of the family regression in response to Sarah's beginning autonomous moves. In this first period of separation–individuation, there was an increased projective use of the child, who was seen not as an infant—in keeping with her real attributes—but as a devouring representation of the parents' denied dependency. What had been tolerable demands in the symbiotic phase became overwhelming in the face of separation issues ("such a strong attachment—I panicked," says the mother). The family abruptly turned the child out, telling her to look elsewhere for supplies ("she would be better off playing with other kids"). Mrs. Blackwell, reliving her own separation conflict through projective identification, experienced her insistence on Sarah's independence, not as a rejection, but as a move necessary for survival. Sarah's demands increased, however, in response to what *she* experienced as a rejection, and the family—confronted with their own lack of supplies—responded with an attempt to control the projected insatiability with the use of a sedative. Tempered by the sedative (phenobarbital at age 2, alcohol as an infant), the interaction between mother and child became tolerable

("This became a big thing for Sarah—asking for the medicine").

During latency, Sarah was a well-behaved, all "A" student. Throughout this period, she had one "best girlfriend," from whom she was inseparable. Her demands on the family were moderate and, with no impending threat of separation, the family's projected use of her subsided. She saw this as the "best time" in her life.

At the beginning of adolescence, however, things began to change. Because of a new assignment for Mr. Blackwell, the family moved to a foreign country. Upset at her sudden separation from her friend, Sarah found herself confronted with her changing body, a stressful period in the family, and the need to make new friends. When boys began to look at her in school, however, telling her that she was the "prettiest girl there," she found herself both frightened and angry at their glances, and remembers having the fantasy of spitting at them as she passed them on the street. In her individual therapy she had a similar fantasy of spitting at the therapist at a time when she was beginning to acknowledge the presence of warm feelings for him. This, for Sarah, is a derivative of the paradigm seen in Excerpt 3, where she hopes for warmth and becomes angry at the (now anticipated) rejection. In a denial of her oral wishes, she spits out at the sources of supply.

In high school Sarah found herself increasingly attracted to boys who took drugs, skipped school, and were involved in illegal activity. She was unclear about the nature of this attraction but attempted on several occasions to discuss it with her family—without success. Once, invited out by the son of the local Mafia leader, Sarah asked her parents for permission to date him, expecting them to disapprove. Frightened and uncertain about this date, she hoped her parents would forbid it. Unable to recognize this request for guidance as appropriate to beginning individuation, the Blackwells experienced it as a threateningly dependent demand and withdrew from the request by saying, "We trust your judgment." In this beginning adolescent encounter, the parents could not provide a holding environment in which appropriate dependence could be tolerated without being considered an exploitation. In a shared, unconscious way, Sarah's request was seen as a threat to the parents' need to see themselves (in their projective identification with her) as able to manage alone.

Unaware of her own rage and despair at her parents' lack of support, and driven by unacknowledged, intensified dependent yearnings, Sarah's behavior deteriorated. She began to stay out all night, fail in school, and take drugs and alcohol to control her anxiety. In the two years prior to her admission, she would be brought home stuporous from alcohol intoxication several times a week. Her alcohol use, a gross reenactment of her parents' earlier attempts to control and respond to her dependent needs, was the only way in which she could allow herself to experience any needfulness in relation to others. Hesitant parental questioning of her behavior evoked Sarah's rage (see Excerpt 3).

Although individually distraught over Sarah's continual self-destructive drinking and possible promiscuity, the parents found themselves unable to confront her with it or to discuss it with each other. Although he stayed awake trembling at night, awaiting Sarah's return, Mr. Blackwell remained elusive with her. Mrs. Blackwell was apparently oblivious to Sarah's distress. Their responses reflected defenses against parts of themselves. In order to confront their child, they would have needed to acknowledge and reintegrate their projections: Mr. Blackwell would have had to acknowledge his own rage, as well as admit the possibility that he could *not* give enough (a position he had assigned his wife); Mrs. Blackwell would have needed to acknowledge the possibility of loving and supporting a needy child (thus opening her to the possibility of experiencing what she had lost by her own separation). Their inability to assert themselves in the face of Sarah's anger (the equivalence during adolescence of the infantile holding environment in this family) is clarified by the following interchange, in which the parents discuss their lack of response at finding Sarah intoxicated during a weekend pass:

EXCERPT 4

Mother: One way of showing you care, too, is . . . through a confidence, you know, in another person's judgment . . . you know, I think that kind of . . . caring . . . as much as always making. . . .

Sarah: Well, yeah.

Father: [Pause] Well, every time you or Peter—or Margaret . . . all this is still not quite fair, but you go off somewhere, ah, we, you know, worry . . . or . . . that everything will be all right. Well, it may turn out to be not all right. But we cannot say automatically "no" to everything.

Sarah: Well, what do you care?

Because of the pervasive defensive splitting and the shared unconscious assumption that requests for support at times of separation mean that separation will not take place, the Blackwells cannot provide a holding environment for their daughter. Their unconscious equation of dependent need with hostile, draining demand greatly intensifies the interaction with Sarah. For Mr. Blackwell, withstanding Sarah's "instinctual assault" (in Winnicott's terms) means to threaten his defensive detachment by the perceived demand for him to take over *all* responsibility ("We cannot say . . . no to everything"). Mrs. Blackwell has similar fears. For her to provide support would reawaken painful longings: She rationalizes her withdrawal into "caring" by wishfully accepting Sarah's "judgment." Sarah, however, angrily recognizes their failure ("Well, what do you care?").

On several occasions during her adolescence, Sarah

ran away from home. With increasing tension at home, she would begin to hate her parents and would take off with a boyfriend for "the road." After several weeks away, she would begin to talk to her friends about her "wonderful parents" (especially father) and would get homesick. She would then return, and the cycle would begin again. In these sequences, Sarah would repeat both aspects of her split in internalized object relations. In leaving, she was acting on the bad self–object relationship (as did her mother); in returning, she hoped for the good one. In the following excerpt, she confronts her parents with the meaning of separation:

EXCERPT 5

Sarah: Mom, I was just thinking. Is that why you told me . . . something like . . . Margaret's out of the family now. She's not part of the family and, uh, she doesn't consider herself that way, and . . . that you sort of implied that when you get a certain age you shouldn't . . . that you didn't like going home. Sort of . . . and that's the way it should be, you shouldn't want to come home. And like I should be out and not want to come home.

Mother: No, not that it was the way it should be, but that was kind of my experience and. . . .

Sarah: [Interrupting] And you sort of implied that that's the way it is with Marg . . . and that's the way it should be with . . . me.

Mother: No, I didn't! Well. . . .

Sarah: Yes, you did.

Father: Yes, you did, that's the way you usually . . .

Mother: Well. . . .

Sarah: And Dad didn't agree with that.

Mother: Well, it's never been very pleasant for . . . me . . . to go back and . . . uh . . . my brother was home . . . uh . . . and I'm sure that at one point that was a great concern of mine, you know, about . . . Sarah. Uh . . . and also the burden it would be on me, as well . . . I mean, it was a self-centered interest as well.

In the relatively secure environment of family therapy, Sarah is able, in the foregoing excerpt, to directly
challenge one of the shared Blackwell assumptions: "You
shouldn't want to come home" (or else you will never
leave — and we cannot provide.) In response to the threat
of the confrontation, the parents split along familiar lines:
Sarah and father unite ("Yes, you did!" they say), father
assigns the rejection to his wife ("That's the way you
usually . . ."), mother acquiesces ("Well. . . .") and Sarah
quickly rushes to protect the "good" relationship ("And
Dad didn't agree. . . ."). Mrs. Blackwell acknowledges
her fear of the increasing demands of a symbiotic child
(her own split-off dependent self, who "burdened" her
own mother), noting "the burden it would be," and is able
to recognize the parallel she has constructed with her
mother and brother.

TRANSFERENCE

The nature of the separation dilemma and the internalized
split is graphically demonstrated in a dream Sarah had in
her sixth month of therapy, shortly before her therapist's
vacation:

I am in an old abandoned house with Professor X., an old friend
of my father's who was able [when the students were rioting] to
help them get what they needed without demonstrating. There
are some people outside. A voice calls me and I get frightened
and cling to Professor X. A woman's hands with long fingernails
reach out of the darkness and pull him away, and I scream. Then,
I am outside the house and there is a shapeless form — dead, I
think — under a blanket on the porch.

Sarah's associations to this dream present a picture of
herself as separated from a warm, providing figure (the
therapist, or good father) and thrust into an unknown and
threatening independence. In separating, she must leave

the "good" relationship *completely* behind her. The dream is an oedipal elaboration of her preoedipal conflict over the wish for gratification and its "bad" consequences.

In her positive transference relationship with the therapist, she can "get what [she] needs without demonstrating" (that is, her dependency is accepted as neither hostile nor exploitative and her reactive rage and escalating protests over rejection are not required). The therapist's vacation is taken as a withdrawal and rejection, however, mobilizing her latent anxiety that the therapist will perceive her as too demanding and ravenous. This causes a sharp alteration in her view of him and evokes the negative transference.

At the end of her first year of therapy, in response to the discussion of the possible setting of a discharge date from the hospital, Sarah acted out the conflict expressed in the dream she had six months previously. She split her experience of the therapist into that with the good therapist (who was providing a sanctuary for her) and the bad therapist (who was discharging and rejecting her). Furious at the perceived rejection (from the bad therapist), she "demonstrated" by running away from the hospital in a manner that communicated both her need and her rage (as in Excerpt 3). While away from the hospital, she was robbed and found herself hungry, drunk, and abandoned. By the time she called the unit to inform her (now good) therapist where she was, she had spent the night alone on a beach, huddled in the rain under a blanket—a representation, as in her dream, of the consequence of a pathological separation, which is a denial of all dependent needs and consequently destructive of relatedness.

Sarah interprets all separations, including the therapist's vacation and the anticipated discharge from the hospital, as confirmation of the rejection she has feared. This is the consequence of her underlying anxiety, derived in part from the family's unconscious assumption that need gratification represents a hostile, draining demand which will be repudiated. The gradual mastery of these anxieties is central to the work of therapy and to the achievement of more integrated internalized object relations, and to a more advanced level of personality organization.

Summary

Parents of borderline adolescents fail to provide the holding environment necessary to facilitate their off-spring's integration of positive and negative internalized relationships. This failure results from their own residual symbiotic ties to their families of origin and their unresolved conflicts over autonomy and dependency. In these families, autonomous or dependent behavior from the child confronts the parents with denied aspects of themselves and evokes in them an aggressive response. Parental interpretation of the child's instinctual needs and aggressive assaults constitutes a developmental interference. Conflicts over separation–individuation evoke a family regression in which critical aspects of intrapsychic conflict in each of the parents are reenacted in their relationship with the adolescent. In this chapter we have examined a case of a borderline adolescent girl—transference, retrospective history, and current family interaction—in order to define more specifically these experiential aspects of the interplay between environment, drive, and ego apparatus in the formation of the borderline ego deficit.

9

The Implications
of Projective Identification
for Marital Interaction

JOHN ZINNER, M.D.

Of the many variables that influence the marital interactional system, the focus of this chapter is on those operating at an unconscious intrapsychic level. Less accessible to observation than are sociocultural values and conscious expectations, these unconscious forces are nevertheless as potent as they are obscure. They exert a significant influence on marital object choice (Dicks 1963) and continue to affect the moment-to-moment quality of the relationship. Moreover, the unconscious fantasies that determine marital interaction extend to include perceptions of, and behavior toward, children, and hence have important consequences for their psychological development (Zinner and R. Shapiro 1972). This issue has been elaborated upon in Chapter 7. More specifically delimiting our topic, we will draw here on our psychoanalytic understanding of the individual to examine the interpersonal consequences for the married couple of the defense mechanism of projective identification.

DEFINITION OF PROJECTIVE IDENTIFICATION

Projective identification is an activity of the ego that modifies perception of the object and, in a reciprocal fashion, alters the image of the self. It occurs as a defense to rid the self of an unwanted or dangerously overvalued part that can then be attacked or glorified when it is located in the object. So far, I am describing a purely intrapsychic process. Again through projective identification, the individual may locate the object not inside the self, but as if it were inside the other partner in a relationship. These conjoined changes in perception influence and may in fact govern behavior of the self toward the external object found in the other person. They are so powerful as to evoke in the external object of the projection a collusive response that is appropriately gratifying to needs for pleasure, praise, punishment, or pain. Projective identification originates from both partners in the relationship, and thus they form a mutually gratifying collusive system. Thus projective identification provides an important conceptual bridge between an individual and an interpersonal psychology, since our awareness of the mechanism permits us to understand specific interactions *among* persons in terms of specific dynamic conflicts occurring *within* individuals.

PROJECTIVE IDENTIFICATION WITHIN
A MARRIAGE

The projection of disavowed elements of the self onto the spouse has the effect of charging a marital relationship with conflict that has been transposed from an intrapsychic sphere to an interpersonal one. One woman whose "cat-and-dog" marriage was undergoing conjoint treatment stated, "I feel better when my husband hates me than when I hate myself." While it is certainly true that projective identification has lessened the anxiety occasioned by her own self-recrimination, such a defense wreaks havoc on the marriage because it requires, to be effective, a continuing state of conflict within the dyad. This conflict need not be overt but may be implicit in the form of polarized perceptions that marital partners have of each other. These polarizations preempt the possibility of sharing feelings and of collaborative behavior. Hence a wife might experience herself as emotionally labile and her husband as cold and logical. Similar polarities within the marriage are strong–weak, frigid–lusty, helpless–effective, rageful–even tempered, depressed–cheerful.

CASE 1

Mrs. A. possessed strong phallic assertive strivings, although their expression was inhibited by guilt and a fantasized fear of their destructiveness. On the other hand, Mr. A.'s own active aggressiveness was in conflict with passive longing. The defensive economy of each mate was served by projection of the wife's aggressiveness onto the husband and by reciprocal projection onto her of his view of himself as helpless. Mr. A. could thereby experience the fulfillment of his own passive wishes through his wife, while she likewise obtained covert vicarious satisfaction through his competitive success at work and, more intimately, his phallic potent orientation in sexual relations. Such a polarization of the helpless wife and effective husband can be quite stable and self-perpetuating and finds considerable reinforcement in contemporary society. This apparently robust system could be easily destabilized, however, by Mrs. A.'s assuming the initiative during intercourse. At this point, her husband would become anxious and lose his erection, since her behavior would undermine his defensive view of her as the passive one.

For similar reasons, it is a familiar experience in the individual treatment of married persons to learn of the reawakening of intrapsychic conflict in the untreated spouse as the mate in psychotherapy begins to internalize previously projected conflict.

The operation of projective identification within marriage is more than a matter of externalization of disavowed traits, however. We find that the contents of the projected material contain highly conflicted elements of the spouse's object relationships with his own family of origin. Although it is commonplace to think of a husband selecting a mate who is "just like the girl who married dear old Dad," we are referring to the unconscious striving to reenact conflicted parent–child relations through such an object choice. Highly fluid role attributions occur in which a husband, for example, may parentify his spouse, or on the other hand, infantilize her by experiencing the wife as the child he once was. The externalization of aspects of old conflicted nuclear relationships serves not only a defensive need but also a restorative one—a need to bring back to life, in the form of the spouse, the individual's lost infantile objects, both "good" and "bad." Jaffe (1968) has similarly commented on this dual function of projective identification.

It follows from what has been said that the operation of projective identification in marital relationships bears close resemblance to the transference that forms in psychoanalytic therapy. Barring an unanalyzed countertransference in the therapist, however, the treatment situation should not be characterized by the collusive interplay of mutual projections that obtain within the marital dyad. Nevertheless, just as we anticipate some degree of transference in treatment, we likewise always find some elements of projective identification operating within the marriage. We may speak of a continuum of projective identification in the relationship. At one end, the most primitive form of the mechanism is at play; self and object representations are fused, and perceptions of the object may be so distorted as to be frankly delusional. At the "healthy" end of the continuum, the self may achieve an empathic grasp of the subjective world of the object by the selective use of the self's own prior experience within his own nuclear family. The location of a particular relationship along this continuum is determined by the quality and developmental level of internalized nuclear object relations, by the capacity of spouses to experience each other as separate, differentiated individuals, and by the intensity of the need for defense. To the extent that a spouse uses projective modes less as a way of externalizing conflict and more as an instrument for approximating shared experience, the marital relationship approaches the healthy end of the continuum.

Effects on the Family

Our recognition of the importance of projective identification derived from our studies of families of disturbed adolescents carried out at the NIMH. We found that within our population of troubled families, parents' images, or *delineations*, of their offspring were often distorted and that these distortions served the defensive economy of the parents. These parental defensive delineations of adolescents were projective identifications and led to reenactments of the parents' earlier experience with their own families of origin. Our adolescent subjects tended to identify with their parents' distorted images of them, and this led to significant developmental problems in the formation of adolescent identity. We frequently observed that the use of projective identification by individual family members caused them to appear as if they were psychologically unconflicted, since the elements of conflict were externalized and distributed among the family members through projection (Zinner and E. Shapiro 1975, Zinner and R. Shapiro 1972). Meanwhile, the family, as a whole, appeared to be the equivalent of a single conflicted psychic entity. We have illustrated this phenomenon in the case of the family of an acting-out adolescent (Zinner and R. Shapiro 1974). The adolescent's behavior represented the unconflicted expression of impulse, while the parents, disavowing their drives, spoke for the harsh directives of the superego. As a unit, however, the family could be viewed as a complete psychological organism in which both drive and prohibition were represented.

Marital Therapy

Our therapeutic methods involve conjoint marital therapy as well as individual and conjoint family sessions. We found that the very processes involving projective identification that were found to operate within the whole family group were active as well within the marital dyad. The seminal work on the implications of projective identification for marital object choice and subsequent marital interaction was performed by Dicks (1967) in the Marital Unit of the Tavistock Clinic. Dicks's comprehensive clinical studies of marriage have not received the attention they deserve in the United States; they merit being a basic reference for all students in the field. Dicks treated a number of what he called "collusive marriages" (p. 68) in which interaction was, to a large extent, determined by mutual projective identifications. He viewed these dyads as if they were a "joint personality," characterized by "a kind of division of function by which each partner supplies a set of qualities, the sum of which created a complete dyadic unit" (p. 69). Here it can be seen how our observation of the family as a "single psychic entity" converges with Dicks's formulation of the marital "joint personality." The phenomena just described is illustrated by the following four excerpts from the conjoint marital therapy of Mr. and Mrs. C.

Case 2

The C.'s marriage was beset by overt conflict from its inception 25 years before. During courtship, warnings from friends that the relationship was doomed only seemed to strengthen the couple's resolve to be married. Each spouse perceived himself and his mate as if they were polar opposites. Mr. C. was seen as exceedingly rational, ruminative, incapable of affectionate, intimate ties, contemptuous of emotional display, and indifferent to sex. In contrast, Mrs. C. was viewed as volatile, impulsive, clinging, and erotic. Each of the partners could maintain such single-minded percepts of himself and the other through the projection of conflicting aspects of his personality onto the mate. Hence, Mr. C. feared the destructiveness of his anger and vicariously experienced the volatile temper of his wife while he simultaneously criticized her outbursts. At times, the intensity of his hostility would overwhelm his projective defense and he would fly into rages. These were experienced as dissociative lapses, as not a part of himself, and he would finally repress the rage.

Faced with the growing independence of and eventual separation from their daughters in late adolescence, both parents struggled to maintain a positive alliance with their children. Mr. and Mrs. C. shared the fantasy that the filial ties could not endure parental ambivalence. Therefore, each competed to be the "all-good" parent while envisioning the mate as the "bad" one, whose relationship with the daughters was one of unmitigated hostility. Their competition is demonstrated in an excerpt from couple's therapy that followed a family session attended for the first time by Cheryl, the eldest daughter, who lives away from home.

EXCERPT 1

Husband: Well, poor old Cheryl was, of course, somewhat at a disadvantage yesterday, in that she'd never been here before. That was not her only disadvantage, I guess. Those two girls are real antagonists, as you could see. Or I don't know that you could see. Cheryl was very mad afterward. She said she would leave the family, and I wouldn't be responsible for her finances, and so on.

Wife: And she wouldn't—she didn't talk to me. Arthur [Mr. C.] told me that she hated me.

Husband: She was very mad because of Barbara's [Mrs. C.'s] outburst about her not cooperating yesterday at home.

Wife: And that he was the only one who she liked.

Husband: No, she didn't say that.

Wife: That's what you told me.

Husband: No, no, she didn't say that.

Wife: No, she didn't say it, you did.

Husband: Well, she was . . . she said that she hated you.

Wife: Yeah.

Husband: And that she'd been home at Christmas and she'd tried to do something, and you chewed her out. And so she wouldn't take it anymore, and so on. And I said, well, you'd better come on back now. She said she was arranging to stay in Wilmington this summer.

Wife: But she arranged that a long time ago.

Husband: I like Cheryl—I like them all. I think it's just a pity that they're so antagonistic. I was very pleased that you [the therapist] intimated that maybe they both had a battle of inferiorities rather than a battle of, to some extent, the exchange of superiority on one side crushing a weaker force on the other. Because I don't think either one of them are that superior. Cheryl likes to score points on doing the proper thing. And, of course, doing it, as many children do, more outside of the home than in—that kind of thing.

Wife: Well, anyhow, you did tell me last night that it was because I was so bitchy that she was this way.

Husband: Well, I think you do the extremes of violent outbursts, which are rather crushing. And maybe I'm the Caspar Milquetoast in the deal, although I have my outbursts, but not so often, I think.

Wife: So you see where the blame is placed. Ask him.

Husband: Well, I think . . . I would say just as a matter of fact, and maybe this is a normal thing, I think these kids look upon me as a . . . well, Joan [the younger daughter] said something about they were getting to know me better. This sort of surprised me.

Wife: Because of this?

Husband: Yes, that's right. She said this. And, they look upon

	me as someone who can help them with their. . . .
Wife:	No, they don't. They just dread asking you about anything, because you go on at 30 miles an hour and. . . .
Husband:	No, I think they ask me more—they've asked me more in the first . . . in this year than they have in a long time.
Wife:	I remember when Cheryl would ask you something and you'd go on. Finally you would end by hitting her over the head or slapping her on the cheek. And. . . .
Husband:	That was in high school. She used to . . . they used to annoy me if they came to me and then wouldn't accept anything.
Wife:	And then you slapped her. Yeah.

In this excerpt, each member of the couple is vying to be the loving, giving parent in contradistinction to the angry, depriving one. The shared ambivalence they might feel toward their children is obscured by their regression to a preambivalent state in which the loci of love and hate are split, through projective identification, between the partners in this collusive dyad. Mr. C. blames Cheryl's alienation from the family on his wife's "crushing" "violent" outbursts, while he perceives himself as "someone who can help" his daughter. In defense, Mrs. C. tries to reverse this polarization by reminding her husband of his striking Cheryl in her high-school years when she "would ask you for something." Insofar as he was the "crusher" then, she can experience herself as the "good" mother who retains the positive tie to her daughter.

In Dicks's terminology, the division of function is accomplished by the parceling out within the C.'s dyad of the affects of love and hate. The psychological incompleteness of each partner is manifested by the lack of ambivalence. They do represent a "joint personality" in the sense that the dyadic unit contains the ambivalence that is lacking in each individual.

A crucial aspect of the therapeutic work is to encourage the internalization of conflict within each partner in the marriage. After all, the intrapsychic conflict is only perpetuated by virtue of its externalization, whereas resolution can occur only when the struggle is experienced as residing within the individual. In the case of Mr. C.'s fear of his anger, for example, interpretations are directed with this in mind. During another marital therapy session, Mr. C. accused his wife of "blowing her cool" at a pair of very provocative house guests who happened to be close relatives.

EXCERPT 2

Therapist: So you feel that anger and love can't reside in you at one time, because one pushes the other out—love pushes out any possibility of anger and anger pushes out love and when the two can't reside in you, well, I think you have to take one of the feelings and put them in Mrs. C. [*Mr. C.*: Yeah.], in this instance, so that Mrs. C. is the angry one and you're the loving one because it's very difficult for you to say, "I'm loving and I'm angry."

Husband: Yeah, [tearfully] yeah, you're cooking with gas. I think, and it may relate to the fact, I mean as far as . . . in my amateurish use of the term of . . . of really getting boiling mad where I'm dangerous, as Wendell Willkie said, and this I don't really do because I would—I don't trust myself. I can remember as a kid, my sister and I used to have some royal battles like the . . . like when I threw the books, and maybe this is the key motif of . . . of the symphony of my existence, that I have a trigger. Certain things are like that. I mean this might never have happened . . . you know . . . well, we'll work on this business.

Mr. C. has tentatively begun to internalize the "boiling mad" aspect of himself previously projected onto his wife. The Caspar Milquetoast self-definition yields to a more authentic one of a man who is deeply concerned about control of his hostility, recalling earlier experiences within his family when his anger led to schisms between himself and his sister.

Having thus illustrated the defensive division of function within the marriage that is effected by projective identification, let us look at some ways in which this same process led to reenactment of earlier relationships within Mrs. C.'s family of origin. We will focus, in this example, on her experience of being devalued or "crushed" in the marriage and, reciprocally, of her own prominent devaluation of her husband. Both Mr. and Mrs. C. have acquired superegos of the harshest variety. Taking advantage of this structural condition, it was painfully common to discharge hostility by generating guilt and self-hatred in the spouse. In order to lighten the burden of their punitive consciences, each perceived its recriminations as emanating from the mate rather than from within themselves. On one occasion, a third and younger of the C.'s offspring began to do poorly at school. Mrs. C. was agonized by this, blaming herself severely for being a "bad mother." In the midst of this torment she turned to her husband during a family session, asking, "Arthur, where have I failed?" Mr. C. willingly enumerated her faults until the therapist intervened. Nevertheless, the husband's criticism relieved her considerably of the anguish that followed from her blame of herself. Now she was able, with great indignation, to fight with her critic, and she was single-minded in her defense of her mothering capabilities.

In the following excerpt from a marital therapy session, Mrs. C. has grasped that her relationship with Arthur recreates her interaction with her mother, who "made me feel completely worthless." She does not yet appreciate how she evokes this devaluing behavior in others, but this becomes apparent in her transference attitude toward her therapist.

EXCERPT 3

Wife: I mean, my parents must have been very unhappy people, too, or they wouldn't have behaved the way they did. And I won't ever know why or so forth, but maybe these are kind of basic . . . just feelings rather than any specific incidents. Until I am able to understand them and try to cope with my feelings toward them, I don't think I'm going to be able to cope with my feelings toward Arthur. Does that make sense to you?

Therapist: Well, why don't you elaborate.

Wife: This is just about where I've gotten. And now I'm . . . and I'm working back. I'm . . . I hate to take the whole . . . this amount of time away, we need to discuss things. Okay?

Therapist: Away? Take it away from what?

Wife: From Arthur. You . . . shall I go on?

Husband: Shall she go on? Or would you rather hear a few words. . . .

Wife: I figured. . . .

Therapist: Well, I'm just . . . I'm confused about. . . .

Wife: Okay, I'll unconfuse you, I think.

Therapist: I'm confused by your guilt a little bit. In other words, you're in a little bit of a box anytime you start reflecting on your own life and feeling sad about it. Then you start hating yourself because you're pitying yourself.

Wife: Yeah.

Therapist: That's a trap for yourself, because you can't. . . it's hard to do thinking if you start feeling that you're indulging yourself too much just by thinking.

Wife: Well, I. . .

Therapist: And then you feel you're taking up too much time in here, as if all of . . . and that may reflect one of your own earlier feelings that you didn't have rights to feeling bad, didn't have rights to your anger, and. . . .

Wife: And any time, you see, when I was a child I would get so angry that I would say something back to my mother, I was instantly told, "You don't talk that way to your mother." And, consequently, I guess I still feel this. And I don't think this way about your mother or your father or . . . and so forth. But last night I was thinking, well, goddamn it, my mother was able to make me feel completely worthless, all of my growing up. And maybe what has happened is that I . . . Arthur was able to bring these same feelings out. And consequently I felt quite comfortable with Arthur. Because these were feelings I had lived with for so many years. No, I . . . I feel I am gaining the strength to face these feelings for the first time that my mother has felt for me. And I was again . . . oh, my God! I mean, go back into the past! I do remember when I was a freshman in college and I was rehearsing for a play, and the head of the drama department was directing it, and the play was coming up Sunday. Anyhow, things were very, very tense, and he turned on me at one point and screamed and ranted and raved. And my first reaction was, "Oh, my God, I've done something horrible again." Then I looked at the script and I saw that I was right. And that he was wrong. And I told him so. And I can remember still that glorious feeling: "By God, I didn't take the blame for something I was right about." And, of course, he quickly then said, "Oh, my God, I, I'm sorry," and so forth. So that . . . it was the very first time in my conscious recollection that I was able to talk back and say, "I'm right, you're wrong." In a very concrete situation. Now probably in feelings . . . I still wasn't able to feel not guilty about something that somebody jumped on me about. Well, anyhow, that brings us up to this feeling that I am wondering if it's a part of me Arthur has supplied over the years, is this need of mine that, that I had

Therapist: grown up with. Now is this a logical kind of reasoning of mine, or am I on the wrong track in my analyzing?

Therapist: It makes sense to me.

Husband: I'm a mother substitute as a crusher? Is that what you're. . . .

Wife: I am saying that I seem to have a need to feel uncomfortable with myself, that I am not a worthy person, et cetera. I've said it once, hell.

Husband: You mean that your . . . that in order to be comfortable you feel uncomfortable. That was like what someone said about people that are so bored, that they don't know that they're bored, which I've been working on.

Wife: Arthur, don't you hear anything, huh?

Husband: Yes, but. . . .

Wife: Well, what did you hear?

Husband: You're saying that you grew up feeling uncomfortable and crushed down, and, therefore, you got used to it and so now you still have to be that way. And I stand in the locus of your mother, making you feel uncomfortable. I was just saying it's an irony that you only feel comfortable when you're uncomfortable. It seems to be a little illogical.

Therapist: Well, it is a puzzle. I mean, that is, you know, another one of the reasons that it makes a lot of sense to me that what you say is . . . that I see you right here soliciting criticism.

Wife: From who?

Therapist: For example, by asking me whether you're on the right track in your discoveries of yourself.

Wife: Well, I honestly. . . .

Therapist: "Am I right or wrong?" And that is really soliciting. . . .

Wife: Well, what I'm doing to you is what I . . . my students do to me and what I've done to my teachers. If I'm practicing something in a certain way, I don't want to go through a whole damn week practicing it wrong.

Therapist: But this isn't the theater. This is about self-discoveries and about yourself. I think you really are soliciting my judgment about you. And it fits in with your saying that perhaps one of the needs that has . . . that you have asked to be fulfilled and has been fulfilled is that judgments are made about you or criticisms, and then you for some reason have a need to experience this bad feeling about yourself. And if I had said, "No, it sounds like you're on the wrong track," I think you would have felt terrible.

Wife: Then I'd have to go through the whole damn process again and start all over again.

Mrs. C. speaks, in this interaction, of the parallel between her mother's and husband's devaluation of her worth. She attributes her tolerance of Mr. C.'s derogation primarily to habit—that is, ". . . because these were feelings I had lived with for many years." We would go a step further, however, to say that she is actively seeking to reenact through Arthur her experience with her mother. Because she has been successful, she feels "quite comfortable with Arthur." Evidence for her attempts to recruit a collusive partner to relate to her as her mother did is found in her behavior toward the therapist. At an unconscious level, her reflections constitute a perfor-mance in his behalf—"Does that make sense to you? . . . Shall I go on?" She associates, in a metaphorical vein, to her conflict with the drama-department chairman and her need to be told whether she is right or wrong. Soon thereafter, she turns to the therapist to ask, "Now is this a logical kind of reasoning of mine, or am I on the wrong track in my analyzing?" At first, the therapist does collude as her mother-judge by responding, "It makes sense to me," but he subsequently extricates himself from the collusion by interpreting her efforts at "soliciting criti-cism." As much as Mrs. C. wishes to disassociate herself from the familiar interaction ("It was either right or wrong. It wasn't a matter of anything else"), she is nevertheless reluctant to relinquish it ("If I'm practicing something in a certain way, I don't want to go through a whole damn week practicing it wrong").

Almost obscured in this excerpt is a glimpse of the other side of the coin—that is, Mrs. C.'s own inclination to devalue, to derogate: "Arthur, don't you hear anything, huh?" The reenactment of the mother–daughter relationship allows for a fluidity of identifications. Mrs. C., identified with her mother, is quite accomplished in making her husband feel worthless. In this situation, Mr. C. becomes for her the devalued child she once was. The common denominator then is the quality of the relationship between Mrs. C. and her mother. Which member of the marital dyad assumes which role is of secondary consequence as long as the subjective experience, the affective tone, of the earlier relationship is recreated. In the following excerpt, Mrs. C. discusses her concern that she is doing to her husband what her mother has done to her father, and through her identification, the scope of the reenactments is expanded to include now her own marriage as a reliving of her parents' marriage.

EXCERPT 4

Therapist: What you've said makes me wonder about your own father. You rarely mention your father.

Wife: I feel that my mother was the stronger one there, and I think she did a beautiful job of castrating him, and I suspect I have doubts about my doing the same thing to Arthur. Maybe the right word isn't *doubt*, but I expect I do the same thing to Arthur. Guilt—I feel guilty every time I fight back.

Therapist: How do you mean castrated? She cut him down?

Wife: Constantly. He just wasn't any good. He wasn't anything according to her.

Therapist: Just what?

Wife: Complete failure as far as she was concerned, and I thought that—I remember when they came to visit us, must have been about ten years ago. It was the first time I got . . . saw my mother . . . as a lady that had done a real swell job.

Therapist: What did you really see?

Wife:	That I don't think . . . that he was perhaps not as bad as she led him to think.
Therapist:	Well, what's your perception of him?
Wife:	Oh, he's very good, very kind. He's never been able to make a lot of money. See why I'm comparing? Why I'm doing the same thing to Arthur? My mother's always acted and . . . he had many of the same characteristics as Arthur—constantly talking and nobody listens. He writes beautiful letters, elegant letters, they ought to be published, just like Arthur. When you talk to him, it's completely undisciplined thoughts, just like Arthur, going on and on and on. And I think my greatest fear is that I do to Arthur what my mother did to my father.

This excerpt, in addition to demonstrating Mrs. C.'s identification with her mother as a severe appraiser of the worth of others, also expresses a secret admiration for a devalued father: "Oh, he's very good, very kind." "He writes beautiful letters, elegant letters, they ought to be published." We see that in being married to Arthur, Mrs. C. is also reliving a relationship with an overtly denigrated but covertly valued father: "He was perhaps not as bad as she led him to think." This element of positive attachment to her father—obscured out of allegiance to mother—provided the leverage for a substantial revision, during treatment, of her perception of and behavior toward her husband.

Because of schisms between her parents, Mrs. C. had come to feel that a positive tie to one precluded intimacy with the other. During the transference relationship, the therapist–mother did not abandon Mrs. C. because of her affection for her husband–father. Mrs. C. came to understand that she could care for both, and without retaliation.

No attempt has been made here to present a comprehensive picture of the rich unconscious underpinnings of the C.'s marriage. Rather, we have selected excerpts that illustrate our main themes. Mr. C.'s intrapsychic conflict over his anger (*Excerpt 1*) is transposed onto the interpersonal field through the mechanism of projective identification. He discharges his hostility through the vicarious experience of his wife's volatility, which he disavows in himself. This disavowal permits him, in fantasy, to sustain a relationship with his daughter that is seemingly free of ambivalence. By virtue of the integration of his severe prohibitions on anger and her unbridled expression of hostility, the couple become, in Dicks's term, a joint personality. Interpretation by the therapist of this process of externalization (*Excerpt 2*) leads to an internalization, albeit tentative, of Mr. C.'s own conflict and to the elaboration of pertinent genetic material. The marital interactions generated by projective identification represented the reenactment of earlier object relationships in the spouses' families of origin (*Excerpts 3 and 4*). This process bears a strong resemblance to the formation of the transference, and, in fact, efforts are made to recruit the marital therapist as a collusive participant in this reenactment (*Excerpt 3*).

Although this chapter is not directed primarily at the treatment process, some comments stimulated by the aforementioned clinical material are appropriate. We hope that we have demonstrated how an appreciation of unconscious forces enriches our understanding of the marital relationship. Beyond that, this understanding illuminates the path for our therapeutic interventions. Intrapsychic conflicts that have been externalized through projective identifications must be reinternalized with the aid of our interpretations, since the process of working through can only be achieved at an intrapsychic level. Interventions that are aimed at modifying the behavior of the spouse who is the recipient of projections so that he is no longer a collusive partner have their parallel in individual therapy in the form of the analyzing of the countertransference. The transference in conjoint marital therapy must be closely attended to since the unconscious forces that influence the marital dyad are equally at play in the triad that now includes the therapist. For these reasons we concur with Dicks (1967), who emphasized "the importance of grasping the meaning of unconscious communications as the essential part of marital therapy worthy of the name" (p. 118).

10

Who Are You and What Have You Done with My Wife?

JUSTIN A. FRANK, M.D.

The title of this chapter reflects a question a husband might ask his wife. He no longer knows her; she's changed, somehow, from the woman he married into someone else. The motivations to marry, and the characteristics of marriage itself, are largely unconscious. Herein lies the root of a not uncommon predicament: Unexpected marital complications ensue when unconscious elements governing the choice of marital partners emerge. Broadly speaking, unconscious processes play two dynamically distinct yet similar roles in marriage, resulting in two types of couple relationships. In both instances, the paradoxical relationship between intention and result is dramatic.

People marry for conscious and unconscious reasons. They unconsciously seek either to gratify forbidden incestuous wishes or to supplement parts of the self that are covertly felt to be deficient. For example, a man may have in mind an unconsciously idealized parent or idealized self, whose role he assumes his wife will play. She may at first happily comply, in part because of her own unconscious needs. As they grow and develop, husband and wife depart from unacknowledged unconscious perceptions and no longer overtly meet each other's needs. Eventually each spouse no longer matches the other's conscious expectations. When the differentiated person emerges, the other partner has several options: He may withdraw and seek an idealized person elsewhere; he may get depressed or angry; or he may decide to face the new reality.

A man who was uncertain of his masculinity—a former football player now an aggressive businessman—had married a beautiful, intelligent, but promiscuous woman. Over the years of their marriage she had many affairs, about which she told her husband everything. This suited him well, but when she gained enough self-confidence to attend professional school he became anxious, and upon her impending graduation he began to have homosexual affairs. Possessing a desirable woman had consciously allowed him to feel masculine, while his homosexual fantasies were being gratified during lovemaking, which had unconsciously offered him imagined contact with the penises of her lovers. As she became less dependent on him, he began to fear that she had been gaining strength by taking away his phallic powers. Unconscious contact with men was no longer sufficient. He turned instead to conscious action to reassure himself against his castration fears and thus began a homosexual affair with someone who in fact had the same first name he did.

In contrast to the marriage aimed at conserving idealized images, there is a second type, in which the couple marries to resolve past unconscious conflicts through repetition in the present.

A woman married five times, not consciously knowing beforehand that each of her husbands would be alcoholic. She had had an alcoholic father and was consciously trying to escape painful memories of being brutalized by him. Nevertheless, she had an unconscious sixth sense for recognizing alcoholics (despite their overt dissimilarity from her father) and repeated her childhood conflicts with them.

One spouse may also attribute unwanted personal characteristics to the partner through projection. Thus a person may consciously marry one person but find himself entangled with another who is hauntingly reminiscent of past conflicted significant relationships or of aspects of himself he wishes to disavow. While the first type of marriage is liable to disintegrate when a partner differentiates and fails to live up to unconscious expectations, the second type results in "wedlock," a stalemate in which any attempt at differentiation is stifled. The couple becomes locked into a hated but comfortable and familiar collusion.

A woman raged at her husband at home and in therapy for his passivity, for his constant attention to the television set. When she married him, her husband had been a cynical yet outgoing and politically active college student. Now, despite the fact that he worked daily at his profession, his sedentary television-watching at home reminded her of her father, whose passivity she despised and whose interest in television sports made her jealous. The husband often finished work early, cooked the meals, and then waited passively for her to get home from her job. Through treatment, she eventually discovered a feared passive side of herself against which she had struggled for many years. She had projected this unwanted part of herself onto her husband and maintained her perception of him as unambitious and weak.

Object relations psychotherapy is psychoanalytic in that it is interpretive rather than instructive. It focuses on unconscious processes that occur both within and between each member of the couple. Unconscious interactions between spouses often reflect projective identificatory mechanisms of the sort first described by Klein (1946) in the mother–infant relationship. Klein recognized that, early on, the infant internalizes his objects—that is, the mother's face, breast, and so on—and that feeling responses to these objects are based on the infant's own internal aggressive feelings and on the circumstances of maternal care. For example, a colicky infant who cannot get comfort from the mother may experience her as persecuting. The infant sees two kinds of objects, good and bad, based on good or bad feelings within or in response to the care provided.

The good and bad internal objects that form the infant's unconscious world have relationships among themselves. The infant initially splits objects into good and bad to protect himself from overwhelming anxiety, lest one object destroy another or destroy his entire inner world. Perhaps he fears that his greedy hunger will deplete the internalized mother and invite her retaliation. To defend against this felt inner danger, he projects his greed outward and perceives the object as greedy. Projective identification serves to help the infant achieve safety as he projects part of himself into the object both for self-protection and with an aim of controlling the object. The self is relieved and the inner world is safe, but the ego is depleted and now needs the dangerous object close at hand. Thus, as in the marriage just described, a harmful part of the self may be housed in the spouse (the "passive" husband), who is then perceived as necessary, yet potentially threatening. The spouse is then forced to remain in a role that supports this projection, and growth and change become restricted.

In normal development, the mother, through her holding and handling of her infant, accepts and survives his rage and projections. In a sense, the mother bears the various frustrations of the infant without retaliating, and metabolizes them so that they can be reintrojected in a more benign form. This maternal function, called "containment" (Bion 1967) or "the holding environment" (Winnicott 1960), enables the infant to establish with confidence his good inner objects and to feel safe that there are limits to his destructive powers. So, too, in the healthy marriage, each spouse offers the other a similar opportunity that can be growth promoting.

The focus in couple therapy is on the relationship between various feeling states and between subjects and objects, and on the manner in which these relationships are satisfying or not. A point that bears repeating is that object relations theory refers to unconscious fantasy, not to external human relationships per se. It refers to the fantasies that affect those relationships, which can interfere with or augment their development. The following example further illustrates the concept of projective identification of unconscious object relations.

INDIVIDUAL INTERVIEW WITH MR. CARSON

Mr. Carson, a fastidious, controlled, organized, and purposeful man, complained that his messy wife was ruining his life and their marriage with her massively disorganized behavior. Their problems had been longstanding, but it was only bouts of acute gastric pain that forced Mr. Carson to seek psychiatric consultation.

Mr. Carson was a well-dressed, slim, short, dark man. His angular face was decorated with a well-groomed moustache. Upon entering the consulting room, he offered me his card and in an obsessional manner detailed how disorganized and disturbed his wife was, how she could never accomplish any task. He complained that the house was a mess and that things were strewn everywhere. It was only with great effort that I could get him to talk of his own background.

He was from a strict Jewish family dominated by a rejecting, highly critical, self-centered mother. His father was described as ineffectual and passive. His closest childhood relationship had been with his grandfather, actually his mother's stepfather, who provided young Mr. Carson with cultural input, encouraging him to read philosophy and literature. He had always hated his younger brother, who was more athletic and better able to get along with his father than he. That Mr. Carson blamed his wife for all their problems was clear enough, and when asked if he felt he contributed, he said, "Yes, by not knowing how to help her change."

I asked if I could meet with her and he readily agreed, but he warned me that Mrs. Carson was so disorganized that she would be unable to find my office or might forget the appointment time.

INITIAL INTERVIEW WITH MRS. CARSON

Mrs. Carson arrived for her session on time after all. She was dressed in a shapeless burgundy outfit of loose-fitting pants and jacket, hair a mess, and old brown, loose-fitting clogs over which her white sweat socks were flopping. Still, there was a twinkle in her eye, and one had the feeling that she was in costume, albeit a familiar one. Mrs. Carson was the second of two children born to working parents. She was often left alone with her older brother, who teased her incessantly and occasionally beat her. She was expected to clean the house and to vacuum the drapes on weekends. According to Mrs. Carson, her mother and father offered her little in life to be pleased about. She preferred to be alone, felt safety in isolation. Her mother was more concerned with order and cleanliness than with other things and could not, for instance, boil an egg without elaborate cleaning rituals. Mrs. Carson made her own way to art school, obtaining a scholarship. She was a top student and, at any hint of praise from a faculty member, produced prolific and creative work. She was extremely resistant, however, to any attempt to impose a structure on her studies, although she did apprentice to a fastidious old European potter.

COUPLE INTERVIEW

The shared fantasy need to split off certain parts of themselves became more obvious when the couple was seen together. Split-off affects, drives, and ego needs were projected in a collusive tangle. In the initial couple interview, the Carsons were barely civil to each other. He kept trying to nod at me, as if to say, "See what she's like,

Doctor!" while she smilingly ignored him, absorbing his not infrequent insults about her housekeeping. His complaining and her provocation were entrenched attitudes. I looked for evidence that Mrs. Carson knew how provocative she could be, as the following excerpt shows:

Mr. C.:	She never has dinner on time. Yesterday when I got home, stomach hurting, I slipped on a block at the foot of the stairs. [Sigh]
Mrs. C.:	I am very busy with our sons. They need tutoring privately because the schools are so inadequate. The oldest one is a mathematical genius. And I helped make him.
Mr. C.:	She always ignores my needs.
Mrs. C.:	I try to please you, but whatever I do is wrong.
Therapist:	I notice, Mrs. C., that when you tell your husband that you try to please him, there is a mischievous twinkle in your eye.
Mr. C.:	I know she does all this to get me upset. But without me she couldn't do anything.
Mrs. C.:	[Looking at the therapist knowingly] He does get worked up, doesn't he?

To get at the feelings of disappointment and loss underlying their rage, I asked about what they were missing. Whom did they think they had married? As they described their premarital hopes and dreams, it became clear that Mr. Carson admired his wife's sensitivity and her artistic and social freedom, and he had hoped to grow through his relationship with her. Mrs. Carson said that she admired her husband's integrity, responsibility, and capacity to organize and take control of his life. She had hoped to find strength and structure from this marriage. Mr. Carson clearly described the irony of his situation when he said, "I vowed I would never have a repeat of my relationship with my mother, yet my wife never listens."

Idealized longed-for parts of each partner had become buried under an avalanche of projections.

Therapeutic Work on Unconscious Projections

As therapy progressed, Mrs. Carson became more aware of her hope that being married to such an orderly person would protect her. Thus she had wanted to supplement her depleted self-image. However, she projected her mother's criticisms into her willingly critical husband. She defiantly provoked him, repeating her childhood experiences of being criticized for her disordered sloppiness. Further, the projections were violent and sadistic, creating such fragmentation in Mr. Carson that they rendered him unable to have any effect on her. She pushed him further and further into excessive orderliness and obsessional fits of rage. She was secretly comforted by the way he reminded her of her early maternal attachment and also by his covert encouragement of her desire to mess and to remain in a regressed, martyred state.

On the other hand, Mr. Carson needed to organize himself obsessively as protection from his intense but anxiety-provoking urges to attack his mother while covertly retaining his primitive attachment to her. He learned in therapy that he wanted revenge against his mother, who had "spoiled everything" with her critical, biting sarcasm, never seeming to perceive his needs. Mrs. Carson, too, criticized Mr. Carson by making brilliant intuitive attacks against which he was powerless, because to defend himself would be to kill.

Session after session uncovered bitter, hateful anger. The focus of therapy was entirely on unconscious fantasies, projective identification, and repetition of early relationships. Although the Carsons could readily acknowledge the validity of the genetic and the dynamic interpretations, each had to work hard to reclaim projections. Yet after numerous sessions, the couple seemed relieved and finally began to make suggestions to each other that helped them both to reclaim split-off aspects of themselves. Mrs. Carson gradually became punctual and began to dress well, and Mr. Carson became a bit more relaxed and reflective. Still, the power of the unconscious repetition compulsion linked with unresolved, gratifying, primitive maternal attachments made the work slow going.

Earlier in this chapter I mentioned the mother's capacity to survive the infant's sadistic, greedy, envious attacks, and her ability to contain safely the infant's projections. This function, so necessary for both members of a couple, was one that the Carsons had been unable to provide for each other. The following excerpt illustrates how some of that function was assumed by the therapist in a transitional way, while the reclaiming process was going on.

Mr. C.:   You dress up for Dr. Frank now. At home you're still a mess.

Mrs. C.:   No matter what I do it isn't right. But it doesn't matter to me. I feel happy at home, and now I feel you attack me here. What's wrong with my clothes now? They are just what you complain about. I think Dr. Frank doesn't mind.

Mr. C.:   You're just hiding the truth. We never eat on time, and the kitchen is a total mess, and the children . . . they are always busy. You just want to impress him how much better you are.

Mrs. C.:   My husband likes all attention to be for him.

Therapist: So which is it? Are you dressing up for him or for me?

Mrs. C.:   I just feel like it. It pleases me to look well.

Mr. C.:   I asked you to dress better for years.

Therapist: Mrs. Carson is doing what you want but not giving you credit for having an effect on her.

Mrs. C.:   Maybe. . . .

At this point in the treatment, the holding function of the therapist enabled Mrs. Carson both to be less overtly angry at her husband and to feel better about her femininity. I refrained from making other triangular interpretations, such as that perhaps Mr. Carson preferred her to be messy so that she wouldn't attract other men, such as me. The central issue was her ability to change her appearance for me, for him, and for herself while at the same time appearing not to listen to his requests. Ironically, he had criticized her so much that she did stop listening, as nothing was ever good enough for him. His wife now revived his infantile experience in which his mother was too self-concerned to respond to his needs. In addition, the sadistic edge to this revival served Mrs. Carson's own purposes.

Couple therapy uses an object relations framework to illuminate unconscious projections and distortions that occur between marital partners. Although the active and regular intervention required of the therapist differs from traditional analytic technique, the content of interventions is similar, aimed at interpreting and working through unconscious issues interfering with conscious efforts to sustain a mutually satisfying and growth-promoting relationship.

PART IV

THE ANALYTIC, GROUP-INTERPRETIVE APPROACH

11

The Family Group as a Single Psychic Entity: Implications for Acting Out in Adolescence

JOHN ZINNER, M.D.

ROGER L. SHAPIRO, M.D.

Our intent is to discuss, from a psychoanalytic perspective, a phenomenon of family life that interferes with age-appropriate development of the child and adolescent. We will consider a kind of family that acts *as if* it were parceling out the derivatives of drive and functions of superego among different family members so that specific members come to represent and act on behalf of one psychic structure over a particular period of interaction. Taken as a whole, the family appears to constitute a single, relatively complete, psychic entity; taken alone, each individual seems to be psychologically incomplete and overrepresentative of one mental structure. Consequently, internal psychological conflict within members is transmuted into interpersonal conflict *between* those who have come to represent the agencies of impulse and superego. We will examine the association of this kind of family functioning with impulsive and antisocial behaviors of adolescent offspring.

The model proposed represents a step in our broader effort to relate particular qualities of family interaction to specific kinds of functioning in children and adolescents nurtured within that family.

We have previously outlined a theory of family organization (R. Shapiro and Zinner 1971, Zinner and R. Shapiro 1972), which characterized families as functioning on two levels. Our conception represents an extension into family life of Bion's (1961) psychoanalytically derived theory of small groups. The first of these levels consists of behavior appropriate to developmental issues and tasks within the family and is regulated primarily by the reality principle and mediated principally through secondary-process thinking. At another level, in a fashion that may interfere with fulfillment of developmental tasks in family members, behavior is determined by shared unconscious fantasies and unconscious assumptions generated by instinctual needs and defensive requirements that provide a "hidden agenda" for family interaction. Within the family group, the shared fantasies are "played out" by members who are both implicitly and explicitly assigned roles in the unconscious family drama. The fundamental mechanism of role attribution is projective identification, by which members split off disavowed or cherished aspects of themselves and project them onto others within the family group.

These projections govern family members' perception of and behavior toward one another when family group behavior is dominated by unconscious fantasies. Family members relate to the projected aspects of themselves in the same manner as they would were these projections internalized. Hence internalized neurotic conflict *within* individuals may be externalized, assuming the form of interpersonal conflict *between* family members. The relationship between parents and split-off aspects of themselves projected onto their children frequently serve to recapture the lost nuclear family relationships of the parent when he was a child. An example will illustrate the latter point. A woman patient, now in middle age, experienced a difficult adolescence in which, after a long struggle with a tenacious mother, she reluctantly relinquished her yearnings for autonomy and plans to strike out on her own. She made a choice on one side of her ambivalence; she remained inseparable from her mother, who subsequently died many years later while living in the patient's home. Now the daughter of our patient has reached adolescence, and the girl is perceived quite unrealistically by her disconsolate mother as repudiating the family and yearning for separation. In the intensity of the struggle that ensues between mother and daughter, we experience not only a dramatic reliving of mother's adolescent conflict with her own mother, but also an almost palpable sense that this interaction serves the function of conserving the relationship with the deceased grandmother and bringing her back to life.

The clinical material from which these intra- and interpersonal observations are made is derived from families of adolescent patients who were hospitalized in a residential treatment and research unit located in the Clinical Center of the NIMH. Therapeutic modalities include intensive individual psychoanalytically oriented psychotherapy for the adolescent, weekly conjoint marital therapy for the parents, and conjoint family therapy for all family members. All families participated as well in a weekly multiple-family group, and the adolescent inpatients joined in a weekly study group of peer and authority relations. As one might expect in such a setting, a number of our patients were admitted with problems related to impulsivity and a variety of troublesome behaviors, including stealing, truancy, running away, and heavy drug use. Coming primarily from middle-class homes and engaging in their disturbed behavior generally in a solitary fashion, they are comparable to what is generally described as the "individual delinquent."

More than two decades ago, antisocial youngsters and their parents were studied and treated in "collaborative" individual psychotherapy by Johnson (1949) and Szurek (1942), who noted the association between delinquent behavior in the children and defective superegos (superegos with "lacunae") in the mothers.

The investigators stated in their thesis that:

> [A]ntisocial acting out in a child is unconsciously initiated, fostered, and sanctioned by the parents, who vicariously achieve gratification of their own poorly integrated forbidden impulses through a child's acting out. One or both parents, in addition, unconsciously experience gratification for their own hostile and destructive wishes toward the child who is repeatedly destroyed by his behavior. [Giffin et al. 1960, p. 624]

The concepts of unconscious sanctioning of delinquent behavior and vicarious parental gratification have become a part of general psychiatric knowledge and find repeated confirmation in practice. The opportunity to work intensively and conjointly with all family members provides an additional perspective on these phenomena not readily available to those who treat only individual members and are not privy to direct observation of their interaction. The observations of Johnson and Szurek were drawn from concurrent psychotherapy of two family members; the delinquent child and one of his parents. As a consequence of this method of data collection, the concepts developed relate essentially to a dyadic relationship in which the behavior of one member, a parent with a static defective psychic structure, impinges upon a second member, the child, in a rather unidirectional, noninteractional fashion.

The notion of a "punched out," or "lacunar," superego denotes the absence of an aspect of psychic structure. This defect is presumably transmitted across generations in "mirror image" fashion. Our whole-family observations indicated, however, that what appears to be a "lacuna," or hole, in the superego is, in fact, an illusion produced by transactional processes of projection and identification within the family. We find that the antisocial behavior of one member is not just a consequence of a disturbed dyadic parent–child relationship. Rather, this behavior is a dynamically necessary product of shared unconscious fantasies and unconscious assumptions concerning expression and satisfaction of drives within the family as a whole. The family *acts as if* integration of impulse and restraint *within* each member—that is, intrapsychically—was beyond his capacity. The family as a whole assumes responsibility for this integration by distributing the functions of impulse and restraint among its membership so that, at any moment, family member A might be involved in relatively unmodulated drive-discharge activity while member B is serving as the critic and source of restraint on A's activity. We observe that while the so-called delinquent child is the most usual agent for the family's drive-discharge activity, this is by no means always the case. Not infrequently will the parent, in what he considers a "lapse" from his usual moral stance, act out in egregious fashion, while the supposedly wayward child assumes the limit-setting and critical functions of conscience. Thus the unconscious assumption calls for some *one* member to satisfy impulse in behalf of the entire group; this person is then repudiated by the remaining family members, who simultaneously gratify their own drives vicariously through his activity. By virtue of where members direct their projected impulses, the family can "choose" the agent of its drive activity. Thus not all offspring of such a family will exhibit hedonistic behavior; rather, the troubled sibling is likely to be the one who holds a prior special meaning for his parents and is experienced by them as a repository of their projected drive derivatives.

We can bring coherence to this view of the family and

its dispersal of psychic functions by understanding the parents' experience as children within their own nuclear families. The phenomenon of projection—at one moment of the drive, at another moment of the internalized parent–critic—is characteristic, as A. Freud (1936) has shown, of the phases of superego development, which culminate in an intrapsychic integration of drive *and* parent–critic productive of modulated and socially appropriate instinctual gratifications. When internalization and integration of both agencies within the psychic apparatus does not occur, there is a perpetuation into adult life of what should have otherwise been only transient evolutionary stages in the maturation of the superego. When the individual projects his impulse and becomes the parent–critic in relation to these projected drives, A. Freud refers to a process of "identification with the aggressor." Similarly, the projection of the critical functions of the superego represent a regression to an earlier period when controls were, in fact, exercised entirely from the outside. We have found that the parents in the delinquent families under consideration have failed in their own development to bring about a relatively harmonious integration of drive and prohibitions. To defend against severe intrapsychic conflict, they identify with the aggressor—that is, their own parents as authority–critics. In a similar vein, Olden (1953) has cited identification with the aggressor as an explanation for some parents' excessive aggressive behavior towards their own children. In our families of delinquent adolescents, parents also project onto their symptomatic adolescent their own poorly integrated impulses, recreating a conflict that began to be waged a generation previously.

Thus this perception or delineation of their offspring as impulse-ridden and action-prone, and their covert instigation and sanctioning of his misbehavior serves three functions. First, impulse gratification is experienced vicariously through the acting out of the adolescent. Second, parental defense is served by externalizing unresolved conflict between drive and inhibition. Third, the ambivalently held old relationship between parent and grandparent is brought to life by externalizing it onto the adolescent, with roles generally reversed.

Collusion of the adolescent in this family drama is motivated by untrammelled opportunities in the adolescent to gratify his own resurgent impulses by projecting his critical functions onto his parents. This externalization of conscience complements his parents' attribution of their impulses onto the adolescent.

One must not overlook as a motive force, in addition, the adolescent's responsiveness to the parents' defensive needs. At some level the adolescent discerns that his acting out protects his parents from neurotic conflict. Their defensive delineations of him as delinquent thus assume an imperative quality that commands him to continue his behavior as a way of sustaining the psychological intactness of his parents.

In summary, we are proposing that in the families under study, impulsive, antisocial behavior of the adolescent be viewed as a compromise formation that is a product of the family as a whole. The conflicts generating the family "symptoms" have the appearance of interpersonal, rather than intrapsychic, strife. In actuality, they derive from unresolved intrapsychic conflicts waged within each family member between impulse and prohibition, and date back in their origin to conflicts waged in the parents' own nuclear families.

In the following case description, we wish to illustrate the distribution of psychological functions within such a family and the dynamic requirements for the adolescent to act out.

From her parents' point of view, Carol's wild behavior seemed to come from out of the blue, and indeed one can understand their perplexity. Nurtured in an upper middle-class family with a professional father and a socially ambitious mother, a strong sense of propriety and decorousness, plenty of material comfort, why should their 15-year-old daughter stand in such an ungrateful and defiant posture toward their cherished values, and why is she behaving the way she does — truant, thieving, "speeding" on amphetamines, promiscuous, and running away?

Prior to her puberty, there seemed little cause for concern. In fact, during latency, her own fantasies were quite congruent with her parents' ambitions; she imagined herself a debutante, the "belle of the embassy ball," a source of pride to her parents. She achieved satisfactorily at school, enjoyed playmates, fulfilled the image of a pretty, promising, and precocious little girl, in particular the "darling" of her father. Changes in the family, however, came hard on the heels of puberty and menarche during Carol's twelfth year. Concurrently, Mrs. Barlow became pregnant with Ann, the third Barlow child and the first-born in the decade since the birth of Carol's brother, Ralph. A few days before Mrs. Barlow's confinement, Carol left home without parental consent for the first time. Ann was born on the day that Carol entered junior high school. Mr. Barlow heralded the event by announcing that "our new little Carol is born." On the same day, Carol's father took her shopping to purchase her first brassiere. From that time on, Carol and her relationship with her family rapidly deteriorated. During her twelfth and thirteenth years, her school performance fell. She affected "way-out" dress and cosmetics and smoked long, multicolored cigarettes. She kept late hours, drank, and dated boys much older than she. Carol saw this as her "crazy" period, in which she felt herself to be like "putty," without standards and values of her own. Aware of a persistent feeling of guilt and need for punishment, she cut her wrists superficially on several occasions. She was anxious about sexual sensations, sustaining a secret wish to be a "hermaphrodite."

From age 14 until her hospitalization at 15, conscious feelings of guilt and anxiety diminished and her impulsive behavior increased. At 14, an intense and tempestuous sexual involvement with an 18-year-old boy culminated in two suicidal gestures, marked ambivalent parental entanglement in the doomed affair, and ultimately her hospitalization at the Clinical Center.

Mr. Barlow reflected that "behavior such as Carol's gone to would have been as foreign to me as life on another planet." Indeed, both parents recall in their own background that the highest priority was "knowing right from wrong." Both came from families in which parental authority went unchallenged throughout childhood and adolescence. Even in adulthood, Mr. Barlow's abstemious parents cancelled his bachelors' dinner when they heard that alcoholic beverages were to be served. Mrs. Lucille Barlow remembers that limits rarely needed to be stated, since she never dared to approach the boundary. Her mother seemed to be more responsive to Mrs. Barlow's appearance and conduct than to her affectional needs. In spite of Mrs. Barlow's occasional candor, such as blurting out, "I don't like my mother," it is apparent that she has dealt with potential conflicts by identification with these very maternal qualities that she concurrently despises. To illustrate, one of the most troublesome characteristics that Mrs. Barlow describes in her mother is "nattering"—complaining about things "that are not very important," such as a lack of extreme tidiness. Mrs. Barlow vehemently denies any "messy" impulses of her own, avows her "tidiness," and appears to have expressed in her parental home her hostility to the rule by overcompliance rather than rebellion:

Mrs. B.: But I was perfectly willing. I don't remember ever having to be told, over and over and over and over to do it. . . . and uh—but I used to *love* to clean out dresser drawers. And they used to always say if there was something in the house that they couldn't find, "Well, ask Lucy, she probably put it some place." But I always enjoyed that. I don't know what it means, now. [Laughs loudly]

It is, however, in relation to Carol that this conflict is played out with great clarity:

Mrs. B.: Carol is—no, Carol is terribly untidy, and when I get angry, you say what do I do, I take all her dresser drawers and dump them on her bed! And say, "Now clean 'em out!" And uh . . . the difference between us is she'd throw half of the things away and then I have to go through the trash to make sure because I can't *stand* her throwing out things that are worthwhile.

In this recounting of her interaction with Carol, Mrs. Barlow is most manifestly identified with her own mother, while a polar delineation is made of Carol as "terribly untidy." Mrs. Barlow's unconscious identification with the "untidy" Carol is played out in her "dumping clothes" and "rummaging through trash," a good example of return of the repressed expressed through an interpersonal drama. Mrs. Barlow experiences herself as "perfectly willing" and not "ever having to be told," only insofar as she can project her unwillingness and defiance onto Carol. Infrequently, Mrs. Barlow will reinternalize some of her "dislike" for her mother's rigidity. This is demonstrated in the following excerpt, in which she shows how she has covertly communicated to her family that she neither expects nor insists upon being obeyed:

Mrs. B.:   And I'm sure I've often thought that this, the little issues that have come up between—Carol and myself, this . . . is just a difference in people that . . . that I . . . I like things like that and I can't stand it messy and I like things done, when I ask them to do it they *all* have learned . . . that if I ask about three times for something to be done, they don't do it, I go do it myself because I—and my mother was this way . . . and I . . . I used to dislike it in my mother, I know, that she wanted things done when she asked you, but we *did* it, as far as I can remember.

During adolescence, Mrs. Barlow experienced her familial home as "too peaceful," drab, and uneventful. She relinquished a strong romantic attachment with one boy to marry Mr. Barlow, who had a "good future." She feels that, unlike Carol, she was able to sacrifice short-term satisfaction for long-term pragmatic considerations.

Similarly, Mr. Barlow experienced his family as severe and unyielding. His occasional efforts to defy parental authority during adolescence were responded to with vigorous beatings. He generally adhered to the austere family morality and throughout college felt unsophisticated and immature in comparison with his peers. Unwillingness to break the family codes markedly limited his sexual experimentation, so that he saw himself as inadequate as a man yet too anxious to do anything about it. It appears, therefore, that both Mr. and Mrs. Barlow failed to work through important developmental tasks during their own adolescence. Their eldest daughter's entry into puberty rekindled unresolved conflicts in them, particularly concerning authority relationships and sexuality. This was especially burdensome for Carol who, with the birth of a sibling, "our new little Carol," lost a more felicitous parental definition of herself—to gain another delineation as hypersexual and defiant, both fabricated heavily upon parental projections.

In the following excerpt from a family therapy session, the Barlows discuss an evening in which Carol had gone out with two male friends, Burt and Todd, and the trio had engaged in some drinking:

Mr. B.:   There are several things I'm expert on. One is smoking cigarettes, remember? The other is drinking. Very experienced at that. And a rule . . . that I have used—successfully—before I ever met your brother [*sic*]—if a girl drinks, she'll get drunk, sooner or later.

Carol: I didn't get drunk. . . .

Mr. B.:   You—didn't let me finish. If a girl drinks, she'll . . . you can get her drunk, sooner or later. And *then* you've got her! If you want to make her, you can have her! And this is a rule I've applied quite successfully in my uh—younger days! *Invariably*—it works [*Carol:* Invariably—in my experience . . .]

Therapist: So the drinking also gets—connected in your concerns, Mr. Barlow, with Carol's sexual behavior.

Mr. B.:   It *can't*. Whether . . . I'm not talking about specific whether or not . . . but if a girl drinks . . . sooner or later she . . . anybody who drinks . . . will sooner or later get drunk. Maybe it will only happen once or twice—but it will happen. And *then*, if the

	circumstances are right, a girl then can be had. Maybe she doesn't even *know* it. Can be had sexually, to be brutally specific. Did you ever . . . did that consequence ever cross your mind?
Carol:	Umhmmm. But they're not that way.
Mrs. B.:	[Protesting tone.] Oh, Carol, come on! [*Mr. B.*: Who's *they*, for Christ's sakes?]
Carol:	Burt and Todd—they're not that way.
Mr. B.:	What do you mean, they're some kind of queers? They don't like girls?
Carol:	No. . . .
Mr. B.:	What do you mean, then? [silence] You can call that Barlow's rule: Anybody who drinks will get drunk. [Pause] And if you're drunk . . . then . . . anything can happen. Meaning to me that you—at least—didn't consider some of the consequences, that, from personal experience I know can arise out of situations like the kind you were in. Because I've *been* in situations like 'em myself. [Pause] Sounds impossible, doesn't it?
Mrs. B.:	Maybe he does remember when he was young. I keep telling him he never was, Carol. [Cheerful tone as compared to woebegone voice she has used up to this point]
Mr. B.:	[Confidential tone] Sounds impossible, didn't it? You never thought me capable of it, did you?

As this interaction has evolved, it becomes clear that Carol's sexual behavior assumes a critical role in Mr. Barlow's subjective assessment of his own sexual competence. He has here created a categorical equivalence between a girl who drinks and sexual promiscuity. Carol is delineated as unable to control her own sexual impulses—or, perhaps more accurately, as the inevitable victim of a man who "wants to make her." Whether or not her actual current behavior confirms the delineation is irrelevant to him insofar as it is bound to occur in the future. If, on the other hand, Carol's associates are not so ruthless as Mr. Barlow imagines, then she must be guilty of affiliating with "some kind of queers" who "don't like girls." These delineations, which are impervious to Carol's refutations, create a double-bind restricting parental confirmation of Carol's identity to that of a person who is either sexually promiscuous, on the one hand, or sexually inadequate, on the other.

In order to understand the manner in which Mr. Barlow's delineations serve his own defensive needs, we must recall his own constricted adolescent experience in the area of hetero-sexual relationships. His intellectual development was precocious and resulted in his associating with a school group that was almost two years his elder. He never felt free to drink or to smoke until he was 19 or 20, and his first significant sexual experience occurred at about age 20. Although Mr. Barlow's father taught him about "reproduction," it was not "sex in a sexy way," like "what a boy and girl do in the back of a car." He feels that Carol "seems to be getting it all—15 or 16 in comparison to me would have been 19 or 20." This slow and uncertain development in his own adolescent experience tends to belie Mr. Barlow's boastfulness about his expertise in the preceding excerpt. We know that he is conflicted about his own sexual competence, between the feelings of a shy, unsophisticated adolescent and the hypermasculine, rather gran-diose adult whose potency has established an eponym—Barlow's rule—in the annals of sexual behavior. In the light of these dynamics, then, it appears that his previous interaction with Carol represents more a dialogue with a part of himself than with his daughter. His delineation of her falling prey to her male friends is a demonstration of his potency and capability. Her denial of this behavior challenges his own self-image and threatens him with being "queer." As she perseveres in denying the delineation, Mr. Barlow begins to internalize his projection and avows his own experience in this area. At this point Carol represents to him that part of himself accusing him of harboring sexual impulses, and it is to this part that he addresses his argument, "You never thought me capable of it, did you." Here the roles have become reversed, although drive and superego functions remain dissociated within the group as a whole. This excerpt demonstrates the intensely defensive nature of the father's delineation as well as the binding influence it has on his daughter. If she is promiscuous, then he is potent; if she is restrained, then he is incapable. It is clear, therefore, that it is acting out rather than restraint in Carol's behavior that is in the service of her father's defensive needs.

In another brief family excerpt, we see how Mrs. Barlow

likewise responds to Carol's behavior with barely restrained admiration and envy of her daughter's rebelliousness. The family is discussing Carol's having jilted a quite proper boyfriend by sneaking away from him while they were on a date. Initially in the hour, Mrs. Barlow maintained that she was upset by this behavior and fearful that Carol was again going to run away when she heard she had precipitously left her boyfriend and disappeared. She soon shifts in her discussion, however, from reproaching Carol to apparently admiring her.

Mrs. B.:　[Laughs] How you have the nerve to do these things, I'll never know!

Carol:　[Laughs] I know—it's really kinda funny.

Mrs. B.:　It *is* kinda funny [sounds amused; coughs], *but* . . .

Carol:　[Delighted tone] Then we opened the back door and Barabara and I—went running away from Phil—and we went to the movies.

Mrs. B.:　But then you left me in tears. Because, see, Phil called me and said, "Mrs. Barlow, I left Carol off at the drugstore and went to look for her and she's gone."

Moments later, Mrs. Barlow comments on the deserted Phil, "He really kinda in a way . . . no one really deserves it, but he deserves anything he gets—in a mild way." At this point, Mrs. Barlow's identification with Carol's behavior is so nearly overt that Mr. Barlow must interrupt to attentuate it and restore the family to its prior dissociated state. "Nevertheless," he says, "I'll be the spoilsport. You weren't with whom you were supposed to be and you upset your mother very much."

These excerpts of family interaction indicate the marked extent to which the family task of facilitating adolescent maturation has been subordinated to group functioning according to unconscious fantasy. Unconscious assumptions in which impulse expression is equated with messiness and sexual license, and in which loss of control and inhibition of impulse is equated with inadequacy, may be inferred from the family behavior in the excerpts. Failure within the parents to achieve a better integration of superego characteristics and instinctual forces leads to dissociation and dispersion of drive and superego functions within the family which is inimical to the major integrative challenge of superego realignment that the adolescent must accomplish. The resurgent oedipal complex of the daughter finds its complement in the reawakened unresolved oedipal conflicts of her parents. All family members exploit their situation; all are victims and all are victimizers. For while it is true that the adolescent's strength of drive and proneness to action makes her a vulnerable agent for her parents' impulses, she likewise abdicates responsibility for her own actions by projecting her self-criticism onto her parents.

In summary, we have attempted to show how symptomatic behavior in some delinquent adolescents may be the product of transactional processes within the family as a whole.

These transactional processes involve the acting out of shared unconscious fantasies and the dispersion among family members of aspects of drive and superego by mechanisms of projection and identification. The adolescent's impulsive behavior is found to have its roots in his parents' own experience within their nuclear family.

Summary

The authors have engaged in investigations to determine how family behavior facilitates or inhibits the satisfactory completion of developmental tasks by the adolescent offspring. In this report, impulsive acting-out behavior in certain adolescents is viewed as a product of transactional processes occurring within the family as a whole. The family of the delinquent youngster behaves *as if* it were a single psychic entity, with derivatives of drive and functions of superego dispersed among family members.

Internal psychological conflict within family members is transmuted into interpersonal strife between those who have come to represent the conflicting mental structures. By the mechanism of projective identification, the family generally comes to perceive the adolescent as the agent of its impulses. This is not invariable, as family roles may be reversed, with the adolescent speaking for the superego.

The roots of parental dissociation of drive and prohibition lie in their own unresolved conflicts around sexuality and authority relationships, which are rekindled by the onset of adolescence in their offspring. The parents are viewed as recapitulating with their child the very conflicts that they had experienced with their own parents.

12

The Adolescent, the Family, and the Group: Boundary Considerations

ROGER L. SHAPIRO, M.D.
JOHN ZINNER, M.D.

BOUNDARY CONCEPTS

In this chapter we will discuss the boundary concepts that have given orientation to our work in a research treatment program for disturbed adolescents and their families. *Boundaries* are demarcations that are crucial to the definition of any system, in that they separate it from its environment and from other systems in its environment (Miller and Rice 1963, Rice 1967, 1969). As such, boundary concepts are central in explicating a psychology of the individual personality system, of the family system, or of the group. Boundaries are also constructs that speak of the relationships between parts of a system and thus provide an essential framework for conceptualization of differential aspects of psychological processes within the individual or family or group (Landis 1970).

We assume that there is an important correspondence in the structure of the personality system and its subsystems and the structure of external reality—especially the social system and its subsystems—that impinges on that personality (Edelson 1970). The same concept, then, would be expected to have an important homology in each system. The correspondence between the boundary concepts of individual psychology and the nature of boundaries in the family system and the group is the focus of our study. The aim of this study is to define the relationship of boundary characteristics of the family system—in particular, characteristics of the boundary between the family and the individual adolescent—to the nature of self boundaries that have developed within the adolescent himself (R. Shapiro and Zinner 1971). In addition, we consider how characteristics of self boundaries in the adolescent relate to the role boundaries he establishes in new interpersonal and group situations. When there is pathology in the adolescent and in the family, we design treatment situations so that the manifestations of pathology in boundary problems, or the origins of pathology in boundary problems, can be explored (R. Shapiro 1966, 1967, 1968, 1969).

The Individual Boundary of the Ego

The major boundary concept in psychoanalytic psychology is the ego. Freud (1923) defined it as the coherent organization of mental processes that relate the individual to his drives and to the external world. Certain boundary characteristics of ego functions are conceptualized as self boundaries, a structural concept that refers to boundary properties of the self-representation, which differentiate the phenomenal self from other aspects of the personality and from the world of reality external to the person as subjectively experienced (Hartmann 1950, Jacobson 1964, Landis 1970). Throughout development, biological maturation and experience bring changes in the functioning of the ego and its discriminations of internal and external reality, and related changes in the boundaries that differentiate the self. Our research concerns aspects of experience that effect these differentiations of self and determine characteristics of self boundaries in adolescence.

New capacities for abstract thought in the adolescent are clearly demonstrated in the work of Inhelder and Piaget (1958), who describe a consistent change in the individual's ability to conceptualize and to generalize between ages 11 to 15. Concrete operations in the thinking of the child progress to abstract thought in the adolescent. The capacity for hypothesis formation develops with the use of hypothetico-deductive reasoning and experimental proof. We consider this cognitive growth in early adolescence to be evidence of autonomous ego development (R. Shapiro 1963). It is the cognitive basis of the abstract differentiation of the self that occurs in adolescence, resulting in a new definition of boundaries of the self.

Jacobson (1964) has conceptualized adolescent development in terms of remodeling of psychic structure and increase in the secondary autonomy of the ego. This implies increased strength and definition of the boundary between conflict-free ego functioning and ego functioning that continues to be determined by the internalizations of experiences of anxiety and conflict in childhood. Increased autonomy of the ego is also evidenced in increased strength and definition of the boundary between the adolescent and external objects. Reorganization of roles and modifications of libidinal investment within the family are seen. The adolescent is also redefining himself in his peer relationships and in the group life of social institutions outside of the family. His increasing freedom to act in new roles in society is a further aspect of the increased strength and definition of his self boundaries.

Erikson (1956, 1958, 1962) has conceptualized alteration in the self and new definition of its boundaries during adolescence as the establishment of ego identity.

In Erikson's formulations, change in the ego of the adolescent and in the definition and resilience of self boundaries is a precondition for extensive change in the adolescent's experience with his family, with his peers, and with other groups in society. Familial and societal response to adolescent maturation facilitates or interferes with the development of ego identity and with stabilization of new self boundaries. When either the internalizations of childhood experience or the lack of nutriment in current adolescent experience interferes with ego reorganization and increasing autonomy in the adolescent, there is a failure in the coherent differentiation of the self, with chaotic boundaries and a clinical picture of identity confusion.

During adolescence, there is important change in the individual's relationship to the family, to the peer group, and to other groups in society (R. Shapiro 1963). This change follows maturation in the ego and the id during puberty, which results in new cognitive and affective capacities (A. Freud 1936, 1958, Inhelder and Piaget 1958). These capacities may or may not be free to develop, depending in part upon the nature of internalizations of family experience that have occurred through infancy and childhood (Schafer 1968). Adolescent development brings about a reorganization of childhood internalizations in relation to ego–id maturation and new experience. Disturbances of adolescence are thus a consequence both of the continuing power of internalizations of disturbed family relationships of childhood causing ego impairment in the adolescent, and of failure of the current family and group relationships of the adolescent to facilitate progressive differentiation and integration of the self.

BOUNDARY REGULATION BETWEEN SYSTEMS

These considerations regarding disturbance in the individual adolescent determined the design of our research

and residential treatment program at the NIMH from 1960
to 1974. This program for adolescents aged 14 to 21
included individual psychotherapy for the adolescent,
conjoint family therapy, and study of the hospital group
in which the adolescent lived and worked. It combined
three hours a week of individual psychotherapy for the
adolescent with a weekly one-hour conjoint family
therapy session; one hour a week of marital therapy for
the parents; and four patient–staff meetings a week,
including a study group examining peer relationships and
authority relationships on the psychiatric unit. In designing the program, we attempted to articulate the
psychological maturation of the adolescent with his experience within the family, within the peer group, and
within the social institution of which he was a part. The
task of our program was to design and manage the
conduct of situations for study and treatment that promote relative ego autonomy in the adolescent, leading
to individuation and psychological separation from the
parents.

In this discussion and review of boundary concepts
we have used in our work, we want to define the following subtasks within the overall task of the program.
First, we explore and modify the internalizations of childhood experience that are manifested in disturbance in the
development of relative autonomy in the adolescent's ego
and impairment in individuation. This is the task of
individual psychotherapy.

Second, we explicate and modify the actuality of
current family dynamics that are interfering with adolescent individuation and separation. This includes clarifying the nature of the boundary between the parents as
a marital pair and the adolescent. This is the task of
conjoint family therapy and marital therapy.

Third, we study and modify the adolescent's functioning in a new social organization (away from the
family) in which he has the opportunity to develop a more
mature and responsible relationship to peers and to

authority figures than was present in his family relationships. This is the task of the unit study group.

What boundary considerations are involved in the implementation of these tasks? We investigate how chaotic self boundaries in the adolescent are related to the nature of his internalized objects and their boundary characteristics; how they are related to the current dynamics at the boundary between the adolescent and the family; and how they are related to the boundaries of the roles he seeks to assume or is put into in new interpersonal or group relationships. Individual psychotherapy, family and marital therapy, and the unit study group are situations in which we explore these questions. In these therapy situations, we investigate characteristics at the boundary between two interacting psychological systems. This study is facilitated by recognizing that these may be considered intergroup situations. Each of them involves two systems in a situation of mutual exchange. We observe and define characteristics of boundary regulations between them and infer the relationship of these regulations to the inner coherence of each system.

Rice's group therapy model has helped us to recognize and articulate this situation (Miller and Rice 1963, Rice 1967, 1969). Rice's basic propositions in applying to individual and group behavior a system theory of organization are, first, that every relationship—between individuals, within small and large groups, and between groups—has the characteristics of an intergroup relationship; and, second, that the effectiveness of every intergroup relationship is determined, so far as its overt purposes are concerned, by the extent to which the groups involved have to defend themselves against uncertainty about the integrity of their boundaries. A corollary of this is that the making of any intergroup relationship carries with it the possibility of a breakdown in authority, the threat of chaos, and the fear of disaster.

Rice's formulations about the intergroup situation thus specify an interrelationship between the integrity of the boundary—that is, the adequacy of boundary regulations between two systems—and the state of internal coherence within each system. Integrity of the intergroup boundary implies that each system has a clear inner sense of differentiation from the other. This depends upon the presence and effectiveness within the system of sufficient internal authority for integrated functioning. Here, authority is defined as the capacity within each system to be able, to some degree, to determine task definition, to be self-regulating, and to control task implementation, including intergroup transactions.

Conditions at the boundary between the two systems are determined by covert definitions within each system of the intergroup task. If each system has a different definition of the intergroup task, or if change in one of the systems requires a change in definition of the intergroup task, authority in each system is strained, with anxiety arising over the possibility of breakdown in authority in each system. The integrity of the intergroup boundary is threatened if there is insufficient differentiation between the two systems to promote clear intergroup transactions, or if authority is too fragile within either system to maintain integrated functioning, or if authority is too inflexible within either system to find a framework for intergroup transactions within a changing situation. Under these circumstances, abrupt separation from the intergroup situation occurs, or there is breakdown of boundaries between the two systems, with accompanying chaos.

Conceptualized as intergroup situations, individual psychotherapy, conjoint family therapy, and the unit study group highlight different determinants of the self boundary problems of the developing adolescent. We have defined three tasks that these intergroup situations are designed to accomplish. We will next discuss our efforts to implement these tasks through study and modification of the characteristics of the crucial intergroup boundary in each situation. This involves a focus upon the interrelationship between the nature and extent of boundary integrity, and the state of internal coherence within each system in these intergroup situations during a period of rapid change — the period of adolescence.

THE PATIENT-THERAPIST BOUNDARY

We return to the first task we have defined for our research and treatment program: to explore and modify the internalizations from childhood that have rendered the adolescent's ego vulnerable and unable to achieve relative autonomy and individuation. We use the individual psychotherapy situation to implement this task. In Rice's terms, this is an intergroup situation between two individual personality systems in which the task of therapy and the patient and therapist roles are clearly defined. Here psychoanalytic theory provides conceptual means in the structural, dynamic, and economic theories for articulating phenomena within each individual personality system; and the theories of transference and countertransference explicate the phenomena of the intergroup boundary between the individual personality systems.

In the individual psychotherapy situation, the internalizations of the adolescents are studied through their projections in the transference. These internalizations may interfere with capacities maturing in the adolescent that alter his potential for individuation and for finding new libidinal objects outside the family. If characteristics of the adolescent's internal objects militate against this development by engendering separation anxiety, sexual anxiety, or anxiety deriving from deficient models for adult roles and relationships, these characteristics of internal objects will have manifestations in the transference relationship. The phenomena of the transference–countertransference boundary elucidate these internalizations and related anxieties that have determined weakness and confusion in the adolescent self boundary. The experience of psychotherapy involves the interpretation and working through of transference distortions in the context of a new relationship. As a more realistic perception of the relationship to the therapist occurs, the itensity of anxieties determined by old internalizations is diminished, with consequent alteration and consolidation of self-boundary definition. The present is less pervaded by the past, chaos within the adolescent is reduced, and the adolescent develops sufficient inner authority for integrated functioning. This allows progression in development of relative ego autonomy and individuation, with increasing coherence and integrity of self boundaries.

TRANSACTIONS AT THE BOUNDARY
BETWEEN ADOLESCENT AND FAMILY

We use the conjoint family therapy situation to implement the second task defined earlier—that of explicating and modifying the actuality of current family dynamics that are interfering with adolescent individuation and separation. Study of the conjoint family therapy situation poses new conceptual difficulties. It is a more complex intergroup situation than is the individual therapy situation. The intergroup boundary between the adolescent and his family is the major boundary to be examined in relation to the task. We conceptualize transactions across this boundary through use of the concept of delineation and through a related concept, that of unconscious assumptions in the family as a group. We observe interaction in family therapy with these concepts in mind in order to clarify the phenomena at the boundary between the adolescent and his family. We will discuss these concepts briefly in this chapter. They have been discussed at length and with detailed clinical examples in previous publications (R. Shapiro 1966, 1967, 1968, 1969, R. Shapiro and

Zinner 1971, Zinner and R. Shapiro 1972) and in Chapters 4, 5, 6, and 7.

Delineation is a concept closely linked to observable behavior. Delineations are behaviors through which one family member communicates explicitly or implicitly his perceptions and attitudes—in fact, his mental representation of another family member—to that other person.

The work of conjoint family therapy is an articulation of the ways in which family members delineate one another. In particular, we attempt to elucidate the dynamics of parental delineations of the adolescent and the relationship of these delineations to a dynamic of shared unconscious assumptions of the family as a group. The maturation of the adolescent has altered the intergroup situation between the adolescent and his parents, in that adolescent individuation involves the finding of new libidinal objects and gradual separation from the parents. However, the families with whom we work resist the changes required by the adolescent's maturation. The dynamics of this resistance are conceptualized in terms of the unconscious assumptions of the family as a group. These assumptions determine delineations observed at the boundary between the adolescent and the family. Disturbances in the adolescent and in the family are manifestations of the breakdown in authority and the threat of chaos described by Rice in an intergroup situation in which unconscious assumptions militate against necessary change and determine uncertainty about the integrity of boundaries within a changing situation.

In addition to conjoint family therapy, we use marital therapy to implement the second task of explicating and modifying the actuality of current family dynamics that are interfering with adolescent individuation and separation. In marital therapy, we want to clarify the nature of the boundary between the parents as a marital pair and the adolescent. We explore problems in the marriage that have resulted in pressures against change and characteristic efforts to hold the adolescent in particular roles related to the parents's difficulties and dissatisfactions with each other. The boundary between the generations is often uncertain and unstable, and this adds to the anxiety within the family as the adolescent matures. The generational boundary is made explicit in the design of our program by having a separate session each week of marital therapy for the parents. This in turn helps us to clarify in the conjoint family therapy the problems and uncertainties at the boundary between the parents and the adolescent and the contribution of this to the adolescent's problems. Weakness and failures in the generational boundary are problems at an intergroup boundary within the family group that generate specific pressures against adolescent individuation and separation.

Another intergroup boundary in the conjoint family therapy is that between the therapists and the family. The adolescent's individual therapist and the parents' marital therapist shift roles to become co-therapists of the family as a group in the conjoint family sessions. We study the ways in which parents and adolescent relate to the role shift. For example, there may be denial in the family sessions of the psychological presence and availability of the experience of marital therapy or individual therapy even when it is clearly relevant to what is happening in family therapy. Or there may be a perception of one of the therapists in family therapy that is dominated by his role as an individual or couple therapist and relates to attitudes toward the individual or couple therapy that are not being made explicit. Issues such as these become evident and interpretable through focusing on the intergroup boundary between therapists and family and between the therapy subgroups in the family session. The transference issues in this situation are complex and must be approached with the recognition that family therapy is an intergroup meeting with a number of subgroups present. The family's techniques for dealing with boundary problems in the meeting are studied to elucidate the unconscious assumptions that govern its management of boundaries both within the family and between the family and the world of relationships outside.

THE ADOLESCENT IN RELATION TO GROUPS OF PEERS OR AUTHORITIES

The third task defined earlier is that of studying and modifying the adolescent's functioning in a new social organization, away from the family, in which he has the opportunity to develop new roles and a new relationship to peers and to authority figures. The situation we developed in our program for implementing this task is the "unit study group" (R. Shapiro et al. 1975). In this situation, we study transactions at the boundary between the adolescent and the group that are expressions of the role the adolescent takes or is put into in a new group situation.

There were several one-hour administrative meetings each week in our psychiatric unit, during which the unit administrative psychiatrist and the nursing staff met with all the patients to discuss the problems of living and working together in the hospital. In these meetings the rules that regulated life on the unit were evolved, issues concerning implementation of the school and work program were discussed, activities away from the Clinical Center were decided upon, and community passes and privileges were requested and discussed. Efforts were made to examine the responsibility each patient was taking for therapy, school, work, and behavior in the hospital and outside community.

Separate from the administrative meetings, the unit study group is an intergroup meeting consisting of all the patients, the chief psychiatric nurse (representing the nursing staff), the unit administrator (representing the individual and family therapists), and the clinical director (representing the research project chiefs and senior psychiatric staff). The task of this meeting is the study of authority and peer relationships in the group life of the psychiatric unit. It is explicit that this is not a decision-making meeting; rather, it is one in which the dynamics of roles and role relationships are studied, including the nature of attitudes toward those in authority. The work of the meeting is the examination of the roles individuals take or are put into by the hospital group with whom they live and work. Patients are able to reflect upon the roles they take in relation to people in authority and to examine the dynamics of their relationships to peers and to authority figures. Staff members in authority roles are able to (1) articulate role differences among themselves, (2) experience differences in roles they take with the patient group and the ways in which they are related to by the patient group; and, (3) despite definitions of difference, see and work with projections through which they are experienced as monolithic in the group. A range of issues of group life in the hospital are discussed in the meetings. In particular, phenomena defining the boundaries of the self are attended to in the group. These phenomena include the roles taken by the patients and new roles that evolve in their relationships with one another. Transactions at the boundary between the individual adolescents and authority figures are studied, with attention to real and fantasied characteristics of this boundary and its consequences for group behavior. The adolescents define themselves in a variety of ways, and as their experience in the group evolves, shifts occur in their transactions with peers and with authority figures. Interpretations focus upon the dynamics of new roles patients take and the nature of transactions that eventuate in definition of new behaviors and role boundaries.

The following excerpt from a unit study group meeting contains transactions from which we infer different definitions of patient role. The excerpt exemplifies the kinds of themes that emerge in the group and the kinds of transactions that occur across the boundary between the adolescent, the authority figures to whom he relates in his group life, and his peers.

Unit Study Group Meeting

EXCERPT

Dr. S.:	One consequence I was thinking of is that if less talk has to do with having less authority, then the patients feel low man on the totem pole.
Bruce:	Yeah, but you know, the way I see it is that you cats can tell us things forever, you know, but it wouldn't do any good, you know . . . like cause each person is an individual and you can't . . . like if you're going to help somebody with their problems or something, you're going to have to know that individual pretty well, and like you can't just come and tell people what's happening, they have to tell *you*, you know; if they don't tell you then you really can't do a very effective job. So you can sit and talk forever and it's not gonna do any good. And you can tell 'em where it's at. It might even *be* that way . . . but you really don't *know* where they're at 'cause they won't talk to you.
Dr. S.:	I couldn't agree more!
Bruce:	Well . . . that's where it's at, I think. . . .
Dr. R.:	It's not clear why you want to, for instance, leave me as unit administrator uh . . . not knowing where you're at so that it makes the administration not accurate, sort of imposed.
Bruce:	Well, I don't *know*, I just think, you know, *you* might feel it starts off like I'm leaving you there, but *I* feel like it starts off like you're imposing on *me*. You know what I mean?
Dr. R.:	So it's a debatable question as to who started imposing on whom, and there's a battle going on? . . .
Bruce:	[Interrupting] It really doesn't matter. I don't see any battle, really . . . you know. . . .

Dr. R.:	Sounds like it.
Bruce:	[Snickers]
Dr. S.:	I think it's clarifying. Because you're speaking *for* the group at the moment. I have a lot of feeling of people feeling imposed on. Even Dr. R., as the administrator of the unit, has felt imposed on in here. But you're also saying something about your knowing best of all where it's at for you.
Bruce:	That's right.
Dr. S.:	And that's true for everyone in this room.
Bruce:	[Low voice] That's right.
Dr. S.:	And . . . [pauses, does not continue]
Dr. R.:	You know, it's interesting. I think that Fred was empathic with the position he felt me to be in; at least he could see that I was sitting alone.
Dr. S.:	His empathy's put him to sleep, apparently. . . .
Dr. R.:	[Interrupting] Yeah, that's what I was going to say, it's almost as if pointing that out uh and making an effort seems to have worn him out. Takes a lot of work. Ann points out everybody's alone to some degree. Sounds like she felt very alone. Yet to work on what that's about . . . maybe it's about being with . . . people who tend to talk too much so you feel like they're imposing. It takes more effort than it seems to be worth.
[Pause]	
Ann:	Well, I think each person in here was . . . attempting to . . . bound their own territory; you know . . . create . . . their own world, their own boundaries.
Dr. R.:	I think that reflects the feeling I've had. Certainly I've felt that in a way Dr. S. has come onto the unit. Then I've been having to say, "Hey, wait a minute, let's get clear at least if you're gonna come on the unit, in what way, and what our relationship is. I am here daily. You're my boss." I run the unit directly in terms of being administrator—but it's not a usual experience until this kind of group for me to work this way and as closely with you— so I've had to do a lot of thinking about that, sort

out my feelings about it. [Pause] How do you go about doing that, Ann?

Ann: What?

Dr. R.:   Sorting out—your place.

Ann: I haven't been involved in that here. . . .

Dr. R.:   You haven't at all? . . . sounds like you've been thinking about it.

Ann: About my—place?

[Long pause]

Dr. S.:   I have the impression, Ann, you felt undercut by Dr. R. because you were trying to define your thinking here, your boundaries, your territory. I thought what you said implied you have been thinking about it. And he took your lead maybe to try to define his place and his task.

Ann: Well, that's—that's cool.

Dr. S.:   [Interrupts] I thought it was. But I thought you felt undercut by it in some way. I think that may be one of the problems in a group. Did you experience it that way?

Ann: [Slight pause] No, not . . . not really. No. . . .

Dr. S.:   Because then when he asked you, it was brought back to you, and you said, well, you really hadn't been thinking about it, but you just had . . . *told* us you had been thinking about it.

Ann: Well, I was . . . thinking more in terms of my own place, not . . . with other people, but with myself. Your way . . . of forming boundaries is talking and . . . getting everything in form, all your actions and interactions, so . . . [pause]

Dr. S.:   Are you saying that's not your way?

Ann: I'm just saying that it's one way.

Dr. S.:   It is one way.

Ann: Yes.

Dr. S.:   I wonder what the problem is around defining one's self with words. Does it feel that it's just my way or Dr. R.'s way? Bruce said he forgot what the meeting was for. Ann said it's one way and I don't think it is the only way, but I wonder what's wrong with the one way. There's something about it that seems to make for reticence so that Rennie, you, for instance, you listen and take it in but you don't find a way to work actively for quite a long time in this group. Sometimes it's interesting to listen and take in, but why does that role seem the only one for you? . . . It's better than sleeping, but there might be something better yet. Bruce has become the group artist; he draws people, doesn't talk about *them* but he talks about me and you today. Doesn't . . . really say much about the other patients he lives with. You're all very careful with each other.

Arnold: [Pauses] Uhhh . . . I'm becoming an observer again.

Dr. S. You are, Arnold. You came in feeling released, but what happened?

Arnold: Lots—I couldn't . . . maintain concentration. One thing I have noticed about this meeting is that it seems to be a rather odd relationship here between staff and patients in that they do interact but they never seem to work quite properly. It never seems to get anywhere, and I was wondering why. I just was reading the autobiography of Malcolm X; you know, the more you read, the more you get turned on to the fact that the audience in certain parts of the countries that Malcolm X was visiting were actually putting on little vignettes; they were acting, so Malcolm X would be struck by this, just as Nixon was struck by that girl who was holding up the sign some place in Ohio. There is a definite interrelationship between the actor or the audience, and uh . . . the leader. Like they are two parts of the whole. And I was wondering why it seems that there's never that type of dialogue between staff and patients here. I think it's because . . . all we talk about is why we don't talk about anything. And we never seem to . . .introduce anything from the outside that might be useful, to start up, you know, to get a little bit of conversation going into something that wouldn't be directly personal or wouldn't antagonize anybody. Then you'd, you'd also have the personal relationships the way people are interreacting as well. I don't know. You can't just talk about a vacuum for too long.

[Pause]

Dr. S.: One could say that your model of Malcolm X and the countries he visited, or even President Nixon for that matter and the girl he saw saying "Bring us together"—that there is something going on in this room similar to that.

Arnold: Similar, yeah, but it seems to be descending, spiralling downwards as opposed to the opposite, spiralling upwards.

Dr. S.: I think it's felt so much as a slap in the face, for instance, I called Bruce the group artist and . . . he . . . winced as if I'd struck him and insulted him. I myself don't know what's wrong with being the group artist.

Bruce: I don't want to be the group artist.

Dr. S.: But I was saying what my perception was of you. You didn't say that you didn't want to be that or what you did want to be or anything. You winced and looked angry.

Bruce: Yeah, man, you know, you can just go on saying whatever you want to say, it's fine.

Dr. S.: I don't say whatever I want to say.

Bruce: Maybe you should.

Dr. S.: Maybe I should? No, I try to think about what I say. There is a job we are trying to do here. Some things I think don't have anything to do with that and I wouldn't say them.

Aronld: Must we have such areas of controversy? There probably could be things we could talk about going on outside of the unit.

Dr. S.: Outside of the unit.

Arnold: Of course, it's probably too irrelevant to what's happening. I think it's a better idea than sitting around here sighing and being afraid to talk.

Dr. R.: It sounds like you're onto the drama going on right in here.

Arnold: How so?

Dr. R.:	Malcolm X comes to mind. . . .
Arnold:	Well, it's just, just that I happened to be reading it.
Dr. R.:	It seems apropos.
Arnold:	Well, it's like . . . I mean he, he thought that the audience was reacting strictly to him. He didn't realize that the audience, people who were watching him, were trying to impress something upon his mind also. By the way the audience as a whole was reacting. He never considered this, how his policies were changed by the people he talked to. You know, the reception he got influenced his mind and his actions.

In this excerpt, Bruce is manifesting new behavior in transactions with authority figures. The excerpt starts with Bruce stating that the patients are responsible for defining and articulating the boundaries of their individuality. They are the authorities on who they are and what their problems are. There is clear recognition that unless they let staff authority figures know how they think and feel, the staff are unable to do their job. However, feelings of being imposed upon and anger at the imposition lead to concern over differentiation and a continuing tendency of the patients to keep themselves anonymous. Ann adds to the understanding of patient anonymity. She says that she is too preoccupied with establishing her individual boundaries to be able to deal with the group at all at this time. Arnold says that leaders can discern the group's needs and wants from the group's behavior. He implies that the group's behavior is motivated by an effort to get something from the leaders and to control them. This is more important than defining the boundaries of the self. He is disturbed by Bruce's fight with Dr. S. and Dr. R. and wants to lead the group away from internal areas of controversy. He protests about the doctors' refusal to accept the patients' messages that they are helpless and must be cared for.

What dynamics of the group as a whole can be inferred from this excerpt? The group appears to be dominated by a covert (and often overt) assumption of dependency upon the staff. This is the pervasive dynamic, to which the patients relate in a variety of ways. They all appear to feel needful and dependent. This results in their feeling highly vulnerable to authority figures, perceiving them as extremely coercive. In this excerpt there is some shift in Bruce, who is manifesting new role behavior in his assertion of the authority of the patient role in the group if it is to be a work group. This fragile leadership exemplifies the kind of transaction on the boundary between the adolescent and authority figures upon which we focus.

Arnold is an articulate spokesman for the usual patient position of basic-assumption dependency. He emphasizes the patients' covert communications, which in this group seem to express a need for protection and care from authority figures, demonstrated by acting helpless and fearful. His contributions define the boundary between patients and staff as an area of struggle in which patients repeatedly attempt to evoke from the staff a basic-assumption dependency leadership. This takes precedence over self-definition as the patients' task in the group.

How do we accomplish work in this group with the powerful basic-assumption dynamics that exist in it? Work is promoted through our position that the patients are as responsible for their participation and contribution in the group as they are responsible for their behavior in the hospital. Their participation in our program is voluntary and represents a choice for which they are responsible. The patients often want to deny this responsibility and to put it on their parents or on us. They often want to insist upon their helplessness and their inability to behave responsibly and at the same time to express hatred toward the professional staff for exercising control over them. They want to deny that they themselves have any role in giving away their own controls and their own responsibility. Rioch (1971) discussed the central importance of dynamics similar to these in educational situations. These group dynamics are clearly not specific to a psychiatric unit.

The patients tend to repeat in the unit study group roles they have taken and are taking in their families. The ongoing task of the group is to work interpretively on these roles in the many ways in which they are manifested. This facilitates the adolecent's conscious experience of new possibilities in role behavior in relation to peers and authority figures in a social organization away from his family. In this way, his group experience helps him resume the task, interrupted in the period of identity confusion, of learning and integrating appropriate, mature, and responsible social roles.

Summary

We have described a program of research and treatment in which we have studied changes that occur in the adolescent's internal psychological boundaries, and in the characteristics of the boundaries between the adolescent and his family, peers, and social institutions. These changes are initiated by the psychological maturation of puberty, with ensuing reorganization of the individual's internal psychological boundaries. They are also determined by experiences that occur within the boundary areas between the adolescent, his family, and his social groups. The program is designed to help the adolescent articulate and integrate his experience at significant social boundaries and relate this to confusion within his own self boundaries. This allows progression in the development of ego autonomy and individuation, with increasing coherence of the adolescent's self-identity and integrity of self boundaries.

13

Family Dynamics and Object Relations Theory: An Analytic, Group-Interpretive Approach to Family Therapy

ROGER L. SHAPIRO, M.D.

Psychoanalysis became an object relations theory when Freud (1923) proposed the structural hypotheses in *The Ego and the Id*. Prior to that, in psychoanalytic theory, interest in objects was limited to their role in affording need gratification through drive discharge, and identification was conceived of as a mechanism of defense. Freud's increasing recognition of the role of identification in mental life led him to propose that identification was a crucial factor in the formation of ego and superego. This was a change in his conceptualization of the role of object relations in development.

In structural theory, internalizations of object relations were crucial constituents in the formation of psychic structure (Loewald 1966). The structural theory established psychoanalysis as a developmental theory. Subsequent contributions to psychoanalytic theory in ego psychology and the work of the British school of object relations were built on the foundation of structural theory. These contributions continued the effort to comprehend the relationship of the individual to reality through conceptualizing processes of internalization of object relations during development and their persistence and state of organization in both conscious and unconscious mental processes (R. Shapiro 1978).

This position is consistent with that of Kernberg (1976), who states:

> In the broadest terms psychoanalytic object relations theory represents the psychoanalytic study of the nature and origin of interpersonal relations, and of the nature and origin of intrapsychic structures deriving from fixating, modifying, and reactivating past internalized relations with others in the context of present interpersonal relations. Psychoanalytic object relations theory focuses upon the internalization of interpersonal relations, their contribution to normal and pathological ego and superego developments, and the mutual influences of intrapsychic and interpersonal object relations. [p. 56]

Psychoanalysis was established as a personality theory and as a therapy before the structural theory was formulated. The methods of psychoanalysis as a therapy were based upon prior topographic theory. Although the structural theory soon led to important changes in analytic technique—specifically, the methods of defense analysis (Settlage 1974)—other modifications of technique, derived from developmental considerations and from the role of object relations in personality formation, have evolved more slowly in the years since the structural theory was formulated. These modifications have been particularly significant in the treatment of children and adolescents. The methods of child analysis are one example of such technical development.

This chapter is concerned with another technical development that addresses specific problems in the treatment of adolescent disturbances. In it I will discuss methods of analytic assessment and treatment of the family of the disturbed adolescent. I believe treatment of the family may be required because of the body of findings, predicted by structural theory, relating pathology in children and adolescents to disturbances in relationships within the family.

First, I will discuss the need for an analytic framework for the assessment of families of disturbed adolescents and indications for the application of such a framework to the group interpretive treatment of certain of these families concurrent with the individual psychoanalytic psychotherapy of the adolescent. I will then outline an analytic theory of family functioning that conceptualizes family regression and is derived from Bion's (1961) theory of small groups. Finally, I will describe findings in families of adolescents with borderline conditions or pathological narcissism that are indications for combined individual and family treatment.

ASSESSMENT OF FAMILIES OF DISTURBED ADOLESCENTS AND INDICATIONS FOR CONCURRENT FAMILY THERAPY

In one of Freud's (1917) last discussions of theory of the therapeutic effect of psychoanalysis, he says that most of the failures of psychoanalytic treatment are due, not to unsuitable choice of patients, but to unsuitable external conditions. He notes that, while the internal resistances to therapy, the resistances of the patient, are inevitable and can be overcome, the external resistances to therapy that arise from the patient's environmental circumstances are also of great practical importance. Freud writes:

> In psychoanalytic treatment resistances due to the intervention of relatives is a positive danger, and a

danger one does not know how to meet. One is armed against the patient's internal resistances, which one knows are inevitable, but how can one ward off these external resistances? No kind of explanations make any impression on the patient's relatives; they cannot be induced to keep at a distance from the whole business, and one cannot make common cause with them because of the risk of losing the confidence of the patient, who—quite rightly, moreover—expects the person in whom he has put his trust to take his side. No one who has any experience of the rifts which so often divide a family will, if he is an analyst, be surprised to find that the patient's closest relatives sometimes betray less interest in his recovering than in his remaining as he is. When, as so often, the neurosis is related to conflict between members of a family, the healthy party will not hesitate long in choosing between his own interest and the sick party's recovery. [p. 459]

Freud says in conclusion that he followed the rule of not taking on a patient for treatment unless the patient was not dependent on anyone else in the essential relationships of his life.

Clearly, the conditions Freud recommends as optimal for psychoanalysis are by definition not possible in the treatment of adolescents. The shift from the adolescent's dependency on his primary objects (the parents) to the finding of new objects is a central aspect of personality reorganization throughout adolescence (Jacobson 1961, R. Shapiro 1963). Difficulty in this process is among the important causes of disturbance in the adolescent. It is, therefore, essential to design a therapy that helps the adolescent to manage difficulties in family relationships that interfere with the transition from preadolescent dependency on parents to a new level of autonomy in relationships inside and outside the family in late adolescence. Such a therapy requires work with the external resistances to analytic therapy described by Freud. The nature of the adolescent's dependence on his parents dictates a redefinition of the task of his treatment to include management of the external resistances. The boundaries of adolescent therapy have expanded, then, to include methods for the maintenance and repair of a working alliance with the parents.

Adequate assessment of an adolescent patient involves careful evaluation of the internal resistances, of defensive organization, and of the causal relationship between the state of ego functioning, defenses, and symptomatology (Laufer 1965). Assessment of the adolescent must also include evaluation of the external resistances, the nature of the adolescent's dependency on his parents, and the nature of evidence of the parents' interest in and conflict over the adolescent's changing or remaining as he is. I believe that these factors are best assessed through interviews with the parents and adolescent together (conjoint family interviews), in addition to individual interviews with the adolescent (R. Shapiro 1967, R. Shapiro and Zinner 1971). In addition to their value for assessment of external resistances, conjoint family interviews have the goal of forming a beginning working alliance with the parents as well as with the adolescent. It is important that this alliance be established and that the general goals of treatment be agreed upon. Family interviews establish a working situation that can be held in reserve and, in the most favorable cases, may not be needed again.

If, however, the situation is one in which neurosis in the adolescent is related to conflict between members of the family, change in the adolescent may lead the parents to define the situation in a way that assumes their interests are opposed to the adolescent's; they may choose their own interests over his, and new external resistances may arise. This possibility should be anticipated in the assessment phase. A reconvening of family interviews is then indicated to attempt to manage the external resistances interpretively in a way analogous to management of internal resistances through defense analysis. In conjoint family interviews, exploration of the nature and the sources of the impasse between parents and adolescent is possible. The therapist is aided in his effort to maintain a stance of neutrality because he can orient himself to the goals of therapy agreed upon by the family. He may then proceed to examine the interferences with the accomplishment of these goals. The framework of conjoint family interviews established during the assessment phase is the foundation that authorizes the therapist to work interpretively on this task. He attempts to understand and interpret unconscious assumptions activating resistances in the family to change in the adolescent, both from the side of the parents and from the side of the adolescent. The psychotherapy of adolescents with severe neurosis or higher-order character pathology may then be preserved through analysis of external resistances to treatment when they arise in the family.

The more severe disturbances of adolescence—the borderline conditions and pathological narcissism—present a specific indication for ongoing treatment of the family, concurrent with individual psychotherapy of the adolescent, because of the severe pathology in the family in the area of separation–individuation.

Interest in problems of separation–individuation in early childhood has led to new recognition of their links to processes of individuation during adolescence, which Blos (1967) has called the second individuation phase. Disturbances in separation–individuation, studied by Mahler in childhood (Mahler 1971, Mahler et al. 1975), have been shown to determine borderline and narcissistic pathology in the adolescent in the work of Kernberg (1975) and Masterson (1972), and my research group (Berkowitz et al. 1974a, 1974b, E. Shapiro et al. 1977, E. Shapiro et al. 1975). These disturbances are seen both in the parents and in the adolescent and are treated most effectively by concurrent individual and family therapy.

THE THEORY OF UNCONSCIOUS ASSUMPTIONS

Our research into the origins of adolescent disturbance has used evidence from direct family observations to explore the family contribution to pathologic outcome in adolescence (Berkowitz et al. 1974a, 1974b, E. Shapiro et al. 1975, 1977, R. Shapiro and Zinner 1971, Zinner and R. Shapiro 1972, 1974). This evidence leads us to conclude that, during the course of his development, and depending upon his particular emotional meaning to his parents, the adolescent who is disturbed has not been supported by his parents in his efforts to accomplish phase-appropriate life tasks. On the contrary, his parents have responded to his development with anxiety and repudiation of change in their relationships with him. In the face of progressive individuation in the developing child and adolescent, characteristic defensive behaviors are mobilized in these parents which distort their perceptions of the child and adolescent and dominate their responses to him. We find that the nature of disturbance in the adolescent is related to, and in part determined by, the characteristics of regression and the nature of defenses that dominate his parents' behaviors with him. Furthermore, our evidence suggests that these episodes of regression and related defenses in parents are activated by their unconscious fantasies regarding the child.

Our findings from observations of family interaction indicate that the nature of character pathology in the adolescent is related in specific ways to the characteristics of defenses, regression, and consequent distortions in the relationships between the parents and the developing child. In order to specify what characteristics in families are related to specific adolescent character pathology, we assess the level of regression and characteristics of defense in family transactions and the nature of unconscious fantasies that are the motives for defense. We find evidence within families for an organization of shared or complementary unconscious fantasies and related higher-level repressive defenses or lower-level defenses, including denial, splitting, and projection. These shared or complementary fantasies and related defenses serve to maintain equilibrium among family members and constitute external resistances to change. The underlying assumptions of the family based upon unconscious fantasies are conceptualized as the unconscious assumptions of the family as a group. We observe repetitive family behaviors that appear to militate against change, development, and individuation of the child, and we infer that shared unconscious assumptions in family members motivate and organize these repetitive behaviors. These unconscious assumptions are assumed to derive from the internalized developmental experience of both of the parents in their families of origin. An organization of motives and higher- or lower-level defenses evolves, then, in the marriage, conceptualized as the unconscious assumptions of the family. These are operative throughout the development of the adolescent. Depending upon their centrality and coerciveness as the family develops, unconscious assumptions are powerful determinants of disturbance in the maturing adolescent.

The concept of unconscious assumptions of the family group is a construct originating in clinical observation. It derives from Bion's (1961) small-group theory and facilitates an integration of family-systems theory and psychoanalytic concepts of individual psychology. It has proven useful both in the differentiation of families of neurotic, borderline, and narcissistic adolescents and in the clinical understanding and treatment of these families in conjoint therapy.

Bion's small-group theory derives from psychoanalysis and is a conceptualization of both the conscious functions and tasks that define groups and the unconscious motives that are also present in group members and that may dominate group behavior. Our effort to conceptualize family behavior has been facilitated by using a similar framework—that of family functions and tasks and of a variety of unconscious motives that interfere with their accomplishment. From the point of view of adolescent development, we conceive of the family as having an important function in promoting specific developmental tasks. These include the promotion of individuation and relative ego autonomy, resulting in an integrated identity formation in adolescent family members, which leads to a substantial alteration in the quality of their relationships to parents and to peers (Blos 1967, Erikson 1950, 1956, Jacobson 1964, R. Shapiro 1969). Adolescent development is interfered with by unconscious assumptions in the family that militate against these changes. Unconscious assumptions inimical to the task of adolescent individuation activate anxiety and defense in family members in response to manifestations of individuation. Regression and symptomatic behavior are then seen in the family, often most markedly in the adolescent member.

A brief review of Bion's small-group theory will help us to clarify its application to family process. Bion proposed a group theory that articulated two levels of group functioning; a mature and a regressed level. In Bion's terminology, the mature level of group functioning is called the *work group*; the regressed level is the *basic-assumption group*.

Bion brought the concepts and framework of Kleinian theory to his work with groups. The Kleinian concept of positions facilitated a conceptualization of the two levels of group functioning as being present simultaneously in all groups. Depending upon the relationship of the members of leadership in the group, either the mature or the regressed level of functioning might be the chief determinant of the group's behavior. This framework is also useful in conceptualizing mature family functioning and family regression, two levels of family functioning potentially present in any family situation.

Through the concept of position, Klein (1935) emphasized that the phenomena she was describing in individuals as belonging to the paranoid-schizoid position or the depressive position were not simply a passing stage or phase. Her term implies a specific configuration of object relations, anxieties, and defenses that persists throughout life. The depressive position never fully supersedes the paranoid-schizoid position; the integration achieved is never complete, and defenses against depressive conflict bring about regression to paranoid-schizoid phenomena, so that the individual at all times may oscillate between the two. Some paranoid and depressive anxieties always remain active within the individual, but, when the ego is sufficiently integrated and has established a relatively secure relation to reality during the working through of the depressive position, neurotic mechanisms gradually take over from psychotic ones (Segal 1964).

Bion applied Klein's concept of position to groups in his conception that in every group, two groups are present; the work group and the basic-assumption group. The work group is the mature group, defined by its work task. But the work group is only one aspect of the functioning of the group; the other aspect is the regressive level of group functioning, the basic-assumption group. We postulate that mature and regressive aspects of family functioning are present in any family, just as both aspects of group functioning are present in any group and primitive positions of mental functioning are present along with mature functioning in the individual. Bion's capacity to effect a shift in perspective from the individual to the group as a whole was crucial to his method of working with groups and to his articulation of shared levels of regressed functioning, as well as mature functioning, within groups. The same shift in perspective from the individual to the family as a group is crucial in analytic family treatment.

In Bion's work, a group is defined by the task it is gathered to perform. Consciously motivated behavior directly implementing this task in reality terms is called *work-group functioning.* The group is behaving at a mature level in that it is working at its task, its relation to reality is good, and communication among group members is logical and clear. In contrast, Bion observes that much behavior in groups appears to have some other organization and motivation. This is behavior that suggests a level of regression dominated by unconscious assumptions on the part of members that the group is gathered for quite different purposes than the realistic accomplishment of the work task. Bion postulates unconscious mechanisms in group members, which are mobilized in group interrelationships and which result in behavior unconcerned with the considerations of reality, such as task implementation, logical thinking, and time. He calls these *regressive states*: Group behavior appears to be determined by wishful and nonrational unconscious considerations—basic assumptions. In such states, a group appears to be dominated and often united by covert assumptions based on unconscious fantasies. Bion outlines three general categories of basic assumptions that he frequently sees dominating the regressive behavior of groups. One is the unconscious assumption that the group exists for satisfaction of dependency needs and wishes: another is the assumption that the group exists to promote aggression toward, or to provide the means of flight from, real tasks, issues, and objects; the third is an assumption of hope and an atmosphere of expectation that is unrelated to reality considerations and is frequently seen in relation to pairing behavior in the group. The basic-assumption mode of group behavior is, then, regressive behavior that implies covert and often unconscious assumptions in group members about the purpose for which the group is gathered. These assumptions, which have little to do with considerations of reality, have powerful unconscious determinants and are conceptualized as expressions of shared unconscious fantasies in group members. Shifts in direction and power of basic-assumption fantasies and behavior, and work, are observed in groups; it is important to investigate the conditions under which these shifts occur.

Turquet (1974) has emphasized that basic-assumption group behavior is mobilized for defensive purposes having to do with the difficulties of the work task and disturbance in relation to the work leader. The work of the group, its functioning and task performance, is impaired, with deterioriation of the ego functioning of the members. The realities of the situation and the task are lost sight of, reality testing is poor, secondary-process thinking deteriorates, and more primitive forms of thinking emerge. There is a new behavioral organization that seems to be determined by fantasies and assumptions that are unrealistic and represent a failed struggle to cope with current reality. The group thereby survives as such, though its essential functioning and primary task are now altered in the service of a different task.

We derive a framework from Bion, then, an orientation to clinical observation of the family. States of anxiety, defense, and regression in the family are conceptualized as consequences of unconscious assumptions, in which an organization of meanings and motives is inferred. These assumptions are in opposition to the developmental tasks of the family with respect to its children and adolescents. Family group behavior now appears dominated by assumptions that particular meanings of childhood and adolescent individuation represent a danger to family requirements, cohesiveness, and even survival. These assumptions are generally unconscious and may be denied by family members.

The family group is different in essential ways from the "stranger" small group conceptualized by Bion. In considering the family as a group, the fact that its members have a shared developmental history and have specific role relationships through development results in a differentiation and specificity of shared assumptions, motivations, and defenses that cannot exist in the randomness of the stranger group. In this sense the complexity and differentiation of family process is much closer to individual psychodynamics than it is to group process. However, the study of the family is greatly facilitated through observing the shifts from family behavior implementing reality tasks to family behavior dominated by unconscious assumptions. It is possible to characterize the level of family regression, to define shared unconscious fantasies and assumptions with precision, and to describe the characteristics of shared and complementary higher-level or lower-level defensive behaviors between and among family members. In contrast, Bion's formulations about basic-assumption behavior in stranger groups are global and generalized conceptualizations of group regression and of regressive group wishes in relation to the leader.

Let us now consider the evidence in family interaction that leads us to infer that unconscious assumptions are dominating family behavior. When the family is in a situation of anxiety as a consequence of mobilization of unconscious assumptions, we find clear analogies to small-group basic-assumption behavior. Behavior showing conflicting motivations, anxiety, and higher- or lower-level defenses is seen in family members with evidence of ego regression. Behavior in the family appears to be determined more by fantasy than by reality. Work failure is evident in the family situation, similar to basic-assumption functioning. There is emergence of confused, distorted thinking, failure of understanding and adequate communication, and breakdown in the ability of the family to work cooperatively or creatively in relation to developmental issues and tasks. It becomes impossible to maintain a progressive discussion in which family members understand one another or to respond realistically to the problems under discussion. In short, when the family is in a situation in which unconscious assumptions are mobilized, associated anxiety and higher- or lower-level defensive behaviors are seen, and there is disturbance in the family's reality functioning. In contrast, in the absence of mobilization of unconscious assumptions, the family does not manifest anxiety and prominent defensive behavior, is clearly reality oriented, and relates well to tasks facilitating the maturation of children and adolescents.

UNCONSCIOUS ASSUMPTIONS, DEFENSIVE DELINEATIONS, AND PROJECTIVE IDENTIFICATION

In order to characterize the family contribution to adolescent disturbance, we carefully study episodes of family regression determined by unconscious assumptions. We observe behaviors of the parents with the adolescent and behaviors of the adolescent with the parents in order to define the defensive meanings of their relationships implicit in their behaviors. And we infer from these defensive behaviors unconscious meanings of the adolescent to the parents and parents to the adolescent, from which we formulate unconscious assumptions of the family as a group.

We use the concept of delineation to formulate the dynamics of the parents' relationship to the adolescent and the adolescent's relationship to the parents. This is a concept closely linked to observable behavior. Delineations are behaviors through which one family member communicates explicitly or implicitly his perceptions and attitudes—in fact, his mental representation of another family member—to that other person.

Delineations may communicate a view of the other person that seems to be predominantly determined by his reality characteristics. Or, delineations may communicate a view of the other person that appears to be predominantly determined by the mobilization of dynamic conflict and defense in the delineator. We call the latter *defensive delineations*. For example, let us consider parental defensive delineations of the adolescent. When parental delineations are observed to be distorted, stereotyped, over-specific, contradictory, or otherwise incongruent with the range of behaviors manifested by the adolescent, we make the inference that these delineations serve defensive aspects of parental personality functioning. That is, they are not simply realistic characterizations of the adolescent. Further, we find that the parents, through their defensive delineations, seek to hold the child and adolescent in relatively fixed roles throughout development, in the service of avoiding their own anxiety.

The predominant mechanism underlying parental defensive delineations is projective identification. The concept of projective identification provides a highly useful means of conceptualizing phenomena of regression and elucidating dynamics of role allocation in families. In family regression, there is rapid reduction in usual ego discriminations. Dissociation and projection are increased, with confusion over the ownership of personal characteristics that are easily attributed to other family members. When one individual assumes a role compatible with the attributions of others in the family at the regressed level, he quickly becomes the recipient of projections which tend to fix him in that role. Family members project this aspect of their own personal characteristics onto him and unconsciously identify with him. The power of these projections, with their accompanying unconscious identifications, may push the individual into more extreme role behavior and into feelings that are very powerful and may be experienced as unreal and bizarre.

Bion (1961) observes that Freud's view of identification is almost entirely a process of introjection by the ego. To Bion, however, the identification of group members with the leader of the regressed group depends not on introjection alone, but on a simultaneous process of projective identification as well. The leader is as much a creature of the basic assumption as any other member of the group. Group members project onto the leader, on the basic-assumption level, those qualities required and mobilized in shared basic-assumption fantasy. This is also true in families, in which projective identification results in the projection onto a child or adolescent of those qualities required and mobilized by the unconscious assumptions of the family.

These parental projections have a critical effect on the individual child maturing within the framework of family assumptions. Developmental theory emphasizes identification processes as internalizations that are major determinants of structure formation in the child. In addition, we believe that the child internalizes through development characteristics of parental relationships with him. The child's dynamic meaning to his parents, attributions made to him, and attitudes toward him are delineations that modify his self-representation and are determinants of structure formation. Parents'delineations of the child and adolescent, where the parents' regression is at a level of impaired self–object differentiation and primitive projective identification, are particularly coercive. Behavior in the child that counters these parental delineations leads to anxiety in the parent. The child is then motivated to behave so as to mitigate this parental anxiety. Internalization by the child of the parent's defensive delineations of him moves the developing child and adolescent into a role that is complementary to parental defensive requirements. Defensive delineations are, consequently, dynamic determinants of role allocation in the family. The role allocated is necessary to maintain parental defense and mitigate parental anxiety. The dynamics of role allocation operate in a broader framework of unconscious assumptions of the family as a group. Over time, these establish a pattern of internalizations within the self-representation. Unconscious assumptions within the family, and related experience of defensive delineations, impinge upon the reorganization of internalizations required by ego–id maturation during adolescence. These influences may interfere significantly with individuation and the consolidation of identity in the adolescent.

In the families we have studied, we find evidence that each family member participates in the regression we have described. It is through the participation of all family members in these regressive episodes that the level of family regression and higher- or lower-level defensive organization achieve their stability and their power.

In family assessment and family therapy, we attempt to articulate the unconscious assumptions of the family as a group and to discern the participation, contribution, and collusion of each family member in the episodes of family regression that are dominated by unconscious assumptions and higher- or lower-level defensive organization. We consider these factors to be decisive for the developmental disturbances we are discussing.

FAMILIES OF ADOLESCENTS WITH BORDERLINE CONDITIONS OR PATHOLOGICAL NARCISSISM

In families of adolescents who manifest borderline or narcissistic disturbances, we consistently find evidence of a powerful cluster of unconscious assumptions that equate separation–individuation with loss and abandonment. Thinking and actions of family members that are not in accord with these assumptions are then perceived and reacted to as destructive attacks (E. Shapiro et al. 1975, R. Shapiro and Zinner 1971).

There are important areas of similarity in the characteristics of regression in these two types of families. In both types of families, regression is activated by behavior in family members signaling separation–individuation and loss; in these circumstances there is clear evidence of anxiety in the family and efforts to restore the previous equilibrium. There is regression to an organization of lower-level defenses of denial, splitting, and projection, and an active splitting of aspects of self and objects. These split self and object representations are then distributed by projective identification. There is, however, a difference in the nature of the split in the self and object representations found in these two types of families, and, consequently, there is a difference in what is projected onto the separating and individuating family member.

In families of borderline adolescents, individuation, manifested in either autonomous or needful behavior in one family member, activates unconscious assumptions in other family members about the nature of relationships containing good experiences. Such behavior is unconsciously perceived as a threat to the survival of the family as a group, leading to anxiety and projection of destructiveness onto the individuating family member.

In these families, a structure of internalized object relations is found in family members in which there is splitting of all good and all bad self and object images. Family members split off those bad aspects of themselves, which are associated with painful and aggressive experiences with objects in the past. In particular, painful responses to autonomous strivings within individuals, or to needs for nurturance and support, give rise to shared unconscious assumptions in the family about the dangers of such behavior. Through projective identification, they relate to the separating and individuating adolescent as they would to a repudiated part of themselves, rebuffing him in episodes of aggressive turmoil and withdrawal. The result in the adolescent is an identity formation dominated by negative self and object images, a continuation of splitting of positive and negative internalized relationships, and a clinical picture of identity diffusion.

In contrast, in families of narcissistic adolescents, the unconscious assumptions focus on the specific meanings of a narcissistic relationship between parent and adolescent (Berkowitz et al. 1974b). If parents project valued aspects of themselves onto a child or adolescent and use him as a self-object, the narcissistic equilibrium of the parent is disturbed when, during individuation, the child or adolescent moves into a position no longer complementary to the parents' narcissistic needs. This disruption of a central narcissistic relationship in the family disturbs the self-regard of other family members, whose narcissistic equilibrium depends on the parent who is now suffering an abrupt disturbance in self-esteem.

In families of narcissistic adolescents we find a structure of internalized object relationships in which there is an active splitting of grandiose and devalued self and object images. Real, ideal, or devalued images of self and object are not integrated in family members into a self-concept with stable internal regulation of self-esteem. An effort to stabilize self-esteem is seen in the activation of a narcissistic relationship within the family. In these families, such a differentiated narcissistic relationship is found between a narcissistic parent (grandiose self) and the adolescent (idealized self-object). This external relationship helps maintain the split in both parent and adolescent. The adolescent who is used by the parent as a self-object, also evolves a pathological narcissistic self-structure and requires the relationship to an omnipotent parental image to maintain narcissistic equilibrium. Separation–individuation produces narcissistic disequilibrium in both parents and adolescent, with episodes of narcissistic rage and projection.

Family regression militates against further differentiation of the adolescent from the family. Instead, through projective identification, boundaries between family members become even more blurred, with parents and siblings projecting onto the adolescent who is attempting to individuate those feelings of devaluation denied within themselves.

These findings lead us to combine psychoanalytic psychotherapy for the adolescent with analytic, group-interpretive family treatment in borderline conditions or pathological narcissism of adolescents. In family treatment, the continuing problems of projection and loss of differentiation between parents and adolescent are interpreted, and there is an opportunity for working through

the meaning and experience of separation over time. Less
bound by the projections of his parents, the adolescent
has a new possibility for individuation, which he is able to
explore more fully in his individual therapy (Berkowitz et
al. 1974a, E. Shapiro et al. 1977).

Conclusion

   In the treatment of adolescents, unconscious assumptions in the family lead to external resistances to analytic
therapy. The patient's family relationships frequently
interfere with therapy more than do the patient's own
internal resistances. This is a central problem in treatment. Methods of conjoint family interviewing have been
described for the management of external resistances in
the treatment of adolescents. Such interviews should be
part of the initial assessment of the disturbed adolescent,
as they help to establish a working alliance not only with
the adolescent, but also with the family.
   I have presented concepts and methods that we have
used to study families of disturbed adolescents. An organization of shared or complementary unconscious fantasies and related higher- or lower-level defenses within
family members which maintain equilibrium among them
is postulated. Anxiety and intensified defensive activity
are activated by behavior that challenges or contradicts
the underlying assumptions determined by these unconscious fantasies. These unconscious assumptions of the
family as a group are evidenced in repetitive family
behaviors that appear to militate against change, development, or individuation of children. Shared unconscious
assumptions in family members that motivate and organize these repetitive behaviors derive from the internalized developmental experience of both of the parents in
their families of origin. An organization of motives and
higher- or lower-level defenses evolves, then, in the
marriage. These are operative throughout the develop-

ment of the children and have critical effects on their personality development.

For neurotic adolescents, conjoint family interviews should be resumed when the external resistances interfere seriously with treatment.

For adolescents manifesting borderline conditions or pathological narcissism, when serious disturbances over separation–individuation, found in both adolescents and parents, are profoundly interfering with adolescent development, concurrent psychoanalytic psychotherapy for the adolescent and group interpretive family treatment is indicated.

14

The Influence of Shared Unconscious Fantasy on Family Communication

Verbal communication with and within families poses an inherent dilemma for family therapists. They rely on the communicative and expressive functions of speech to effect therapeutic change in the family. Talking is the vehicle for the therapist's interpretations, and it is the means by which family members will share their feelings and increase their understanding of one another's fears, longings, and perceptions. This view of talking as an invaluable resource is often not shared by the emotionally disturbed family, however. To them, talking is not a path toward making things better; rather, it is a hazardous venture portending catastrophe rather than cure. To such a family, talking has lost its positive communicative and expressive value. Instead, speech has become an instrument of unhappy interactions—a vehicle for expressing aggression, for engendering guilt, for acting out competitive urges, for lowering self-esteem. As a consequence of this negative valence attached to talking, communication in disturbed families is substantially impaired. At the outset of the treatment, the therapist is likely to encounter blaming, bickering, interrupting, or, alternatively, silence. Members may refuse to take in and mull over what the others are saying or may talk exclusively to the therapist rather than to one another. Misunderstandings are inevitable, and individuals tune out and lose themselves in solitary reverie.

The first challenge for the family therapist, therefore, is to help the family regain confidence in the healing powers of talking. This is no mean task, however, because the failure in communication represents far more than a nonspecific by-product of the overall deterioration in family functioning. In fact, the family communication problem is firmly embedded in the family pathology in a highly specific and systematic way.

With this in mind, I would like to focus on two propositions:

1. that problems in family communication are specifiable. They are coherent derivatives of shared unconscious fantasies within the family and are subject to analysis and interpretation in a manner similar to any other family behavior.

2. that the analysis of family communication problems provides a therapeutically useful access to these guiding family fantasies. This means that problems in talking together are not merely obstacles to overcome before the so-called real interpretive work can begin. Rather, these communication difficulties, in and of themselves, offer a springboard for deeper understanding of the family dynamics.

Starting with a prototypic nuclear family consisting of two parents and their children, let me review the impact of shared unconscious fantasies and assumptions on family life. These formulations of family group behavior are extensions of Bion's (1961) psychoanalytically derived theory of small groups. In Chapter 6, R. Shapiro and I (R. Shapiro and Zinner 1971) have conceptualized two levels of family functioning. The first level involves a family behavior that is phase-appropriate to developmental issues and tasks within the family. Family interactions are empathically tuned to the particular developmental needs of the child and provide the appropriate degree of optimal tension that stimulates individual maturation. The reality principle and secondary process thinking are dominant. Family communication facilitates developmental maturation, enhances empathy, and provides sublimated expressive outlets.

In contradistinction to the task-oriented behavior of the family just described, there is a second level of group functioning that is governed by shared unconscious fantasies, fears, and assumptions. Family interaction is not geared to the phase-appropriate developmental requirements of the child. Instead, members relate to one another in ways that will serve their own defensive economy. Members' perceptions of one another are dominated by projection more than by realistic appraisal. Interactions reflect reenactments of conflicted object relations of the parents' own nuclear families rather than being attuned to the here and now of the current family situation. Family communication at this level does not facilitate developmental progression or empathy. Instead, talking is in the service of perpetuating the unconscious assumptions that dominate family life. For example, on the more superficial task-oriented level, a family member might communicate anger by saying, "I'm mad at you because you were late." At the deeper level of unconscious assumption, the spoken word becomes, not a vehicle for expression, but rather an instrument of aggression. The word itself is used to hurt. A family member might berate another as "worthless and no good" or abandon him with silence.

In the following family therapy excerpt, a diabetic mother is soon to be admitted for a brief elective medical hospitalization. Her 17-year-old daughter, Ruth, has been silent in recent sessions and now expresses her fear of talking in the family. This family is dominated by an unconscious assumption that adolescent individuation is tantamount to abandonment and rejection of the family. A powerful fantasy exists that if the daughter upsets the mother by taking independent action, the mother's blood sugar will rise, leading to a heart attack and death.

EXCERPT 1

Dr. B.:	Is that what keeps you a lot from saying what's on your mind, because you fear your mother's reaction?
Mother:	[Reassuringly] You don't have to worry about my reaction.
Ruth:	I have to worry about your reaction a lot.
Mother:	Like what? As much as I have to worry about your reaction?
Ruth:	I don't know . . . I say something here. When we get home, you say, "That's not true, you just said that for attention."
Mother:	How long ago, Ruth?
Ruth:	The last time I ever said anything. That's how long ago.
Mother:	How long ago, how long ago, Ruth?
Ruth:	A long time ago.
Father:	Like what? Can you remember what it was?
Ruth:	I don't know . . . It was something about my parents.
Dr. A.:	Did you make some kind of a promise with yourself that you weren't going to speak again?
Ruth:	No, I didn't make a promise. It's just that every time I think of something to say, I remember. . . .
Dr. A.:	. . . what happened, and you don't say it?
Ruth:	I remember what has happened before and what will probably happen again.
Dr. A.:	Is that why you've been so quiet the past couple of months?
Ruth:	It wasn't that I didn't want to say anything; it's just

	that I'm afraid to say anything.
Father:	I wish you'd get over that fear.
Ruth:	I'm feeling it right now.
Father:	Why?
Ruth:	By the way she's acting.
Mother:	Who?
Ruth:	You.
Mother:	Me?
Ruth:	I feel like as soon as we get out of here, you're going to say, "Why were you saying all that?"
Mother:	I'd like you to come to the point and speak and say what you want. I've told you that many times, too.
Father:	I don't think your feelings are justified, Ruthie.
Dr. A.:	That's just what Ruth is concerned about.
Mother:	[Aside] Probably an excuse.
Dr. A.:	. . .being told that her feelings are not justified or it's an excuse. I think, if she says what she feels, she doesn't want to hear that it's an excuse or that it's not justified.
Mother:	I don't know. She's not afraid of upsetting me. Whatever she feels like she wants to tell me, she tells me. She had me all upset today by her comments this morning. [Begins to cry]
Father:	This morning? What did she say?
Mother:	I told you.
Ruth:	What did I say?
Mother:	Who's going to drive you to school when I'm in the hospital and how are you gonna sleep in the house by yourself while Daddy's working? Get your hands off your face.
Father:	Ruth, we only have an hour and we're stagnant right now. Why don't we speak up?
Mother:	[Sharply, in a trembling voice] No, I don't know why she's hesitating to say what's on her mind. She doesn't hesitate to tell me what's on her mind and I don't think she's worried about upsetting me, because she didn't think about whether it would upset me this morning when she just blurted out to me, "Who's going to drive me to school in the morning and do I have to sleep here at night alone?" I told her I drive her girlfriend to school every morning, maybe her mother would drive them to school, and that

maybe one of the dogs could go upstairs with her. I don't like the idea of her being alone at night either, but I don't think it's her worrying about my reaction because she didn't worry about it this morning, because it upset me all day.

Ruth: [Weeping silently]

Mother: Ruthie, move your hair away from your face and talk—would you please?

Father: Ruth, I don't like to see you sitting there with your face masked either. Come on.

In this excerpt, the family is paying lip service to the therapeutic "task" of saying what one feels. Both parents exhort Ruth to speak up without worrying about their reaction. They delineate her as unjustifiably fearful of retaliation, which, if it ever occurred, did so in the remote past. A contradictory injunction, however, reinforces Ruth's anxiety about speaking. That is, Ruth doesn't worry about her mother's reaction *enough*. After all, as her mother said, if she was so worried, why did she then say what was on her mind that morning and upset her mother all day? Speaking up about differing with her parents is an intrinsic part of Ruth's developmental process of individuation. Insofar as individuation of its members is devastating to the family, Ruth's speech becomes viewed by her parents as an instrument of hurt and abandonment. As a consequence, her parents refuse to hear her, disqualifying Ruth's feelings by accusing her of using words to seek her parents' attention rather than to express her ideas. Her words are also endowed with the power, in fantasy, to kill her mother by upsetting her. Ruth's silence protects her mother by not expressing the upsetting feelings; at the same time, the silence serves to punish her parents by deserting them.

The deficiencies in family communication illustrated by the excerpt can all be understood and integrated by attending to the underlying assumptions governing this family's interaction. Consequently, the talking or silent behaviors become a window providing access to family dynamics. Opportunities for therapeutic intervention abound. In this instance, the therapist's act of noticing and exploring Ruth's silence facilitates her renewed participation and joins the issue of how different ideas among family members are experienced as threatening and potentially destructive to others.

A second illustration will be provided by a study of communication in the Haynes family. In this case there is a family-wide failure in basic trust: That is, there is very limited confidence in the good will of important others. Consequently, speaking one's thoughts and feelings is seen as making oneself vulnerable to attacks, humiliation, and loss of a sense of self. You will not be surprised to discover, therefore, that Tim, the 19-year-old son and psychotic index patient, is selectively mute. He speaks guardedly with only a few individuals, while regarding others to whom he refuses to talk as a "pack of hungry wolves." As an introduction, note the way in which Tim's 16-year-old brother, Frank, experiences family therapy.

Frank: [Sighs] Well, I feel kind of dredged in these sessions and kinda excavated on, you know, taking out everything that I really have. It's almost like having your phone tapped, you know, and everything that's private or important to you seems to come out and all your feelings. I just don't see really that we've gotten much of anything out of it—I don't think that. There's a lot of talk about the family betterment, but I don't think the family can go anywhere but down. Not only just Tim, but all the rest of us. You mentioned how it's been affecting all of us and really we've lost a little bit of ourselves in this seven or eight months, with all this strain of having him ill.

In a similar vein, at another time, the mother responds to the therapist's comment:

Dr. S.: What was it, though, Mrs. Haynes? Is it that you are feeling again I'm being unjust because you're very willing to talk and you don't feel that you keep things back? Or because it should be obvious to me that it's hard to talk, or what?

[Pause]

Mother: I think you psychiatrists think you could talk down Mt. Blanc, and I just don't believe that! I think the elks are still there no matter how much you talk about them or how much you study them and all of that and—the Swiss don't do that! Long ago they found the passes and tunnels through the Alps, and then they go up and live in their beautiful little country. And that's what I think we should be doing here, but instead of that we go plugging up the mountains every week, bruising and falling back and all of that kind of thing. I don't think we're helping one another. I think we're just destroying each other! [pauses, lowers voice] I just think so, I really do.

Other comments made by this family about talking in therapy are equally graphic in describing the destructive aspects of speech:

"You'll dig your grave with your mouth."
"I'll sink my own ship with my words."
"Words are like a broken jar; once said, they can never be unsaid."

These family aphorisms convey the conscious sense of hazard in expressing one's thoughts and feelings. The damage can be absolute, permanent, and emotionally lethal.

The following excerpts from a family session illustrate how failures in basic trust are manifest in family communication. The parents have learned that Tim was greatly disturbed over an unrequited fantasied love affair with a young, attractive, married female inpatient staff member. Tim had been making anonymous telephone calls to her at her home. His parents now broach the subject by vague allusions but are very reluctant to be open—allegedly because of the presence in the session of Tim's brothers, Frank and Joe, particularly Joe, who is 15 years old. In the excerpt, the therapist works with the communication problem toward arriving at the underlying fantasies. You can imagine how such difficulties in family talking would impair the mastery of the developmental tasks pertaining to adolescent sexuality.

Dr. Z.:   [15-second silence] I sense a sort of vagueness about what you're talking about.

Father: Yes, intentionally, because I don't feel that I'd be very comfortable plunging into all of Tim's internal business with a couple of carping younger brothers, who were not of an age where perhaps they'd have much understanding.

Dr. S.:   I wonder if it's only Tim's internal affair, now that it certainly has involved the family.

Father: Well, it hasn't involved *them* because it wouldn't normally, any more than the trouble they get in involves him. [Pause] It's not my normal practice, in other words, to give these kids the ammunition to snipe at one another with.

Dr. S.:   It does seem that it's one of the problems of family therapy too, because family therapy then becomes a place where ammunition is manufactured somehow for sniping at one another. I think it is seen that way.

A short while later in the session, the therapist speaks to the mother.

Dr. S.:   I again have a feeling, that I remember from another time when I said you looked depressed, that you're not quite with us today and are feeling something that you're not sharing much with the group at all.

Mother: [Short pause] Well, I guess I have sort of an ortho . . . unorthodox view of what is appropriate to a family session because I've been hearing all week out here about gaily bringing things up and [deep sigh] I feel like Edward, that the age of the participants has

something to do with it. And I think compassion is
something that most people learn by suffering. And
that it's not very realistic to expect it in younger
brothers and I *have* some feeling of compassion for
our young Werther and some regret from him too that
there has to be a Carlotte, but I don't really expect that
they will. And I would be reluctant to bring it up.

Dr. Z.:   I'm not clear about what your metaphors . . .

Father: [Rather loudly, interrupting] *The Sorrows of Werther* is
a novel that . . .

Frank: [Not a very strong voice] Yeah, so *we'll* know what's
going on.

Joe: [Amused] You don't know what's going on either?
[Family members laugh]

Mother: You're not a student of Goethe?

Dr. Z.   I would be interested in understanding what you
meant. . . .

Mother: [Delicately smug tone] I thought it was quite *clear*.

Dr. Z.:   Well, apparently Joe, at least, was also somewhat
confused by it.

Frank: Yeah, I was confused, too. Let's make it more
general?

Dr. S.:   Frank and Joe were *supposed* to be confused, though.

Mother: That's right.

Frank: The sufferings of who?

Father: [Chuckles, as does Mother] *The Sorrows of Werther*.

Frank: I'll look it up just to spite you.

Father: It's an old, very old-fashioned story.

Dr. Z: But you're feeling that Joe and Frank shouldn't be
involved in this discussion?

Mother: I don't think it would be very meaningful to them.

Dr. S.   That is, I think, a big assumption because I think that
if you talk about Werther and Carlotte, you're apparently talking about a young man and a young woman
. . . and about the suffering of a young man, I
suppose, over a young woman. And I think that it's
not *only* Tim who might know something about that.
I think Joe and Frank also *might* have some inkling of
what it's like to care about a young woman or suffer
about a young woman or feel some kind of compli-
cation in that kind of relationship. . . .

Mother: [Interrupting] Frankly, I doubt that, but you may be right. . . .

Dr. S.: [Interrupting] Your mother doubts that either of you have any idea of what the suffering might be—in relation to a young woman and a young man.

Frank: What she doesn't know won't hurt her. [All laugh]

Dr. S.: This feeling runs through the session, that what everybody doesn't know won't hurt them. My impression is that people are hurt quite a lot by that attitude in this family.

Mother: [Pause] Yes, that can work both ways. You can also find information that you might have expected to have, exploding in your face. And I personally believe that there are levels of communication and I assumed that that was the belief out here because even the simplest question doesn't get an answer.

The individual therapist learns that Tim has fallen in love, but that it is unrequited. Tim feels devastated and acts out. Two younger teenage brothers are witnesses, each with their own strivings and fears regarding sexuality. This scenario is the grist of family life, presenting the group with a challenge and opportunity for growth despite the pain. But this family maintains that the younger boys have nothing to contribute. In the excerpt, the therapist works directly with the fear of talking. As in dealing with resistance in psychoanalytic treatment, we cannot simply direct or bludgeon the family into being candid, in this case about romantic attachments. The impairment in communication must be dealt with as a resistance. Working through the communication barrier paves the way for further exploration of the protected underlying content.

A family functioning at the first, phase-appropriate level would provide empathy, support, education, and limits. A sense of perspective and confidence, through identification, in particular, would be offered by parents sharing their own experiences as adolescents. Such is not the case with the Haynes family. Their interaction is determined by a shared fantasy that sexual feelings are an explosive "internal business." To expose such feelings in the group would only provide "ammunition" for "sniping" attacks. The group is paralyzed in its effort to deal with Tim because his problem can only be discussed vaguely and by obscure allusions to a tragic figure who commits suicide. The family is attempting the improbable task of coping with an urgent matter while deliberately confusing its membership about the nature of the problem. Both brothers are denied the family as a resource in dealing with their own emerging sexuality. Furthermore, parents cannot achieve a new integration of their own sexual conflicts through the reexperiencing of their own adolescence.

Summary

The family therapist's major healing resource is often experienced by the family as an instrument of harm. The disparity in attitudes toward candid communication must be worked with explicitly and empathically from the very outset of treatment. Handled skillfully, what was once a barrier becomes a pathway to a deeper understanding.

PART V

INTEGRATION
OF INDIVIDUAL
AND FAMILY THERAPY

15

Concurrent Family Treatment of Narcissistic Disorders in Adolescence

DAVID A. BERKOWITZ, M.D.
ROGER L. SHAPIRO, M.D.
JOHN ZINNER, M.D.
EDWARD R. SHAPIRO, M.D.

The concept of narcissism, from its inception, has been related to family dynamics. In his initial formulations on narcissism, Freud (1914) stated that parents attempt to recapture the lost narcissism of their own childhood by looking to their offspring to fulfill their own unrealized aspirations. For some youngsters, parental expectation has provided the fuel for ego-syntonic accomplishment and success. For others, achievement is obtained, but at a price, and is accompanied by neurotic suffering. For still others, alienation from the family, regressive retreat, and profound disturbances in self-esteem result, with an associated sense of failure. It is the treatment of this last group of adolescents and their families, which we shall address in this paper.

Benedek (1959) has proposed that in each "critical period," the child revives in the parents their related

261

developmental conflicts. This revival can lead either to pathologic manifestations or to a new level of integration in the parent. For example, it has frequently been noted (Benedek 1959, Rangell 1955, Searles 1959) that the resurgent oedipal situation in the adolescent may lead to a rekindling of unresolved conflicts around sexuality in the parents. Zinner and R. Shapiro (1974) have presented evidence from family observations that this revived oedipal conflict in parents results in their dissociation of drive and prohibition during this period.

We have observed in the families of narcissistic adolescents that, parallel to a reawakening of sexual conflicts, there is a reawakening in parents of conflicts concerning self-esteem during the period of their children's adolescence. We have been impressed in these families with the great pressures brought to bear by the parents on the adolescent to achieve, perform, and succeed in order to stabilize parental self-esteem.

In a previous report (Berkowitz et al. 1974b), we concluded from clinical observations that parents with serious conflicts in self-esteem experience the adolescent as if he were an extension of their own psychic organization and use him, in specifiable ways, to support their self-esteem. They are overinvolved in the adolescent's life and demonstrate an excessive need to control him. In order to maintain their own precarious narcissistic equilibrium, these parents project into the adolescent unacceptable aspects of their own negative evaluations of themselves. Such family interaction represents one form of pathological self-esteem regulation in the parents—namely, the externalization of conflict between contradictory views of the self through the use of the child as a narcissistic object.

In cases in which the child is used to maintain parental self-esteem, we have found it useful to employ conjoint family therapy concurrently with individual therapy for the adolescent. Analytically oriented family therapy allows observation of and therapeutic intervention into the massive pathological externalization of conflict characteristic of these families. In this chapter we intend to explore the use of this technique in assisting family members to acknowledge as part of the self that which has been projected, a process which may be referred to as *reinternalization*. We shall focus specifically on the utility of family therapy in promoting the reinternalization of conflicts around self-esteem. Not only does reinternalization help the narcissistic adolescent, but it also facilitates growth in all members of the family.

EXTERNALIZATION OF CONFLICT

Externalization of individual dynamic conflict has frequently been noted as a basis of intrafamilial psychopathology (Brodey 1965, Dicks 1967, Framo 1965, Wynne 1965, Zinner and R. Shapiro 1972). Intrapsychic conflict in an individual is transformed into interpersonal conflict through the unconscious defense mechanism of projective identification (Zinner and R. Shapiro 1972). Members of the family split off disavowed or cherished aspects of themselves and project them into others within the family. These projections govern family members' perception of and behavior toward one another when family behavior is dominated by unconscious fantasies that determine meanings of family members to one another. Family members relate toward others into whom they project aspects of themselves in the same manner as they would were these projections internalized. Thus internalized conflict *within* individuals is externalized, assuming the form of interpersonal conflict *between* family members.

An example will illustrate the externalization of narcissistic conflict resulting in pathological maintenance of self-esteem. The father of a patient with a severe narcissistic disturbance showed to this adolescent son a report card from his own childhood on which the father had received all A's. The father led the son to believe that this

was a "typical" and "usual" report card for the father
when, in fact, it was the *only* one of its kind. The father
hid all other information to the contrary in order to "set a
good example" for the son. The father's rationale for this
behavior was, "If people don't think I'm better than I am,
they will think I'm worse than I am." The father's statement reveals an underlying discrepancy between two
contradictory perceptions of himself. He appears to attempt a resolution of this conflict by projecting into others
his own poor view of himself. It is as if he were saying, "I
must inflate myself in order to overcome my poor view of
myself that is reflected in others' opinions of me." Moreover, when the son brought home his own report card
with a C, the father would not permit the boy to show it
to his siblings for fear that they would "tear [him] apart."
In this statement, the father sees his inadequacy in his
son, and the projects his intolerance of that inadequacy
into the siblings, creating a reenactment of his internal
struggle within the sibship.

By locating his own problems with achievement in
the son, the father mitigates any inner distress at not
living up to his own expectations. By projecting his own
poor self-esteem into his adolescent son, the father encourages the son to feel that he is inadequate and can
never live up to the father's expectations in the same
fashion as the father himself feels that he cannot live up to
the expectations of his own ego ideal. The father has thus
externalized internal conflicts in self-esteem. He has temporarily defended against the depression that would
ensue from an acknowledgment of his own sense of
failure. In this manner, the depression and loss of self-
esteem that the parent experiences when failing to live up
to his ego ideal is transformed into anger at the adolescent, who has come to embody the poorly performing
self. The discrepancy within an individual between the
actual self and an ideal, aggrandized version of the self
has thus been transmuted into interpersonal conflict between family members.

In the process of viewing family interaction, the

therapist may obtain valuable clues about the origins of narcissistic vulnerability in the parents. The relationships between parents and split-off aspects of themselves projected into their offspring frequently serve to recapture lost nuclear family relationships that bore on the self-esteem of the parent when he was a child. Parental dependence on the adolescent, we have found, derives significantly from the parents' own relationships (now internalized) with primary objects that led to early narcissistic fixations. In these families, a basic function of the child is to maintain parental self-esteem by colluding in reenacting with the parent these unresolved relationships from the parents' families of origin that significantly affected the development of their self-esteem.

For example, we have previously reported extensively on another case in which the mildest display of rebelliousness from the younger of two adolescent daughters remobilized for their mother an earlier source of narcissistic fixation, a relationship to a rival sibling with whom she had competed desperately and in vain for her *own* mother's approval (Berkowitz et al. 1974b). The current raging battles over household chores between our present mother and, in her words, her "rejecting" daughter now served to replicate in almost exact detail this earlier relationship with the mother's triumphant and hated sister from her own childhood.

SELF-ESTEEM REGULATION IN THE FAMILY

In normal development, given an environment of "optimal frustration" (Kohut 1971), the early dependency on parental figures is gradually relinquished as the child develops increasing autonomy from these objects. The growing child gradually internalizes regulatory functions performed by the parent which, in depersonified form, become part of enduring internal psychic structure. For example, first the mother soothes the infant and, by regulating tension for him, keeps traumatic anxiety from occurring. As he develops more autonomy, he takes this tension-regulatory function over for himself. Gradually, in similar fashion, the individual acquires the necessary structure to monitor his self-esteem internally so that states of impending narcissistic disequilibrium are apprehended through signals of anxiety (see Tolpin 1971), depression, or shame. The healthy ego, using these signals, can then restore homeostasis by acting to effect change in the self or in the environment.

In successful development, derivatives of primitive overestimations and underestimations of the self are gradually blended together into an integrated, cohesive self in which modulated regulation of self-esteem has become an internalized function. The developing child feels neither wholly omnipotent and grandiose nor totally helpless and inferior. Rather, the self-representation contains modulated, more realistic evaluations of assets and liabilities. In normal development, omnipotence and grandiosity are gradually transformed into healthy pride in realistic achievement. Similarly, feelings of helplessness are tempered into the capacity to experience realistic disappointment in the self without feeling overwhelmed and utterly devalued. However, failure in this development of psychic structure for self-esteem regulation leads to wide mood swings and excessive dependence on the confirming approval of external objects to maintain narcissistic equilibrium.

We find that parents of narcissistic adolescents have themselves failed to develop adequate psychic structure for relatively independent self-esteem regulation. Under careful scrutiny, they can be found to demonstrate the two classic hallmarks of narcissistic vulnerability (Kernberg 1970, Kohut 1968, 1971, Reich 1960). First, they evidence extreme vacillations in self-regard with, on the one hand, haughty, grandiose, and controlling behavior, preoccupation with attempts to feel great and important, and an omnipotent, inflated self-concept. On the other hand, they experience themselves as weak, powerless, worthless, inadequate, and inferior. Second, and intimately related to these alternating states of self-regard, they demonstrate an inordinate overdependence and intense hunger for the confirming approval of others, coupled with an extreme sensitivity to overt criticism or the mere absence of praise. They thus rely excessively on the behavior of objects to determine their own subjective experience of self-esteem.

We find that parents with defective psychic structures of this kind have not achieved a true autonomy from early objects. Instead, they tend to depend on their present offspring as representatives of these objects for narcissistic supports in order to maintain their precarious self-esteem. The situation becomes very difficult when their children reach adolescence, as the phase-specific task of separation becomes particularly threatening to them. A new scrutiny of his parents is an integral part of the adolescent process of separation from the family. Normatively, the adolescent challenges his previous idealizations of them by questioning their values and lifestyle in an attempt to formulate his own. This questioning, we have observed, can be experienced by a narcissistically vulnerable parent as a devastating challenge to his omnipotence. Just as parents must allow themselves early in the child's life to be idealized (Kohut 1971), so too must parental self-esteem be sturdy enough to withstand the adolescent's onslaughts in his attempt to disengage from them and develop his own identity.

We have found, in the families we have studied, that this aspect of children's separation and individuation is experienced at levels of unconscious fantasy as a threat to parental self-esteem. Behaviors that herald separation and autonomy are experienced by the parents, not as a desirable goal for the adolescent, but rather as a narcissistic injury, to which the parents react with narcissistic rage.

What in the developing child motivates his active participation in the parents' self-esteem system? Certainly the mechanism of projective identification cannot function without a willing recipient for the projections. We have previously suggested that the child unconsciously attempts to modify his subjective self-experience and self-evaluation in accord with parental projections. He will do so to the extent that he cannot tolerate parental anxiety or his own anxiety over the consequence of the parents' narcissistic rage and withdrawal when he does not comply.

Equally important, however, is the narcissistic gratification that accrues from the child's participation in this type of relationship. To be a narcissistic object for the parents is a role that holds a powerful and seductive appeal. Indeed, feeling so vital to one's parents' existences while figuring so prominently in their vacillating self-esteem provides fuel for the child's omnipotent grandiosity. The child's realization of his power to determine his parents' self-experience contributes to a heightened regressive pull to maintain this situation and his vital role in it. The adolescent finds himself in a dilemma. If he moves out of this role, the consequence is painful because the parent becomes furious and might, he fears, abandon him. Yet, to stay in the role, gratifying as it may be on one level, comes into conflict with the adolescent's developmental need to separate.

The adolescents in these families thus perceive only two alternatives in the relationship to the parents. Either they continue to be a narcissistic object for the parents or they risk alienation from the family and loss of the relationship. Not infrequently, we observe that when in therapy the nature of the parents' relationship to the adolescent begins to change and they allow for more independence and separateness, the adolescent will experience this as a loss and attempt to reinvolve the parents by some new acting out.

CONCURRENT FAMILY TREATMENT

Despite advances in the psychoanalytic understanding of narcissistic character pathology (Kernberg 1970, Kohut

1968, 1971, 1972), it is commonly agreed that this type of patient presents special problems in treatment. Because of a developmental failure in the autonomy of their self-esteem, they depend upon others for regulatory functions that would normally be part of internal psychic structure. It is therefore characteristic of the transferences formed by narcissistic personalities that they deprive the therapist of a recognition of his own separate existence (Kernberg 1970, Kohut 1968). The therapist is often treated, in a variety of "mirror transference," as an extension of the patient's self, or merely as an impersonal function (Kohut 1968). At other times the therapist may be idealized, in which case anything that deprives the patient of the therapist creates unbearably diminished self-esteem (Kohut 1968). The patient therefore responds to the slightest separation, rebuff, or most minute disruption of the transference with hostile devaluation of the therapist (Kernberg 1970) and withdrawal into a cold, narcissistic rage (Kohut 1968).

These special problems of treatment are compounded by adolescence itself. Prior to adolescence, the parental ego is the child's legitimate ego extension, a condition that is an "integral aspect of childhood dependency in the service of anxiety control and self-esteem regulation" (Blos 1967). In adolescence, however, psychological separation—the loosening of infantile object ties—is a central developmental task.

Separation is greatly complicated in families of narcissistic adolescents because the parents require the adolescent to perform a self-esteem regulating function, as we have described. In these families, parental need for narcissistic control results in drastic responses to the child's attempts to separate. The adolescent's either–or alternatives are made more extreme by the narcissistic rage arising in the parents in response to the erosion of control over him. Adolescents struggling to complete the normative developmental task of separating from the parents in such families are thus likely to experience intense feelings of isolation and alienation.

From our perspective, the disordered self-esteem of the narcissistic adolescent is an internal problem deriving from early family relationships. However, it is significantly exacerbated by the nature of the current family interaction. These current interactions, as they reflect implicit parental perceptions of the adolescent as a narcissistic object, form a major basis for his developing identity (Berkowitz et al. 1974b, R. Shapiro 1967). To the extent that these current relationships are based on externalizations of parental conflict, we believe that there is a specific indication for concurrent individual psychoanalytic therapy for the narcissistic adolescent *and* conjoint treatment for the family.

The establishment of a reliable working alliance with both the parents and the adolescent is the task of the initial phase of concurrent individual and family treatment (E. Shapiro et al. 1977). The formation of this alliance is facilitated by family members' increasing use of the therapist's capacity to observe, thus allowing members to observe their regressive behavior in the family in comparison with their transference behavior in marital and individual therapy. Once perceived as helpful in this task, the therapist is in a position to help family members both to acknowledge as part of themselves what has been projected and to begin to internalize the previously projected conflict. Intrapsychic conflict is perpetuated when it is externalized; in contrast, resolution is possible when the struggle is experienced as residing within the individual.

The process of reinternalization enables each family member to achieve a greater degree of separateness from the others. As the narcissistic interactions—the ways in which one member of the family uses another to regulate his own self-esteem—are clarified and interpreted, the separate existence of each family member is defined. The possibility then becomes available for new and more mature relationships among the members of the family, which allow increased autonomy of self-esteem for each.

For adolescents, family treatment provides a path out of their either–or dilemma. It facilitates the normative developmental task of separation–individuation without the threat of total alienation. It helps to free them from parental pressure and from their own complicity with parental projection. Thus they can no longer define themselves as forced into a particular position by their parents but must bear the responsibility for their own actions and choices.

For the parents as well, family therapy facilitates their increasing separateness. It helps to increase their autonomy, freeing them from their dependence on the adolescent as the measure of their worth. The reinternalization of conflict in the parents makes possible its gradual resolution, facilitating psychic growth as the relevant genetic material is recalled and worked through. The family session is not the only arena for this work. In our work with these families, we provide for marital therapy for the parents, using a second therapist who is also co-therapist in the family sessions with the adolescent's individual therapist.

When reinternalized, parental conflict in the realm of self-esteem, revived during the adolescence of their offspring, can lead, in Benedek's (1959) phrase, to a "new level of integration" in the parents. We find, in fact, that in families who derive benefit from treatment, improvement in the adolescent is usually paralleled by a related progressive development in the parent. For example, one mother constantly sought to raise her own self-esteem through the accomplishments of her husband and children. She continually berated her adolescent daughter for poor grades in school and felt that all the problems resided with the daughter. In family treatment, however, the mother came to realize that she was herself feeling impoverished. Having acknowledged this, the mother was able through the marital therapy to discover within herself dormant interests and talents. She struggled to overcome her anxiety in entering a complicated and creative professional endeavor, which provided her much satisfaction in the long run. She gradually became able to support her self-esteem, mitigating to an extent the previous reliance upon her husband and daughter for narcissistic sustenance.

CLINICAL OBSERVATIONS

We will now present family and individual excerpts to illustrate the use of long-term concurrent conjoint family therapy for the reinternalization of conflict in the area of self-esteem. Our case examples and excerpts are drawn from over fifty adolescent inpatients and their families treated by our group on a residential unit at the NIMH. Treatment modalities include intensive psychoanalytically oriented individual psychotherapy for the adolescent, weekly conjoint family therapy, and conjoint marital therapy for the parents.

Hal is an adolescent patient with serious narcissistic disturbance who was admitted to our unit at age 18 with a history of school and work failures, truancy, delinquency, and drug use. Of above average intelligence, Hal had dropped out of high school. He became outraged at each of his successive short-lived jobs when he was not afforded special privileges, pay raises, or rapid promotions. He felt entitled to go "right to the top," complaining that most jobs were "beneath [his] dignity" and "for peasants." He raced cars and motorcycles in order to feel powerful, and described how dealing drugs made him feel important because he carried "that much worth" in his pockets. His frequent drug use enabled him to entertain grandiose fantasies, such as his having an entire city named after him with endless roads upon which to race his cars or his being a great artist waiting to be discovered.

Hal's father is a serious, quick-tempered man who is prone to vacillations in self-esteem. He has been very critical of his children, especially of Hal. At the same time, he has been intensely concerned and involved in their lives. When Hal had delivered newspapers early in his adolescence, the father had frequently arrived on the scene to inspect his work and severely criticize whatever imperfections he could find.

Hal's father was abandoned by his own father at a very early age and raised by a depressed and withdrawn mother who was subsequently hospitalized on several occasions. Constantly searching for approval as a youngster, Hal's father felt overshadowed and worthless in all endeavors by comparison with his favored brother. He frequently complained that Hal was "ripping [him] off," just as he had felt "ripped off" by his brother.

The following excerpts from two audiotaped conjoint family sessions at different stages in the treatment will illustrate the use of family therapy in the reinternalization of narcissistic conflict.

EXAMPLE 1

This session occurred early in the treatment and reflects a typical interaction in the family. The father, in an angry tone of voice, opens the session by berating the son for his appearance. In his statement, the father protects his own self-esteem by maintaining a view of himself as more successful, while he sees his son as the one who is more self-depreciating. He further portrays his son in contrast to himself as capitulating to these self-depreciating feelings: Hal cares so little about himself that he will surrender to a life of drugs.

Thus the son is used to preserve the father's self-esteem. By perceiving Hal as the one who gives in to his feelings of low self-esteem, the father projects into the son his own derogatory picture of himself, thereby ridding himself of those feelings. The father's anger at first appears to be a response to the tendency he perceives in Hal to capitulate to these depressed feelings and turn to drugs. However, this anger also represents the narcissistic rage that is aroused by the son's associating with his peers, seeking relationships outside the family, and separating himself from the father.

Father: [With increasing anger] The thing that bothers me is I don't think you give a damn enough about yourself or what you're doing. When I saw you last Thursday you looked extremely disheveled and hangdog. And you look pretty much that way this afternoon, although not quite so much. And I . . . I feel . . . and your . . . your manner . . . you care nothing about your appearance. You know it bugs us. It bugs your mother, and in particular, probably me more than anybody, but this . . . I feel the way you, the way you dress . . . your appearance reflects how you feel about things. You don't *give* a damn. That's how you . . . that's how I think you feel. And with an attitude like that, I feel you're just gonna go . . . the chances are, with you walking around with some of the friends that you've been associated with in the drug business.

The son explains that he is not feeling badly about himself and in fact has been neat and appropriately dressed when he is out on a pass. However, the father angrily continues to portray Hal as the one who needs to do some thinking about himself. The therapist recognizes a repetitive theme of the father speaking about himself through his son and intervenes:

Therapist: It seems to me . . . your father feels you are so lacking in concern about yourself—he feels it's something about your not valuing yourself, your seeming depressed and looking disheveled. I thought you [to father] were talking about yourself again when you were talking to Hal, and about your own feeling belittled, when you're feeling very depressed or very unimportant.

Father: Oh, when somebody puts me down I get angry! But I usually don't show it. And it comes back and bites me during the night and in my own thoughts and

> nothing gets resolved by that. But that's what—I do get angry. And you're right. Most of the time I think that I feel I don't do things well. There's something about . . . very tense here, and I don't remember what you were saying in the first place. What you were asking me, I don't remember that.

In the preceding dialogues, the father begins by belittling the son and accusing him of not caring about himself. The therapist interprets this as largely a projection of the father's feeling belittled. The father replies first that he feels belittled by others ("Oh, when somebody puts me down, I get angry") and then acknowledges that he *does* experience much self-doubt ("You're right. Most of the time I think that I feel I don't do things well"). He then becomes anxious and represses this thought.

It is evident that after some interpretive work is done on the projection into the son and its relationship to the father's own self-esteem, the father begins to acknowledge the source of the projection as emanating from within himself. At this early stage in the treatment, however, the father is not able to tolerate for more than a moment the reinternalization of his projection. The interpretation has resulted in increased anxiety rather than in the father's further self-reflection.

Hal's sister has found the therapist's interpretation pertinent, however, and attempts to further the therapeutic work of the session:

Sister: [Turning to the father] I think that what the doctor says is true—that you very much underestimate yourself. I mean, how often did Mom and I, when you were writing these little things, suggest a writer's course, or say, "Why don't you write a book or something?" And you'd say, "Oh, I couldn't do that."

At this point, the mother effectively derails further exploration of this issue:

Mother: Well, back to this discussion of the week-end passes.

By shifting the focus from an exploration of the defensive functions of the father's perception of the son, the mother protects the father from further examining his own unconscious motivations. An appropriate therapeutic intervention at this juncture would be to note the collusive interaction developing and to work on understanding the shared anxiety that has generated this shift.

EXAMPLE 2

Several months later in the treatment, members of the family have begun to identify with the therapeutic task. The therapeutic alliance has been more firmly established, so that family members are able to perform ego-observing functions that had initially been performed exclusively by the therapists. In the session from which the following excerpt has been taken, the father has been bitterly expressing his anger and disappointment in both Hal and Hal's brother, Jeff, each of whom he feels is a failure for dropping out of athletic competition.

Therapist: What was so disappointing to you when he quit the team?
Father: Well, I guess ah . . . well, I guess I put myself in his shoes, I would have felt great finding out that I could swim so well and ah. . . .
Mother: It just hit me—that I think it's the reverse of that— when you say that you put yourself in his shoes and you would have felt great if you found out that you were that good a swimmer. I remember back at college, when you didn't follow through on the shot-putting, and you were . . . you felt so badly that—I forget who the coach was—disappointed at you dropping out. . . .
Father: Yeah, I. . . .
Mother: I think there's a connection there. You didn't follow through on something and that's why . . . it may have brought back memories of. . . .
Father: Yeah, maybe this is a sort of . . . substitute for my

	own not following through . . . that if he would have stayed then he would have . . . uh. . . .
Mother:	[Laughing] Compensated, in a way.
Father:	Yeah, yeah, I hadn't thought of it that. . . .
Hal:	I was thinking of me throwing the shot . . . and ah . . . how, how to not. . . .
Father:	Well, the kiss of death seemed to be when I worked with you, with it for a while and—then you dropped it.
Therapist:	I wonder how it makes you feel to have the feeling that your father is so dependent on your successes?
Jeff:	Like a burden, you know. Kind of like a burden, in a way, because then . . . if you don't succeed, then you feel bad about it.
Father:	Well, when he said "burden" there, that rang a bell with . . . that's everything it really is, the burden to see Hal quit and the burden to see Jeff quit. And I guess . . . I'm sure it would [half-laugh] be easy to say uh . . . I'm looking for them to up my [laughs] opinion of myself.

In this particular excerpt, it is the mother who initially makes the observation that the intensity of the father's disappointment and belittling rage arises from his own dropping out ["I remember back at college, when you didn't follow through on the shot-putting . . . you felt so badly . . ."). At this point in the treatment, however, all members of the family are engaged in the therapeutic process. The sons are now at greater liberty to express their experience of the father's pressure to achieve (". . . kind of like a burden . . .") and to introspect on their reactions to this pressure (". . . if you don't succeed, then you feel bad about it"). The father is able to recognize the internal source of his distress ("Yeah, maybe this is a sort of . . . substitute for my own not following through") and, with a sense of humor, to acknowledge and reinternalize the projection of his own poor self-esteem ("I'm sure it would be easy to say that uh . . . I'm looking for them to up my opinion of myself"). Very little intervention is necessary on the part of the therapists.

In this second family session, the discrepancy between the father's actual and ideal self becomes more readily apparent. He feels that *he* has been the failure and disappointment. Earlier, this discrepancy had been transmuted, through externalization, into interpersonal conflict between himself and his son. During the session, with the mother's help, the father is able to recognize that his excessive dependence upon the achievement of his offspring is really in the service of increasing his own precarious self-esteem.

Example 3

A shift in the family dynamics between the first and second family sessions has allowed Hal to become more observant of himself. In the earlier session, the father was preoccupied only with criticizing his son, while the son was preoccupied with defending himself against this criticism. Reflection was impossible for either of them. In the later family session, the father was able to reflect on his narcissistic use of the son, so that he no longer needed to rely on him for the maintenance of his own self-esteem. He no longer needed to perceive the son as the embodiment of unacceptable aspects of himself. It is this shift in the family which makes possible the kinds of self-observation that Hal demonstrates in the following excerpt. If this shift had not occurred, Hal would have continued to be thrown back on a perpetual, unmodified narcissistic relationship in his family.

In individual therapy a few weeks after the second family session, Hal demonstrates a new comprehension of his own narcissistic sensitivity. The individual therapist is soon to go on a vacation, and Hal has observed within himself a coincident recent increase in the intensity of his dependency in his relationship with a girl. In the session, he begins to compare this relationship to previous ones.

Hal: Monday it seemed like what I was trying to fight was somehow finding a comforter, you know, or another mother or another therapist in her or something. But

> I think if I feel good about myself inside, there isn't
> a feeling of if she isn't there that I can't exist. The
> way I'd go about it before was just latch on, make the
> other person my life—that's my father. He takes me
> and my sister and brother and pretty soon he loses
> his sense of value from himself or something and
> makes the kids his life; if they fuck up, he fucks up.
> . . . The scary part is when I notice myself turning
> someone like a girl into my own mind or something
> . . . if I get dropped or jilted, it destroys me. I just
> feel I'm trying to build something up for myself
> where you have a certain foundation and the rest of
> it's built up. And if all that falls down, you still have
> your foundation. But I think . . . the usual pattern of
> before is where it's destroyed all the way down to
> the foundation and then there's nothing.

Hal's insight into his own narcissistic vulnerability,
while precipitated by the forthcoming separation from his
individual therapist, draws heavily on his observations of
and experience in the concurrent family treatment. He
recognizes in himself the tendency he has, like that of his
father, to depend excessively on external objects for the
maintenance of his self-esteem. Moreover, Hal demonstrates in his statement an awareness that this dependency on a "comforter" (therapist, girlfriend) has been
vital to his very existence and that it is related to his
internal estimation of himself. In this example, a separation from the therapist that might ordinarily have precipitated an acute withdrawal from therapy was, indeed,
used by the adolescent to further his understanding of his
own conflicts in self-esteem.

Summary

We have described the dynamics and treatment of a
form of pathological self-esteem regulation characteristic
of the families of narcissistically disturbed adolescents.
The parents themselves demonstrate a failure in the

development of adequate psychic structure for self-esteem regulation, which leads to an overdependence on external objects for the maintenance of self-esteem. This externalization of intrapsychic conflicts around self-esteem in these families results in the use of offspring as narcissistic objects. Shortcomings perceived in the child are experienced as reflecting the parents' own inadequacies and are responded to by narcissistic rage and devaluation.

Because the child is used as a narcissistic object, the parents are compelled to control him. The period of adolescence is particularly threatening to the parents because of the adolescent's phase-specific disengagement from the family and search for new objects. The narcissistic rage resulting from the perceived threat to the parents leads to an intensification of their devaluing projections into the adolescent. The adolescent complies with the parents' narcissistic use of him because of both his anxiety about abandonment and the gratification of his own grandiosity which participation in this intense relationship affords him. Consequently he has greater than normal difficulty in separating, and his own self-esteem is further impaired through identification with these parental projections.

Psychoanalytically oriented conjoint family treatment, concurrent with individual therapy for the adolescent, provides an intervention into the externalization of intrapsychic conflicts by family members. It can produce dynamic shifts within the family that allow the adolescent to develop increased insight into his own narcissistic sensitivity. Reinternalization—acknowledging as part of the self that which has been projected—of narcissistic conflict makes possible its gradual resolution. The separate existence of the developing adolescent and of the parents is established, providing the possibility of increased autonomy of self-esteem for each.

16

The Borderline Ego and the Working Alliance: Indications for Family and Individual Treatment in Adolescence

EDWARD R. SHAPIRO, M.D.
ROGER L. SHAPIRO, M.D.
JOHN ZINNER, M.D.
DAVID A. BERKOWITZ, M.D.

Our intent is to explore the effect of certain ego deficits of the borderline patient on the working alliance, with an aim of understanding the indications for technical modifications in the therapy. In our study and treatment of borderline adolescents and their families, we have consistently observed a facilitation of the working alliance by the active participation of the individual therapist in concurrent conjoint family therapy. This chapter presents our understanding of this facilitation in terms of the developmental impairment in the borderline patient's ego functioning and its vicissitudes during his adolescence.

Contemporary psychoanalytic investigations into the early development of the borderline patient (Kernberg 1966, 1967, 1972, Mahler 1968, 1971, E. Shapiro et al. 1975) suggest that this pathological outcome represents a fixation in ego development that initially occurs during the

281

early childhood stage of separation–individuation (Mahler 1968, 1971). The consensus of these investigators is that pathological factors in the interplay between experience, drive, and ego disposition interfere with the child's progression from a symbiotic relationship with the mother to a position of relative separateness. This interference is presumed to occur following self–object differentiation but prior to the development of object constancy.

Developmental impairment during this period results in a pathologic continuance of splitting as a defense—that is, a sharp dissociation between self and object representations that are libidinally tinged from those that are colored by aggressive tones (Kernberg 1966, 1967, 1972). This continued defensive use of splitting results in limitations in the capacity to test reality, to tolerate anxiety and frustration, and to sustain a stable, integrated object relationship with an underlying attitude of basic trust.

These capacities are essential for the formation of a "therapeutic," or "working," alliance (Greenson 1965, Zetzel 1958), in which part of the patient's ego is focused on reality and collaborating on a work task with the therapist. Such an alliance allows both a continuing recognition of the therapist as a separate individual and a positive attitude toward the therapeutic task when the conflicts revived in the transference bring disturbing wishes and fantasies into consciousness. The ability to achieve this "dissociation within the ego" (Sterba 1934) between observing and experiencing is generally considered to be a precondition for classical psychoanalysis (Greenson and Wexler 1969, Zetzel 1968).

Basic to the working alliance is a necessary continuing perception of the therapist as helpful. Due to a defensive inability to integrate positive and negative aspects of the same internalized object, the borderline patient is inordinately sensitive to minor frustrations in the treatment. In the face of such inevitable frustrations, his characteristic response is to withdraw all affectively positive perceptions of the therapist and reinvest them in another object. At this point, the patient, through the mechanism of projective identification (Kernberg 1967), experiences the therapist as attacking and rejecting and responds defensively in order to control his now projected rage. The urgent need to control a therapist distorted by aggressive projections interferes with the patient's ability to use him in the work of examining and integrating behavior. The therapeutic task must therefore include a constant struggle to keep in the foreground enough of the working alliance to limit this destructive use of splitting and projection of unmodified rage.

During regressive episodes of negative transference with such patients, interpretation of the splitting alone is often inadequate both to control the patient's unmodified fury and guilt and to prevent destructive acting out. Intensive therapy or psychoanalysis with patients who have early ego deficits that interfere with solid alliance formation risks the possibility of an uncontrolled ego regression with loss of reality testing and a possible transference psychosis (Kernberg 1968, Little 1966).

MODIFICATIONS IN INDIVIDUAL THERAPY

One school of thought suggests that such ego deficits are relatively irreversible and preclude the use of intensive psychotherapy or analysis. Zetzel (1971) recommends the use of infrequent but relatively interminable psychotherapy for these patients. The goal of such treatment is to facilitate the patient's use of the therapist–patient relationship in a supportive manner, hopefully leading to some internalization of its positive aspects, including its stability and limitations.

Other analysts (Eissler 1953, Frosch 1971, Kernberg 1968) recommend the introduction of "parameters of technique" to enable the patient to manage potentially regressive intensive therapy. These parameters usually involve some type of structuring or "limit setting," either within the treatment hour or in the external environment (Adler 1973, Masterson 1972).

Underlying the patient's defensive use of splitting is an anxious, unconscious perception that his aggressive impulses are so powerful as to destroy the internalized "good" object. Limit setting is designed to correct this perception by providing sufficient external structure and support for negative transference responses to be contained without allowing them to become destructive to the actual object relationship. Empathic containment, as opposed to retaliation or withdrawal, is a type of "holding environment" (Winnicott 1954), in which negative projections can be examined and integrated without being acted out. Providing a safe place for self-examination is intended to help strengthen the patient's observing ego by confronting him with the discrepancy between his projections and reality, instead of allowing him to alter his reality to conform with his projections.

Greenson (1965) defines transference as *both* a repetition of the past *and* inappropriate to the present. This necessary distinction between transference and current reality can be further blurred by the therapist's countertransference involvement in the patient's primitive defenses. In the midst of a regressive negative transference involving the use of splitting and projective identification, for instance, the therapist may become involved in a process of "empathic regression" (Kernberg 1965) in order to maintain his emotional contact with the patient. If, for example, the patient is screaming in rage at the therapist whom he perceives as attacking, frustrating, and rejecting, the therapist may, through guilty introspection, find within himself the person at whom the patient is yelling. Such a counteridentification could result in a limited blurring of ego boundaries with respect to the patient. In addition, the unexpected and uncontrolled intensity of the patient's rage may make the therapist vulnerable to anxiety potentially disruptive to the therapeutic work. Disruptive anxiety in the therapist may be related to the possible loss of the relationship with the patient (with specific countertransference implications) or the need to control his own tendency to retaliate. Kernberg (1965) recommends the use of external structure and limit setting within the hour as part of the analytic work with such patients in order to sustain the *analyst's* identity in this relationship and support the alliance.

Some therapists attempt to manage both the patient's powerful use of projective identification and their own countertransference collaboration in this process by the use of manipulation. Roland (1967) suggests that in the treatment of patients with character disorders, the therapist must "accentuate" those aspects of himself that will allow the patient to differentiate him sufficiently from internalized representations of familial objects and relationships. Eissler (1950) reports the use of manipulative interventions aimed at demonstrating his omnipotence to the patient. He considers such manipulation early in the therapy as crucial to the establishment of an alliance with adolescent "delinquents."

Although we agree that in order to sustain a working alliance it is essential for the patient to be able to differentiate the therapist from his internalized objects, we do not advocate the use of manipulation in the treatment of these patients, particularly during their adolescence. In adolescence, increased instinctual turmoil and the urgent search for new objects make it difficult to establish a stable working alliance (A. Freud 1958). Because of the persistent defensive use of splitting in adolescents with borderline personality development, transference and countertransference problems are exacerbated, as we have discussed. These conditions have also led us to consider modifications in treatment in order to help stabilize the alliance. Our examination of the family's contribution to the formation of the borderline patient's internalized objects and our observation of family interaction during adolescence have, however, indicated an alternative approach—the use of concurrent family therapy.

BORDERLINE ADOLESCENTS
AND THEIR FAMILIES

Work with families of borderline adolescents (E. Shapiro et al. 1975, R. Shapiro 1967, Zinner and E. Shapiro 1974) reveals that the adolescence of the borderline child becomes a period of family regression as well. During separation–individuation periods (ages 2 to 3 and adolescence) of the borderline child, family group behavior becomes dominated by unconscious fantasy, which requires defensive operations.

These families demonstrate a tendency toward splitting which parallels that of their borderline adolescent. Within the family group, attributes of "goodness" (providing, gratifying, loving) and "badness" (depriving, punishing, hating) are separated one from the other and reinvested in different members so that each family member appears relatively preambivalent and single-minded in relation to the troubled adolescent. The family group, taken as a whole, appears to be a single, ambivalent entity, loving and hating, giving and withholding, rewarding and punishing. Individual members, however, act as if they *were* the unidimensional, unconflicted, preambivalent objects their borderline offspring perceive them to be. These defensive operations are founded on the unconscious fantasy that there is unmodified aggressive intent behind the borderline child's autonomous moves or his needs for nurture and support.

Parents of these children, because of critical interactions with their own parents during separation–individuation, have unconsciously associated either autonomous or dependent behavior with either libidinally or aggressively tinged self–object representations (that is, autonomy is associated with "good" experience and dependency with "bad," or vice versa). Because of an unstable integration in each of the parents of positive and negative ego states, each has resolved his original conflict about issues of autonomy and dependency by an identification with the libidinally influenced self-perception (that is, each sees himself as "lovingly dependent" or "strong and autonomous") and a denial and projection of the aggressively tinged alternative.

In these families, both the integrity of the marriage and the integrity of each parent's personality is dependent upon the use of projective identification (E. Shapiro et al. 1975, Zinner and R. Shapiro 1972). Through the use of this mechanism, the borderline child is chosen by the parents to participate with them in a relationship that embodies their denied, aggressively tinged self–object representations. In other words, if each parent sees himself in his own way as "lovingly dependent," the borderline child is seen in a shared unconscious manner as ruthlessly independent. If each sees himself as "strong and autonomous," without dependent needs, the designated child is perceived as ravenously demanding and totally dependent.

These perceptions have particular impact during the periods of separation–individuation, when, depending on their own self-perceptions, the parents unconsciously view the child's independent moves as hostile rejections or his needs for nurturance and support as draining demands. The intensity of this interrelated system of splitting and projective identification contributes developmentally to an impairment in the child's ego formation. Motivated by his inability to tolerate either parental anxiety or his own anxiety over the possible loss of parental love, the borderline child unconsciously attempts to modify his subjective experience in accordance with these projections (Zinner and R. Shapiro 1972).

Early interactions between parent and child that are dominated by unconscious assumptions become one important basis of his internalizations (R. Shapiro and Zinner 1971). For example, if the parent withdraws from the infant's dependent needs because of an unconscious perception of them as draining demands, he will increase the intensity of the infant's perception of him as the "bad" object. In an anxious attempt to retain his vitally needed perception of the parent as the "good" object, the infant will defensively prolong his use of splitting and internalize an unmodified frustrating parental image—an image which is subsequently difficult to alter. If the parent withdraws support in response to the toddler's autonomous moves because of an unconscious perception of them as hostile rejections, a similar unmodified internalization will result. The intensity of these interactions threatens to overwhelm the loving relationship with the parent and requires the continued use of primitive defenses, leading to the continuance into adult life of primitive, poorly integrated ego and superego.

In individual therapy with borderline adolescents, these transference paradigms are reawakened with all their primitive intensity. The patient experiences the therapist as alternatively devouring and rejecting. With his fragile ego further weakened by the instinctual stresses of adolescence, he is threatened by the possible loss of distinction between therapist and internalized parent in a transference psychosis. The therapist must find a way to collaborate with the patient in distinguishing reality from overwhelming fantasy.

THE USE OF FAMILY THERAPY

Indications for the use of family therapy have been discussed at length in the literature (Boszormenyi-Nagy 1966, Framo 1965, 1970, Williams 1973, Wynne 1965). We will not attempt to review this complex subject here but will concentrate instead on one aspect: its usefulness in facilitating alliance formation with the borderline adolescent.

Masterson (1972) uses conjoint family interviews *after* the individual alliance with the adolescent is formed. He feels that if such interviews are begun early in the treatment, they will "create greater conflict and feelings of abandonment, which will produce further acting out by the patient" and interfere with the therapy. Masterson suggests that the conflicted symbiotic tie within the family is so intense that a therapeutic alliance with the adolescent cannot be formed unless the family is excluded from contact.

In over a decade of work with borderline adolescents and families at the NIMH, it has been our experience that the concomitant use of family therapy does not interfere with the individual therapy or make the individual alliance unworkable. On the contrary, the early perception of the therapist as helpful in the family group provides a quality of flexibility in the individual situation that allows a shift from an unworkable transference, as previously described, to a situation in which transference and observing ego can coexist.

In families of borderline adolescents, the family's regression to behavior dominated by the unconscious assumptions we have described makes the parents' actual behavior more closely approximate that of the adolescent's internalized objects. In this setting, projective identification between parent and adolescent becomes the main pathological focus and the therapist is less intensively the locus of transference distortions. The task of the therapist in this situation is to provide the family with an opportunity, in the midst of the most highly regressed interactions, to use his capacity to observe. In addition, the therapist can more easily maintain his objectivity in the family session, since the intensity of his countertransference response to the adolescent is mitigated by the presence of the family. The shifting focus of interactions allows the therapist to clarify more readily the nature of family relationships for interpretive use in managing the individual transference and stabilizing the alliance.

To put this phenomenon more specifically, during periods of regressive negative transference in individual therapy, the patient experiences the therapist as not helpful in furthering his autonomous development (that is, the alliance is lost). In the family setting, both patient and therapist share an experience with the family in which the adolescent's behavior evokes anxiety in the family, leading to defensive operations. During such an interaction, the thinking of family members becomes dominated by unconscious assumptions rather than realistic perceptions. In response, their behavior becomes, *in fact*, not supportive to the patient's developmental needs. In the face of a shared regression, family members require support for their powers of critical observation. For the adolescent, the therapist's clarification of the reality of the family interaction and the underlying shared family fantasies strengthens his ability to distinguish between therapist and parent and supports the working alliance.

CLINICAL OBSERVATIONS

In the following discussion, we will examine excerpts from one family session and a subsequent individual session with a borderline adolescent. These interactions, though representing only a minute portion of the therapeutic work, capture a quality of alliance-building that we find characteristic of concurrent family and individual therapy with these patients.

Sarah B. is a 19-year-old borderline girl with a three-year history of running away, promiscuity, serious alcohol abuse, and other provocative acting-out behavior. We have previously discussed in Chapter 8 her family history and dynamics of interaction (E. Shapiro et al. 1975). Much of her disturbance is related by her to a recurrent feeling of being "spaced out." It is in response to this peculiar affect of nonrelatedness that she resorts to alcohol, which allows her to engage in both sexual and aggressive behavior.

Her family, as a group, is unable to tolerate the acknowledgment of dependent needs, particularly those expressed by Sarah. Historically, this inability to tolerate dependency can be seen as an aspect of the family's regression during Sarah's adolescence. It is a reenactment of similar difficulties experienced during her early childhood separation–individuation period (E. Shapiro et al. 1975).

After six months of individual and family therapy with a focus on the patient's need to act out painful feelings and the family's tendency to avoid them instead of discussing them, Sarah spent a long weekend at home. In the family session that followed the weekend, each family member described the weekend as "nice." In fact, Sarah was feeling quite depressed.

In the following excerpt, Sarah remembers an unusual attempt on her part to communicate this feeling of depression to her father. The excerpt illustrates the needful quality of this communication and the father's inability (with family concurrence) to acknowledge it. In their response, the members of the family appear to unite in a statement that Sarah *must not* be needful, because it would signify an intolerable demand on the family and necessitate their acknowledgment of their own denied needfulness.

FAMILY THERAPY EXCERPT

Sarah: [To father] You said something to me and I said that I was depressed. And you said, "Why don't you go to sleep; maybe you'll feel better." And I said, "No, Dad, I don't think sleeping will help," and then you just walked out.

Therapist: You wanted some other response?

Sarah: I suppose I . . . suppose I wanted to talk . . . about it.

Father: And I walked away?

Sarah: Yeah.

Therapist: You don't remember this incident?

Father: I remember . . . that "I am depressed" . . . yeah.

	But I certainly don't . . . [Long pause]
Therapist:	And how do you remember your response?
Father:	[Pause] I remember some . . . vague . . . ah . . . obviously unsuccessful attempt to . . . I . . . find out what it was about.
Sarah:	[Softly] No, Dad, your reaction was that I should go to sleep.
Father:	[Pause] I can't believe, Sarah, if you tell me that you were depressed . . . I find it almost impossible to believe that I would have done that . . . Saturday night.
Therapist:	[To mother] Do *you* believe it?
Mother:	What? . . . [low voice] I don't know.
Sarah:	Look, I'm saying that this is what happened. Don't you believe me?
Mother:	You're saying that, he says it didn't. . . . I didn't hear . . . [to therapist] I'm surprised to hear that Sarah would come out and say that she was depressed.
Therapist:	Me too. But do you believe her?
Mother:	[Pause; low voice] I don't really know.
Therapist:	[To brothers] Do you believe her?
Steven:	[Pause] I don't know.
Joseph:	No.
Mother:	I guess he *could* have said it, but then again he wouldn't necessarily have said it.
Father:	[Pause] I wish I could be a . . . because I can honestly not believe it, Sarah. I . . . I'm sure that it happened . . . in some fashion . . . and that you heard it that way. I'm also sure that . . . I didn't *say* it that way. You know?
Therapist:	Why are you so sure?
Father:	Because I would *not*! I just would *not*!
Therapist:	You have a tendency, you have said, not to see . . . painful things.
Father:	I also have . . . uh . . . fought the tendency very hard. I realize it sounds weasly, but . . . ah . . . there, there was . . . there *had* to be . . . in between . . . "I am depressed" and "Why don't you," I mean, I can believe that both statements were said. . . .

Sarah: [Shouting] You didn't even ask me what it was
                about, Dad! You did not! Last night, when you
                called me and were willing to talk, it seemed really
                funny because you hadn't before, on the weekend,
                you know. I couldn't understand last night when
                you were talking to me!

    Sarah's attempt to verbalize her hitherto acted-out
depression is a piece of new behavior in the family. It is a
product of six months of work in both individual and
family therapy. The mother says she's "surprised" that
Sarah would "come out and say that she's depressed." In
fact, neither she nor any other family member can acknowledge the possibility of such behavior from Sarah.
This inability represents each family member's denial and
projection into Sarah of needful aspects of himself. Sarah's expression of dependent needs is unconsciously
experienced by family members as a hostile, draining
demand on meager resources. For their own protection,
then, they unite to deny the possibility of such behavior.
    Additional motivation for the group reaction comes
from father's insistence that his response (that is, his
withdrawal) *could not* have happened. In this family, the
father is the generally acknowledged "good" parent. This
perception is achieved by the use of splitting mechanisms
in the family (Zinner and E. Shapiro 1975) and is maintained by a group denial of any evidence of the father's
inability to provide. In presenting such evidence, Sarah is
challenging an important defensive family assumption.
Their anxious response to this challenge is to attempt
unconsciously to alter the reality in conformity with their
defensive needs.
    With his interventions, the therapist is attempting
both to point out the defensiveness in the group and to
support Sarah's new behavior. In addition, his investigation of the shared family denial underlines the actuality of
family relationships and their repetitive patterning.
    In this session, the family's united denial left Sarah

confused and angry. Their insistence that she could not undertake any behavior that contradicted their defensive use of her left her doubting her own perception of reality. In addition, she was hurt and angry at their refusal to provide requested support.

In the individual session later in the afternoon, Sarah began by discussing how angry she was at the "rigid" staff rules under which "nobody [was] allowed to see [her]." In fact, the staff had limited her visitors and required them to check in since several had brought drugs on previous visits.

In reading the following excerpt, it is important to keep in mind Sarah's hurt and angry response in the family session when family members suggested that what she perceived was not so. Her opening statement in the next excerpt ("Nobody is allowed to see me") is, unconsciously, a needful request of the therapist parallel to her attempt to talk with her father about her depression. The therapist does not immediately hear the parallel however, and responds only to the manifest content. Sarah's angry response is immediate, uncontrollable, and seemingly inappropriate.

INDIVIDUAL THERAPY EXCERPT

Sarah: Nobody is allowed to see me!

Therapist: That's something of a distortion, that visitors are *not allowed* to see you.

Sarah: Joe had to talk to a staff member.

Therapist: That doesn't mean he's not allowed to see you.

Sarah: Fred was kicked off the unit.

Therapist: You say that in a tone . . .

Sarah: [Shouting] Oh, fuck you!

Therapist: . . . that indicates that it's an arbitrary staff that would just kick Fred off the unit for no reason at all.

Sarah: [Softly] Of course there's some reason.

Therapist: You were hurt when I said that. What are you angry about?

Sarah: [Long pause, then angrily] "It's a distortion," just like everything I say is a distortion.

Therapist: Everything you say is not a distortion. [Sarah, swearing, angrily runs out of the room, slamming the door.]

The therapist did not recognize Sarah's opening statement as an unconscious reference to the family setting in which nobody is "allowed" to see her *as she is*, because of the family's defensive structure. In his concrete response, he unwittingly replicated the family's reaction by suggesting that she was distorting reality. The experience with the family was sufficiently powerful and the parallel sufficiently close that Sarah momentarily lost the distinction between therapist and internalized "bad" parent. This fleeting loss of distinction, representing a momentary ego regression, transformed her experience of the alliance with the therapist into an earlier experience with a depriving, rejecting, hostile object. Overwhelmed by pain and rage, she fled from the room. When she returned ten minutes later, her rage was unabated.

[Sarah re-enters, slamming the door]

Sarah: [Angrily] I'm not gonna let you fuck up my passes. . . . I don't have anything else to say to you. I want to go out with Joe this weekend, so I came back.

Therapist: I don't know why you left.

Sarah: [Tearfully] Because I'm sick of hearing my "distortions of the truth," and that I "lie," you know? Because it *is* the truth. There may be other things, you know, but they're *not* allowed on the unit for various reasons. It may be my fault, but it's still the truth, and I . . . I told them why they weren't allowed on, it's not like I said it was other people's fault, you know. [Crying] I said it was my fault.

The transference repetition was more fully recreated when Sarah angrily announced her determination to go on pass ("I'm not gonna let you fuck up my passes"). Her

parents' continuing inability to accept appropriate dependent needs serves to push Sarah into an angry pseudoindependence in which her words declare autonomy but
her affect and behavior demand support. Sarah's tearful
response to a gentle attempt to examine her behavior
allowed the therapist, who had initially experienced her
rage as bewilderingly inappropriate, to recognize her
appeal. With this recognition, he could realize the
repetition of the earlier family dynamic in the current
transference:

Therapist: You thought I was saying to you what your father
said to you this morning?

Sarah: [Shouting] Yes!

Therapist: [Pause] I can see why you ran out.

Sarah: [Tearfully] You just sit there laughing, "distortion of
the truth," you know. It's real funny.

Therapist: I understand now why you were so hurt. [Slight
pause] I'm glad you came back.

Sarah: [Tearfully] I didn't want to come back, you know, at
all. But I'd just be fucking myself over and I've done
enough of that, you know.

Therapist: That was confusing for you this morning when
nobody believed you

Sarah: [Tearfully] Yeah it was, I was just *flipping out*, you
know! Like maybe I didn't hear it, but *I know I did!*
[Crying]

Therapist: I believe you. [Long pause] In fact, that was the first
time that I understood what you meant about
things being very strange—spaced out—because I
felt you were being extruded by everyone in the
family.

Sarah: Afterwards my mother said she believed me, you
know? [Pause] That's how it is in my family, everybody just floats around all the time . . . gotta
pretend everything's fine.

Therapist: And when you know that it isn't, it makes you feel
crazy?

Sarah: After awhile, I don't know anymore. . . . In
thinking back, I just thought it was all in my head,

you know. I really didn't even know if it's just me or
what! [Crying] I just didn't know! You know, it's
sort of like when I first started getting spaced out
and I didn't understand what was going on. It was
like people were talking . . . would talk to me and I
didn't know whether they were talking to me or
somebody else even if they were looking right at
me.

Therapist: Well, that's what was happening this morning in
family therapy. Did you have that same feeling
when I said that what you said was a distortion?

Sarah: You said it sort of laughingly, you know, like . . .
like I was saying things crazy or something, like I
didn't know what I was talking about. Just that
word stuck in my mind, you know, like I can see
now what you were saying. It was just the way it hit
• me . . .

In this excerpt, the therapist used a number of
interventions, including rapid and concrete interpretation
of the negative transference ("You thought I was saying to
you what your father said"), clarification of reality ("you
were being extruded by . . . the family"), and support for
her appropriate libidinal needs ("I'm glad you came
back"). This combination of interpretation, clarification,
and support allowed her to work on the psychological
determinants of her symptomatology ("it's sort of like
when I first started getting spaced out"), observe the
pretense demanded in the family ("gotta pretend everything's fine"), and reestablish the working alliance ("I can
see now what you were saying").

On first reading, one might view this excerpt as
evidence of the therapist's deflection of the negative
transference in the service of becoming the "good" parent.
It is important, however, to note that the emphasis of the
interpretations is in the direction of increasing observation and understanding rather than simply providing
support. Although initially overidealized, the therapist
emerges over time in the therapy as "helpful" rather than

"all-good" because of his consistent refusal to exploit the family on his behalf by labelling their behavior as "bad" Such an exploitation, often seen in hospital staff members caring for borderline patients (Adler 1973), is an ever-present danger in treating patients who use splitting as a defense.

In the excerpt, the therapist's interventions were indicated by Sarah's regressive use of splitting and projection, which threatened the working alliance by compelling her to run from the room. Although the therapist, in his defensive remark ("That's something of a distortion") *was* both insufficiently perceptive and affected by guilty countertransference feelings about limiting her privileges, Sarah's response was excessive. Because of the projection of her own aggressiveness, the therapist's defensiveness was perceived as assaultive. With a capacity for more integrated (that is, good *and* bad) internalized object relations, she might have been able to hold on to the perception of the therapist as basically helpful despite his seemingly hostile comment. Such an alliance would have facilitated her ability to tolerate the anxiety aroused by the therapist's comment so that the interaction could be more intensively worked on.

In the absence of such integration, the therapist might have responded to her overwhelming rage and defensive flight by some additional form of limit setting, with the hope of containing her projection in order to examine its intensity. However, excessive limit setting has the disadvantage of not mobilizing the patient's own capacity for controls.

The shared experience with a regressed family, in combination with its profound repetition in the individual transference, allowed Sarah, through affective and verbal communication alone, to use the therapist's observations to confirm her sense of reality. The consequent strengthening of her own capacity to observe allowed her to make a tension-relieving and mutative distinction between therapist and internalized parent.

DISCUSSION

In his classic paper on the therapeutic action of psycho-analysis, Strachey (1934) suggests that the mutative effect of interpretation depends in large measure upon the ability of the patient's ego to "become aware of the contrast between the aggressive character of his feelings and the real nature of the analyst, who does not behave like the patient's 'good' or 'bad' archaic objects" (p. 13). Recognizing that the analyst, however careful, may be unable to avoid all behavior that may confirm the patient's projections, Strachey states that "the patient's sense of reality is an essential . . . ally" (p. 146) in the analytic process.

This ally is extraordinarily frail in patients with bor-derline personality development, particularly during their adolescence. Serious ego weakness, with the pathological use of splitting as a defense, combined with a shared family regression and consequent lack of parental ego support, markedly weakens the borderline adolescent's reality sense.

With individual therapy alone, the use of technical variations (limit setting, manipulation, and so on) may prove inadequate to sustain a working alliance. The patient's difficulty in distinguishing the therapist from his projections of internalized (split) objects can be severely aggravated by concurrent regressive family interaction, which, during adolescence, repeatedly confirms these projections.

The actual experience in the family therapy session can clarify the reality of this regressed interaction for both patient and therapist, with the aid of the therapist's observing ego. Observation and clarification are then used in the individual session, not to take sides with the patient against the family, but to help solidify the patient's own capacity for observation. With this increased capac-ity, the adolescent can sustain an alliance in the face of both the reality of the regressed family behavior and his projected distortions in the individual therapy.

In family sessions, therapists and family members can together observe behavior determined by the shared unconscious fantasies and assumptions that provide a "hidden agenda" for family interaction. Such observation reveals how these shared fantasies influence the behavior of family members who are both implicitly and explicitly assigned roles in the unconscious family drama.

In the individual transference, when the patient's regression evokes a reenactment of these interactions with the therapist, this shared experience can be called upon to supplement and support the individual alliance. Use of the therapist's capacity to observe assists the patient in the assessment of reality, the articulation and integration of previously overwhelming affects, and the maintenance of an alliance in the face of an intensely regressive negative transference.

The collaborative participation by the family in the borderline patient's use of splitting and projective identification indicates to us the advantages of treating all participants. Because of the powerful interpersonal pull of these defenses, strengthening the adolescent's capacity to observe his responses is enhanced by a parallel strengthening of parental capacity for self-observation. In our work with these families, we provide a second therapist for marital therapy for the parents. This therapist also works in the family sessions, allowing the parents to use his observing ego in a manner similar to the adolescent's use of the individual therapist. With increasing capacity for observation and integrations, both parents and adolescent can begin to use each other in a more mature way to support the potential of each to become autonomous.

It should be noted that our approach is in contrast to the one advocated by Masterson (1972). In his book on borderline adolescents, Masterson suggests that conjoint family sessions be employed only after the patient's "latent observing ego" has been reached and an alliance formed with the therapist. Masterson employs an initial period of behavioral control for these adolescents with no family contact and little or no psychotherapy until the patient has finished "testing the limits." It is only after this is achieved and an additional period of individual psychotherapy undertaken that he will allow conjoint family interviews. Since Masterson does not believe that parents of these patients can be effectively treated, his approach is aimed at a corrective experience with temporary but active substitution of therapist for parent. Following this substitution, conjoint family sessions are oriented toward further reducing the pathologic bonds between patient and parent by allowing "verbalization of anger about the abandonment" the patient has experienced at their hands.

Our experience in treating both family and borderline adolescent concurrently suggests that such a substitution is not necessary. Understanding and treatment of the pathologic system of family interaction in which the borderline child represents to the parents disavowed aggressively tinged aspects of themselves allows for change in the family as a group. The capacity of family members to reinternalize and integrate projections (Berkowitz et al. 1974a) allows for the possibility of a corrective relationship between parent and child, with therapist as facilitator rather than new object.

After the working alliance is stabilized, the two poles of the individual transference relationship can be integrated over time. As this integration proceeds, concurrent family work allows an increasing recognition of a new and more modified relationship between parent and child in which each may find increasing autonomy without the threat of abandonment.

Summary

The borderline patient is characterized by serious ego weakness, with a pathological use of splitting as a defense. During his adolescence, the patient's difficulty in distinguishing the therapist from his projections of internalized (split) objects can be severely aggravated by concurrent regressive family interaction, which repeatedly confirms these projections. Because of this family regression, there may be increased difficulty in sustaining a stable working alliance with the use of individual therapy alone, despite the use of technical modifications (decreased frequency of sessions, limit setting, manipulation, and so on).

The authors suggest that in the treatment of borderline adolescents, the presence of the individual therapist in concurrent family therapy can clarify the reality of the family's regressed behavior for patient and therapist with the aid of the therapist's observing ego. In the individual transference, when the patient's regression evokes a reenactment of these interactions with the therapist, this shared experience can be called upon to supplement and support the working alliance.

17

The Effects
of Parental Self-Esteem
on Adolescent Individuation:
A Dimensional View

JOHN ZINNER, M.D.

In this effort to delineate what a family does to facilitate or impede the psychological growth of its offspring, let me start with reflections of five individuals on their own evolution. These five broadly reflect degrees of success in internalizing psychic structure along a continuum of individuation. At the healthier end of this dimension is Bob, a 17-year-old adolescent whose developing sense of himself he describes as follows:

I'm sorta now like at the point where I think I'm starting to try to take what my parents say more . . . objectively. You know, this objectivity thing. When you grow up it's a matter of increasing or of quantitatively changing compensation in the interpretation of other people and what they say. And so now I'm sorta at the point where I'm very erratically and unevenly more and more breaking away from a sense of the other people in my family purely as parents or brother in the way I take in their advice to me. Whereas I may have taken it always with the idea that since obviously they had a lot more experience than I had—they are, you know, my parents—all my decisions regarding their advice would be affected by that . . . now I take it more as an objective act rather than as if they are making the whole decision.

Rick, Bob's younger brother by two years, adds his introspective comment.

Well, I was just gonna add I feel a lot the same way. I don't know what age it's considered normal to begin to look at your parents as another person. If I got a piece of advice from someone else—say a teacher or another student—I would obviously have to weigh it against their background and what made them say it and how they think it would be applicable to me, and then say, well, how well do they know me, and therefore, how well do they think our experiences match so they think I could use this, finally, to decide whether or not to use their advice. . . . I think this is a process you always make, but not necessarily with parents until you realize that they're people with their own background. I mean if you grow up with people, you consider they know a lot about you, and it's only when they make several wrong decisions that they *don't* necessarily know all about you and their advice is not necessarily 100 percent accurate. Oh, you know, you have to go through the same process with parents. Only it's harder because up 'til then, you did not.

In response to Bob, the father says, "Do you understand what he said? I think he said that he doesn't necessarily do what I say because I'm a parent. He may do it and he may not." The mother adds, "Which I would consider a compliment. Because this is what he's *supposed* to be doing at this age, I think."

Despite the fact that "breaking away" from parents is described as "hard," "uneven," and "erratic," both Rick and Bob evidence a sense of confidence in the successful completion of the task. Further excerpts from their family work are in press (R. Shapiro 1989).

Consider, on the other hand, the reflection of Edmund Gosse (1963), British essayist and critic, as he recalls his twelfth year of life, 120 years ago. Gosse is commenting on his reactions to his father's intense preoccupation with the boy's fulfilling a divine mission as a member of a fundamentalist sect.

It was not in harshness or in ill nature that he worried me so much; on the contrary, it was all part of his all too anxious love. He was in a hurry to see me become a shining light, everything that he himself desired to be, yet with none of his shortcomings. . . . I felt like a small and solitary bird, caught and hung out hopelessly and endlessly in a great glittering cage. . . . I saw myself imprisoned forever in the religious system which had caught me and would whirl my helpless spirit as in the concentric wheels of my nightly vision. . . . (Yet) through thick and thin I clung to a hard nut of individuality deep down in my childish nature. To the pressure from without, I resigned everything else, my thought, my words, my anticipation, my assurances, but there was something which I never resigned, my innate and persistent self. Meek as I seemed, and gently respondent, I was always conscious of that innermost quality which I had learned to recognize in my earlier days, . . . that existence of two in the depths who could speak to one another in inviolable secrecy. [pp. 156–158]

Gosse did go on to achieve a consolidation of his "persistent self" but only at the cost of a profound and permanent alienation from his father.

John Stuart Mill (1969), nineteenth-century British philosopher, is our fourth spokesman. Educated entirely by his father, Mill reflected on the consequences in an unpublished portion of his autobiography.

The only person [father] I was in communication with, to whom I looked up, I had too much fear of.

... To have been, through childhood, under the constant rule of a strong will, certainly is not favorable to strength of will. . . . The things I ought *not* to do were mostly provided by his precepts, rigorously enforced whenever violated, but the things which I ought to do I hardly ever did of my own mere motion, but waited 'til he told me to do them; and if he forbore or forgot to tell me, they were generally left undone. I thus acquired a habit of backwardness, of waiting to follow the lead of others, an absence of moral spontaneity, an inactivity of the moral sense and even to a large extent, of the intellect, unless roused by the appeal of someone else. [pp. 33–34]

This awareness of a continuing dependency on others to compensate for a failure to develop his own inner structure and a sense of self is elaborated upon by our final commentator, Hal, who at 19 has been in psychotherapy on an adolescent inpatient unit. The following monologue is excerpted from one reported in Chapter 15, where Hal's individual and family treatment is described at length (Berkowitz et al. 1974a). His individual therapist is soon to go on a vacation, and Hal has observed within himself a coincident recent increase in his dependency on his girlfriend. In this statement, Hal compares this relationship to previous ones before his gains in therapy.

Monday it seemed like what I was trying to fight was somehow finding a comforter, you know, or another mother or another therapist in her or something. But I think if I feel good about myself inside, there isn't a feeling of if she isn't there that I can't exist. The way I'd go about it before was just latch on, make the other person my life—that's my father. He takes me and my sister and brother and pretty soon he loses his sense of value from himself or something and makes the kids his life; if they fuck up, he fucks up. . . . The scary part is when I notice myself turning someone like a girl into my own mind or something—if I get dropped or jilted, it destroys me. I just feel I'm trying to build something up for myself where you have a certain foundation and the rest of it's built up. And if all that falls down, you still have your foundation. But I think—the usual pattern of before is where it's destroyed all the way down to the foundation and then there's nothing.

These statements display a panorama of varieties of individuation. At one end Rick and Bob begin to see their parents as fallible, no longer omniscient or superhuman. The parental fall from their pedestal is not abrupt, total, or traumatic, and both boys feel confidently that they are learning to supply from within themselves what was previously accepted unquestioningly from without as their parents' advice and decisions. Their parents respond to their statements with conscious awareness of the timeliness and appropriateness of their development; for example, their mother says, "This is what he's *supposed* to be doing at this age," and then adds doubtfully, "I think"—a tinge of her ambivalence about her fall from power.

Edmund Gosse traversed these developmental stages more rockily than did Rick and Bob. Despite the resignation of his thoughts and words, he "clung to a hard nut of individuality" that had developed in his earliest years. Ultimately his "innate and persistent self" prevailed and flourished, but it required a severe breach in the relationship with that crucial parent, his father. John Stuart Mill suffered far more. That "hard nut of individuality" was never acquired and he continued to wait "to follow the lead of others" and was left with an "absence of moral spontaneity . . . unless roused by the appeal of someone else." Finally, in an even more malignant way, Hal's sense of himself and his worth was fused with the narcissistic system of his father. Hal says, "I would latch on, make the other person my life—that's my father."

While the emphasis in these quotations has been on the sense of self of the individual speaking, a great deal can be inferred about the character of parenting associated with this variety of outcomes. It is my aim to define some general relationships that exist between an individual's psychological growth and qualities of family life. The foregoing quotations highlight the principle that development largely involves the gradual acquisition of the capacity to do for oneself what was previously done for one by one's family. Thus we are talking here of psychological growth as the building and refinement of the intrapsychic structures. The line of development of the superego is a case in point. Fundamentally, this structure provides a frame of reference for the psyche, a set of standards of right and wrong, and a detailed picture of an ideal to which one aspires. In infancy, when there is no such internalized structure to speak of, the essential guidelines are established and executed through the activity of external objects—that is, the parents. The suckling who bites the breast or strikes out is moved out of reach by the mother or is restrained by the target of aggression. The toddler who hits or throws food is likewise subject to external control but now with the incrementally increasing importance of the verbal injunction "no." As time passes, the injunction becomes incorporated as psychic structure, first in the form of imitation, then in identification by being spoken when the child repeats "no" in the presence of the mother but not necessarily in direct imitation. Internalization progresses as object constancy evolves so that the parental injunction of "no" is experienced even in the absence of the parental object. Numerous concurrent events and refinements occur that are interdigitated with other lines of development, such as that of emotional object constancy.

Perhaps most important here is the capacity to integrate good and bad self–object representations, which allows for the capacity for remorse and empathy. In this process, the child is able to maintain a picture of, and concern for, the good object even in the face of the child's own rage at the inwardly perceived bad object.

What begins as disjointed parental introjects of approving echoes or restrictive injunctions become integrated into an expanding self-representation. Particularly during the oedipal period, major gains are made in a crucial transition: There is the acquisition of a conscience in which the system of guidance shifts from fear of parental reprisal to a basic inner sense of morality based on guilt. This newly consolidated superego structure remains brittle and easily capable of being reprojected into the parents. Impulse expression filters through and, regressively, fear of parental reprisal is again the dominant guidance system. Likewise, the particular attitudes incorporated into the conscience bear the imitative stamp of the parental values. Crucial remodeling of the superego structure occurs during adolescence, prodded by a resurgence of preoedipal and oedipal drives and linked to the newly acquired capacity for hypothetico-deductive reasoning. The optimal transformation we hope for is a stable structure that bears the unique stamp of the individual rather than rigidly mimicking the parents in terms of its function as both a conscience and a set of ideals. The superego system should permit the sublimated expression of the drives and maintain a relative autonomy from external objects.

This highly condensed summary of superego development is intended to illustrate two central principles. First, we see how maturation involves the internalization of parental functions over time. Beginning with the mother removing the aggressive, biting infant from the breast, we end up with a refined unique ethical system in the young adult. The process is time-consuming, gradual, and inextricably intertwined with events occurring along other developmental lines. Second, we are convinced by the many steps during superego development of the potential for multiple points at which parental behaviors might impact on the maturation of this structure.

The classical psychoanalytic view tends to deemphasize the actual events of family life as having an important influence on individual development, as long as the family behavior falls broadly within what is referred to as an "average expectable environment"—that is, in the absence of obvious trauma. Variations in the outcome of development are more likely ascribed to characteristics of the individual. In our present example, severity of the superego might be viewed, classically, as due to a particularly strong aggressive drive which powers the superego with sadism. A family-oriented psychoanalytic view, on the other hand, places great importance on the impact of family interaction on development. Each developmental task in the individual is viewed as cogwheeled by complementary phase-appropriate family behavior in order for that task to be successfully mastered. This family behavior, then, is specifically attuned to the child's current developmental need. A high degree of empathic understanding permits the parents to provide an environment of optimal tension and support that will nourish the efforts of the child to experiment and explore with new and increasingly independent elements of intrapsychic structure. We can see the tentative progressive process at work in Bob's efforts: "I try to take what my parents say more objectively," he says. He sees his change in attitude as both erratic and uneven. His parents respond in a way that is empathic and phase specific. The mother views his statement as a "compliment" to her conscious goal of raising children who think for themselves. The father, in a noncritical way, indicates his awareness that Bob "may not necessarily do what we say." The parents' voluntary willingness to relinquish control involves their tolerance and acceptance of the fact that their youngster will make mistakes and experience temporary failure. Later in the interview, Rick and his father demonstrate this.

Rick: I don't feel oppressed. I know one case in point—I
          believed you advised me to take Latin?
Father: French.
Rick: Okay, French. And I happened to take Spanish, and
          there were no recriminations. I think I should have

taken French now. But he certainly has not used us in any way. . . ."

You will recall that I referred to a family environment of "optimal tension and support." Parents must empathically sense which situations are beyond the grasp of their child's development. Too much anxiety does not stimulate, it paralyzes and retards. Bob's father senses this in the following:

If I were able to say, "Look, would you please *do* this, and let's not discuss this. I think this is very important." I have no *doubt* they would do it. I do it very, very rarely. . . . You know, in an emergency I say, "Look, would you discuss this later but do it now anyhow, just trust me." I have the feeling they would trust me, period. I don't know. I hope I have not often misused this type of authority."

Just as too much anxiety promotes regression, too little takes away a necessary stimulus for the acquisition of new structure. In the case of John Stuart Mill in relation to his father, he experienced too much in some situations and too little in others, resulting in significant impairments in superego formation and in the capacity for initiative. A review of Mill's (1969) statement indicates his sensitive awareness of his father's impact on his development.

I was so much accustomed to expect to be told what to do, either in the form of direct command, or of rebuke for not doing it, that I acquired a habit of leaving my responsibility as a moral agent to rest on my father, my conscience never speaking to me except by his voice. [p. 33]

Mill's fear of his father's rebukes discouraged him from developing a conscience that spoke to him in his own voice. That degree of individuation was so frightening in its consequence of his father's anger that allaying anxiety by not differing from father took precedence over the development of a personal ethical system. At the same time, Mill's father did not permit enough tension in the realm of initiative and self-motivated activity, since he was always imposing new instructions as to what was to occupy his son, a situation which encouraged Mill's continuing dependency such that he "hardly ever did things" of (his) own mere motion, but waited " 'til he told me to do them.' "

What could explain the great disparity between the empathic phase-appropriate behavior of Bob's parents and the striking lack of congruence between John Mill's developmental needs and his father's offerings?

During development there are a wide variety of behaviors required of parents in order to complement the child's phase-specific needs. Parental tasks appropriate for a child of one age are inappropriate at another phase. The constant vigilance and preparedness to intervene in parenting an infant or toddler must give way in the adolescent years to an increasing noninterventionist stance and an acceptance of the teenager's having a life of his own out of the purview of the parent. Similarly, the same parent who must be capable of accepting his child's idealization of him in the early years is required to tolerate empathically the devaluation and frequent rejection characteristic of the adolescent years. Despite the multiplicity of parental behaviors needed at various times, a consistent thread runs through the parental interaction with the child's developmental vagaries—that is, the capacity in the parent to perceive the child as a separate individual with needs, desires, fears, and aspirations unique to that child.

When parents respond to their child's development according to this principle and attune their behavior to a realistic perception of the child's phase-specific developmental needs, we say they are fulfilling the "work function" of the family group (Bion 1961, R. Shapiro and Zinner 1971).

When the work function fails, as it did in Mill's relationship with his father, another important and consistent dynamic factor can be seen to operate. For a clue to this dynamic, let us return to several of our spokespersons and their families.

Keep in mind the following: Bob's mother takes it as a "compliment" to her that her son is developing a mind of his own. Edmond Gosse says that his vexation with his father "was all part of his all too anxious love. He was in a hurry to see me become a shining light, everything that he himself desired to be, yet with none of his shortcomings." Hal, the teenage inpatient, states that his father "takes me and my sister and brother and pretty soon he loses the sense of value from himself."

In seeing these parents along a dimension—Bob's mother, Gosse's and Hal's fathers—there is a progression of involvement of their child's development with the parent's self-esteem system. In increasing degrees, these children—Bob, Gosse, and Hal—are perceived as narcissistic extensions of their parents. It is interesting that this phenomenon does not seem to impair significantly the work function of Bob's family. This is true because his mother takes pride—that is, feels personally enhanced—*because* Bob is following a normal timetable of development. Problems could arise should Bob depart from this timetable because mother's affirmation of herself as worthwhile *does* depend so much on her son's following a timely progression. The narcissistic investments of Gosse's and of Hal's fathers are far more problematic. Each of them sees his son not as a differentiated and separate person, but rather as an extension of himself. In Gosse's case, this is only a partial situation. His father's blurred perception of his son was limited to certain areas. The region of distorted self–object differentiation in the father cited here pertains to the son as an extension of the father's grandiosity. He strives for his son to achieve the perfection that eludes him and that he requires for the affirmation of his own self-esteem. He loses his capacity to empathize with his son as a person with his own strengths, weaknesses, and aspirations. As a result, he is impatient with and intolerant of any deviation from the "divine mission" in the ministry that the son is intended to fulfill. Operationally, this meant not permitting Edmund to play with peers, to play at all, or to read fiction, and totally ignoring his son's sexuality. At the same time there was a great deal of physically expressed love and affection and considerable shared laughter and companionship within the Gosse family, but always within the confines of rigid religious prescriptions.

In Hal's case, the area of impaired self–object differentiation in the father was much more global. In numerous areas of self-esteem, especially, Hal was used by his father as an object to either affirm or invalidate the father's worth. As Hal says, "He makes the kids his life. If they fuck up, he fucks up." The notion of the father making the kids his life conveys the degree to which the father perceives his children as extensions of himself rather than as separate individuals.

You will note that the sequence in which I have presented these children conveys the impression that the child's developmental outcome is a function of the degree to which the parent is able to perceive the child as a separate entity and to behave accordingly. This implication is intentional. Although the sequences do not provide proof, they are illustrative of our findings: that the severity of deviation from normal development is in direct proportion to the depth and breadth of the parent's use of the child as an extension of himself. At one end of the spectrum, Bob generally hewed the line of successful development. He was affected by some not uncommon problems, however, having to do with guilt over falling short of very high standards of achievement. This was certainly related to the extent to which his success was to echo and affirm parental self-esteem and aspirations of perfection. At the other end of the spectrum, Hal is severely impaired in the acquisition of internal sources of self-esteem. He longs for the "certain foundation" that will prevent his utter devastation whenever he gets "dropped or jilted."

Heretofore, I have concentrated upon dyadic relationships—one parent and one child—because of the nature of the clinical material I have presented. In fact, the principles refer to the family as a whole. We find that within the family there are *shared* perceptions of the individual members, of their relationships with one another, and of the family's relations with the outside world (R. Shapiro and Zinner 1971). Again, we employ Bion's terminology (1961) in calling these shared family perceptions and fantasies "unconscious assumptions." Thus when we find that the family, as a system, is functioning in such a way as to encourage the progressive psychological development of its individual members, we refer to it as "a work group." In contrast, when unconscious fears and fantasies predominate and assert primacy over developmental requirements, we say that the family is functioning at a "basic-assumption" level.

Shared unconscious assumptions within the family lead to perception and behavior that is phase-inappropriate and inhibitory to mastery of a child's developmental tasks. What is the origin of these assumptions, and how are they communicated? The answer lies in the ways in which parents have failed to master similar tasks within their own families of origin. Hal's and Gosse's fathers' failures to achieve stable intrapsychic narcissistic structures led to reenactments with both sons of the same developmental disturbances. Perception of Edmund as imperfect or of Hal as a "fuck up" are shaped by parental perceptions of themselves and *their* parents during parallel phases of their own development. Who Edmund is, who Hal is, and what their actual capacities are, are colored by the experiences of an earlier generation.

The psychological mechanism that determines parental perceptions in basic-assumption functioning is called "projective identification." Parents project an aspect of themselves onto their children and then relate to them according to that perception. If what is projected is one side of an intrapsychic conflict, then inner conflict becomes an interpersonal struggle, in this case, between parent and child. In place of anxiety experienced in a state of intrapsychic conflict, there is anger and recrimination in a relationship between two people. For many individuals, interpersonal conflict is more tolerable than inner anxiety, because the source of pain is externalized—that is, experienced as being outside the self. We know this phenomenon as "scapegoating," in which "bad" projections within group members are located within an individual who is then ostracized from the community. Both Hal's and Gosse's fathers' mollified their own internal pain by projecting their imperfections and failures onto their sons.

Troubled families are characterized by the *collusion* of family members with projections that are spread about the group. Because of their dependency and immature psychic structure, children are particularly vulnerable to internalizing parental perceptions of them, however distorted. Beyond that, there may be certain gratifications associated with accepting a parental projection distorted by parental projective identification. Adolescent strivings for autonomy are fitful even in the normal course of development, as Bob has so aptly described. There is an experience of loss and mourning associated with relinquishing dependent ties. One patient described her mother's efforts to keep her at home as "like holding candy out to a baby." It is hard work to take the initiative, and if Mill's father was always there to direct his course, this certainly interacted with Mill's own regressive passive tendencies to produce his "habit of backwardness, of waiting to follow the lead of others." These collusive forces, then, indicate that the adolescent—at least—must be viewed as an active participant in his own developmental failings, not merely as a victim of parental misperceptions.

At this point, I would like to enliven the concept of family unconscious assumptions by talking about Barbara, a 19-year-old girl who was hospitalized after a suicide attempt during her second year at college. Her parents' marriage was described in Chapter 9 (Zinner 1976). In the following excerpt from a conjoint family therapy session, the mother is furious because Barbara greeted her coolly when she walked into Barbara's room shortly before the session. Barbara had been talking to her friend, Linda, and had asked her mother to wait outside until she finished her conversation. The mother goes on to vent her hurt and rage at a number of perceived rejections by Barbara. Note especially the underlying assumptions expressed by the mother that govern the family's response to Barbara's independent activity.

Mother: [crying] You haven't liked me for a hell of a long time. I thought we used to be so close. I really did. I thought you were the closest one of all of them to me. I felt closer to you than to anybody. And for the whole past year. And then you said, "Well, I didn't come home for Thanksgiving last year." Well, you did come home for Thanksgiving. Or no, didn't you? No, you didn't. And I wanted to straighten that out. You had come home two weeks before with five other kids for the demonstration downtown. Of course you didn't come back two weeks later; it costs a hell of a lot of money.

Dr. R.: You felt the closeness to Barbara. What is that?

Mother: I don't know. She was just such a wonderful kid [crying]. And such an easy child to love, if I just had something to hate 'cause she's always been my pet. And it's all gone and I don't know where it's gone. And I don't think it's on me.

Barbara: I don't think it has gone. I think you're assuming that it has.

Mother: Well, okay.

Barbara: And then I have to prove it to you, that I do care about you.

Mother: So when you walk in a room you say, "Oh, hello."

Dr. R.: Barbara, get over your tears now and tell your mother what you're thinking also.

Barbara: Well, I think back to when we started into family therapy. Your response to my being in the hospital was this was something personal that I had done to the family. Uh . . . I remember specifically when you felt it was because of your having to miss art lessons to pick me up at Smith, having to revamp your whole schedule, you know, to come in for family therapy. And things like you told me not to smoke marijuana, but I went ahead and did it anyway. Taking all these things that I'd done, you know, really personally. Like my whole life has been to hurt you. Well, this immediately makes me feel I've got to prove that this isn't so.

Dr. Z.: You also felt unloved, though, by your mother.

Barbara: Yeah. I felt very hurt, if my mother, you know, looks at an attempted suicide in terms of missing an art lesson. And since then I have felt bitter, because you look as if my presence here and everything I've done has been designed to hurt you, which isn't the case.

Dr. Z.: But now that your mother says it differently, though, what do you feel about what she just said?

Barbara: In a sense, you know, I've known it all along. I've felt it.

Dr. R.: Felt what?

Barbara: Felt, you know, that mother did have very strong feelings toward me. And did feel very close. And I guess part of what's happening now is that, you know, I have felt very close to you all too. In order to get out from underneath that presence, stepping out on my own, it ends up being taken as a slap in the face, which it's not meant to be. But it's hard for both of us. And yet when I see you, I still feel in some way, I have to demonstrate how much I love you or something, to an extent which will satisfy you in terms of your strong feelings toward me. But you're working on the assumption that I don't like you.

Mother: That's what seems to come across. And I think so far as breaking away. . . .

Dr. R.: Do you feel it comes across now? What are you experiencing now as . . . as she talks to you?

Mother: Sort of an intellectual exercise.

This excerpt illustrates the failure of the work function in a family, and the preeminence of behavior dominated by unconscious assumptions. Barbara's mother's rage is evoked by Barbara's involvements with others outside the family and with her movement away from what mother had perceived as the "closest" relationship of all. Barbara is burdened with guilt for seeming to be such an unloving person, and she is caught in a dilemma of having to demonstrate her love at the expense of her own autonomy. Knowing about adolescent development, we would say that Barbara's acts of separation were phase-appropriate. Her mother reacts quite differently, however. Barbara's cool "hello" and her not coming home for Thanksgiving are experienced by her mother as a devastating rejection of her and of the family. The underlying assumption at work is that Barbara must be leaving the family because she hates it, not because she is growing up.

Summary

I have described a continuum of individuation in adolescence. I have posited a relationship between the successful completion of this developmental task and certain attitudes and behaviors within the family. If adolescent individuation is experienced as a threat to brittle parental self-esteem, adolescent development will be impeded and perhaps arrested. On the other hand, when parental self-esteem is enhanced by adolescent individuation, the achievement of that task is greatly facilitated.

18

The Use
of Concurrent Therapies:
Therapeutic Strategy
or Reenactment

JOHN ZINNER, M.D.

The structure of psychotherapeutic treatment involves
ground rules and both explicit and implicit mutual expectations of and limitations upon the relationship of patient
and therapist. The totality of this structure, or "frame," as
Langs (1976) elaborates upon it, offers a secure and
consistent environment in which highly sensitive, private
feelings and fantasies can be expressed and explored
without the threat of actualizing the feared consequences.

ESTABLISHING A FRAME

A therapy structure provides more than security, however. The frame itself becomes an area of struggle, in
which the patient's effort to change the therapist into the
actual object and grantor of childhood wishes is met by the

therapist's efforts to enable the patient to change and grow in psychological maturity. Once the presenting crisis has simmered down and a treatment relationship has been established, much of the work of psychoanalytic psychotherapy centers around the patient's efforts to bend the frame, and his frustration at the therapist's unyielding adherence to the agreed-upon structure. This area of tension and struggle provides the grist and generates the emotions necessary for effective exploration, interpretation, and, ultimately, growth. In a situation in which the patient seeks constant critical approval and praise from the therapist, it is the very maintenance of empathic neutrality by the therapist that generates the tension and strong emotions in the patient that serve to stimulate exploration of the patient's lack of a solid internal source of self-esteem and dependence on affirmation from without. Should the therapist alter his role and accede to the imperative to provide approval and praise, the therapeutic tension is not generated, and it becomes the therapist who changes rather than the patient. In modifying an agreed-upon neutral posture, the therapist actually *becomes* the external source of self-esteem, and no impetus develops for the patient to build an inner self-esteem system relatively autonomous of others.

The frame of the treatment is equally important in conjoint family therapy. We establish ground rules about attendance of all members at all sessions whenever possible. Not infrequently we will enter our waiting room to discover a family member absent without advance discussion. The following week another member will not show. We soon realize that it is characteristic in such a family that members do not function as a team but rather capriciously go off separately, leaving their kin to shoulder the burden of whatever task is at hand. We feel the tension inherent in this family's effort to bend the frame. Do we meet with the family when there are no-shows? If we alter our own ground rules, then the conjoint therapy becomes more like the family; that is, *we* change rather than the family. On the other hand, if we do not permit the frame to be bent, then the pressure remains within the family group to get all of its members to the appointment. Once the group is assembled, the family is changing. Thus, in psychoanalytic psychotherapy, structure and function are inseparable. It behooves the therapist to ensure that the treatment program recommended serves the emotional growth of the patient and does not perpetuate the already-existing problem.

The establishment of a truly salutary framework seems difficult enough in the therapy of a single individual with a single therapist; the task becomes considerably more complex when a patient is to be seen in more than one therapy at the same time and by more than one therapist for the different therapies. The vulnerability of the structure to the patient's regressive imperative is multiplied. A therapist may deal with the problem by avoiding it altogether—that is, by not participating in a program in which the patient is in more than a single therapy. Such an attitude may be held by a psychoanalytically trained therapist who is convinced that the transference is contaminated by the patient's being concurrently treated in conjoint family therapy. The converse, negative view can be heard from the family systems therapist who rejects any concurrent individual therapy because it is thought to single out and label one patient as the problem, thereby indicating that responsibility is not shared by the entire family.

CONSEQUENCES OF TREATMENT DESIGN

Let us define concurrent therapy as contemporaneous use (1) of conjoint family and individual psychotherapy or (2) of several conjoint therapies within the same family, such as a combination of couples treatment along with the conjoint therapy of the whole family. I have been impressed with the diversity of impacts of such therapeutic combinations. On the one hand, I have seen the addition of concurrent conjoint family sessions provide just the right impetus to energize the sluggish and unrewarding individual treatment of one of the family members. On the other hand, I have observed therapists in states of despair over the disastrous results of combined therapies they have concocted. In such cases, the therapist, feeling like a co-conspirator, burdened with secrets he cannot share, is torn by conflicting loyalties to those he is treating. Sometimes a combined treatment may be a crucial ingredient of a successful outcome, while at other times, the concurrent therapy may lead to a worsening or perpetuation of the problems it was designed to overcome. I will try to make some sense out of this disparity.

REQUIREMENTS FOR SUCCESS

Concurrent therapies that are successful derive from a strategy carefully designed by the therapist and based on a thoughtful formulation of the dynamic problem at both the individual and group level. The choice of a particular combination of therapies is aimed at selected interpersonal or intrapsychic trouble spots where it is felt that intervention will lead toward the fulfillment of these two joint goals:

1. to enable the family group to become once again a resource to its membership,
2. to remove the blocks to each member's further emotional development.

Furthermore, the selection must be parsimonious; that is, although a variety of combinations of treatment might make theoretical sense, a choice has to be made as to which will be most efficient in accomplishing the task. After all, it is generally not feasible to have every family member in individual treatment in addition to conducting a conjoint therapy for every group and subgroup. Some therapists try to avoid the necessity of making such choices by deciding to alter membership of the group on a week-to-week basis, a practice I consider to be of dubious value because it substitutes changing the external structure for arriving at a solution from within the group.

THE THERAPEUTIC RATIONALE

In psychoanalytic family psychotherapy, both the individual and the group are considered simultaneously. The individual is seen to deal with intrapsychic conflict by projecting conflicted aspects of the self onto the family or onto certain members. The projection of unwanted aspects of the self leads to conflict among family members because a struggle that was previously internal to one member has now become externalized. Through the mechanism of projective identification, the intrapsychic conflict now becomes interpersonal. Furthermore, vulnerable family members become burdened by what has been projected onto them so that they may, in fact, become *like* the projections at the expense of the development of their own identities. Concurrent individual and conjoint therapies are particularly suited for a family whose members are adversely affected by projective identification. A central function of the conjoint portion of the treatment is to facilitate the reinternalization of members' projections. This results in the reduction of interpersonal conflict within the family group, but it enhances individual intrapsychic conflict by virtue of the taking back of unwanted parts of the self that had been previously externalized into the group. The selective inclusion of individual psychotherapy along with the conjoint work permits these individual reinternalized unconscious conflicts to have a more detailed exploration in a one-to-one relationship between affected family member and therapist.

Another justification for concurrent psychotherapy is the need for the maintenance of appropriate boundaries within the family. Frequently, where there is a problem with the whole family group, there is also significant marital difficulty between the parents. Although it is important and appropriate to discuss in the conjoint family sessions the perception and impact of the marital conflict on the family, it is also fitting that the parents have the opportunity to work out their problems in meetings that do not include the children. It is likely that the anxieties of the children have been generated in the first place by the spilling over of tension from within the marital dyad into the family as a whole. Combining conjoint family meetings with couple therapy frequently results in a rapid reduction of anxiety and symptomatic behavior in the children as they feel relieved of the necessity of mediating their parents' difficulties.

Thus far I have given two important rationales for the use of combined therapies. The first indication involved the need to reinternalize projective identifications and to work them through intrapsychically. The second indication involved the consideration of appropriate boundaries within the family, so that the membership boundary of the therapy be selected to be appropriate to the problem requiring attention. This discussion of the indications for concurrent treatment would not be complete without mention of the potential benefit derived from the interactive effect of the combination. The whole surpasses the sum of its parts, as each therapy generates insights and activity to stimulate the other concurrent treatment. For example, new perspectives gained by the disturbed adolescent in his individual therapy are introduced into the family group sessions for experimentation. Family reactions, both favorable and unfavorable, to more age-appropriate adolescent behavior can be assessed, interpreted, and modified.

BENDING OF THE FRAME

Given this potential for benefit, why is it that concurrent psychotherapies may also come to grief? Combinations of therapies may come into being not as part of a thoughtful, customized strategy, but rather as an act of wantonly bending the frame. The problematic combination evolves when the family changes the therapy into something that is more like the family's own pathological self. In the following example, the therapist who colludes with such an imperative begins to feel like a member of the family, as her treatment program becomes shaped by the very family forces that she is trying to influence.

Therapist Ms. A. experienced rough sledding in her conjoint work with the B. couple as Mr. and Mrs. B. found it difficult to open up with each other around their vulnerable areas, their wishes, and their fears. Each of the B.'s suggested that it would be easier to speak with Ms. A. alone, without the spouse present. Rather than analyzing the resistance to and fears of talking openly as a couple, Ms. A. added individual meetings with each partner to the treatment regimen. In these individual meetings, Mr. and Mrs. B. each tried to establish an exclusive confidential relationship with Ms. A. by divulging secrets that Ms. A. could not feel comfortable sharing with the absent spouse. As a consequence, in the conjoint sessions, Ms. A. became part of the failure of open communication because of the knowledge to which she was privy but could not share. Then, instead of two, there were three people in the room with fears of talking openly. Unless the therapist can find a way out of that dilemma, the therapy has lost its viability.

An interesting situation occurred when a combination of individual psychotherapy and conjoint family treatment took place with two family members. With one member, the combined therapy was part of a carefully formulated treatment plan. For the second family member, the manner in which the combined treatment evolved was an interesting example of an effort to bend the frame. A description of this case elucidates the distinction I make between concurrent therapy as a treatment strategy and, in contrast, as a reenactment of pathological relating.

Mark Green, at 15, asked to see a psychiatrist in his junior year of high school because of severe and persistent anxiety. The first session revealed that he was in an anxious, obsessional state, fearing that his life was at the point of permanent ruin because his grade point average seemed not sufficient to gain him entry into an Ivy League college. He had an explicit fantasy that his economic and physical survival depended on acquiring such an education. The best college would lead him to the best graduate business school, which, in turn, would make him a wealthy executive. Only as a wealthy executive would he feel safely self-sufficient and finally achieve a life free of profound worry.

The more anxious he became, the harder it was for him to concentrate. Soon his grades were falling, and Mark realized his worst fears. At the same time, on the home front, Mark was engaged in a bitter struggle with his parents, who were quite restrictive, he felt, in regulating his social activities in the form of rigid curfews and limitations of where he could go with friends on weekends. He had recently been grounded, to which he responded with intense feelings of rage and helplessness. He felt rejected by his parents, who, he was convinced, preferred his younger brother, Sam, as their "perfect little angel." Mark felt most controlled by, and therefore most angry at, his father, who he claimed spent no time with him alone in any shared activity. Mark said that his father had rejected him in recent years, although they had previously attended some sporting events and used to play together.

As part of the evaluation, Mr. and Mrs. Green, Mark, and Sam attended a conjoint family session. Mark and his father were at each other's throats in arguments filled with rage. Mr. Green castigated Mark for his sadistic treatment of Sam, for not doing his chores, and for not wanting to participate in family activities. Mark argued that he hated Sam for his parents' partiality toward the brother and accused his father of not wanting to give him things or spend time with him. Mr. Green countered that he didn't want to give Mark things or spend time with him precisely *because* of Mark's arguing about his unfair treatment of him compared with Sam. Mr. Green called this "the Mark shit."

In a subsequent individual evaluative interview, Mark explained his intense argumentativeness. He compared himself to children in a story who created their own reality, which led to their becoming unaffected by their own parents. He said he insulated himself from the hurt of parental rejection by being his "own controller"; that is, he could get "self-satisfaction" by "proving" through his own arguing that he was right and his parents were wrong. This protective device stabilized his self-esteem, which was unreliable because his parents, by their criticism, had failed to affirm his worth. He recalled how, when he began to experience the deterioration of his relationship with his parents at 8 years of age, he built himself a fortress within his closet where he would hide.

Based on the clinical data, the therapist devised a treatment program, which included individual weekly psychotherapy for Mark as well as weekly conjoint sessions for the entire family. The therapist would conduct both forms of psychotherapy. The problem clearly required intervention at both the group and individual level. Within Mark there were significant blocks in the evolution of his self-esteem system. Because of the failure to find affirmation of his worth in the school setting, as well as at home, he was developing a private world in which he grew increasingly remote from reality—where his brittle sense of worth could find a confirming echo. Meanwhile, many of his own negative self-images were being projected onto Sam, whom Mark had come to see as "the curse of the earth." The step-by-step blending of Mark's private grandiosity as an unrecognized 4.0 student, with his devalued self-image projected into others, required both the time and private attention available in individual work. On the other hand, the salutary effects of individual therapy would be undermined by the persisting failure of the family to confirm Mark's essential worth and to provide the necessary phase-appropriate echo to his aspirations. For example, his wish to spend time with his friends was taken by his parents as a rejection of the family. This feeling is parallel to Mark's sense that his father found him not worthwhile since he seemed to spend no time with him.

The concurrent therapy recommendation was accepted, and symptomatic improvement in both the adolescent and the family occurred rather rapidly. The sequence of this change is of interest. Mark quickly developed an idealizing transference with the therapist, which served to stabilize his self-esteem. That is, Mark began to value himself more as a consequence of being in a relationship with an admired adult. As a result of his enhanced self-esteem, Mark had less need for his own defensive argumentativeness in the conjoint sessions. He opened up, then, to his parents about his worries and his pessimism for the future, and expressed a longing for a relationship with his father in a more poignant manner than he had in his previous demands for compensation through parental punishment of Sam. The vociferous conflict within the family sessions began to yield to instances of parental empathy for Mark and generated new clinical data.

Mr. Green acknowledged that he knew little about how to *be* a father to Mark because his own father seemed so unavailable to him. Mark's paternal grandfather had been poor, worked long hours, and seemed to have no personality independent of the grandmother, for whom the grandfather was a mere "rubber stamp." Mr. Green became aware that he experienced Mark as rejecting him much as his own father had, and he realized he was retaliating in kind. The rejection he felt from Mark was in Mark's not wanting to do things that Mr. Green wanted to do, such as travel and concerts. Thus Mark's father was reenacting with Mark his relationship with his own father through the mechanism of projective identification, at various times experiencing himself as his father or his son.

Important parallels evolved in Mr. Green's transference to me as well. While he was generally respectful of me at a distance, he explicitly indicated that he saw me as withholding myself from him, not providing guidance, answers, or support. Thus I was experienced as the depriving father and son.

In the family sessions, episodes of sharing and of empathy were often punctuated by recurrence of outbursts, particularly between Mr. Green and Mark. The extreme sensitivity of each to the potential for criticism by the other led to a tenuous situation in which an effort to reach out by one would be misinterpreted by the other, and recriminations and retaliations would ensue. Mark and Sam noted that Mr. Green seemed to have no opinions of his own and that, like their paternal grandfather, he merely rubber-stamped their mother's views of family decisions. This observation, together with his growing awareness of the relevance of his own childhood experience to his current relationship with Mark, led Mr. Green to consider individual treatment for himself.

One day, in a surly and aloof mood, Mr. Green announced in the family session that he had entered into individual treatment with a psychotherapist. Rather than discussing such a planned action with me in the family group, he had sought out the recommendation of a female friend who was a "mother earth" and would certainly suggest a supportive therapist.

The individual therapist with whom Mr. Green had contracted was not psychoanalytically oriented. His method seemed to be to provide unconditional explicit support of Mr. Green's world view without exploring its roots. He answered Mr. Green's questions and gave him advice on how to interact with his family. Furthermore, the new therapist did not seek to make contact with me at the outset to see whether his involvement would enhance or complicate the psychotherapy in which Mr. Green was already engaged.

The introduction of Mr. Green's psychotherapy into our mix was part of a fascinating and problematic reenactment. Bolstered by his good father-therapist, Mr. Green began a rebellion against me and Mrs. Green. He raged against us frequently, regarding us as "dry holes," the people on whom he was most dependent, providing nothing for his needs. He was often angered by my observations, remarking sharply, "I'm sick of you. I don't get what I want from you. What I get from you I don't want." On the other hand, he said of his individual therapist, "He is the only person I've met who will understand."

An additional important phenomenon was that in his anger he began to lump me and his wife together. In one session he saw me as "eating up" Mrs. Green's viewpoint "like it was chocolate cake." This picture of me as having no mind of my own independent of his wife's was exactly the one he had had of his father. His father, he felt, totally withheld himself from him and spoke to him only through his mother. Thus Mr. Green had, in his self-initiation of his individual therapy, re-created his own family constellation. He was the child of the two "dry holes"—his wife and me. The idealized good parents were his new therapist and the "mother earth" who had recommended him. Mr. Green's angry rebellion intensified and began to spill over into some further acting out against our conjoint sessions in the form of lateness.

I interpreted the split I felt he was making between his two therapists such that the other appeared all good while I seemed all bad. I requested and was given his permission to discuss the situation with his therapist in order to hear his perspective on the problem. The other therapist and I discussed the state of the treatment, and I explained the split that was occurring and the problems that it was generating. Needless to say, being the good one, the other therapist had not experienced a problem with the therapy. However, Mr. Green's therapist was responsive and did grasp the transference configuration and the split that was occurring. Not long after this discussion, the escalation of rage and acting out toward Mrs. Green and me began to reverse directions. It appeared that Mr. Green's therapist was providing less advice and answers and leaving Mr. Green "to figure more things out" for himself.

The resolving of the split transference generated new and important material: Mr. Green's rebellion against me and Mrs. Green was also an effort at self-healing. He revealed how punitive his parents had been with him. Their usual sanction was to frighten him into submission by playing on his fears of being cast off. At an early age, for example, his mother had told him that she would send him to reform school if he didn't finish his meal—and finish he did. He realized that he carried over this punitiveness in the restrictions he placed upon Mark—an identification with the aggressor. It was a revelation to Mr. Green to be told that he actually envied and admired Mark's rebellion against him because that is what he wished he had done with his parents instead of permitting himself to be intimidated. Thus, Mr. Green's attacks on Mrs. Green and myself, while bolstered by his good therapist, represented an enactment of his childhood wish to revolt against the "absolute authority" of his own parents. As this identification with Mark became conscious and explicit, the relationship between father and son dramatically improved, and the two once more began to spend time together in shared activities.

As Mark was applying for college two years after his therapy began, Mr. Green was tearful in a conjoint session. He said that he would like it if Mark would stay home for another year because they were getting along well now and he had "lost" six years with his son. Mark responded that he didn't want to hurt his father's feelings, but that the relationship with his father couldn't be his highest priority. His focus had to be on work and eating—work in order to give him the best chance to go to the college of his choice, and eating to ensure his survival. Mark said that although he still feels some urgency about college and about the world, he figures he's grown up enough to ensure his own security.

The complex of concurrent therapies described here illustrates the distinction between a planned treatment strategy and an impulsive bending of the frame in the service of a reenactment. Although it is fortunate in this case that the reenactment could be explored and the integrity of the frame restored, the outcome could just as easily have been the premature interruption of the family treatment. The final judgment as to whether combined therapies have enriched the treatment or perpetuated the problematic past rests on how carefully the therapists have thought through the indications and implications of such an intervention.

19

The Re-creation of the Family in the Mind of the Individual Therapist and the Re-creation of the Individual in the Mind of the Family Therapist

ROBERT WINER, M.D.

INDIVIDUAL THERAPY

Reality and Fantasy

In individual treatment which is much concerned with fantasy, subjectivity, and internality, the therapist needs to discover and hold in his mind a concept of the patient in his factual present and past, including the relationship to his family. And in family treatment, in which factuality, objectivization, and externality predominate, the therapist must be able to imagine the individual family members' private lives behind their public faces.

In individual therapy, we ultimately want to understand

1. what the trauma was,
2. how the patient experienced it,

3. how he elaborated it defensively and in fantasy,
4. what impact that elaboration had on his development,
5. how that structure of meanings was altered by further experience.

The discovery of historical reality is in itself therapeutically meaningless until it can be brought within the patient's sphere of responsibility. Only for his inner world can the patient be totally responsible. As McDougall (1978) wrote, "psychoanalysis can do nothing to modify the effects of catastrophic events if they cannot also be experienced as omnipotent fantasies. . ." (p. 250).

Let me illustrate the complexity of the problem with a brief example from the psychoanalysis of a young man.

When the patient was 13 years old, his father died after many years of chronic, debilitating illness that had ostensibly been concealed from the patient and his siblings. In the analysis, it became clear that the patient, although a successful young professional with an active social life, was suffering from a variety of inhibitions in both his work and his relationships with women. Consciously, he felt proud to be self-reliant. Unconsciously, he believed that he was not entitled to live a full life. In addition to having no memories of his father's illness, he maintained an idealized, thoroughly unambivalent image of him. In the course of the analytic work, it became apparent that as a child he had been aware of his father's condition and had felt burdened by it, much as he now felt burdened by his analyst, and that he had even wished for the ordeal to end. His guilt about those death wishes had kept the entire conflict repressed and had caused him to feel unentitled to his own life.

The reality he needed to reclaim was that he had wished, at moments, for his father's death, that he had in part felt relieved by it after a time of mourning, and that he may have played a small part in its ultimate timing by engaging in roughhousing with his father on the day of his death. He also needed to recognize that despite his death wishes, he had also very much not wanted his father to leave him. Unable to make those distinctions as a child, he had repressed the illness and his ambivalence, leaving himself with faceless guilt. Now reclaiming the experience in a new context of meaning, in the analytic transference, he could potentially assume responsibility for contributing in small measure to the death of a father whom he both loved and felt burdened by. The illness and death were tragic circumstances of fate beyond his control, and his unconscious hostility, in that sense, was beside the point. This is a particularly difficult truth for children to bear, and they often, as this patient did, find it more tolerable to feel guilty and retain their personal illusion of omnipotence than to feel helpless.

The Therapist's Experience of Subjective and Objective Stance

What makes it so difficult for us as individual therapists to discover historical and current reality is that we are, of necessity, captives of the patient's subjective experience. At the same time, this is what makes discovery possible in individual therapy, and especially in psychoanalysis. At the center of therapeutic technique is a movement back and forth between subjective and objective stance. Let me describe this oscillation first subjectively, in terms of the therapist's experience, and then objectively, in terms of the theory of treatment.

Therapists' reflections during the therapeutic hour range between subjective and objectifying thoughts. Objectifying thoughts occur during the active mode of listening, in moments when we sit up straight and try to sort out what's been going on, or when we try to connect the present and the past, or the transference and the marriage, or when we strain to consider what Kernberg or Mahler had to say that might be relevant to the problem at hand. Subjective thoughts include experience in the areas of empathy, reverie, and countertransference. I might find my thoughts drifting to what my wife said at breakfast, or what Sylvia Plath said. Our poignantly prized discoveries during the conduct of therapy invariably come from these latter areas. In these moments we feel the therapeutic quickening.

This is intrinsic to the dyadic nature of individual therapy. The original dyad knows only a shared subjectivity. McDougall (1978) observed that "a baby's earliest reality is his mother's unconscious" (p. 251). His mother, in her empathic responsiveness, gives meaning to his cries, *creates* their meaning. That we feel moved more by our subjective discoveries (or, aptly, creations) than by our deliberative insights does not repudiate formal thought; the two modes of experience support each other. It does, however, underscore the developmental root of individual therapy in the mother–infant communion.

Part of the appeal of our vocational choice is the opportunity to move into and reemerge from similar states of union. Balint (1959) has observed that parts of the external world that are felt to be firm, resistant, and sharply contoured are called by a somewhat aggressive name, *object*, whereas parts that are not solid, do not resist much, and have no real contours are called by nonaggressive names such as *substance* or *substrate*, which link to *subject*, denoting ourselves, or *matter*, which derives from a root denoting *mother*. We move between the compelling and fearsome nonobjective world of subject and mother and the arousing and dangerous world of objects. Therapy is driven by the fantasies of primary union and of objective encounter.

The Structure of Individual Treatment: Movement from Subjectivity to Objectivity

I will now turn to the theory of individual treatment, specifically focusing on psychoanalysis. Patients reliably re-create their inner object worlds in their current lives, recruiting family members, friends, and co-workers to take part in the staging of their internal dramas. The inner object world is largely unconscious. The process of its re-creation is also mainly unconscious. The patient would say, "These things just happen to me."

The strategy of psychoanalysis is to create a situation in which the analyst becomes the patient's primary object of dependency in a safe and permissive relationship. In this context, patients are encouraged to make reclamations from two directions. First, they are helped to view the circumstances of their lives as events they largely participated in creating. A vivid understanding of family dynamics will be quite useful to the analyst here—in understanding, for example, just how the patient's wife got to be so surly. Second, they are to reclaim the unconscious, to bring the ghosts of the internal object world into daylight (Loewald 1960). The patient must come to know this, not as a static inventory, but in all its dramatic, haunting intensity. This happens as abandoned desires come to life again in the space between patient and analyst, creating the transference–countertransference neurosis. Stated another way, the patient's private subjectivity is dramatized in the shared subjectivity of the transference relationship. This is a form of transitional relatedness, described by Winnicott (1951), in which the analyst does not ask the patient whether the desire was created by him or given to him; it is accepted without question for the moment in the space between them. The analyst functions (primarily unconsciously) as a container for the patient's projective identifications, processing them in the context of his own development and therapeutic motivation.

But the analyst must also ultimately understand the forces that underlie the construction of the internal world. That world was formed, not prehistorically as it seems, given the nature of repression, but rather out of the patient's actual life, experienced under the sway of the feelings and motives then present in him, and distorted to meet defensive requirements. The analyst now more wittingly moves back and forth between subjective and objectifying modes, aided in this by his ability to re-create in his mind the possible childhood family experiences of the patient, prior to their defensive distortion. In the act of interpreting, the analyst speaks from outside their shared subjectivity as he objectifies the patient's experience for him, objectifying both the internal world and the distortions of the actual world. In so doing, he calls upon their suspended, but never lost, separate existence as analyst and patient sharing a treatment endeavor. Let me stress again that refinding the actual world is not important in and of itself; it is important insofar as it allows the patient to appreciate what he had to distort, how he distorted it, and why the distortion was necessary. Thus the tide in psychoanalysis (and to a degree in all individual psychotherapy) flows from shared subjectivity to objectifying realization. This is uniquely possible because analysis is a dyadic endeavor; I will later argue that in family therapy the tide flows in the opposite direction.

I would like to explore the relationship between subjective and objective reality, and between the therapist's subjective and objectifying stance, by considering the consequences of a circumstance shared by several of my patients—namely, living in the parental bedroom past the nursing stage. Each patient was kept in the bedroom for distinctive reasons. In each case it had a major, unique impact on the patient's development, the reverberations of which are felt in the patient's present life and in the transference–countertransference. I will present the relevant aspects of one of these treatments.

Alice initially requested marital therapy. She complained that her husband was making her miserable by not following his medically imposed diet. Indeed, he seemed quite unconcerned about his health, while she felt tormented by it. I quickly learned that her father had had a long illness and that her mother had kept him alive for ten years by scrupulously monitoring his diet. Alice dreaded the prospect of being in a similar relationship with her husband and yet seemed unconsciously invested in re-creating the depressive tie her parents had had during her adolescence. Depression was an acknowledged long-standing problem for Alice. A brief analysis had been interrupted when her husband took a new job, a move seemingly motivated in part by a refusal to share his wife with an analyst.

I understood that Alice's husband was managing his anxiety about his health by denial. I also understood that the situation represented for her an enactment of an internalized object relationship. During this evaluation I tried to return an ostensible objective conflict into each partner's subjective world, such that the partner had the possibility of taking ownership of it either in marital therapy or in individual treatment. Given that her husband refused any form of treatment and that Alice's substantial depression was a function of far more than the marital conflict, I recommended to Alice that she reenter analysis.

Alice spent the early months of her analysis in drowsy, long silences, content to just be with me, determined to keep me a silent, uncritical, undemanding presence. I discovered that, among other meanings, this was intended to re-create the many evenings in the shared bedroom when she lay on her cot and watched her father work at his desk. It also soon became clear to me that this transference was a defense against a dreaded development in the treatment: coming to terms with her hateful relationship with her mother. Her behavior on the couch was thus overdetermined, reflecting her internalized idealized romance with her father, her internal paralyzing identification with her critical mother, and probably an identification with a brother recently deceased from a mysterious chronic paralyzing illness. When I discovered that she had spent seven years in her parents' bedroom despite the availability of other space in the house, I became curious about why that had been. She hadn't made a great deal of it, but I soon found out that she had resented the infringement on her autonomy. In fact, she became quite a private child, keeping her thoughts and feelings to herself, and savoring special niches she could create for herself in their large home. I recalled to myself the nights when my son, at age 3, ordered me out of his bedroom after I'd finished reading to him, wanting his room to himself. In having this thought, I was reaching for her unconscious anger. I was also, however, engaging with my son in my mind to fill the void left by her annihilating exclusion of me. That her bedroom experience contained both father-longing and privacy-denial was directly discoverable in the transference from my subjective responses at different moments to her silence on the couch.

At the same time, this woman, who had initially been powerfully beguiling in our face-to-face hours, had become remarkably flattened out on the couch. This led me to wonder about the disappearance of Eros, and I started speculating about the effect of presumed primal-scene exposure on her development. From what I could determine, her father had been quite attached to her and might have enjoyed her more than his wife, or so she'd have me believe. Yet she also remembered an unusually lively conversation with her mother in which she was told that she could have her father's top half and mother would get his bottom half. This led me to think that her parents had had sex when they thought her asleep, and that this must have had a significant impact on her. She remembered angering her parents by wetting her bed once; she assumed that she had been responding to parental intercourse, but the anger in the memory was theirs.

I was also preoccupied by an event she thought unimportant. At age 4, she and a friend had set a basement fire which did enough damage to put the family out of the house for three months. I imagined that this was related to the bedroom situation, but I noted that expected memories of her anger, and anger in the transference, were conspicuously absent. "My son has been more aggressive with far less provocation," crossed my mind. These objectifying thoughts, which I am also referring to as my attempt to create her actual family in my mind along with my transference-derived construction of her internalized family, lay dormant for a time.

Her analysis became increasingly difficult, with prolonged silences and resistance to pursuing any topic in depth. If we seemed to be on the track of something in one analytic hour, I could count on her to be elsewhere the next hour. While she did not challenge my interpretations, she also did not work with them.

I found myself feeling irritated with her withholding. It also struck me that she determinedly never had feelings or fantasies about my life outside the office or about my other patients. My irritation turned into a realization that she was systematically destroying all connections in our work together, both of relationship and of meaning. Monday sessions were particularly difficult for her because she had more to destroy than usual: She had to obliterate the weekend interruption, with all its implications about my life away from her. It was in this destruction of connection that her aggression was hidden.

Putting this countertransference discovery together with my objectified thoughts about her family, I speculated that it was specifically the conjugal linkage in her parents' bedroom that she was attacking. In challenging my authority, she was challenging her mother's claiming of prerogative. The father she watched from the cot was kept separate from the father who shared a bed with her mother. Her analyst was not the analyst of other patients.

I now began to hear more about her anger at men. Her rejection of her mother had made her particularly dependent on her father and vulnerable to his depressive withdrawals. Repudiating any identification with her mother, she tried to make herself a phallic extension of her father; this was ultimately unsupportable. Her attack on linkages was also an attack on phalluses as linking organs. Since, from her point of view, she could not have a permanent connection to or identification with me, she systematically attacked my potency by undercutting my efforts to analyze her. No one would have a phallus, and there would be no connections to envy.

My current understanding of Alice's childhood family experience and of her internal object relations is as follows. It seems to me that her father was always somewhat depressed and her mother rather depressed, masochistic, and controlling. Nonetheless, the parents seemed to have found substantial pleasure in their life together, and the mother probably enjoyed her husband more than her children. Alice's internal experience of a forbiddingly cold mother represents both a projection of coldness toward her mother and a disavowal of her mother's sexuality, which evoked Alice's envy and jealousy. Alice's disavowal made it easier to keep her anger at her parents under control, although I suspect it momentarily erupted in the fire setting. Alice is identified with her internal experience of a controlling, masochistic, depressed mother, and she enacts this in the transference. Her depression keeps her aggression at bay, and her anger is expressed in her attacks on linkages.

Once these connections were clearly interpreted to her, Alice became more available for analytic work.

FAMILY THERAPY

Unconscious Aspects of Family Process

Couples and families typically immerse their therapists in the vicissitudes of their current functioning. Therapists get a full dose of objective reality. They hear at length about who did what to whom. Reality drowns out awareness of unconscious aspects of family process. Yet those unconscious aspects determine the reality in ways that can be summarized as follows.

Both husband and wife use the marriage and subsequent family life as theaters in which they can enact their internal object lives and thus create external confirmation of their inner experience. The original casting for the role of marital partner generally results in sufficient fit for the creation of a drama that integrates and externalizes the object worlds of both partners. To the extent that initial fit is missing, each partner's projective identifications, over the days and years, eventually shape the other partner's performance to create an interlocking fit. The children, given their relative plasticity, are easily recruited to fit assigned parts. The children develop their own internal object worlds, which in turn have impact on their parents' functioning. Virtually all of this is unconscious, and the result of these processes is the set of shared unconscious family assumptions that underlie both adaptive and pathological family functioning.

The family tries to get the therapist to take its overt reality as its ultimate reality, thus brushing unconscious motivation under the rug. For example, the mother may point out dramatically to the therapist: "See! My husband's doing it again! He's humiliating our son!" Indeed, the father has just humiliated his son. What this accounting might leave out is the mother's identification of her disparaged self with her impotent son, her need to have her husband humiliate her son so that she can repudiate him, and her disowning her own helplessness by projecting it into her son (where her husband can attack it and where she can defend it, thus creating power for herself by triumphantly showing the world what a jerk he is).

This possibility is not considered because everyone is seized by the force of the moment: The father has just stunningly humiliated his son. In fact, if the therapist tries to formulate such a thought, he will find himself going considerably against the grain of the family's process, which intends to keep the unconscious unconscious. The therapist may even feel in danger of being humiliated. By this time, the father has a stake in his arrogance, the son in his masochism, and the mother in her moral superiority. The shared investment in maintaining this externalization is profound, and it tends to seduce the therapist into playing some complementary part, most obviously by siding with one of the characters. Less obviously, the therapist may maneuver them into ceasing this behavior without understanding it; in so doing, he is agreeing with the mother's view of herself as helpless and incapable of genuinely mastering a conflict. The therapist's best inroad to a subjective appreciation of the conflict is his own felt response: He was himself afraid of being humiliated. Working forward from that point, he may begin to consider the subjective experience of each family member.

The Structure of Family Therapy

That family therapy "feels" different than individual therapy is a consequence of its structure. In going beyond the dyad, it inescapably introduces small-group process, with oedipal elements of jealousy and competition. At one extreme this may result in blatant rivalry to see who will be the therapist's favorite, with members missing sessions to express jealous hurts. The family may exclude the therapist as though they are parents closing the bedroom door on the child. At the other extreme, the rivalry may be absolutely denied as the family forms a quasi-symbiotic idealizing union with the therapist, a defense which may also serve the therapist's oedipal anxieties. The therapist will not intrinsically feel the power invested in him that he experiences in individual therapy, with its dyadic structure. The therapist's potential strength in family therapy is that of the parents' oedipal authority, which feels quite different from that of the nursing mother's omnipotence which is so often experienced in individual therapy. Consequently, the individual therapist feels a particular vulnerability to annihilation and separation anxiety when the treatment is at its full intensity, while the family therapist feels more the threat of castration and parricide. In a more immediate sense, the call the individual therapist feels is to "be with" the patient, while the call on the family therapist is to "fix it." In other words, there is a quality at the heart of individual therapy that corresponds to Balint's "subject," and a quality in family therapy that corresponds to his "object." Objectivization is an oedipal phenomenon; subjectivity is dyadic.

In noting that family therapy has a core oedipal dimension, I am referring to the structural elements of the treatment situation, not to the family dynamics, which may include the entire range of developmental conflicts. What I am suggesting is that whether the family therapist is interpreting separation difficulties or oedipal rivalry to the family, he will feel a core countertransference anxiety that his authority to interpret will not be acknowledged by the family, and that he will thus tend to feel impotent, castrated, or usurped. Analogously, an individual therapist making an interpretation will experience a core countertransference anxiety that the interpretation could rupture his underlying union with his patient. The interpretation is experienced as a fundamental preoedipal separation or annihilation threat.

Movement from Objectivity to Subjectivity

The tide of family therapy moves from objectivization to subjectivity, as the therapist, bombarded with concrete expressions of the historical and current reality of relationships among family members, holds alive in his mind the world of possible meanings. The movement in individual therapy is from being to meaning; in family therapy, from action to meaning. The therapist can pursue meaning only as he is free to imagine meanings.

A couple came to treatment expressing the notion that there should be no privacy in their marriage, that everything, including thoughts and fantasies, should be shared. The wife eventually began a campaign of weight loss, which ceased to progress after she'd lost fifty pounds, half her excess weight. At this point she announced that she wanted to live separately for a while and started looking for roommates. Her husband was beside himself. She stated that her need for separation was not to be taken as criticism of him, although her timid husband, whom she customarily berated for being sexually indifferent, had recently been unpleasantly sexually aggressive.

In the midst of their painful discussion of a marital separation, I had the temerity to ask whether either remembered a dream from the past week. I asked about dreams in order to gain access to the couple's shared unconscious because I was not satisifed with the wife's conscious explanation that she was merely experimenting with independence. The husband told me that he'd dreamed that a man stabbed a woman in the back in the street and that no one came to her defense.

Putting the dream together with other considerations, it seemed to me that the husband, enraged by his wife's breaking their bonds of mutual dependency by her weight loss, was actually feeling murderous toward her, and that the wife was unconsciously fleeing for her life. While this explanation oversimplifies the dream and the current dynamics of their lives, it does create a model for imagining their inner lives, and moves toward elaborating unconscious meanings. Such dreams and other associations create images of the individual in the mind of the family therapist.

The initial vulnerabilities are different in family and individual therapy. In the former, each family member is vulnerable to being embarrassed or shamed by the others; in individual therapy, self-exposure can be controlled. In family therapy, the therapist presents a threat to the current modes of adaptation, which (as is true of all defenses) the family is invested in protecting. Thus the family will initially tend to close ranks and insist that the therapist can enter only on terms unique to that family. The anticipated danger in individual therapy focuses on the fear of the therapist as an omniscient, omnipotent, penetrating wizard, and the patient manages this fear by trying to make the therapist manageable and safe. Thus the family is initially interested in protecting its interactional reality, while the individual protects his subjective autonomy; these become the embarkation points for the treatments.

I will further illustrate these processes by presenting and analyzing my countertransference experience in a family therapy hour. This session took place eighteen months into my work with the Talbotts. The family included the father and mother, both middle-level executives in a large corporation, and their young-adult children Samuel and Kate. Both children had failed in a variety of efforts to succeed at college and in jobs, at times requiring hospitalization. Samuel now lived at home and Kate had recently left the family again, this time to live with a close relative; both were in intensive individual therapy.

The family arrived ten minutes late, and when I greeted them, Samuel was missing. Mrs. Talbott explained that he had warned them that he didn't intend to come. She revealed that she had called Sam's individual therapist during her son's therapy hour that afternoon to raise her concern about this with his therapist. I cringed when I heard about her intrusiveness and yet admired her persistence. Samuel had been complaining in recent family therapy sessions that he wanted these meetings to end, and I felt a mixture of apprehensiveness, mild relief, and resignation facing the prospect that he might be implementing that intention. Moments later, Samuel arrived and informed us that he had been on time and had waited for the rest of the family in his car. He had driven off when they were late but then decided to return. I felt relieved and reprieved. On the whole, I was pleased with my work with this family, despite the children's continuing immobilization. I felt particularly close to Samuel, who was articulate and carried the ball for the Talbotts in the sessions. While I experienced his wish to terminate as a rejection of my efforts, I was also concerned that I might be holding onto him inappropriately, out of my own dependency needs. I thus felt the twin dangers of being too constraining or too rejecting.

Samuel said he hated the family sessions and complained about his sister's resolute silence: "I shouldn't have come, because then Kate would have talked more." He revealed that he had been in a rage during the week and had destroyed "some carpentry" at home, but added that they had managed to get through it and that he didn't want to discuss it further. His father compliantly agreed, "Maybe we should come less often," and Samuel added that that would be a start. I commented ironically, "Where there's death, there's hope," implying my sense that the family's inability to separate was paralyzing its members' development. I tacitly agreed with Samuel's thought that his presence inhibited his sister. Inquiring about the carpentry destruction would have seemed intrusive, since Samuel had declared that problem resolved.

Mr. Talbott said that he was tired of coming, that he was frustrated by his inability to engage his daughter. He said, "We've talked about a lot of substantial and real things with Sam, but much less with Kate." I had become resigned to Kate's silence, experiencing it as a primitive but seemingly indispensable effort to defend herself against her fear of her family's control over her.

Samuel observed, "There's a certain telepathic nature to my relationship with Kate. It's in the whole family—there's a lot of silent monitoring. There was a time when we had a telepathic relationship as kids, but that ended when Kate started to make new friends. It's half and half now. It's probably the same problem I have with other people." He then turned to reflect on his relationship with his father: "I can tell what my father is thinking, and what he thinks I'm thinking. Sometimes he's correct and sometimes he's wrong. I feel I should make the corrections when he's off, but it would upset him, so I sit here and grind my teeth."

I heard Sam's thoughts as consistent with my sense that individuation was experienced as destructive. Mr. Talbott added, "Showing affection can be a reassuring, strengthening thing, or a threat."

Samuel then spoke about his mother: "She's observant, but she doesn't follow what people are seeing or thinking. It's almost as if she just lets it go. If I'm in a depression, my father is sensitive to it and he gets depressed too, which isn't so great. My mother doesn't get involved."

With my understanding guided by my aforementioned countertransference experience, I commented on the family's double-edged problem with attachment. I observed that closeness, while appealing, was soon felt as an interfering imposition, but that its withdrawal felt like rejection, and that as a consequence of this each family member felt anxious when relating to the others. I was acutely aware in this session of both the intensity and the pervasiveness of Samuel's paranoia and the degree to which I blocked out my awareness of his mistrust. Despite the clarity of his communication, and my sense of understanding him, I realized that he was constantly scanning me for hidden meanings and was suspicious of my motivation. Appreciating this felt like a loss to me, because it made me aware of the gap between us, and I realized that I had been defending myself against this sadness by maintaining an illusion of greater intimacy between us. I realized that I had also experienced his mother's mistrust of me at unexpected moments, and had then pushed aside that experience. Kate's mistrust was more evident at the surface, and Mr. Talbott had always seemed inaccessible to me. It had been possible for me to discover my feelings of estrangement and sadness in this hour because the family was functioning in a more differentiated and open manner. Throughout this process of introspection, I found myself moving beyond the surface of their interactional conflicts to sense a core aspect of the family's subjective reality— their pervasive loneliness.

As the session continued, Mrs. Talbott said that Sam had been angry at her for criticizing his cooking in front of relatives: She had said that he needed to increase his repertoire of spaghetti sauces. Samuel argued that his mother had decided that certain people make certain sauces, and that only Kate was given meatballs to use in sauce preparation. He added, "I haven't been given the ingredients since I've been here. She gives me a false identity publicly." While this complaint had unconscious historic validity as a judgment about his mother's constricting view of him, he was also using it defensively to blame her for his stuckness. He caught himself and said, "When I lived with Cathy [a former girlfriend], I was an adult for a while; now I'm in an imploded state. I get to feeling closer to her [his mother] these days, then I get caught off guard. I think I ought to have the capacity to love my family much more fully than I do."

Sounding a bit weary, Mrs. Talbott replied, "I think Sam is showing more of his gentle side. For a long time he's been angry and upset. My children are competing over everything— our time, attention, and love— they're all out measuring."

Mr. Talbott added that a third, better functioning child, Mike, seemed to compete the most, although he felt that he'd disappointed Mike by not helping him more with his career. In a rare moment of differentiation from Samuel, he volunteered, "Sometimes my ideas about Sam make me uncomfortable."

We can hear in these comments toward the end of the session increased self-containment and differentiation in the family members, mixed with moments of sadness.

Both their ability to think about leaving me and my capacity to anticipate the time when I would let go of them facilitated and resulted from their progressive emergence as separate persons in the family.

COLLABORATION

I will close with some brief comments about the problems of collaborative therapies. When discussing with a colleague two related treatments that we are each conducting, I have caught myself feeling appalled by my colleague's awesome naiveté and his capacity to be led on by his patient. Of course it is obvious to me, the objective outsider. I remember that I too may well have a similarly subjective view of my patient. In part, this is a necessary development, reflecting the requirement that I be accessible to my patients, taken over for a time by their subjective realities. Although I need to work my way forward from that absorption, it can equally be a problem if I hold on too tightly to my notion of the objective reality, thus resisting my patient's appeal.

Although collaboration can be enormously helpful to the therapists, it can also interfere with their necessary absorption in their patients' subjective reality. In other words, collaboration can give an oedipal cast to individual treatment by introducing a third party (the other therapist) who has, in part, competing interests. This shift may be useful or interfering. At times in such situations, the key process may be the therapists' work at integrating their collaboration, with the patients as accessories and the therapeutic outcome hanging in the balance. In such a situation, the dynamics between the therapists bear the structure of the conflict between their patients as surely as when two therapists together treat a family. In both situations, the therapists expect to work with that process as part of the therapeutic task.

In working with an intelligent, sensitive couple, I

reached a point at which I felt they were at the edge of a violent explosion and phoned the husband's individual therapist to share my concern with him. He tried to reassure me that my worries were exaggerated. Later that week the explosion occurred, complete with a brandished gun, threats of violence, and a marital separation.

To say that the husband's therapist was naive misses the point. He was absorbed by his patient's construction of the world, in which aggression was experienced mainly as an unexpected ego-alien impulse. This event may have given the therapist a valuable, vivid realization of just that. Meanwhile, I, like the wife, was sharply attuned to imminent violence. Her attunedness was based in part on her unconscious projection of violence into her husband, in ways of which she was totally unaware. She simply saw men as potentially violent—not including her son, who had grabbed for the rifle. In this particular case I do not know whether my call to the husband's therapist precipitated his violence. It may not have, but I must certainly be open to thinking about that possibility, outrageous as it seems, if our collaboration is to be constructive.

Conclusion

The internal object world is always part history and part fiction, combining, as it must, fantasy, the motivation of the drives, and life experience. Inescapably, in family life the inner object worlds of the members are given flesh as they are re-created in the interactions of the members. In that sense, all relating in the family is infused with transference. That relating, in turn, gives new shape to the internal object worlds of the family members, thus contributing to an ongoing cycle of interplay between internal and external reality. Individual therapy and family therapy intervene in that cycle from different vantage points—the former starting from the psychological experience of the person, and the latter, from the interactional process of the family—but if either is effective it should have repercussions throughout the cycle. The danger is that each therapy can become self-encapsulated. Family therapy may become preoccupied with interactional process and lose sight of the person; individual therapy may become immersed in the intersubjective intensities of the transference and countertransference and lose track of the life being lived. The therapist's alertness to these hazards keeps these forces in balance and promotes growth in the ecosystem of the roots and branches of inner and outer life.

PART VI

AN OBJECT RELATIONS APPROACH TO SEXUALITY IN FAMILY LIFE

20

The Role
of Transitional Experience
in Development in Healthy
and Incestuous Families

ROBERT WINER, M.D.

The task for the family, put most simply, is to promote the development of its members throughout the life cycle. In this chapter I examine the family's unique contribution to personal development—its capacity to create a *condition of transitional experience* in the service of individuation and differentiation—and then explore the ways in which this process is undermined by incest.

PROTECTION OF TRANSITIONAL EXPERIENCE: THE FAMILY'S ROLE IN DEVELOPMENT

The Transitional Object and Transitional Experience

Winnicott's (1951) pioneering observations in this area concerned the infant's attachment during the latter part of its first year of life to a typically soft, durable, comforting, inanimate object, its first "not-me" possession. To Winnicott, the infant's experience with the object had a peculiar quality: The object seemed to be both an extension of mother, carrying a link to her, and at the same time an extension of the self (or, one could equally say that, for the infant, the object was neither self-made nor mother-given). The infant's experience of the object thus lay between subjectivity and objectivity, between narcissistic relatedness and true object relatedness. Winnicott conjectured that the importance of the infant's play with this object was that it facilitated the child's growth toward autonomy by creating an intermediate zone in which the child could, in fantasy, move fluidly back and forth between primary attachment and independence. He described the infant's experience with its "transitional object" as occurring in "potential space." I prefer to call this the "transitional space" to emphasize its developmental importance.

This period of the transitional phenomena, which Winnicott located at "about four to six to eight to twelve months" (p. 4), contains the infant's emergence from the at-oneness of the mother–infant unit. Winnicott described the earlier initial months after birth as the time in which the mother, in a state of "primary maternal preoccupation," intuitively anticipates and responds to her newborn's needs with such attuned sensitivity that the infant experiences the illusion that need does not exist. The infant is in a seamless oneness with its mother. "The mother is able," in Ogden's (1986, p. 173) words, "to provide the infant with what he needs, in the way that he needs it, when he needs it, as if he had 'created' the object." For the infant, at this point, external reality and internal reality are not separate.

Ogden suggests that in the subsequent stage of transitional phenomena, the infant begins to emerge from this oneness by "having the opportunity to play alone in the presence of the absent mother, and in the absence of the present mother" (p. 182)—that is, in the company of the mother who is supportive but not impinging. Out of this experience, the infant comes to internalize the mother-as-holding-environment – the capacity to be self-soothing. As the mother allows the infant to experience dosed unavailability, and thus to feel need, the infant comes to be able to manage the condition of need until help arrives. Through the accompanying transitional play, a sense of a separate self begins to emerge. Ogden observes that if the mother cannot grant her child this transitional space and forces herself on her child out of her own needs, she interferes with his internalization of mother-as-holding-environment and encourages him to become addicted to her as an omnipotent object. Progress toward autonomy is derailed.

From its beginnings in the time of transitional phenomena proper (the second half-year of life), experience in the transitional area serves two goals relevant to emerging selfhood: individuation and differentiation. By creating a way-station, it helps the infant to relinquish complete dependence on the mother and to move toward internalizing self-regulation. In a broader sense, however, traditional space is the stage for creative play, for the trying on of possibilities, free of inhibiting self-consciousness. This facilitates the developmental goal of differentiation, of becoming a particular person through trial action. What makes this possible is the location of transitional experience *between* subjectivity and objectivity. If the experience is simply subjective, it is only fantasy, whereas if it is clearly objective, the burden of facing real consequences becomes inhibiting. In this sense, the infant's relationship to the transitional object is the first true play, if we understand play as the testing of possibilities. We could also say that the transitional object is the first symbol. Symbols, in fact, are themselves transitional objects in that they are both distinct from the objects to which they refer and yet carry their emotional force; it is in the nature of a symbol that it precisely lies between objectification and subjectivity, partaking of both to effect its purpose.

In *Playing and Reality* (1971), Winnicott extended the concept of transitional experience beyond the infant's first play to find it woven throughout the fabric of human experience in a host of ways, facilitating individuation and differentiation. He spoke of the transitional area as "a resting place for the individual engaged in the perpetual human task of keeping inner and outer reality separate yet interrelated" (p. 2). I am about to argue that the protection and facilitation of transitional experience is preeminently the role and task of the family. In so doing, I am following Winnicott's lead in expanding his original observations about an early step in development to a much broader context: here, the family's role in promoting development through the life cycle. The family stands between fantasy and reality, between internality and externality, between the individual and society. Regarding transitional objects, Winnicott's caution to parents was this: You must not ask of your child whether she created it or it was given to her. My remaining thoughts explicate that advice.

A Model for Facilitating Transitional Relatedness

I am proposing that the capacity to use transitional experience to facilitate one's development is a skill (or "ego function") with its own developmental history ("line of development"). In transitional experience, the individual is located *midway* between fantasy and reality and simultaneously participates in both—thus springs its applicability to family life, which is always simultaneously awash with transference yet colliding with reality. To illustrate the elements of this process, I will first use an example of growth through transitional experience in *adult life* that therapists who have had personal treatment may find familiar: the use of the regressive transference neurosis in individual psychoanalytic therapy.

At the core of the transference experience, and crucial to its success, are the patient's simultaneous (or at least alternating) senses of being back in an old familiar place (the transference anlage) and in new uncharted territory (the analysis). The analyst is both rejuvenated parent, for example, and analyst. The patient's experience of being assisted by the analyst in unfolding an analyzable transference neurosis, through which past and present may be deconstructed and reintegrated, is equivalent to an experience with a parent committed to the protection of evolving transitional experience. The analyst safeguards a necessarily private experience from impingement; this is at the heart of analytic neutrality. In analysis, a process of "serious make-believe" (Stone 1961), the analyst is the mother of separation, who facilitates individuation by relating through speech rather than through bodily care. The same definition applies to the family therapist, who creates a realm of transitional experience in which to explore and rework unconscious fantasy that is affecting current family relationships.

The Family's Facilitation of the Use of Transitional Experience

The family drama is also serious make-believe, and the family must protect its dramatic license. When the oedipal son ardently woos his mother, his father does not inform him that he is a puny 5-year-old shrimp making preposterous claims; nor does he treat him as a full-fledged rival and yield the conjugal bed. By allowing his son the space for creative oedipal play in a context of safety, he facilitates the testing of possibilities, shadow boxing, and trial identifications. The father may get carried away on occasion and arrogantly deprecate his son or inappropriately yield to him, but in reasonable time he will regain his balance. The father does not insist that his son answer the question, "Who do you think you are?" Rather, he takes pleasure in *imagining* the man his son might become, and the son senses and enjoys his father's admiration and the possibilities it implies. The family drama is drenched with possibilities, while life outside the family is marked by consequences.

As another example, when the adolescent daughter manages her anxiety about her new-found freedom by acting recklessly while counting on parental restraint to control the situation, nevertheless mightily protesting the restraint as parental infringement, the parent must provide the control. The adolescent is regressively blurring a boundary between self and other by putting an aspect of ego functioning into the parent, in the service of creating space for experimentation. The capacity to make this split is a developmental necessity; the adolescent who cannot effect the split will likely be unduly constricted. The parents join with the child's developmental need and do not let the child run amok; nor do they act as jailers, or interpret the child's behavior. They do not ask, "Are you ready to go off on your own, or are you going to let us be in charge here?" Nor do they ask, "Do you mean business, or are you just testing us?" These questions are not asked because the answer is always both and neither.

The provision of transitional experience is a requirement not only for the family's young. Each developmental transition is facilitated by the availability of space for creative elaboration. It is helpful to the emerging parent that neither infant nor grandparent makes the challenge, "Do you think you know what you're doing?" As a woman moves into motherhood, she identifies at moments with both her nursling and her own mother, and experiences her infant as both her self and her own mother. In this process, aspects of psychic structure that derived from her own infantile experience are repersonified and projected, fluidly and reversibly, into the novel situation, in the service of facilitating an adaptive step, a new reintegration as emergent "mother."

A final example comes from the passage into midlife. One's subsequent decline may be made bearable by locating one's immortality in one's children. To accomplish this, one must be able at moments to experience a fusion of one's own ambitions with those of one's children, so that their self-realization can be felt as one's own, and at other moments to experience the actual finality of one's own death. Without the objective reality, the immersion in one's children is an act of denial. Without the subjective fusion, one is left vulnerable to despair, or one may try to avoid the despair by becoming a child again oneself. The child's responsibility is to accept her parent's fantasy without either exposing it as fantasy or being taken over by it as a delegated reality. She does not confound her physician father with the question, "Am I being disloyal to you if I don't become a doctor?"; she must tolerate the ambiguity, the lack of closure in transitional space. If, on the other hand, her father is located in the frame of denial, her posing the question to him may be quite useful in opening up the transitional space again, to his and her benefit.

It is a complicating aspect of the regression to transitional relatedness that relevant repressed pathological internal object relations will be activated. These configurations may even dominate the situation, but the potential exists for modifying the repressed object relations in the course of the new experience. Developmental crises (starting school, marriage, the birth of a sibling, an empty nest) breathe life into repressed conflicts that may have been relatively dormant. We know, for example, that every significant experience of separation reopens the scars of every past repressed separation trauma. Each crisis offers a second chance to reopen the earlier developmental impasse. In negotiating these second chances, the *maximal* opportunity arises for alteration of the repressed. The repressed is not changed simply by immersing oneself in it; it is changed by being brought into contact with the objective world in transitional experience. Maintaining a transitional state is greatly facilitated by the support of the family, and the family is uniquely in the position to offer that support. Psychoanalysis can be understood as a laboratory re-creation of this living process in one family member. Family therapy offers a transitional space in which the family can develop its own capacity for providing space for the transitional relatedness so essential to its continued growth.

INCEST AND THE DESTRUCTION OF TRANSITIONAL SPACE

The role of transitional relatedness in family functioning can be further defined by exploring its destruction in incest. I will be exploring two reciprocal developments. Incest, in itself, erodes the individual's capacity to make use of transitional experience in development. The absence of this capacity renders the individual more prone to act incestuously.

The Nature of Oedipal Play

The child's oedipal pursuit of the parents constitutes an intermediate stage between primary identification and mature nonincestuous object choice (Loewald 1979). During the oedipal period, the child experiences object-libidinal fantasies toward a person with whom the child has strong preobjectal identificatory bonds. These fantasies are elaborated both in dream and reverie and in the serious make-believe play of actual family life. The frightening intensity of oedipal fantasies is cushioned by the primary identificatory attachments to the oedipal objects. Children who in the preoedipal era were separated from a parent and then reunited at the time of the oedipal surge lack the buffering effect of the preoedipal relationship and may then be overwhelmed by their oedipal fantasies.

The fantasy enactments and the subsequent transformation of oedipal relations into secondary identifications shape the child's character, determining in particular how he will respond in situations of desire and threat. If all goes reasonably well, the developing child will be able to make object choices that realize his emerging integrated personhood. That is, while they will reflect his primary identificatory and oedipal bonds, they will be more than simply a re-creation of those attachments. They will be a novel, integrated transformation of those ties based on the particular person he has become.

In healthy development, the reliable existence of the primary identificatory bonds protects both parent and child from living out oedipal relations in incest or murder and enables both to ultimately internalize or (for the parent) reintegrate oedipal relations in the service of further development. Oedipal play is thus a crucial form of transitional relatedness in which child and parent experience the interplay of the profoundly subjective mode of primary identification and the objective mode of object relating. Put another way, it is the delicate balance and interplay of being and passion.

The Nature of Incest

Failure to achieve the state of transitional relatedness promotes incest, and incest further undermines the partial equilibrium achieved. In incest, the transitional space is obliterated. When oedipal relations are enacted in reality, the oedipal era is no longer a way-station to mature relatedness, a transitional state facilitating the testing of possibilities. The necessary gap between fantasy and reality has been lost, and fantasy can never again be innocent or safe. In one sense the child has become an adult in the act of living out incestuous relations—an adult capable of enacting lust, jealousy, and revenge—and has been driven to a premature state of autonomy and differentiation. In another sense, the child has been deprived of all autonomy and used by the parent as an extension of the parent's will.

The incestuous father abandons his holding function. Rather than protecting the position between at-oneness and separateness, he assaults it from both sides. On the one hand, he forces his daughter into a pathological merger with him and erases her individuality. He says to her, "You are an extension of me to be used as I wish." On the other hand, he prematurely forces a separateness on her since he is disowning her as his child and taking her as his lover. Maintenance of transitional space in the family is a protection against regressive fusion. Incest, in obliterating that space, leads the family to collapse in on itself.

Incest, of course, is not the only activity that violates transitional relatedness—there are other forms of exploitation in family life—but it is the form, short of murder, with the most devastating consequences. Among the consequences to be emphasized are the loss of the capacity to use fantasy and transitional experience in development, impairment of the ability to symbolize, and the inability to create the boundaries of a differentiated and autonomous self.

This clinical illustration is based on an extended evaluation of an incestuous family, consisting of Bill, 43; Cindy, 23; their 4-year-old daughter, Anne; and Bill's 16-year-old daughter, Susie. Anne had come to medical attention because of complaints of vaginal inflammation and swelling. Sexual abuse was suspected, because it had recently been revealed that her father, Bill, had years earlier sexually assaulted his daughter Susie when she was approximately the same age. When, in a police play-interview, Anne was asked where the father had touched her, she pointed to the doll's genital area. Anne's mother, Cindy, had apparently encouraged Anne to accuse her father, who vehemently denied the incest. It was not possible to be certain of the actual situation. Anne had spent most of her nights in the parental bedroom, often in the parents' bed. In her first months Anne had slept on her father's chest, and her mother worried that he would roll over and suffocate her. The ongoing arrangement was a product of both Anne's own insistent demands that she sleep in their room and her parents' mutual reluctance to establish a boundary. Given that the vaginal trauma was considered to exceed even that which might be caused by compulsive masturbation, one possibility considered was that ongoing sexual interaction occurred at night during sleep or twilight states. Both parents were unusually attached to this child and cherished her as a sacred innocent.

I began to ask the parents about their family backgrounds. While his father was in the army, Bill had shared his own mother's bed from ages 2 to 6, and he had wet the bed frequently. Many nights he awakened to discover that she was missing; she would be off with various men for days at a time while relatives living with them cared for him. Bill's father returned shell-shocked and probably also psychotic; he spent most of his remaining years in psychiatric institutions, occasionally visiting Bill and once knocking him unconscious. At about the time of his father's return, his father's parents had Bill's promiscuous mother declared unfit and took the boy to live with them. He did not see his mother for the next five years. Bill's own military service was interrupted by a psychosomatic illness and followed by recurrent nightmares in which guns failed to work. While in the service, he began drinking to the point of unconsciousness. Over the years he had a series of marriages and was extremely sexually driven, but managed to keep custody of his children and to develop a successful professional life.

Incest with Bill's other daughter Susie occurred, she reported, on several occasions between ages 3 and 7, while Bill and her mother were still married. It involved penetration and was apparently much more aggressive than the behavior with Anne. Later, when Susie's parents were divorced, her mother gave custody of her to Bill and wanted to have little to do with her. Susie described feeling rejected by her mother and unable to please her demanding father. She gave an impression of being lifeless and lost.

I was interested to discover that a psychologist and a physician they consulted had both felt afraid that Bill would attack them in some way—one of them imagining that Bill might break into his house. The sense of threat he engendered had not been initially apparent and both felt surprised by it.

Cindy described her mother as a depressed, self-sacrificing, but uncomplaining religious fanatic who had been married many times. Cindy's father left during the first year of her life, to be replaced a few years later by a stepfather who left when Cindy was 9. Cindy's mother's last husband, of whom Cindy had been most fond, was (like Bill) an army veteran. Like Cindy, her mother had grown up without a father—he had been killed in the line of duty when the mother was 2—and this was taken to explain her marital instability. Cindy had been living away from home a short time when she fell in love with Bill, the dashing, charismatic executive who was dating her roommate. After describing her continuing sexual attachment to Bill, from whom she had separated after the incest revelation, Cindy mentioned that there had been a good deal of family nudity during her childhood.

This case illustrates the continuity of developmental failure from generation to generation. Bill's early years were filled with overstimulation, rejection, and exploitation. It appears that his mother took him to her bed when she was lonely and abandoned him when other men were available. Rather than helping him to work through his dependency needs, she exploited his dependency in the service of her own. As he moved through the oedipal era, it seems inevitable that his sexual desires were aroused, partially gratified, and abruptly cut short in his mother's bed. Without having established a foundation of preoedipal security and relative autonomy, he was thrust into oedipal enactment. The process of finding security thus became sexualized and, because of the rejection, aggressivized. It appears that his sense of phallic capability was always in question (as reflected, for example, in the nightmares), and he sought reassurance in being a warrior and later in conquering virgins (as Cindy had been at 17 when Bill and she met).

In the best-documented incest episode with his first daughter, he was at the time struggling with the fear that his wife was homosexually engaged with a neighbor. When he unexpectedly found his latency-age daughter playing with a girlfriend in bed, he forced her up against a wall and pressed himself against her, angrily telling her that he'd show her how sex was supposed to be done. In this action he confused his daughter with his wife, confused her sexual exploitation and play with his wife's (possible) actual sexual betrayal, and confused parenting and retaliating in his determination to "teach her a lesson." The episode conflated the issues of maternal abandonment and sexual potency and ended in his reassuring himself of his phallic power by assaulting his daughter.

There was no transitional space available for Bill in which he could elaborate in fantasy his responses to his wife's possible transgression. He acted on the basis of what Segal (1957) has called a "symbolic equation" in which "the early symbols . . . are not felt by the ego to be symbols or substitutes but to be the original object itself" (p. 53). His daughter did not symbolize his wife; in his mind she *was* his wife. His daughter's play did not symbolize sex; it *was* sex. And he did not *feel like* a rejected lover; he *was* an injured party who must retaliate. Throughout his adult life, he could feel genitally capable only by endlessly conquering new women: Phallic competence could not be symbolically achieved through work and in relationships. His sense of himself as a father was not a stable internalized role: His children could quickly become simply receptacles for his desire or targets of his fury or objects with which to repair himself. The fear of both therapists that Bill would attack them reflects their sense that Bill would not be able to symbolize his anger at them but would treat them as the enemy and retaliate.

Anne was an anaclitic object for Bill and Cindy. Their inability to separate from Anne at night seemed to reflect their own maternal deprivation; they could not bear to hear her cry. Their primary identification with her precluded their being able to respond to her developmental needs as an emerging separate person. She was to make up for all the prior disappointments and injuries of their lives. As a remarkable expression of the degree to which she had internalized this expectation, Anne said that she hoped the interviewer could help her parents too. In the diagnostic sessions, it was clear that Anne was worried about invasion, loss, and damage, and that she felt overstimulated and anxious. Yet Anne seemed to have suffered less psychological damage overall than her half-sister, Susie. One possible explanation for the difference is that whereas both children were exploited incestuously (although it is unclear whether Anne was ever sexually penetrated), the incest with the older girl was much more aggressive and hateful. She was used as an impersonal object, while Anne was always revered in her parents' minds. Further, Anne was not rejected by her mother. It may be that the parents' capacity to hold a primary identification of the child is the minimum necessity for a noncatastrophic outcome. Bill said that he fended off incestuous impulses toward this daughter by threatening himself with suicide; we might say that he imagined annihilating his own self to safeguard the emergence of her selfhood.

Bill's behavior with these daughters revealed the consequences of his own early developmental disturbance in the transitional area. Ogden (1986) suggests that potential space can be thought of as the area between three points: the symbol, the symbolized, and the symbolizing self. When that space collapses, as Segal (1957) points out, the symbol and the symbolized are the same, and the symbolizing self does not exist. This leads either to an overvaluation of fantasy, as in Bill's experience, in which fantasy is simply experienced as reality, or to a defense against fantasy by overvaluing reality. Bill experienced his fantasies about Susie and his first wife's behaviors as realities on which to act. In his relationship to Anne, he revealed his inability to soothe himself: He could not fall asleep without her. His failure to internalize the mother-as-holding-environment left him addicted to the mother-as-object, represented by his daughter. For Anne, the incest impinged on her developing autonomy and on her capacity to contain herself, leaving her vulnerable to overstimulation.

Transitional play in the early years of life promotes the creation of a rudimentary emerging self, based upon primary identifications. In the oedipal years, transitional play allows for the transformation to a more mature self based upon secondary identifications. Incest during the oedipal years interferes with the development of the capacity for secondary identification and leaves in its wake a deteriorated capacity for maintaining boundaries. I would like to illustrate this by describing certain transference developments in the analysis of a 50-year-old woman.

Rebecca and her older brother had coped with the misery of their childhoods through a nightly experience in which he read to her and they then engaged in sex play, which included intercourse. This had ended at her brother's insistence when she was 7 because he had become afraid of impregnating her. She had never forgiven him for stopping.

In psychoanalysis, Rebecca found the limitations of the therapeutic relationship intolerable. She peeked inside her analyst's car, watered his waiting-room plants, stole food from the kitchen adjacent to the waiting room, inspected his pants for any drop of urine that might stain them, and contorted herself on the couch wishing that he would anally penetrate her. Early in the treatment she brought in a camera and took a picture of him, which she kept in her purse. When he went on vacation, she called his colleague to confirm that he hadn't died. Two years into the treatment, the analyst discovered that he did not feel entirely certain that this woman would not succeed in seducing him, despite his lack of conscious sexual attraction to her.

The analyst felt overwhelmed and persecuted by the patient's demands and intrusions, and was for a time unable to step outside this experience and think about it as her analyst. The treatment process had lost the flexibility of transitional play and was immobilized by her relentless clinging, which obliterated, for both parties, all other motives and meanings. His dawning awareness that she would not seduce him was followed by his realization that she was perfectly capable of destroying the treatment; this double recognition allowed him to reinstate the psychological boundaries of the treatment. Now that he could reflect on his countertransference experience, he could re-create the transitional space of the analysis for himself and for the patient. Then meaning could once more be elaborated.

Rebecca was gradually able to shift the focus from desperately clinging to her analyst, as though he were nothing more or less than the mother (or brother) who would hold or abandon her, to using him as an analyst to help her explore her thoughts and feelings. At the very end of a substantial and useful termination phase, however, she demanded that the analyst give her a gift. Efforts to understand this were to no avail, and she left with some bitterness. Among other meanings, her demand was that the analyst undo the actuality of the separation by abandoning his position as analyst, in actuality. Understanding could not be a sufficient gift on this occasion.

The developmental impact of the maternal neglect is not easily separated from that of the incest, which was in part a response to the deprivation. Some details of her own mothering experience with her daughters hint at the scope of the early difficulties. While Rebecca had felt profoundly connected during her first pregnancy, her infant daughter's subsequent fussing had made her feel helpless, inadequate, and enraged. She managed the situation by quickly adopting a male infant, with whom she felt more comfortable. She became pregnant again, and one month before the delivery of her second daughter, she had an affair with her minister. As adults, one of her daughters was living with a female lover, the other in a religious commune. The patient herself was still caught up in hateful mutual withholding with her own mother. Her early separation difficulties, which came to haunt her own adulthood and the lives of her children, constituted the bedrock on which the incestuous experience was layered.

Rebecca attempted to adapt to the deprivation of her childhood through sibling incest. In normal development, the renunciation of oedipal love promotes internalization; incest interferes with this progression. For Rebecca, adaptation would be based on manipulation of the environment, not on an internal working through of life's difficulties. As a further consequence of her lack of capacity to use transitional relatedness, she was unable to use symbolization as a mode of adaptation. During the regression of the termination phase, she demanded a gift because it was not possible for her to master the loss internally as a way of negotiating the ending. She had never forgiven her brother for beginning to date other girls after he stopped the sex play with her. She had punished her unborn second daughter for preparing to leave her womb by having the affair with the minister. A loss, whether of analyst, brother, or fetus, could not be compensated internally, symbolically; it could only be revenged or, more likely, made an intractable grievance.

The next case illustrates the vicissitudes of aggression in the absence of transitional play and demonstrates the consequent aggressive use of projective identification as a mode of functioning in family life.

If the toddler is excessively anxious or enraged, he will be unable to effectively use transitional play to master aggression. The transitional object in early play can, in Winnicott's words, "survive instinctual loving, and also hating and, if it be a feature, pure aggression" (1951, p. 5). The toddler can use it, tug on it, discard it, pick it up again, tear at it, rub on it, cling to it, and so on. In this case, as with the older daughter in the first case, the incest is very aggressive; the daughter is treated like a rag doll that can be snatched up, played with, abused, and discarded. This utter disregard for the daughter's feelings resembles the child's attitude toward its transitional object. This is the debased caricature of transitional object play that signifies the destruction of transitional space.

Projective identification is, as Ogden (1986) points out, the negative of playing. Through this mechanism, the projector attempts to capture and transform the internal life of the recipient, evoking in the recipient the ejected disturbing mental contents of the projector with such force that the recipient will experience them as her own. Her capacity to elaborate her own subjective experience will be thwarted as she is taken over by experience that properly belongs to the other but is felt to be personally derived. When aggression cannot be tamed through transitional play, the conflict may be managed by

projectively recruiting other family members to internalize it on one's behalf. The following family case study
of Mr. and Mrs. Smith and their daughter Sandy dramatically demonstrates this process of invasion, recruitment,
and coercion.

For Mr. Smith, the crucial issue was intrusion. His sister had been
the first great intruder: She had become the favored child and he
the outcast. Feeling that he had nowhere to turn, he had retaliated
by not talking and not responding to questions: No one would get
inside him. His silence had provoked his father to rage, and his
father, unable to control himself, had lashed back with a two-by-
four board. When his mother wanted to get rid of him, he took off
for Vietnam, where he roamed the countryside in his intelligence
unit, ferreting out the enemy. When his mother wanted him to
return, he angrily volunteered for a second tour of duty. In
Vietnam, *he* was the intruder. But by now the migraines were
throbbing in his head. His attempt to place the conflict outside
himself in the fields of Vietnam had failed.

    He married Mrs. Smith, a woman with a young daughter,
Sandy. She soon became pregnant with their son. His wife's
pregnancy must have echoed his mother's for him. During his
wife's pregnancy, he believed that a tumor had invaded his brain,
and I imagine that the tumor was a concretization of his growing
rage. His inability to comfort his crying newborn son increased his
feeling of helplessness and confirmed his sense that he was
worthless. It seems a reasonable inference that the intruder was
fundamentally the rage by which he felt possessed, and that his
paranoid defenses were ways of trying to control that rage—by
evoking it in his father, by externalizing it in the enemy, by
somatizing it into headaches, by keeping others away from him,
and by inviting the punishment that might subdue him. He said at
one point that if he could spend 99 years in jail, he'd feel better.

    In contrast, Mrs. Smith was unable to let go of her family. She
had clung to a mother by whom she had not felt loved, and
she had been unable to commit herself to her own marriage. She
complained that her efforts to please her mother had always
failed. With her mother's tacit encouragement, Mrs. Smith had
taken refuge in her relationship with her father until he pulled

away when she reached puberty. Mrs. Smith had made her daughter Sandy a surrogate parent — until the birth of her son by Mr. Smith, when she abruptly cut Sandy off and showed less interest in her husband. Shortly after this boy's birth, when she was 10, Sandy began having intercourse and running away. Soon after that, alone on a trip with her stepfather, she submitted to him sexually for the first time. Both seem to have felt cast out by Mrs. Smith, and for both there seemed to be comfort and revenge in the incest. For Mr. Smith, Sandy represented both his wife and his mother. In joining with her he excluded them, but in violating her he also attacked them in her, and perhaps also his sister and son symbolically inside the womb. When the incest was revealed, the Smiths separated for the third time, and Sandy, who was out of control, was hospitalized.

Mr. Smith's actions in Vietnam and with Sandy were enactments of fantasies, his inner life writ large. Where someone with more capacity for containment might simply have experienced *feelings* of disappointment, or anger, or longing, he *engaged* in espionage and incest. The transitional space is, in another sense, the space between the event and the response, a space in which an event can be experienced, felt about, and thought about. That space did not exist for Mr. Smith, nor did it for Sandy.

In the hospital, Sandy created extraordinarily vengeful drama among peers and authorities. She threatened to kill a female rival. She used boys as pawns to hurt other girls. She became a cause célèbre on the ward when a reliable nurse inadvertently poisoned her with an overdose of the wrong medication. When she ran away from the hospital, the policeman who returned her advised her to get a lawyer and sue for her release.

During the hospitalization, she succeeded in pitting her individual therapist against their family therapist and drawing the hospital administrator into the fray. On one occasion the administrator, a man, broke into a family therapy session to discuss the individual therapist's alleged contemptuous behavior with the family therapist, a woman. This invasion of private territory to join forces against a common enemy bears a startling resemblance to the stepfather's invading his stepdaughter to join incestuously with her in an attack on the mother.

At another point, the individual therapist told the parents a dream Sandy had described to him, a recurrent dream of her stepfather raping her. Her stepfather responded to this revelation with a nightmare in which he was falsely accused of rape. The individual therapist, who could not respect confidentiality, was joining Sandy and her stepfather incestuously in their nightmares. Meanwhile, a court official went beyond his authority and suggested to the parents that they split up, sell their house, and use the proceeds to pay for residential treatment for Sandy. The natural order of the legal and therapeutic process was in an uproar in response to the massive projection of primitive, punitive, and grandiose aspects of the family.

A striking feature is the degree of recruitment to their pathological system that this family achieved. A policeman, a nurse, a hospital administrator, a therapist, and a court officer all acted in intrusive, destructive ways. Projective identification of contents related to aggressive conflict occurred both within the family and as a means of negotiating relations with the outside world. The force and effectiveness of the projective identification was such that the outsiders responded without their usual capacity for internal control. This contagion speaks to the fragility of the human capacity for transitional relatedness that underlies effective role functioning, and the universal potential for regression into states of fusion in the face of sufficient provocation.

This recruitment and dedifferentiation is an expression of the pathological object relatedness of the incestuous family. For the Smiths, family members are one another's property, to be used as needed for the maintenance of the individual's balance. The world outside the family is untrustworthy, and adaptation must be achieved through incestuously exploiting the resources of the family. The only love that really matters is the willingness to surrender one's inner object world for that purpose. These dynamics all appeared in the microcosm of the family therapy hour and were evoked in the therapist's countertransference experience, as the following synopsis of a session late in the hospitalization illustrates. At moments the therapist is simply taken over by the projective identifications and responds by joining the enactment, and at other points she struggles to contain the projections and metabolize them for the family.

The session began in an angry mood. Mrs. Smith hoped that Sandy would soon return home, and Sandy told her that she was sabotaging her weekend passes. Sandy was concerned that, according to her doctor, her insurance coverage for the hospitalization was running out. Mr. Smith was furious that Sandy's therapist had discussed this with her and not with him and wanted to take up the therapist's inappropriate action with his administrative superior. It was unclear whether Mr. Smith was identifying with Sandy's fear of being sent home prematurely or was feeling rendered impotent by the implication that he couldn't provide for his daughter's needs. The family therapist, Ms. F., reassured him that she'd discuss the matter with the individual therapist. Frightened by his thundering rage, she had felt that her choices were either to make an interpretation, which seemed quite intrusive and certain to prompt retaliation, or to yield to him, which she did. Thus from the outset Ms. F. experienced pressure both to be omnipotently at the center of their lives and to be a million miles away for their safety and hers. Their psychological reality crowded out her capacity for personal subjective experience; she had no space in which she could experience herself as a therapist, and she could not see beyond narrow choices deriving from their conflicts.

As the angry mood continued, Mrs. Smith earnestly invited Ms. F. to join her tackle football team. Taken aback, Ms. F. declined, commenting on the aggressiveness of the sport, and unconsciously remarking on the aggressiveness of the offer. Mrs. Smith chided her for trying to make something out of a mere invitation. When Ms. F. persisted in talking about how violent the sport was, Mr. Smith asked incredulously, "Do you do this on the *outside,* with *other* people?" Ms. F. acknowledged ruefully that her interpretive style would surely tire almost as quickly on the outside as it did with them. Mrs. Smith's offer appeared to be heartfelt (reflecting her gratitude to Ms. F. for her husband's recent return to their home), concrete (expressing her wish to merge with Ms. F. in a loving tackle), and at the same time self-protectively distancing. Their defensive anger may have been in response to Ms. F.'s acknowledging only the aggressive side of the offer. Mr. Smith then asked why they had come for so many sessions, more than other families did. Mrs. Smith exclaimed, "It's just that Ms. F. loves us so much." Ms. F. was left speechless. Desire and aggression are commingled in incestuous families to a degree that others find both exciting and unbearable.

Ms. F. began to feel depressed. She wondered to herself, "Oh shit, do I do this with everybody?" Her countertransference derived from taking in the guilt that the family disavowed and preferred to evoke in others. Meanwhile, Sandy asked her stepfather if he'd liked the poetry she'd given him. Mr. Smith said he was impressed by it, but the rage in it frightened him and was, he thought, directed at him. Here he was taking on the guilt, as Ms. F. had done earlier. Sandy said that the poem was for a boyfriend at whom she was angry. Only once, she said, had someone broken off with her, and that had felt really bad (at the same time an acknowledgment and denial of her many rejections by her father, mother, and stepfather). She angrily refused to identify the person. Her stepfather thought that one of the poems was sexual, which Sandy denied, and he replied that maybe he just had a dirty mind. Sandy said she wanted to be kept away from one of the boys to whom she felt sexually attracted. Ms. F. was aware of the electricity sparking between stepfather and stepdaughter. Sandy complained about the sex education class she had to attend: The guys weren't mature enough to handle their sexuality — an unconscious dig at her stepfather. Mrs. Smith said that she'd been embarrassed during a college sex education class by a model with a flashing penis. Mother and daughter dissolved in hysterics, and Mr. Smith, feeling the mix of awe and ridicule, smiled wanly, perhaps wondering if he had a penis left at this point.

Ms. F. then raised the issue of their reconciliation, and the parents acknowledged that they had felt ready to give up and that they were worried about how it would all work out. Mr. Smith refused to discuss the issue in front of his stepdaughter, telling Ms.

F., "You've broken into me and you've tried to break me down and you're not going to do it. You're not going to use your tactics on me. I know what you did in the last session. You work on building a relationship! It's not going to happen!" Ms. F. asked if she'd hurt him in some way. Repeating the interaction of his childhood, he refused to talk. Then he explained, "I won't speak in front of my sibling." Then, sheepishly, he caught his slip: "Sibling? I don't know what 'sibling' means!" Ms. F. suggested, "Like your sister?" Mr. Smith replied, "Just because I say 'sibling' doesn't mean anything. It's like when I'm referring to Mom — I mean my wife! And now you're going to make something of that!" Mr. Smith's paranoid response seemed to be due to his fear about the reunion and gratitude to Ms. F. for helping him with it. Ms. F. gently told him he was encouraging her to interpret by giving her his unconscious thoughts, and Sandy teasingly chanted "Freudian slips!"

Captive to the family's unconscious process, Ms. F. felt self-righteous and sadistic pleasure in reaching his unconscious and making it her ally against him. Her countertransference feeling of being in possession of his internal life is analogous to Mr. Smith's exploitation of Sandy's adolescent sexual intensities for his own ends. He could not support the transitional play in which she might safely test out her new-found sexuality, a space in which he might be experienced in fantasy as father and lover in the process of working toward incestuous disengagement and outside object choice. This was especially tragic because Sandy's relationship with her stepfather had the potential for reworking the trauma of her earlier rejection by her father, a potential inherent in adolescent experience. Instead she was again abandoned by a father as he rejected his paternal responsibility for his stepdaughter and instead used her as a vehicle for coping with his own abandonment rage. The only holding possible in this family is from the inside, as a hook holds a fish.

The session ended dramatically. Mr. Smith calmed down in response to Ms. F.'s affectionate humor and said that she had been a catalyst for his reunion with his wife. Ms. F. asked how she had done that, and he replied that after a recent session alone with her, he went home and saw a vision of angels and archangels, representing dead family members at peace. Nonplussed, Ms. F. wondered if he was being sarcastic.

Mr. Smith continued, "I'm not going to let my past ruin my life. That's what I learned in the last session, I'm not going to let my anger with my family [of origin] ruin my life. My anger with my wife has been too intense and it's because of my past family. You helped me to see that." Ms. F., still responding to his earlier pushing away her understanding, could not believe that he really understood that. Bringing positive and negative feelings together at this precarious moment would have run the risk of recreating an incestuous fusion because the family had not yet developed a secure transitional relatedness at this stage of treatment.

The family that is able to serve as a developmental resource for its members will have succeeded in establishing the flexible boundaries which facilitate the use of transitional relatedness, and the regression that entails, while acting as a barrier to incest. The maintenance of these boundaries is a part of the holding process, in which the individual is held *from without*, while the privacy of the inner object world is protected from exploitation. We have been examining families in which holding takes a perverse form: The individual is held *from within*, as aspects of the inner life are appropriated by another to serve the other's ends. Incest both reflects a prior degradation of transitional relatedness in the family, of which it then becomes a manifestation, and contributes to its further destruction.

The following case, which is derived from the psychoanalysis of Faith, a woman in her 30s, illuminates these issues from an unusual perspective: This is a case in which incest was rebuffed.

Treatment had initially been sought because the patient felt overwhelmed by the experience of being a mother to a newborn, alternately trying to be a perfectly devoted mother and then feeling engulfed by her baby's needs and fleeing into outside activities.

Faith's father had been enormously possessive of her, proud of her, enraptured by her. He had denigrated her friends, taken her out alone, and replaced his wife with her. This had suited his wife, who had resolved the difficult problem of what to do with a manic-depressive husband by immersing herself in a career and assigning his caretaking to her oldest daughter. Faith had learned how to soothe his rages and came to find her mission as the family's savior. When her father had found her too arousing, he had demanded that she sit motionless beside him, and had hit her if she flinched. Seized by uncontrollable jealousy when she began to date, he told her that he was sure that she was having sex with her boyfriends (which in fact she wasn't) and proposed that she stay home and have sex with him instead. She refused, and he made her an outcast in the home. No one could speak to her in his presence, and she couldn't eat with the family or bathe when he was home. She finished school two years later, left home, and, until her analysis, had never spoken to him again.

Until Faith's father proposed incest, they had been able to function as a family, in their own way. We could say that Faith had achieved an oedipal victory in the unconscious life of the family. But this victory had not been realized in sexual actuality, and this unconscious reality could be balanced against other realities of the family's life, such as the mother's continuing influence and the support of a helpful grandmother. The father's demand that the fantasy be made an actuality destroyed this balance. Faith responded to her father's attempt to banish her from the family, with which her mother colluded, by setting her sights outside the home. She attached herself to a surrogate family composed of school faculty and classmates and relinquished her position as family caretaker for her father and siblings.

The question of interest for our present purpose is this: What made it possible for Faith to find the courage to reject her father's proposal and, in consequence, accept extrusion from the family? Family life had never offered the children security: Vigilance was the order of the day. The children had to contend with their father's erratic violent outbursts and unpredictable mood changes. Faith remembered that when she was young, her burly trucker father would charge at her, tickle her, and roll over on her. She'd feel suffocated, terrified, and unable to get him to stop. In her analysis she was initially afraid to use the couch, frightened to turn her back to me.

The need to stay in control persisted throughout the analysis: She waited to talk about certain events and feelings until she felt she could manage them; she wrote up her dreams and analyzed them prior to our sessions; she was careful not to let my vacation plans influence hers. She minimized spontaneity and fought against regression. Whereas in the earlier cases, the collapse of transitional space led to taking fantasy as reality (the symbolic equation), Faith used reality as a defense against fantasy. Sexual feelings toward me were particularly threatening. On the surface, loss of control represented a dreaded, submissive yielding in a sadomasochistic relationship. More profoundly, it meant loss of her sense of identity.

To deal with both the overstimulation and the threat of being overwhelmed and losing her selfhood, Faith developed the defense of compartmentalization: Experiences, feelings, and relationships were kept separate from one another. This defense was evident during her second pregnancy, an ordeal for her because she was threatened by the normal degree of fusion between fetus and self. From a series of dreams we learned that she felt she had to contain in her uterus all the old tensions of her family's life, including her fascist father and all the insurrectionist and ungrateful children. The attempt to encapsulate experience appeared starkly in a dream just before she took a month's vacation from the analysis. She was holding her daughter frozen in a block of ice which created pools of water on the floor. Faith wished to preserve our relationship in suspended animation, at a secure distance, but was afraid that she would lose control. She said that her parents had power over her, but that they couldn't control her feelings or her mind. Faith defended herself by compartmentalization, a tendency transmitted to the next generation: When Faith's daughter reached the toddler stage, she took to carrying a set of bags with her everywhere she went, and spent hours each day sorting all manner of objects into them.

Her parents also managed their lives through compartmentalization. Her mother stayed out of the home and kept a distance in all her relationships, finding security in the accumulation of property. Even her father's attempt to keep her motionless in a chair was, at one level, an attempt to control and simplify his life. Here we see a shared family defense against despair about being unable to create a reliable, creative transitional space.

Faith's family was unable to act as an appropriate resource to support her development, instead pressing her toward premature self-sufficiency and responsibility for others. Her childhood was disrupted by overstimulation, latent and occasionally overt violence, neglect, and parentification. Nevertheless, aided by internalization of more adaptive aspects of her parents' and grandmother's functioning, she was able to find a way to negotiate life through controlling her mind and behavior. Although adequate to enable her to establish a productive career and a rich marriage, the adaptation was not sufficient to allow her to cope with motherhood, and at that point she sought treatment. While in the earlier cases therapy was aimed at containing fantasy and making it responsive to the requirements of reality, for Faith the therapeutic goal was the liberation of fantasy from reality-bound overcontrol, so that fantasy could safely enrich living.

Transitional experience, beginning with the child's play with its transitional object, requires the supportive presence of another who protects the child, or later the adult, in the transitional play. The significant other who does not ask me whether I created the object or received it, but accepts either possibility, is a necessary presence, serving the function of not asking that question and instead being with my experience. That support, for the child, must come mainly from the family. Without it, transitional experience cannot be available as a mode of growth. Then, members of families that cannot protect transitional experience tend to exploit one another as each member scavenges for his own development.

Transitional experience gives birth to a multitude of

present possibilities through which ancient desires may be channelled toward potential fertilization. Transitional space expands the present, making it a transformative now. If that space is destroyed—if the present implodes— then past and future become inseparable. In the timeless lives of the families described, the past reigns unopposed into perpetuity. These families, like black holes, collapse time for those who come near them. Without the dynamic potential of transitional space, past and future are in circular linkage, and the only continuity is that borne by Sisyphus, for whom tomorrow promised to be indistinguishable from yesterday. The incestuous family, in turning back on itself, attempts to destroy time, individuation, and differentiation. The family that can serve as a resource to its members bursts the present moment into its infinite possibilities.

21

Adolescent Sexuality in Family Therapy

John Zinner, M.D.

When I first encountered 16-year-old Cathy, she was indeed lost in every emotional sense of the word. She felt abandoned by her "soul"; she sought a personified "Jesus Christ" who would make her one again; she was "two people." On the one hand, she was tormented by sexual impulses and by guilt for past transgressions, which she believed had made her sterile. She worried over her incapacity for orgasm and felt she would never find a man who would love her. On the other hand, she yearned for a time long ago when she "didn't have to pretend to go into beautiful thoughts within myself," when she could embody the family's idealized view of relationships, with no anger, no fights, and no disturbing physical sensations within her body.

Her recent troubles began shortly after the onset of puberty in the eighth grade, when she made a conscious effort to come out into the world of her peers, emerging from a rather isolated but saintly shell. The ensuing two years were disastrous for her, as her impulses took hold. She became involved in a relatively delinquent peer group in junior high school. Cathy was introduced to hallucinogens and missed school frequently, and her excellent academic work plummeted. She became promiscuous in a rather passive, masochistic way. She was "passed around" from boy to boy for sexual relations. Because of her immobility in these involvements, she was ridiculed and called a "lazy bitch." Lighted cigarettes and other objects were thrown at her by these same boys, and her self-hatred and shame blossomed.

A brief hospitalization followed a period of intensified sexual activity and the use of angel dust. After discharge, her overall functioning continued to deteriorate and she became phobic such that she was unable to attend school. It was at this point that she was referred to me for outpatient treatment.

I have selected Cathy's case because it demonstrates the failure of the family as a resource in individual development and illustrates some theoretical and technical points in the discussion of sexual issues in the conjoint family treatment of disturbed adolescents. The three main points are as follows:

1. The primary goal of the conjoint portion of the treatment program is to restore the family group to a level of functioning in which it can provide a phase-appropriate resource to the adolescent mastering the developmental tasks related to sexuality.

2. It follows from this goal that specific therapeutic interventions must be geared to those problems in interaction that are interfering with the family's function as a resource. That is, treatment must be individualized based on the therapist's formulation of the problematic dynamics in each case. Thus interventions tailored to

the needs of one family may be quite inappropriate for another.

3. Consideration of boundaries between the generations is especially important in the area of sexuality. The therapist must have a sensitive appreciation of the inevitable tension between the need for candor and openness in therapy and for privacy and separateness in the sexual world of its individual members and subgroups, such as the parental dyad. Such a tension between values frequently dictates a treatment program that includes not only conjoint treatment of the entire family group, but also concurrent individual therapy for the adolescent and marital therapy for the parents.

The treatment program that was developed for Cathy and her family included weekly conjoint family therapy meetings as well as weekly individual psychotherapy sessions for Cathy. The same therapist conducted both the individual and family sessions. Cathy also entered a day-hospital program, which included group psychotherapy and accredited high school instruction. Fran, the oldest daughter, who no longer lived at home, attended conjoint family sessions intermittently for sustained periods.

Cathy's family consisted of her parents and a sibship of three girls, of which she was the middle child. The other daughters were Fran, 19 years old, and Sally, 13 years old. At the first meeting of the entire group, I was struck by the lengthy periods of silence and the stunning lack of interaction among members despite the lack of overt hostility. I pursued this phenomenon with the group to discover that the paramount areas of concern, including Cathy's illness and the behavior of all other family members, were considered upspeakable. The fear of hurting one another or disturbing the fragile integrity of the group was such that only against the greatest resistance was there a glimmer of recognition that anything at all was going wrong. Of course, these fears had to be addressed before other substantive concerns could be considered.

It emerged that the family was regarded as "perfect" and free of conflict. Out of their own unhappy experiences in their nuclear families of origin, both parents established a conscious determination to raise their children in the total absence of anger and conflict. The mother, in particular, believed that "children grew themselves up," and that when differences in values existed, the differences should be erased by parental flexibility, silence, and accommodation. Tension between the generations was conceived as problematic and destructive to the development of children. The mother herself felt that she had been "crushed down" by a "grasping, promiscuous" mother. She forsook her own family as a resource and, with some success, turned for guidance to extrafamilial sources, such as her teachers at school. Fran, the eldest daughter, had chosen her mother's solution of turning away from the family—she had run away three years earlier—and in her case she turned to older men as resources for her own development.

Enormous covert tension existed within the group, but because of the power of the group injunction against conflict, differences were suppressed and a conspiracy of silence evolved. Cathy, for her part, developed a great fear of "totalling" her mother if she shared her hostility and her sexual difficulties. Her silence and inability to ask for help left her in a state of panic that she was adrift, alone in a sea of impulses. Cathy reported a telling dream in which she was in a car driven by an evil woman. The car was swerving dangerously all over the road. Cathy was in the back seat, gripping a child's toy steering wheel, unable to control the motion of the car. She associated the adult driver to her mother and to her own adult impulses.

The initial phase of conjoint family treatment involved exploration of the fears of conflict and differences. Interaction increased as these fears were tested by a tentative sharing of some low-level sexual secrets held by family members. This included the revelation of the father's worries over why Cathy was observed to be using an oral contraceptive and of both parents' monitoring of phone calls to the girls because of the fantasy (which was reality based) that the use of drugs was rather widespread among the children. This had never been discussed. In one powerful emotional moment, the mother confessed that shortly before Cathy's hospitalization, she had entered her daughter's room and read Cathy's diary, which was conspicuously left open on her desk. In her journal, Cathy had detailed her numerous sexual involvements as well as the agonized sense of despair and loss of personal boundaries that followed her affairs.

The mother wept as she reported her discovery, not because of what she learned, but because she feared that her intrusion would destroy Cathy's trust in her. She confessed that reading the diary was "the worst thing I have ever done in my life." This prompted an outburst of weeping from Cathy. She pleaded with her mother that the issue was not that she might distrust her mother because she had read the journal, but rather that she had felt that her mother didn't care what happened to her because she had never mentioned her knowledge of Cathy's sexual relationships and had, by her silence, allowed them to continue. With the door to discussion thus opened, we learned that the mother had on several occasions walked into Cathy's room to find her petting with different boys on her bed. The mother would exit quickly, and no word on the matter was subsequently exchanged. Furthermore, Fran, while she was still living at home at the age of 16, had frequently had her boyfriend spend the night in her bedroom. All family members had closed their eyes to this, and the parents had not even discussed the matter between themselves.

It should be relatively apparent at this point that this family had not been functioning as a resource for Cathy's phase-appropriate need to master the surge of sexual stimulation consequent to puberty. A conspiracy of silence consciously determined by a need to minimize conflict was preventing necessary parental guidance, limit setting, and potential for identification. Cathy felt bereft in her isolated world, her ego overwhelmed by impulses, without the opportunity for support from parental ego functions to shore up from the outside what she was currently lacking from within. This problem of emerging adolescent sexuality was amplified by her preexisting severe character disturbance; developmental failures antedated adolescence. Because of the brevity of this discussion, however, Cathy's underlying borderline personality organization will not be detailed here.

By this time, it may be clear that far more was at play here than simple parental denial of their children's sexual promiscuity. Indeed, by their passivity and unwillingness to set or even discuss limits, both parents were covertly encouraging their daughters' sexual acting out. In fact, both parents had suppressed and compartmentalized their own sexual impulses as a consequence of the harsh superego injunctions each of them had experienced.

Their own marital life was almost devoid of sexual activity. The mother, in an effort to disavow any identification with her own promiscuous mother, had adopted an anhedonic posture for herself in which she was rarely conscious of sexual desires. The father had been restricted by his parents from phase-appropriate sexual activity during his own teenage years. During adolescence, he had periodically run away from home to a nearby city, where he engaged in unspecified, forbidden activities. During family treatment, it emerged that this pattern continued into the present: He absented himself from the home for several weeks at a time to visit a large city, allegedly on business. It was later revealed that these absences did not involve work, but rather were for binges of gambling and, undoubtedly, compartmentalized sexual activity. The details of what he did while away were never clarified during the course of therapy.

It thus became clear to the therapist that an important dynamic was at play in the parents' failure to respond to the sexual promiscuity of their daughters. Both mother and father were enacting their own intraspychic sexual conflict by vicarious gratification of their own forbidden impulses through the acting out of both Cathy and Fran. We refer to this process as *projective identification* (Klein 1946, Zinner 1976). Here, a forbidden aspect of the self is projected onto another. This externalization minimizes intrapsychic conflict by separating the warring elements of the self. At the same time, it permits the individual to experience gratification of the impulse through the hedonistic activities of the recipient of the projections.

Let us look more closely at Cathy's mother to illustrate the nature and impact of projective identification. Throughout her own childhood and adolescence, her mother often brought strange men into the home while her father, who traveled frequently, was away. On a number of occasions she actually witnessed or overheard her mother having sexual relations with these interlopers. Unconsciously these experiences were stimulating to her, and she defended against the sexual arousal by a determined disavowal and repudiation of her mother and of her own sexuality.

She viewed her mother as a sexually driven woman and herself as a saintly and abstinent person. We see now that the mother's covert encouragement of Cathy's and Fran's sexual activities in their own bedrooms represents a highly specific reenactment of Cathy's maternal grandmother's use of the family home as a haven for casual sex.

This is a crucial point to be understood. For the family to function as a resource in Cathy's current sexual development, her parents should have an empathic grasp of Cathy's degree of arousal and vulnerability. In response to this realistic and empathic picture of Cathy, her parents would need to provide guidance, limits, and an open channel for communication, and to offer themselves as objects for identification as sexually active adults and as former adolescents who have encountered similar tensions and temptations. The family is not presently able to provide this facilitating environment, however. Instead, Cathy's entry into puberty has stimulated a reemergence of parental intrapsychic sexual conflicts, and her parents' responses to Cathy's sexuality are dominated by their own efforts to cope with these conflicts. Thus, instead of setting limits on Cathy's involvements with boys, her parents covertly encourage her activities out of their defensive need to externalize their own sexual impulses. I will make the assertion here that whenever the family is failing in a substantial way to provide a facilitating environment for adolescent sexual development, the root cause will be found in the parents' own unresolved sexual conflicts. Thus the restoration of the family to its role as a resource is more than an educational process; it is a psychotherapeutic one in which attention to problems with parental sexuality is a crucial focus.

Up to this point, I have described the opening of communication about sex in Cathy's family by uncovering and working on underlying fears of conflict and aggression. The parents were stunned to be confronted with the impact of their silence and the ways in which it encouraged the behavior and left their daughter feeling unloved, alone, and frightened. What followed was a surge of curiosity on the part of the girls about their parents' social and sexual experiences as adolescents and young adults. As is usually the case, both parents had repressed their own experiences as a part of their overall defensive process of projecting their impulse life onto others. Their mother initially could not recall whether she had ever dated, and with some effort finally remembered that she had "probably gone steady a couple of times." The father recalled only that he was interested in a girl during his late high school years, but that he was permitted to see her only on occasional weekends.

Bit by bit, a sketchy awareness developed that the parents' marital life was not as ideal as had been previously believed. The father's heavy nightly drinking and lengthy absences were discussed for the first time. The crucial process of internalization of parental inner conflicts had begun. The mother urged the father to work with her in marital therapy, but he was adamant in not wanting to delve into himself more deeply. As a result, she requested individual psychotherapy and began treatment with a psychiatrist who was prepared to coordinate his work with the family treatment.

It is an unfortunate development when the spousal partners differ on whether or not to deal with their own inner conflicts and their marital relationship. There is substantial risk that the old defensive marital equilibrium will be shaken and will not be replaced by a new, more gratifying complementarity because the husband and wife are not changing together. We will see the profound effects of such a decision in Cathy's parents' marriage.

The increased awareness of parental sexual conflicts in this family led to a diminished need to use Cathy for their resolution. In a concrete sense, this led to a growing appreciation of Cathy's difficulties in containing her own impulses. A process of limit-setting and parental involvement in her social life began to occur. More ordinary kinds of parent–child confrontations over Cathy's dating habits took place within the family sessions: Cathy was told that she would no longer spend the night out with boys. Cathy objected. Her mother told her that people can be hurt by having casual sex, that they can be exploited, that their feelings are often not taken into account. In another instance, the mother expressed disapproval of Cathy's dating a boy who drank heavily. She worried that Cathy would drink as well and lose control of her impulses. Cathy angrily argued with her, accusing her mother of "an all or nothing" attitude, maintaining that her mother's view was to "avoid the world or be overwhelmed by it." These confrontations were often angry and vehement, but they were important. Both Cathy and her mother felt good, strikingly enough, after the encounter. Cathy remarked with relief that her mother was not "totalled" by her aggression, and her mother was impressed that she, in turn, was not rejected.

The effect of this parental involvement was quite dramatic. Realistic agreements were negotiated and were generally adhered to. Even Cathy's inevitable testing of the limits was within a range of behavior that was not self-destructive and seemed to generate more fruitful family discussion of the issues. Cathy developed the theory that parents should set their expectations "one notch higher" than they mean, so that when children test the limits, their behavior will still be within a tolerable range. This view was directed at her feeling that many of her earlier sexual involvements were a plea for help from her parents and that their lack of response only caused her to amplify her promiscuity in an effort to evoke their concern.

The primary salutary effect of parental support, however, was that Cathy began to exercise a discriminating function of her own with regard to her sexual life. In her individual therapy, she came to examine the pattern of her object choice—in particular, her tendency to gravitate toward sadistic young men. She began to see how her seeming saintliness and altruism evoked sadistic responses in others. "That way I don't have to feel it myself," she said, referring to her own unintegrated sadistic impulses. Previously repressed images of her drunken father leering at her and making provocative remarks came into awareness, and an ultimately unresolved question of some incestuous contact emerged in her individual psychotherapy.

Such material regarding an area of the inner world of sexuality, impulse, and fantasy lies outside the boundary of shared family experience and is not appropriate to conjoint family sessions. Nor is it likely that an adolescent would be willing to share such personal issues with other members. In other families, the failure of family resource functions may be evidenced by *too much* communication and sexual sharing within the sessions and in the home. There may be open discussion of intimate details of the parents' sexual activities during the family therapy meetings, paralleled by such behavior as nudity and exhibitionism within the home. In this instance, the therapist needs to encourage a strengthening of intergenerational boundaries and is in the paradoxical position of analyzing the motives of the family group and *discouraging* the sharing of sexual information within the group.

This is not to say that the concurrent individual therapy is divorced from and not used in the conjoint work. To the contrary, it is the very purpose of such a concurrent individual and family treatment program that the different experiences are closely interdigitated and experience and insight from the one are used productively in the other. For instance, in Cathy's family, her father's drinking became a matter of paramount concern within the conjoint family sessions. Knowledge of his behavior surfaced first through dreams and then in memories in Cathy's individual sessions. It was here that she analyzed her great trepidation at exposing the family secret of her father's drinking within the conjoint meetings. She ultimately did so, and what began as a dream in individual psychotherapy became a subject of general family concern and attention.

The results of the mother's individual therapy were more problematic, though inevitable. She became aware of the degree of her own repressed sexuality and of the variety of her defenses for coping with and externalizing conflicts. She reentered the world after many years of self-enforced isolation. This evolved, first, by her returning to work and in that way finding satisfaction through her own activities, not merely those of her children. She began to become restless over having no social life: She and her husband had no friends and, without hyperbole, never went out or entertained. She formed male and female friendships of her own and urged her husband to join her. He not only demurred but actually encouraged her to develop her own outside relationships. Toward the end of the family treatment, she had removed her wedding ring and was almost certainly involved in a meaningful relationship with another man. Needless to say, there was a period of considerable unhappiness and insecurity for the children as they witnessed what seemed to be an inexorable march toward the termination of their parents' relationship. In the many discussions during the family sessions, however, the father's passive participation in this process was unshakable.

The emergence of Cathy's adolescent sexuality posed both a challenge and an opportunity for her parents. It reactivated old unresolved developmental issues within the parents themselves. With that came the chance that they, as the father did, would simply reenact the old conflicts, employ the old defenses, and remain developmentally as they were before. On the other hand, the problems posed by Cathy's sexuality offered the possibility of new solutions for the parents themselves. The mother chose to follow this path and was able to reintegrate previously projected and disavowed elements of her impulse life. The mother and father became asynchronous in their relationship, and despite the fact that the family came to provide a resource function for Cathy, the earlier complementary equilibrium of the marriage was lost. The old marital equilibrium involved the children in a network of powerful projections that seriously impaired their own development. Children and parents became the casualties of a family group that was defensively structured.

As for Cathy, she terminated treatment at 18, having graduated from high school with her formerly good academic performance restored. Although she herself was without substantial concerns and was free of conscious anxiety and insecurity, the work was far from complete. In particular, I was concerned about a degree of sexual asceticism that was becoming established and by her involvement with an Eastern religious group dedicated to an omniscient leader who seemed to offer his followers permanent respite from threatening dependency issues. This seems to me to represent a compromise formation in Cathy designed to help her cope with the loss consequent to the separation from her family and her home, a form of pseudoindependence. As of today, I do not know the outcome of this stage.

Cathy's story illustrates some technical aspects of dealing with problems of adolescent sexuality in a family context. Ideally, the family is conceived as providing a facilitating environment for the mastery of sexual developmental tasks in its adolescent offspring. When this family environment fails to facilitate, individual development may be substantially impaired. This failure in the family's function can inevitably be traced to the parents' unresolved sexual conflicts which have been reactivated by their awareness of their child's emerging sexuality. There is no simple technical or educational device that can solve this problem. In each case, the particular dynamics of the functional impairment within that family need to be assessed, and technique must be geared to the formulation.

For example, only a sensitive assessment of dynamics can determine whether therapeutic efforts should be directed toward strengthening or toward loosening intergenerational boundaries, toward encouraging more open communication about sex or toward restricting it. An inevitable tension exists between what is appropriately shared within a family and what is kept within the boundary of the self or of the marital dyad. The burdening of the conjoint family treatment with more exclusively intrapsychic matters can be prevented by a program of concurrent treatment which offers the possibility of individual or marital treatment, or both, side by side with the family work. Far from being at odds or in competition with one another, these concurrent therapies are complementary, replicating the natural and appropriate boundaries that exist within the family itself.

22

An Object Relations Approach to Sexuality in Family Life

DAVID E. SCHARFF, M.D.

In early psychoanalytic theory, the unfolding of sexuality and the development of the individual were thought to be almost synonymous (Freud 1905). Fifty years later, Fairbairn, while retaining Freud's term *libido,* applied it, not to sexual energy, but to the forces of attraction in relationships. He thus moved the center of motivation for personal development away from the programmed unfolding of sexual instinct to the series of attachment behaviors (Bowlby 1969) that secure the relationships needed for growth (Sutherland 1963). Innate sexuality, which Freud had seen as the central thread of individual development, could then be related to the vicissitudes of individual and family relatedness.

Recent developments in research and theory offer more specific ways to understand this relationship. This chapter will review the theoretical and observational advances which offer us an updated view of sexual development, its effect on the family, and the family's effect on the sexual development of the individual. These aspects are linked in a cycle of mutual influence.

In Chapter 2, J. Scharff described the application of Fairbairn's theory to an object relations view of individual and family development (see also Scharff and Scharff 1987). The final form of Fairbairn's formulation (1963) is summarized in Figure 22-1, which shows the central ego and its ideal object and the two split-off and repressed areas of unbearably painful exciting and rejecting systems of relating. I want to begin by reviewing and elaborating on this aspect of individual structure because it is critical for sexual relatedness.

The antilibidinal, or rejecting, system, consisting of the rejecting object and the part of the self that adheres to the rejecting object, is characterized by such painful affects as anger, frustration, and anxiety. The libidinal, or

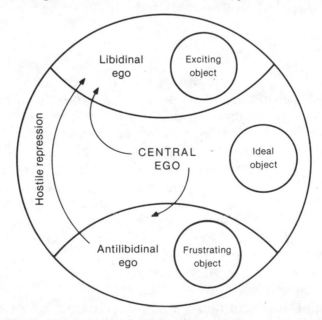

Figure 22-1. Fairbairn's model of psychic organization, by D. E. Scharff, from *The Sexual Relationship: An Object Relations View of Sex and the Family.* Reprinted courtesy of Routledge and Kegan Paul.

exciting, system, characterized by neediness, longing, and anxiety, consists of an exciting object that has also been described as tantalizing (Ogden 1986) and a part of the self that craves satisfaction from it. The object is excessively exciting of need, while the self is perpetually stimulated to long for an unrequited satisfaction. This feeling of longing is just as painful as the rage of the rejecting object system. The exciting object and the rejecting object are both brands of bad object.

Ogden (1982) emphasized Fairbairn's point that an interpersonal experience had been internalized and that an inner relationship not a drive would be expressed in the transference. It is important, however, to keep in mind that these constellations do not represent a simple internalization of actual experience with an external person. They are multilayered representations built up at different levels of development over the years as the growing person takes in the experience of relationships as modified by his own fantasies and by the limited ability to understand that which was present during the particular stage of development at the time of each experience.

Once these internal object relations structures are in place, they have a dynamic relationship to one another. While the central ego is the agent of repression in the first place, antilibidinal ego associated with the rejecting object further represses the libidinal ego associated with the exciting object in the painfully need-excited system. Fairbairn concluded this from his finding that it was easier for a hysterical patient to be in an angry or rejecting posture than to suffer from unrequited longing. A similar finding from couple and family therapy is provided by an adult couple (or a parent and child) who fight endlessly so that we may wonder why they stay together. Dynamically, it is so painful for them to yearn for each other when they do not feel loved that they cover the yearning with fighting. Their fighting often has a sexualized quality and can eventually be understood to constitute a substitute for sexual gratification (see Figure 2-1 on p. 14).

Another observation must be added to those of

Fairbairn, however. It is equally likely that we will see a further repression of the antilibidinal (rejecting) system by the libidinal (excited) system. In this case, a couple or family exudes a sticky sweetness or an overly close, anxious clinging that forbids ordinary separation and individuation. Clinically, we may get an uncomfortable sense of how this way of relating papers over angry wishes to attack or fears of hurt and abandonment (Scharff and Scharff 1987).

While most clinicians are fully familiar with the vicissitudes of the rejecting object, they tend to be less aware of the toll taken by the repressed "need-exciting object." In a theory of sexuality, the exciting system is especially helpful. In giving the need-exciting object the name *libidinal object*, Fairbairn sought to underscore the link between the affect invested in that object and Freud's use of the term *libido* for sexual energy. In the normal personality, the libidinal system is not so heavily repressed. In states of sexual arousal and falling in love, for instance, it is available to color and enhance the central ego and its sexual relatedness to its ideal object, now refound in the lover. Overly preoccupying sexual pining occurs, however, when the urge in sexual relating, which pulls one person toward another, resonates with the excited part of the person's unconscious. This excessive, painful sexual longing is apt either to be repressed or to result in one or another sort of symptomatic sexual behavior. In the remainder of this chapter I will explore the nature and the effects of the interplay of the excitement of excessive longing and the rejection of needs both in individual sexuality and in the family context.

FAMILY INTERACTION

Klein's concepts of projective and introjective identification have given us a way of understanding unconscious communication between the individual and his objects

(Klein 1975 a,b, Segal 1964). The individual projects parts of himself into his primary external objects—sometimes treasured parts to be kept safely, at other times hated or denied parts—to be rid of them or to "cure" them in the other. The other person is then treated as though characterized by these parts. This unconscious form of communication is normally the basis of empathy between parent and child or between two spouses. It is subject to pathological skewing, however, and then forms the unconscious vehicle for pained relationships. The action of mutual projective identification in marriage was described by Dicks (1967), and elaborated in Chapters 9 and 10 by Zinner and Frank. R. Shapiro (1979) described the family as a special small group with shared unconscious assumptions that shape its unconscious life and within which multiple family-wide individual projective identifications take place. In considering sexuality, we will be most interested in those shared unconscious assumptions that bear on the lure or dangers of sexual ways of relating, and on the reciprocal influence of family-wide and individual sexual issues.

THE PSYCHOSOMATIC PARTNERSHIP

A mother and infant have a psychosomatic partnership—an intense relationship, which in the beginning organizes the infant through holding and handling by the mother and interaction with her (Winnicott 1960, 1971). Interactive mirroring is a fundamental part of this: The mother reflects the infant's condition to him, usually while holding the baby in her arms as well as in her gaze. At the same time the infant is the instrument of the mother's own unconscious needs. The mother offers her vision of the infant's identity, and in the process of introjecting this identity, the infant organizes its unformed experience (Lichtenstein 1961).

The mother forms the "container" (Bion 1967) for the

infant's experience, negotiating an active, secure, and loving arrangement, which *from the beginning* also leads to a separation from the mother. We now know that separation and individuation do not begin, as Mahler and her colleagues (1975) described, in approximately the eighth month. The infant is a separate being from the beginning, from the first interactions with its mother (Stern 1985).

As the mother holds and handles the baby, she provides *contextual holding,* the arms-around envelope of security in which she and the infant can relate (Scharff and Scharff 1987). This "holding function" sets the stage for the other aspect of her relationship with the infant: centered relating. In the *centered relationship,* she looks into the infant's eyes, speaks to it, and provides confirmation of its experience and capacity. In this role, she provides the basic building blocks of the infant's internal objects. The infant reciprocates by "holding" the mother with its body, molding, and responding in ways that provide the building blocks for new aspects of her internal object life, now as a mother. The relationship is mutual and reciprocal; on both sides it includes two aspects: holding each other safely and securely, and relating centrally in interaction at the core of being. When I refer to the "mother" here, I mean the person who does the mothering, not necessarily the biological mother. This certainly includes the father when he is handling the infant.

The father has his own primary relationship to the infant, which is similar to the mother's in providing care. But it differs from hers in being more physically and emotionally exciting. Since mothers tend to provide lower-key, steadier rhythms in their relationship to their infants, while fathers wind infants up in a more exciting way, we can speculate that the mother provides a model for reliability and rejection—the antilibidinal pole—while fathers provide a model for excitement and longing—the libidinal pole (Scharff and Scharff 1987). The father also provides an outer envelope of holding around the mother–

infant pair. As they also provide holding to him, this constitutes the family's *shared holding capacity* (Scharff and Scharff 1987).

The beginning of the centered relationship and the contextual holding is in the psychosomatic partnership. The relationship between parent and infant is, at the same time, both completely somatic and completely psychological. As the child develops, the relationship is progressively less somatic and more psychological. The amount of time in physical contact decreases, and psychological, verbal, and symbolic interaction replace the original dominance of the somatic. For most of development, the overriding importance of somatic exchange recedes, except in the case of sexual development. The somatic route to innermost psychological life, to internal objects, is established in the first weeks of life. It is therefore on this bedrock that developmental levels of sexual interaction are built, and it is this fundamental heritage that is drawn upon in the physical sexual exchanges of later life (D. Scharff 1982).

Masters and Johnson's (1966, 1970) work on adult sexual function and dysfunction provides the major data that helps us understand the operation of the psychosomatic partnership in adult sexuality. Their research described sexual physiology—the somatic side of sexuality—while their behavioral treatment format allowed us to study the meaning of the experience of two people in intense interaction. The psychological side of the partnership format provided much fuller descriptions of sexual interaction. Most sexual difficulties, viewed from an object relations perspective, are not really dysfunctions in the sense of a mechanical failure. Rather, they are what I have called "disjunctions"—somatically expressed failures in fit between internal object relations (D. Scharff 1982). The adult sexual partnership echoes the experience of the early mother–infant psychosomatic interaction—the only other time in the life cycle when physical interaction and psychological intimacy are so closely intertwined. Sexual interaction represents the physical expression of primary emotional bonds, inheriting this role from parent–infant interaction. Adult physical experience reawakens and reverberates with the emotional aspects of this earliest set of relationships. Sexual life, however, also absorbs currents from inner object relationships derived after infancy, from latency, adolescence, and adulthood.

THE FAMILY AND SEXUAL DEVELOPMENT

We must now factor in development, both of the individual and of the family as a whole. Growth and change in the individual throughout the developmental phases affect the family; at the same time, the individual is influenced by the changing nature of the family as it moves through the family life cycle. I will elaborate here on those areas of development that are specifically sexual.

At certain phases, genital sexuality leads or at least is closely connected with the developmental push. The first of these periods might be said to occur during the infant's second year of life, when infantile masturbation becomes a regular feature. Infants will play with their genitals during this period provided that they have previously received adequate physical holding and handling within the context of a loving relationship (Kleeman 1966, 1967).

The next sexual era is the phallic-narcissistic period (Edgcumbe and Burgner 1975). Boys and girls become acutely aware of their genitals and those of others before they are yet focused on the problems of triangular relationships. They are equally interested in displaying themselves to excite mother or father or both. This period is introduced by internal sexual energizing of the child and by cognitive advances permitting recognition of difference.

Oedipal development, beginning a few months after the phallic-narcissistic era, is introduced by another cognitive leap. Now the child, who has been aware of the relationship between the parents, tries to solve the problem of his ambivalence about each of them and about their pairing. In deciding that one parent is the sexually desired object and the other is the rival, the child attempts to fashion a solution for the problem of trying to deal with two ambivalently charged objects. In the oedipal struggle, the child usually solves the problem of ambivalence by making one parent the good object and the other the feared bad object, thus separating the pair. The child makes the assignment of good or bad along sexual lines, and this assignment normally changes from the negative oedipal stage, during which the same-sex parent is the good one, to the positive oedipal stage, during which the opposite-sex parent is the good one and the other is the rival. Fairbairn (1952) pointed out that in designing this solution, the child makes up the oedipal situation. We can see, however, that it is not just the child's internal situation that is thus skewed, but that the child actually invents a form of family structure and then imposes it on the family through projective identification. In this way, children actually reinvent their families during the oedipal period, and this internal solution has ramifications for the family as a whole (Scharff and Scharff 1987).

Although the family of a latency-age child has its own sexual issues, sex is not at the leading edge of development. During puberty and early adolescence, however, masturbation and the beginnings of age-appropriate sexual exchange once again bring sexuality to developmental prominence. The "central masturbation fantasy" (Laufer 1976) can be seen as an elaboration of the adolescent's principal object relations issues tied to the physical intensity of masturbation. Finally, courting in later adolescence, mate selection, and reproduction in young adulthood occur during periods of development when sex, individual development, and family development are more obviously closely allied. In each of these periods, a sexual push from inside the individual gives expression to object-related issues in newly sexualized "language."

We can now tie the contributions of psychoanalytic drive theory, first described by Freud (1905) in "Three Essays on the Theory of Sexuality" to the growth of relationships in the family. Sexual drives unfold within the context of the relationship to parents, family, and later successors to these original primary objects. These relationships begin with the original psychosomatic relationship and progress to predominantly psychological relating. Since the drive aspects of sexual development are expressed within somatic and psychological relatedness, sexual development can be understood only in the context of relationships to both internal and external objects.

Sexual Symptomatology

Several types of family factors determine whether symptom expression in children will take a sexual form.

Trauma. If early experiences of object loss, trauma, or neglect occur during one of the periods of heightened genital urgency, the symptoms of loss are apt to take a sexual form.

Context. The family sets the *context* for development. For instance, certain families (that is, mothers, fathers, and other caregivers) stimulate the *oversexualization* of relationships because they, at their relatively more advanced level of development, use sexual interaction as an overriding language for all emotional exchange. They provide a sexually excited, or libidinized, context for general development. For instance, parents who have a sense of having missed something in their own sexual lives pass on to their adolescent children an unconscious message that their sexual activity is longed for (Johnson and Szurek 1952, Szurek 1974). While feeling sexually deprived themselves, these parents encourage the children to form a projective identification with their excited longing for sexual expression. The children then act out sexually on behalf of the parents.

Other families minimize the importance of sexuality in development and in relationships, thereby denying the sexual significance of even obviously sexual aspects, such as a child's masturbation, a 4-year-old girl's excited love for her father, or an adolescent's pubertal development. These families provide an *antisexualizing context* for development, encouraging excessive repression of sexual issues in the growing child.

This minimization of sexual exchange and its significance leads to repression of the libidinal system and results in later inhibitions of sexual life or in the excision of parts of ordinary sexual function. A hysterical woman who says that she would be happy with her marriage if only sex were not required is often expressing the result of this kind of family influence. There are also those who have a split form of sexual repression; they enjoy genital arousal but are terrified of touch elsewhere. For instance, one genitally responsive woman forbade her dependent husband to touch her breast, saying the skin was "irritable." For her, the unconscious meaning of his touching her breasts was that she would be turned into a mother who would be sucked dry and abandoned, a fear which echoed what she felt had happened to her own mother.

Cognitive models. Children contribute to the process of their own growth. They have a progressive fantasy life during development. At each forward move, certain distortions occur because each new step of development is negotiated at first as if the model for prior stages still applies (Scharff and Scharff 1987). But each new stage of sexual development occurs to accommodate something new; thus the old model is not quite right—and it is the parents' job as guardians of the child's growth to correct for the new situation. If the parents are vulnerable at such a point, for instance at the oedipal stage—then the child's development may be sexualized and may in turn sexualize the family's overall climate.

An example of a child's developmental distortion of meaning is the case of a 3-year-old girl who announced to her mother one day that her "bottom" was an alligator with big teeth. She provided an example of the vagina dentata *in statu nascendi*. She modeled her understanding of her vulva on the earlier model of the mouth. The mother, acting as an organizing container, suggested that the vagina did not have teeth and therefore would not bite, thus encouraging the girl to develop a less threatening model of her body. In so doing, the mother contributed to the girl's body identity, not through a physical exchange, but by providing a holding relationship of understanding and tolerance, inside which she took the girl's concern and provided modified building blocks for her self-image.

Both process and content were involved when the mother modified her daughter's image of her body. As she talked in a loving and understanding way, she embodied the vagina as a loving, not a biting, organ. On the other hand, patients whose parents have been forbidding about sexual questions, perhaps snapping "That's dirty!" or "Don't touch yourself there!" when viewing childhood masturbation, have taken in the notion that sexual organs form part of a biting or rejecting relationship. The bodily identity is formed within the contextual holding that the parents offer the child, and the image of the body forms the vehicle for future relating in the sexual psychosomatic partnership. Thus when this mother helped her daughter to soften her image of her own genitals, she was also keeping the child's developmental preoccupation from lending an aggressively tinged sexualization to the relationship with her and with the family as a whole.

Marital relationship. The parents' marriage is the principal determinant of the balance between satisfactory and unsatisfactory internal object relationships in the family. Children are aware, consciously and unconsciously, of the relationship between their parents and indeed internalize an image of the paired good, loving parents and rejecting, hating parents as part of their own internal world. If the parents' relationship is frustrating, either emotionally or sexually, they may turn to the child for the love they miss from each other, thus heightening the need-exciting system between child and parent, and pushing the child toward excited relationships that may or may not be specifically sexualized. Furthermore, the child will be guiltily aware at some level that this heightening of excitement between child and parents covers rejection between the couple, with which the child may also identify.

Transmission of internal object relations. Aspects of the parents' internal object relations affect their children directly through projective identification. If they have experienced deprivation or sexual trauma in their own development, the internalization of these factors will have an independent effect on their relationships with their children.

The following case (also described in Chapter 23 on transference, countertransference, and technique) illustrates many of these points about sexuality and the family.

Mr. and Mrs. Simpson sought treatment for sexual dysfunction. Mrs. Simpson said, "I just hate sex. That's all." Mr. Simpson said that he regretted the strain placed on his wife both of his lifelong premature ejaculation, his intromission of only 1 to 3 minutes, and his sexual desire; he hoped I could abolish the latter with saltpeter. Mrs. Simpson's lack of sexual desire and even avoidance of arousal could be traced to her childhood experiences. Her father had been verbally and physically abusive, while her mother seemed helpless to intervene. She had had a few episodes of sexual interaction with her brother in preadolescence, which, while partly traumatic, also seemed to offer more love than she felt she could find elsewhere in her family. Sex had assumed a threatening yet beckoning quality for her.

Mr. Simpson had no memory of his childhood for the first two years of marital sessions. All he could remember was that his father had been arrested for making homosexual advances in a men's bathroom when Mr. Simpson was 15, and that his parents' marriage had dissolved at that time and he had lost regular contact with his father. For his earlier childhood, he had complete amnesia. Only during family therapy did he begin to remember parts of his earlier life. Once he remembered being strapped by his father at about the age of 12 for being next door alone with a girl. But the most significant recovery of memory was his recollection that his father had forced anal intercourse on him when he was about the same age, and that Mr. Simpson had subsequently committed sodomy on his brother.

When the Simpsons were first seen, they told me of their concern for their 5½-year-old middle child, Alex. He was grossly immature, had school behavior problems, and was both encopretic and enuretic. He had been born after they already had one boy, Eric, and Mrs. Simpson had been devastated that Alex was not a girl. This disappointment contributed to her prolonged postpartum depression, and she felt guilty that her illness might have caused Alex's difficulties. The Simpsons readily agreed to both a family evaluation and an individual evaluation for Alex.

In the family evaluation, Alex demonstrated a combined picture of hyperactivity and attention deficit disorder. The oldest son, 8-year-old Eric, had no outstanding problems. The youngest child, 3½-year-old Jeanette, used immature speech and had a sexualized way of interacting. She was often as disruptive as Alex was, but she got away with it, coyly playing on her charm. Whereas Alex was impulsive and bumptious, she was sly and charming—but to the same effect.

At one point in the interview, Mr. and Mrs. Simpson, speaking obliquely, said that their fights occurred when he wanted sex and she did not. As they talked, Alex built an elongated tunnel out of blocks, which he said was a firehouse. Jeanette took a firetruck with a ladder that could be raised and lowered, and pushed it through the tunnel, wrecking it. When I called this juxtaposition of child's play and adult discussion to the attention of the parents, they laughed in recognition of the theme. Eric offered the opinion that Jeanette would always cause this kind of wreckage, while Alex could drive more skillfully.

This play seemed to represent the children's understanding that phallic activity was felt to be fundamentally destructive to their mother and was therefore to be avoided. However, Eric's comments indicated that girl's were more sexually destructive than boys—a view not consciously shared by the parents but consistent with Jeanette's impulsivity and Mrs. Simpson's barely concealed anger.

Later in the session, the children played out the way in which a father doll or a baby could "drive a ship" by lying down—that is, by being passive. And Alex then played at grinding up the father doll by inserting it into a cement mixer.

While this was going on, Eric drew pictures of cosmic wars in which the good guys fought off horrendous interstellar attacks. He continued to comment on his siblings' play. He seemed to be the "good" and well-adjusted child. However, on reevaluation a year later, he also seemed to view himself as a harmful person, an internalization that had not been observable initially.

As a result of this interview, several characteristics that reflect sexual difficulty in this family became apparent. First, the parents' sexual dysfunction represented the net result of their individual histories. Each had grown up in a family in which hopes for love were frustrated and in which aggressive, but sexualized relationships with family members were substituted. The resultant fear of sex was something they shared, even though both hoped for a sexual life. Mrs. Simpson's openly acknowledged fear and hatred of sex were matched by her husband's unconscious fear of sex. In trying to rid himself of his own sexual wishes in order to protect her, he was, through projective identification, trying to protect himself from the "bad father." The couple shared a fear of sex and an idea that the mother would be harmed by the bad father's penis.

The resulting sexual difficulty and tension between the couple affected the entire family. The children shared the anxiety about the couple's well-being, and each incorporated different elements of the difficulty. The children would often quarrel to draw attention from a potential fight between the parents. Eric, the oldest, tried to be "good," to use rational and latency defenses to combat the masculine forces of evil in the universe and in the family, but he had absorbed the identity of the destructive father. Alex, the middle boy, had attempted to stay his development in order to avoid growing into a destructive man, but his incorporation of an intolerance for aggression, taken from both parents, led him to soil his pants whenever he might otherwise have become angry. He continued to use an anal technique of relating instead of advancing to a phallic or oedipal one. Thus he could disguise his oedipal strivings for his mother and his rivalry with his father, and could maintain a kind of innocent, infantile impulsivity. Seen from the first as the child who could give to everybody, Jeanette now had a precocious seductive quality, which, as Eric noted, frequently caused wrecks but without drawing blame.

Thus, in these various ways according to their different developmental stages, the children had incorporated aspects of the parental problem and were now in turn affecting the family. Alex's birth had triggered Mrs. Simpson's original depression and emphasized her sexual withdrawal. Jeanette's oedipal development was sexualizing the family despite their fear of sex. And Eric's latency defenses were joined by the parents as they tried to do the right thing in therapy to make reason of their difficulties.

The parents' sexual difficulty followed from their object relations history. In turn, their relationship formed the holding context for the family and then provided the object relations material that determined the shape of the children's developmental troubles. The dynamic connections between these elements were demonstrated and interpreted in family therapy. The fact of their dissatisfaction with their sexual life could be worked with in family therapy, but the specifics of their sexual difficulties were not addressed with the children present. Once the family therapy was on course, the Simpsons began sex therapy for themselves. She became responsive and orgasmic, and he became able to sustain intercourse for about ten minutes, long enough for her to be satisfied.

Treatment of this family over a period of two and a half years involved individual therapy for Mrs. Simpson and Alex, family therapy, and sex therapy for the couple. Treatment enabled the couple to reconstruct a satisfying sexual relationship, to work with Mrs. Simpson's severe depression, to partially relieve Mr. Simpson's neurotic memory loss, and to give a developmental boost to each of the children. As we did in this case, we customarily use an understanding of the interrelation of sexual and family development to help such families avoid the transgenerational transmission of general and specific sexual difficulty through solving developmental problems that can otherwise crystallize as internal object relations structure in the children.

THE CYCLE OF MUTUAL INFLUENCE

The experience with this family allows us to see the intergenerational sexual issues from their initial development in the couple, to their transmission to their children, to the children's influence on parental sexuality. Parents bring their own object relations to the marriage, and the unconscious aspect of their sexual relationship is determined by their shared object relations. In turn, parents influence children, both by the individual relationships each parent has with the child and by the kind of couple's relationship they present to the child. Children internalize these elements—a relationship to each parent and to the two of them combined—and split off the painful parts, modifying their internal worlds in complex ways as they do so. The internal object relations thus formed determine the child's emotional path through subsequent developmental stages. In turn, however, the children modify their families from the time of birth, introducing conscious and unconscious challenges to the family, and becoming a new primary object for the parents. As they also internalize experience with the child—individually and as a couple—the parents' internal worlds are forever altered. This alteration may result in sexual or nonsexual symptomatology. When sexual strain in the couple's relationship does ensue, it may in turn have a further effect on the family as a whole. Family maturity and sexuality develop in a cycle of mutual influence.

When as clinicians we are presented with sexual symptomatology, our determination of an appropriate intervention rests on whether it is the internal object relations constellation of a single family member or the mutual projective identification of the couple or family that poses the predominant difficulty. If we are seeing a single individual without a partner or nuclear family, individual therapy or group therapy are our only options. But in circumstances in which there is a partner, spouse, or family, the question of how to balance the intervention is more complex. Many modes of intervention—individual, couples, family, group, and sex therapy—are mutually compatible when each therapist uses an object relations approach. With the family and couple, we are working with their capacity to provide shared holding for the family as a group, and for the growth of relationships and of individual family members. With the individual, we look together at the internal object relations difficulties. In conjoint sex therapy, a symptom the couple shares is used as a vehicle to look both at the failure of their mutual holding capacity and at strains in their combined internal object relations. More than one therapy format can be used simultaneously, as was the case with the Simpson family. These approaches and their integration have been elaborated elsewhere (D. Scharff 1982, Scharff and Scharff 1987).

In families and patients with sexual difficulties, we attempt to link the sexual symptoms with other currents of development—to uncover the object relations issues that have impaired the individual and family capacity. When we are successful, we provide a context in which sexual symptomatology can be traced to its origin in internal object relations. The individual and the family can then improve the quality of their relationships and are all freed to love in new ways and to be loved in return.

PART VII

OBJECT RELATIONS
FAMILY THERAPY

23

Transference, Countertransference, and Technique in Object Relations Family Therapy

DAVID E. SCHARFF, M.D.

Object relations family therapy is a way of working at the core of the family's experience so that the therapist can understand the family's issues by taking in its members' struggles to relate to one another and to the therapist. Opening-phase technique establishes the therapist's capacity for helping the family by sharing that understanding. The aim is to facilitate the family's ability to work as a group and to foster the development of each family member.

Reflecting the Kleinian influence (Box et al. 1981, Scharff and Scharff 1987, Williams 1981), transference and countertransference are at the heart of technique in object relations family therapy. They offer the living bridge between therapist and family through which the family's shared unconscious assumptions, mutual projective identifications, pained relationships, and deficits in providing holding to one another can be experienced, understood, and fed back to the family in modified form. Thus, transference and countertransference are central. It follows that object relations family therapy does not depend principally on an assembly of techniques. There are other aspects to the technical approach, to be sure, but all of them are aimed at securing the treatment alliance and supporting the emergence of transference.

This chapter will outline the basics of the use of transference and countertransference. In addition, it will sketch the aspects of technique that set the stage for their use with families, and illustrate this way of working. (A full elaboration can be found in Scharff and Scharff 1987.)

THE ORIGINS OF FAMILY TRANSFERENCE

Transference, in individual therapy and in family therapy, can be thought of as emanating from two aspects of relating, which give rise to a contextual and a focused transference, respectively (Scharff and Scharff 1987). In the earliest intimate relationship, the first aspect is seen when the mother holds the infant in her arms, providing the *context* of their relationship. She and the infant carry out the second aspect of relating when they look into each other's eyes, converse, and respond to each other with the subtle changes in position that convey the mutual responsiveness of the *focused* relationship that centers on and penetrates to the core of infant and mother. The focused relationship depends on "eye-to-eye" and "I-to-I" contact facilitated by the mother's capacity for *centered holding*, while the provision of the context is characterized by the "arms-around" quality of *contextual holding*.

A patient's transference to the therapist stems from each of these two aspects of relating. First, the patient has expectations based on experience of others' capacity to provide "arms-around" holding in relationships. These expectations and fears of failure in holding form the *contextual transference.* The patient also brings expectations and fantasies based on the experience of centered relating, which are recorded as the internal object relations that form the structure of the patient's internal world. This *focused transference* consists of the projection of these internal object relations into the therapist through projective identification (Zinner 1976, Zinner and R. Shapiro 1972). In the early phases of individual therapy, the contextual transference is prominent and must be attended to in order to facilitate the later development of the focused transference.

Both aspects of transference also occur in marital and family therapy. Spouses or family members bring to therapy their focused transferences, which have already been operating in their relationships to one another. They also bring a shared couple or family transference to the therapist. This shared contextual transference is built around their shared hopes and fears about the therapist's capacity to help—specifically by shoring up their deficient ability to provide holding for themselves. This deficit in the family's ability to provide holding for the family as a group interests us most, because if the family can be helped to do a better job of it, it will then be able to provide for individual needs for development and for centered relating. In object relations family therapy, therefore, the therapist can most easily and usefully organize understanding of the family around the information gained from the family's shared contextual transference.

COUNTERTRANSFERENCE IN FAMILY THERAPY

Countertransference in family therapy, as in individual therapy, refers to the affective experience of the therapist in joining with the family. Its individual and pooled transferences get inside the therapist and resonate internally. While the resonance may at times be with unfamiliar areas of the therapist's unconscious, creating problematic responses, this is not the point of emphasis about countertransference. Countertransference in my view refers to the totality of the affective responses that occur when the family creates an impact that penetrates beyond the therapist's conscious and relatively reasonable capacity to understand. The family's object relations system reaches an area of the therapist's unconscious where it resonates with the therapist's own internal object relations. Training and personal therapy prepare the therapist's psyche as a fertile ground in which these internal experiences can take hold, in which the growth of meaning amidst uncertainty can be cultivated, and out of which is garnered a harvest of intimate understanding of the family from the ripened countertransference. In this way, therapists allow themselves to be the substrate for a newly emerging understanding, which they then feed back to the family in the form of interpretation.

The two forms of countertransference correspond to the two forms of transference. The *contextual countertransference* is stirred by the family's expectations and projections about the therapist's capacity to provide contextual holding, and resonates with the therapist's internal issues as a provider of holding—a sort of parent to the family's growth. The individual family members' focused transferences stir various versions of *focused countertransference* in the therapist, which consist of his own centered object relations issues. If focused transference and countertransference become dominant during the course of family therapy, however, we should regard this as the family's attempt to substitute individual experience for their shared experience—evidence that the family is using one member as a spokesperson for the shared contextual transference. Thus, if we find ourselves feeling bullied by an angry adolescent, it is likely that the family feels bullied by him and that the members' shared feeling that they cannot provide holding to his anxiety is being expressed to us in the parents' collusion to make his bullying the prominent message. In this situation, we use the experience of the adolescent's bullying to speak primarily to *the family's shared difficulty*, not simply to the bullying adolescent. Our work is to understand the reason that the family is needing to speak through this adolescent.

TECHNIQUE IN OBJECT RELATIONS FAMILY THERAPY

I will now turn to what we do on the way to gathering enough experience with the family to be able to have a transference–countertransference experience to work with and feed back to the family. The family therapist's activities fall into a number of categories. They will be listed and briefly discussed and then illustrated with a report of a session. Some of these functions will be obvious; others will be more controversial.

Provision of the Space within a Frame

The therapist provides a literal and a psychological space for the rediscovery of lost parts of the family and of the individuals' selves. Echoing the holding capacity of the therapist, the style of the office (his seating, comfort, and provision of toys) facilitates the work. However, the therapist's attitude can transcend dilapidated surroundings in a clinic, the unfamiliar physical space of the family's own home, or even the invasion of the office by video cameras or students. Ideally, the office should be pleasant, with toys and drawing paper for the children, a sense of privacy and security but not opulence, and a flexible seating arrangement.

In all cases, we are responsible for managing the frame of the therapy—the arrangement of appointments, payment, and other agreements. Consistency in these matters, as discussed in Chapter 18, clarifies the interface between therapist and family.

Management of the Environment

The therapist is responsible for management, but this is not the same as being directorial. While we might occasionally give advice or stop a child from writing on the walls when the parents will not, our management generally consists of the active maintenance of a situation that supports the job of therapeutic holding, understanding, and giving feedback or interpretation. Consider, for example, children who charge into the office at the beginning of the session and fight for the red swivel chair. We don't usually have to grab the 10-year-old loser and tie him down as he kicks his triumphant sister, who turns to complain to her parents that she has been mistreated yet again. Management here consists only of monitoring this opening family gambit and the parents' handling of it. Thus, in this case, the act of management may be to *not* manage the family, but to manage ourselves as we begin our own processing of the events, the seating configuration, and the way in which the family begins the session. In a future session, however, we might well have to actively manage discussion of the parents' attitude about the frame if, for instance, they had allowed that beleaguered sister to miss the next therapy hour.

Modeling Ways of Working Together

It is generally agreed that it is not useful for the family therapist to be a blank screen. While we may want to follow the family members' lead to see how they work and interact, we may also take the responsibility of suggesting ways of working that they had not considered. We need a way of interacting to which they can relate. Vocabulary and manner must be adjusted to accommodate the family's style: Humor and informality may fit one family, while a more formal or even reserved style might be better for the next one. The therapist's choice of language is dictated by his own level of comfort in relation to the family and by his assessment of what to do to make the family comfortable.

Following are various essential components of our way of working, which offer therapeutic experiences that the family then learns to provide for itself.

Questioning about feelings. Some families give a detailed account of family interaction or explain away behavior. These cognitive styles tend to obliterate feeling and substitute explanation for understanding. We use affect and nonverbal communication as our guide to detecting feelings. We follow expressed affect and try to detect unexpressed affect by observing gestures and by commenting on and directly questioning about feelings.

Enlarging the field of participation. We elicit from all family members, especially the children, their points of view. If they participate spontaneously, we do not need to interview them deliberately, but we do check to be sure that everyone has a chance to be heard. This requires that we establish ways of talking with each person. If the family includes young children, then play must be a medium of communication; and we may have to demonstrate to the family how to use and understand play. The young child speaks through play and is most at ease—and most attentive—while at play. Parents can sometimes be shown how to listen to children's play and to speak through it more effectively, if we use play to communicate back to the child and to the family (Scharff and Scharff 1987, Zilbach 1986). (The technique of play is discussed more fully in Chapter 24.)

Enlarging the family's scope of exploration. By observing and asking exploratory and sometimes probing questions, we enlarge our perspective. We encourage conversation from one family member to another, and then perhaps to a third, as follows: "How do you feel, John, as your mother says to your father that she isn't sure she loves him?" Thus we create space for listening to one another. We then help the family to use its group level of experience as an organizer. We also ask for a history of the situation, during affective moments, constructing what Grunebaum once described to me as an "affect bridge" to internal objects.

Aspects of enlarging the scope of family exploration are as follows:

- Enlarging the individuals' observing egos,

- Exploring marital discord and sibling conflict, and the relationship of these to each other,

- Getting a history of the internal objects—the past history of the parents' families of origin, of the marriage, and of the children's development within the present family, including the children's version of that history according to their selective memories,

- Using the family group as a resource.

We do not advocate constructing a genogram in a structured way at a preset time. Instead, we find that a history gathered at a time when an emotional issue is current is likely to provide more meaningful object relations information. Thus, although we do get a brief history of the parents' childhoods early on, we do not fully explore the object relations history until we reach a tense moment or an impasse. Then, with their feelings accessible and attention aroused, family members can respond to our questions about whether this situation brings anything to mind about their developmental histories, or perhaps about the parents' marriage. A dynamic family and internal object history obtained at an affective moment creates a bridge between past and present, conscious and unconscious, and thinking and feeling, and so offers the family an opportunity to develop increased empathy and insight.

In the family in which I was being bullied by the adolescent son as the father looked on helplessly, I asked the father about his own experience at that age. He answered that although he could hold his own with his contemporaries, he was picked on regularly by older boys. His wife then interjected that she felt that he had probably somehow provoked them, because he provoked her and his son. He could then begin to explore his provocativeness, opening the way for the son to do so as well. When I asked whether something had been going on between him and his parents during this period, it occurred to him that his parents' fighting and eventual divorce had begun then, and he became suddenly tearful. The son then dropped his bullying attitude and began to share his own fears and uncertainties.

Reflecting and digesting. This category of activities involves tolerance, taking in, reflecting, and digesting. These absorptive activities give us space to think and to analyze our own responses and countertransference. We model for the family this process of creating space for review. This constitutes the receptive aspect of what Bion (1967) has called *containment*, a concept Box (1984) applied to families. This is our contribution to creating mental and emotional space in which many things happen and can be spoken and felt, but especially in which projections can be reexamined.

Supporting and advising. We can give advice, especially to families with young children, but with older children, it is often preferable to examine the deficits in the family's shared holding capacity that lead the parents to ask the therapist for advice.

One mother presented the problem of endless fights with her 12-year-old daughter when she tried to help her daughter with her homework.

"What should I do?" the mother asked me.

"Well, now you are trying to get me to help you with *your* homework," I interpreted to the mother. She laughed, and the father looked at me and nodded while the daughter gave a mild "I told you so" glance.

Then the mother said, "You mean it's all right if I tell her I won't help her with her homework if she yells at me? And just let her fail the test?"

I gave our tried and true response: "What do you think?"

She replied, "I guess if she does fail, she won't yell at me the next time. Or maybe she'll pass and she won't need me to help at all! Huh! I never thought of that. Okay, I'll try it!" And she looked at me with a tilted head and querying glance, clearly not completely convinced. The daughter voiced no objection, and the father nodded briskly as if he had known it all along.

Feedback and Interpretation

This includes all the functions of clarifying, mirroring, and pointing out inconsistencies and repetitive behaviors in the family. The language we use depends, among other factors, on the age of the children, the levels of the family's understanding, and their alliance with us. There are many degrees of interpretation, from superficial to deep. We usually verbalize an interpretation, but sometimes we interpret nonverbally, say by adding to a child's drawing. Or we might offer a behavioral interpretation, as we do in the following vignette.

A parent is being strict with her 5-year-old daughter, insisting that she sit quietly while we talk. The therapist quietly begins to play with the child and to invite her to move around the room, thus making a nonverbal statement to the parents and to the child—a behavioral interpretation, made without having to defy the parent directly. The rapport and information the therapist subsequently gains indirectly informs the parents about why this activity is helpful for the child.

Interpreting resistance. Interpretation often must begin by focusing on the family's resistance to coming or to working. In these cases, confirmation of shared resistance may come from surprising places, as it did in this brief example of the therapist's interpretation of resistance that is denied by the father and then confirmed by the son.

Therapist:	I think the family is saying that John is speaking for the shared reluctance to come that everyone feels.
Father:	I think you're wrong. I want *them* to come and get this solved. I'm tired of the grief they give me about getting here.
Mother:	Oh, I think my husband and I are together on this therapy.
John:	Well, on the way here, Mom and Dad were arguing, and Dad said, "I wish you didn't speak like that to the kids. That's why we have to go to that goddamned family therapy anyway."

Interpreting conflict. Interpretation is the vehicle through which we actively join the family, demonstrating that we have until then been joining them reflectively. Through interpretation, we reach to the core of the family experience. An accurate empathic interpretation is an ideal toward which we work by trial and error through clarifying comments. The point is not to always make the right interpretation, but rather to work along with the family to get it right.

We look for *confirmation* from them, often finding that it comes indirectly, as it does in individual therapy. For instance, we may assume that confirmation is given by an overly strong negative response, an emotional shift, or an indirect assent—as when a family responds to us by saying "We hadn't thought of that," which often means "We only knew it unconsciously."

Working in the here-and-now. This involves our use of events in the room, often cued by transference and countertransference, to stand for and thus permit work on larger issues. This differs from work on the review of the week's events or on the family's history, which are essentially there-and-then work. Both are standard material for us, but the advantage of the here-and-now is its emotional immediacy. At its heart is something I call the *core affective moment* in the session—when we catch an emotional exchange happening in the room and get the family to explore it.

Understanding the family as a small group. The family is more than a collection of individuals. It functions according to its own small-group dynamics. Its capacity to provide holding and relating to its members is reflected in those dynamics. We must be attuned to this level of interaction and take advantage of it. In Chapter 13, R. Shapiro described his application of Bion's (1961) work on small-group behavior to the understanding of the family's small-group dynamics. These dynamics—in the family as in any small group—are governed by shared unconscious assumptions that determine the nature of their pattern of mutual projective identifications and shared contextual holding. This understanding allows us to build the kind of interpretation that centers on the "because clause."

The "because clause." A useful feature of family group interpretation of conflict is the "because clause." Group analyst Ezriel coined this term when he organized group transference interpretations according to the required relationship the group seeks with its therapist and the avoided relationship it covers because of a calamity it dreads, such as abandonment (Ezriel 1952). We cannot reach this depth of understanding at first, but we can say, "You as a family do this maladaptive thing because you are afraid." The more specific we can be about what is feared, the more helped the family feels. But family members will often provide the because clause after we ask "Can you help me understand what could happen if you don't deal with me this way?" Thus we and they inch toward understanding.

Technique in Later-Phase Family Therapy

Working through. Long-term family therapy enables us to offer a depth of working through of family difficulty that is analogous to that which we do in long-term individual treatment. Chronic interaction patterns and projective identifications have to be undone repeatedly in many forms over an extended period in order to provide fundamental change. Most families will need such an opportunity if they are to experience extensive growth, although some well-functioning families who see us in a crisis may do well with brief therapy.

Termination. Each session has an ending, which relates to issues of loss and separation and prepares the family for eventual separation from the therapy and the therapist. In addition, the work on termination of the overall therapy usually provides review of the issues and an opportunity for further mourning and reworking.

Illustration of Technique from the Midphase of Therapy

The following session is an example of the midphase of treatment of the family that was also described in Chapter 22. It illustrates the use of play and the way in which the interface between the family and therapist can be understood through the therapist's countertransference. It also demonstrates the use of the group level of experience and the application of the here-and-now toward understanding.

The Simpsons had been in treatment for approximately a year. They had initially come for therapy because of sexual difficulty: Mrs. Simpson said that she "hated sex," while Mr. Simpson suffered from premature ejaculation. In addition, Mrs. Simpson was recurrently depressed, while Mr. Simpson had so much trouble with his memory that it interfered with his work as a computer programmer. They readily agreed to a family evaluation as well because of difficulty with their middle child, 5-year-old Alex, who soiled and wet his pants and was generally immature. The evaluation revealed that 3½-year-old Jeanette was also immature, seductive, and overexcited, perhaps oversexualized. The oldest boy, Eric, initially appeared to have solid latency development, but later revealed some unsublimated aggression.

I recommended a combination of family therapy, sex therapy for the parents, and individual therapy for the mother and Alex. The parents at that time elected to make individual therapy for Mrs. Simpson their priority. A year later, when I saw them again, the parents were in better shape: The year's intensive psychotherapy with a colleague had allowed Mrs. Simpson to flourish so that she was less frequently depressed, although she still had severe regressions and had been hospitalized for a few days several months ago. She had taken and maintained a part-time job, and she was now interested in sex. The couple agreed that they still needed sex therapy for their dysfunction, but the first priority for them now was family treatment, which we began while Mrs. Simpson continued in individual therapy.

The family therapy session I will describe came after approximately eight months of weekly family treatment. We had not been able to meet the previous week, but in the session two weeks earlier, we had investigated the centrality in the family of the mother's depression and had been able to understand the role of each of the other family members in relation to it. Today, two weeks after the previous session, they came in, the children leading eagerly as usual. Eric began by showing me pictures he had drawn of transformer robots called "demolishicons," the most powerful of which was "Demolishicor." He then began to build with the collection of colored blocks that all three of the children liked to use. Alex began to draw. The father suggested he draw Donald Duck. When he said he could not, the father said "He can *be* Donald Duck, but he can't draw it." Alex drew a Mickey Mouse face while Jeanette ate candy from a packet. They were all whispering.

I asked about the candy and the whispering. "Is there a secret that leads to the whispering?"

They denied that there was a secret. They had arrived a half hour early, and Mrs. Simpson had bought the candy because her mouth was dry from her antidepressant medication. Further discussion of Mrs. Simpson's medication brought forth memories of her recent hospitalization and the panic that had led to it. As she talked, Alex handed her a second picture he had been drawing of "Monstro the Whale," who, he said, had swallowed Geppetto, Pinocchio's puppet-maker father. Jeanette handed her mother a picture of the primary colors, which she then listed.

Thus far I felt that the activity in the room was avoidant, although not unusually so for the opening part of a session that followed an emotionally charged session and then a missed one. I was absorbing the experience of avoidance without comment.

Eric was now building a small building, which he said was a museum. It was the same sort of structure he had built the last time, and he told me that the same sort of thing was going on there—namely, "Nothing!" Eric wanted more cars and blocks to complete his design, which meant that Alex should surrender some of his. Mr. Simpson and Alex tried to help him think of how he might finish his project with what was available and without taking something from Alex.

Mrs. Simpson said, "Eric, if you can't have it the way you want it, it would be nice to try to have it another way."

Eric rejected her advice and began to pout.

Noting with some amusement that the museum was loaded with toy soldiers holding rifles aimed at me, I said half jokingly, "I see that all those guns are pointed right at me!"

The family laughed.

"Why am I the enemy? What bad thing am I about to do?" I asked.

Eric then took the Incredible Hulk, a great, green, unfriendly looking figure, and had it menace me playfully. It was coming to fight. I thought about the way in which the Hulk had often represented anger in the family. In a session some weeks previously, we had talked about Mrs. Simpson's feeling that she was an uncontrollable Hulk who wreaked damage on the family when she meant to work for its good. I felt I had now penetrated a quietly menacing anger which had first been expressed in Eric's trying to confiscate Alex's supply of toys, but which belonged in the transference to me.

I said, "Wait a minute while I find a toy to talk to the Hulk."

Mrs. Simpson handed me a baby doll, saying "Babies have been known to be vicious."

Her offer seemed to indicate her identification with me as the object of Eric's anger, so I handed the doll back to her and said, "Maybe the baby can find out what I've done wrong."

In retrospect, I could see that handing the doll back to her was also a wish to avoid Eric's anger, to aim it at the mother instead. In this wish I had joined the family pattern of directing angry accusation at the mother.

She obligingly took the doll and, through it, said to the Hulk, "Okay Hulk, what have I done?"

Eric said for the Hulk, "I'm mad because you won't let me rule."

Mrs. Simpson replied, "You can't always have your way, and pinching won't help." The doll and the Hulk wrestled.

Alex interjected, "The baby lost her diaper and she's going to poop all over the floor." He stepped in to fight playfully with the Hulk himself. The parents and I were all aware that Alex's encopresis had now entered the discussion about anger.

I said, "Alex said that when the Hulk attacked the baby, she would lose control of her poops. Can people control their poops when they fight?"

Alex did not answer, but a minute later he stopped the fight and, taking a car, knocked over the museum Eric had built.

Eric got angry, "Alex! Why did you have to do that?" He dropped the Hulk and began to rebuild the museum.

I felt a wash of sadness that the anger had gotten out of hand and that I could not help them stop it. My feelings were complicated. On the one hand, I felt a kind of glee that Alex had been able to be directly angry instead of soiling his pants. On the other, I felt identified with Eric and the beating he was taking. In this confusion of my own feelings, I could sense the family's confusion. I turned to the family to work on it with them.

I said, "When Alex got between the Hulk and the baby, he talked about people losing control of their poops. But instead of losing control of his own poops like a baby this time, he destroyed the museum and Eric got mad. How does this relate to family events?"

Mrs. Simpson said, "Eric acts aggressive, but if you return it in kind, he doesn't like it. He thinks his own actions are okay, but in others, they're wrong."

Lightly touching Eric's shoulder to get his attention because I felt this discussion would be hard for him, I said, "So you're saying, Mom, that Eric expects that he can play like the Hulk without objection. Then he's surprised if someone else gets mad."

Eric said, "Dr. Scharff, please don't touch me on the shoulder. I'm sunburned."

I realized that Eric was hurt, that he was not experiencing what I was saying as sympathetic, and that he'd like me to "lay off."

Eric was now rebuilding the museum. Alex put a family of small dolls in a car and drove over to visit the museum. I realized that Alex was continuing to act maturely, not like a soiling baby, but was playing out the aggressive problem in an age-appropriate way. Eric had Demolishicor attack Alex's family.

Mr. Simpson said, "Jeanette and Alex can't stop Eric. He ignores it when they try to defend themselves, and he overwhelms them."

Mrs. Simpson had now turned red, and she spat out, "I'm livid. When he does this, I get so mad. Right now, I just want to leave the room!"

I said, "Tell me about it instead."

She said, "I can't discuss my anger yet. I feel he's so stubborn, even after you point it out to him. It causes everyone else to be unhappy. He monopolizes things like the blocks. I just want to knock over that museum."

I turned to Eric, with whom I was again suddenly feeling thrown into sympathy as the victim of his mother's anger, and said, "Eric, does this happen at home?"

Nodding slowly with tears in his eyes, he acknowledged that it did.

Mr. Simpson said, "Usually things break down at this point. Eric, give some of the blocks to Alex and Jeanette."

Mrs. Simpson added, "Eventually we intervene. Then he's upset that we have forced his hand."

Mr. Simpson said, "Then Eric feels we favor Alex and Jeanette."

"Is that right?" I asked Eric.

He nodded sorrowfully, putting his head down on a table and becoming inert.

"What is this like from your growing up, Mrs. Simpson?" I asked.

"It's like my father," she said. "We would dread the time he came home. He'd line us up and yell at us, looking for someone who did something wrong. Then if one of us admitted something, he'd yell at that one. It was awful. He had to be in charge. He made the rules, and no one else mattered. And my mother didn't protect us from him. Just like I can't protect Jeanette and Alex."

"So you feel that Eric is like your father—so destructive?" I asked.

She nodded, beginning to sob. "And when I feel that and I get so mad at him, then I feel that I'm like my father, too. I hate that worse than anything in the world. I hated that man. And now I'm just like him. And then I hate Eric worse for making me feel that way."

I now felt sympathy for Mrs. Simpson, too, no longer identified with Eric against her "tyranny" but able to see the internal tyrant that victimized them all and that they dealt with by projecting it into one another. I felt sympathy for all of them, for the suffering they shared.

Seeing Eric now slumping over the table, his father said to him, "Come here, Son."

Eric got up slowly and was comforted by a loving hug from his father, draping himself across his chest while his father stroked his arm and back. I felt comforted watching them. At the same time, it did not get in the way of the work that was going on. I felt grateful to the father for taking care of Eric in a way that let the mother continue to speak. He was managing to hold the family in holding Eric. It let me keep my attention on Mrs. Simpson. Jeanette now went to her and climbed in her lap, comforting her, while Alex continued to play with the remains of the museum.

I said to Mrs. Simpson, "When you feel you're bad like your own father, you hate Eric, but you also hate yourself."

"Yes," she sobbed. "And I feel I've damaged him just the way I felt my father hurt me. And I can't undo it. There isn't any way out."

It was excruciating for me to remain in the room. I wondered what despair I had wrought. And at the same time, I felt almost exhilarated that the family was managing to hold a steady course through these straits of despair. I felt we were beginning to get a whole-family view of the trouble, and I felt less torn between competing sympathies and thus less angry at one family member for seeming to victimize another. I was drawn now to enlarge my understanding of the father's role, a feeling spurred by gratitude to him for comforting Eric so effectively a moment earlier.

Wanting to enlarge the field at this moment to include the father, I thought of how he tended to remain outside emotional moments, so I turned to him and asked directly, "Does this have any echoes for you, too, Mr. Simpson?"

He said, "My childhood wasn't so dramatic. At least I don't remember any events like that. Sometimes we'd be spanked with a belt for doing something wrong. I can't remember anything more."

Thinking of Mr. Simpson's inability to remember so many things, I said, "Of course, your not being able to remember is one of the things you struggle with. What kinds of things did you get spanked for?"

"I only remember one time," he said. "I was spanked for going over to a little girlfriend's house when I was about Eric's age. My dad womped me with his belt. It hurt. I can relate to Eric's sulking now when I think about it."

I turned to Eric. "Did you know about your dad's being spanked with a belt?" I asked. Eric shook his head, but he looked partially revived. I felt he was in touch with his parents' moving histories. Over the next couple of minutes, we established that in the father's recollection, what he had been punished for had had a sexual connotation: He had been strapped at least partly because he had disappeared with a girl.

I had been working to locate each individual in the family

struggle. Now I felt I could draw the events of the hour together, to offer the elements of a "because clause." I said, "Mrs. Simpson, you get so mad at Eric because he reminds you of your father. Then you feel like the bad parent yourself when you get so mad. He feels destructive and hopeless about getting your love. Mr. Simpson feels that insisting on any sexual overture will make you hate him like your angry father. Therefore, he tries to deny those interests to be 'the good father,' but he ends up feeling he's been strapped by his own angry father that he sees in you. So the two of you have a similar struggle, Mr. and Mrs. Simpson, when sexual matters are at issue. But in the setting with the children, it is often Eric who is in the role of bringing up the bad father. When he wants something for himself, he feels bad about it, and he becomes a Demolishicor. But he also does it in a way to protect you, Mrs. Simpson, from feeling that you are the Hulk or the Demolishicor yourself. Strangely, his way of behaving seems at first to protect you from those feelings of hating yourself by taking it on himself."

Mrs. Simpson said, "Yes, you're right. But when I want to bust up his museum because I don't want him to be so high and mighty, then I get to feel awful." At this moment, Alex took the car and broke down the last remains of the museum.

I said, "And it's at those times that Alex takes on Eric for you, Mrs. Simpson. It is part of the reason Alex is so hard to stop in his impulsive destructiveness. He used to do it by becoming an angry, pooping baby. These days he is getting more directly angry."

Jeanette climbed down from her mother's lap and began to play sweetly among the ruins. *In looking back on the session, I realize that Mrs. Simpson had said that it was the baby who could best take on the Hulk, and that I might have added that Jeanette was often put in the role of becoming the sweet baby who could save them from these issues. But one never thinks of all the things that might be said during a session.*

Mr. Simpson was rubbing Eric's head. I asked Mr. Simpson, "What do you think is happening now?"

He said, "Eric's hurt. He has a hard time when his mom's so unhappy with him. There are things he wants to do better and doesn't know how to change."

I asked Eric, "Is that right?"

He nodded.

Mrs. Simpson said, "He probably hates me back."

I said, "So you're afraid he'll hate you like you hate your father? But is there anything else you feel for Eric?"

"Oh, yes! I love him. Really I do. He's a wonderful kid. I don't know what else. I feel hopeless, like all the damage is done. He's already been hurt. I've done it. I hate myself." And she began to sob again.

Alex began to build a simpler house from the blocks, one to house the family car.

I said to Eric, "Do you still feel like crying?"

"Yes," he said. "I feel sad."

"I know you do," I said. "And I think this has been painful for everyone, your mom included. But it's important we talk about all this because it's underneath so much of what goes wrong at home. It gets in the way of the loving. In your family, Mrs. Simpson, you felt your dad hated you and you hated him, but you also wanted his love. What's so painful about being so mad at Eric is how much you care about him too, and feel for him being in a situation like yours. And you also envy him being so competent, getting so much from you and his father, and then wanting more. It makes you remember how you've felt that you had so little. This image of the bad father comes out at these moments of breakdown. It often keeps you, Mr. and Mrs. Simpson, from feeling that you can be good parents. Each of you has felt that you couldn't get enough to go around. It gets played out in the way we've seen. If someone wants too much, it's as though he is taking it from the rest of the family. And finally, I have a lead from Mr. Simpson's memory that this might also be operating in the sexual relationship. But that we'll have to explore with the two of you alone. What's important today is the way each member of the family plays out the anger over what's missing, and the pain when it goes wrong."

DISCUSSION

This description of one midphase therapy hour illustrated, among other things, the use of play for communication and for interpretation. Family and therapist shared an understanding of the children's play and of their interaction during play and talk. The children played while they listened, understood the allusions that their parents and the therapist made to the meaning of their play, and reacted to what was said in a mixure of words, play, and other nonverbal responses. Through the session, a shared understanding of the family's dilemma grew.

This understanding developed as individual contributions to the theme coalesced into an expression of an underlying unconscious assumption shared by the family as a group: that one person could get what was needed only at the expense of the rest of the family, and that parents were bound to be destructive. The countertransference reflected my vacillating identifications, which mirrored what family members felt as they struggled with the consequences of this shared unconscious assumption. I identified at various times with the oldest boy, with the parents as they handled sibling bickering, with the encopretic boy, and finally with the entire family as they struggled to manage their problems in providing centered holding to one another and contextual holding to themselves as a group (Scharff and Scharff 1987). At the end I was able to draw on this experience of shifting painful identifications, felt in my countertransference reactions, to formulate an understanding of the family in its struggle with the vicissitudes of individual needs and relationships, with the invasion of internal object relations into current experience, and with the difficulty of balancing one person's needs for love and understanding with those of others.

The availability of the therapist's own inner experience contributes to the shared venture of object relations family therapy. In this session, I have tried to describe the impact of the family's experience on me by spelling out my countertransference at several points as I tried to join with the family. This meant that when I spoke to them, I did not feel it was from an outside or superior position, but from inside their experience, which I felt in my own version as they felt it. Thus, this kind of work is carried out in an area of overlapping subjectivity, where the family's experience is shared by the therapist, who can then use his own first-hand data to understand the family's struggle from the inside.

The references to the mother's history, and a few moments later the father's, came at the moment of core affective experience in the family. The here-and-now of the therapy was at that moment linked to the mother's and father's internal object relations as expressed in their memories of earlier family events. That the link to the mother's object relations was more immediate makes sense in view of the fact that she was always more in touch with her internal life, but even with the father, who maintained a split-off repression of his early life, we were able to establish some connection to history. These formulations then gave access to the family members' hurt and longing, from which derived the because clause that enabled each of them to feel understood.

My countertransference response became conscious when I sensed that I was becoming overly identified with the older boy and felt in myself the family's worry that I, as a therapist, would also be a damaging parent. Using my countertransference, I joined in the family's struggle with their experience of the previous generation. Working my way out of this dilemma provided an effective way of sharing with the family the therapeutic task of coming to terms with the problematic internal object relations. In this session, the family contributed extensively to the interpretive process and to building the because clause. This is the kind of collaborative work that establishes an alliance with the therapist, allows the family to generate its own insight, and therefore leads to a renewal of the family's sense that it can provide holding for its members. Although much work remained to be done after this session, the family members were already more able to tolerate pain long enough to carry out the work for themselves, a precursor to their eventual readiness to terminate therapy.

Summary

Aspects of technique that were discussed and illustrated can be listed as follows:

- Providing a safe space in which to work,

- Managing the session,

- Using drawing and play to communicate,

- Attending to the contributions both of each family member and of the family as a small group,

- Noting the shared contextual transference of the entire family,

- Attending to the here-and-now experience,

- Participating in the core affective exchange,

- Using an object relations living history, which links the memory of the relationships with the previous generation to the parents' and child's inner object relations, and which ties the overall family pattern to the moment,

- Tolerating, taking in, reflecting, and digesting, all of which form the therapist's receptive containment,

- Using interpretation and countertransference to join the family in understanding.

At first family members feel understood by the therapist in one another's presence; later, in small steps, they feel more understood by one another and can thus feel more understanding of one another. The reciprocal sides of the process are interlocking and mutually reinforcing because the relationship between internal objects and feeling about self are closely interwoven. A change in one affects the other: Object and self are tied together in a never-ending cycle. The projection of parts of object and self into other psyches within the family system ensures that the well-being of the individuals and of the family as a whole go together. The technique of family therapy fosters entry into this projection system, allowing us to experience, observe, and ultimately analyze it, thus creating space within the family for reflection, understanding, change, and growth.

24

Play: An Aspect of the Therapist's Holding Capacity

JILL SAVEGE SCHARFF, M.D.

In family therapy, the therapist's task is to provide a helpful environment in which the whole family can participate and that the family can shape according to its unique expressions of need, thought, and feeling. The environment derives from the design of the office, from the way in which arrangements for consultation and therapy are handled, and from the ability to listen thoughtfully, to engage, to be affected, to tolerate anxiety, to reflect upon experience, and to communicate understanding intent. This ability has been called the therapist's *contextual holding capacity* (Scharff and Scharff 1987). Through this capacity, the therapist provides the context for expression of the family's usual patterns of relating, which derive from the complex interaction of present relationships and previous experience with the families of origin and with the present family during earlier periods of development.

The first step in creating the context is to communicate the expectation of seeing the entire family. To offer "whole-family understanding" (Zilbach 1986), the therapist needs the whole family at the session. If that family includes a crying baby or a messy toddler or an unstoppable 3-year-old, then the context must accommodate to their needs if the family is to feel fully held in the therapist's mind. This is where play comes in. Therapists need to be able to play with families who have young children. The contextual holding capacity has to include comfort with play—and the accompanying noise, mess, and regression, all common features of ordinary family life.

This sounds so obvious, it is a surprise to discover that it needs saying. It seems strange that a family therapist might not think of very young children as part of the family to be seen in treatment. But it is understandable that family therapists trained only to work with adults and adolescents might be reluctant to include younger children in family therapy. Some therapists deal with this by referring the case to a clinician who works with children and families. Unfortunately, others will exclude children under the age of 13 in order to reduce the family to compensate for their lack of experience with child psychotherapy. In such a case, the family, its younger children, and the therapist lose an opportunity. The family cannot express its total experience, the young children are discriminated against, and the therapist cannot share whole-family understanding with the family.

Therapists who are trained in working with children often specialize in individual play therapy and have not been trained in family work. Furthermore, the literature on working with young children in family therapy is sparse. Thus, until recently, many therapists have been uninformed about play in family therapy (Scharff and Scharff 1987, Zilbach 1986).

PROVISION OF THE PLAY SPACE

The family therapist needs an office large enough to allow for six to eight seats and for floor or table play space. It is best if the play space is in the middle of the circle of chairs so that the adults and therapist can watch or play while still talking. Locating the play space at the end of the room or in a corner may give a "go away and play" message, which devalues the play. Play is not a diversion; it is central to the work of family therapy with children.

I suggest that just a few toys be available so that the child is not overwhelmed with choices. Paper and a set of crayons and markers can be used by all ages, although some mothers, for good reason, prefer the markers to be out of toddlers' reach. Blocks are basic and require a few animals and vehicles to expand their usefulness for 4-year-olds and older children. I generally bring along only these materials when I am packing a bag for a teaching interview. But in my office I also like to have large paper, small black-skinned and white-skinned family dolls, a larger doll and doll bed, and some puppets. Intricate interlocking plastic blocks are fun for older children, but the smaller pieces should not be used with infants around. I do not use board games because I prefer to work with fantasy play, but I have supervised a student who made surprisingly fruitful use of them in family therapy.

These selections offer a range of media for self-expression and give the message that the family can have fun while working on serious issues. The provision of play materials creates a play space that reflects a readiness on the part of the therapist to engage in play.

In family therapy, the adults sit and talk while the children are playing; an adult sometimes joins the children on the floor or intervenes in a dispute over a toy. A microcosm of the situation at home is reproduced in the office. The therapist can observe how the parents support or suppress the play, how they manage sibling rivalry, and how they communicate with their children. The therapist models an interested but nonintrusive method of following and exploring the themes that emerge in the play so that the children's contribution is included. At the same time, the parents learn how to listen to their children at play, which improves the parents' capacity for holding the family.

HOW PLAY WORKS

Play is the young child's natural vehicle of expression. Moving, jumping, or crawling around the room with the toys, the child expresses ideas and feelings symbolically in the safety of displacement onto the toy characters or general play media. Both motor and symbolic routes of expression are important in reducing anxiety, thereby facilitating the child's comfort in the session. The importance of motor expression should not be minimized, for the child who has to sit on his need for physical release will hold back other aspects of himself as well. Play also offers the therapist who can follow its message an elaboration of the family's unconscious themes—including its unconscious transference to the therapist—often long before these are expressed verbally by the adults. Play can be taken as a gloss on the verbal themes or as a confirmation of understanding, or may actually lead the way to direct discussion of the family issues and conflicts expressed in displacement through the play.

Play may be more or less central to the family work from one session to another. The character of the play varies depending on the number and ages of the children. In the toddler's family, for instance, the play will not be clearly thematic, but will demonstrate problems of sharing, messing, destroying, getting into things, going to the bathroom, and needing support and discipline from parents; in the family of the latency-age child, on the other hand, the play will be more symbolic and less action-oriented. Adolescents may play with their sneakers, tear at holes in their jeans, shred tissue, or twist hair in addition to scribbling or sketching while talking. The importance of play varies not only from one family to another, but also within the same family and even in the therapist, who just cannot take it in as effectively at some times as at others. The therapist's countertransference is essential to understanding the play, especially when the themes are obscured by dense displacement or by the therapist's own barriers to comprehension.

As different play reflects varying degrees of displacement from the source of the conflict, so the therapist's response to play varies from simple observation without comment to full interpretation. Between these extremes, therapists may silently analyze their responses to the play, ask about the play, intervene through the play, or use the play as a metaphor to illustrate the family's spoken theme. Play may introduce new themes, and it may be a safe area in which to offer interpretation about conflict, relationships, and underlying anxiety. Then comes the work of reconstruction, linking the insights from play to family living and then watching the next piece of play in reaction to interpretation.

PLAY IN A DIAGNOSTIC CONSULTATION

The following case example, taken from two diagnostic sessions that were recorded on videotape, illustrates these varying uses of play in family therapy with very young children. It also shows the usefulness of a co-therapy model in that situation.

Mrs. W. complained to a clinic social worker that her overactive 16-month-old, Brooke, was into everything and was exhausting her. She admitted that Terri, her 4-year-old, was also demanding. When frustrated, Terri threw temper tantrums and refused to listen to reason.

Before the family moved East from Alaska, Mrs. W. had suffered from severe, unremitting migraine headaches for the last two months of her second pregnancy and had frequently taken codeine to relieve them; thus Brooke had gone through withdrawal after delivery. Mrs. W. felt guilty and worried that "being born an addict" had damaged this child so that she now cried too much. Her husband would come home at the end of the day and criticize her management of both children, asking why the toys had not been picked up. She felt bombarded by all of them.

The social worker arranged for a family evaluation by her consultant, Dr. David Scharff (D. S.), and me. (Although we teach together and have written together, he and I usually work alone, but this social worker was interested in having us use a co-therapy model for teaching and thus referred the case to both of us.)

The W.'s arrived with beautifully dressed children. Mrs. W. deftly moved our markers out of reach. Brooke immediately started to scream. Mrs. W. offered a crayon, which was rejected, and a pacifier, which stopped the yelling. Terri began to play purposefully with the crayons, producing a drawing, which the baby then scribbled on until she was pushed away. Every time Brooke was thwarted she opened her mouth and yelled until Mr. or Mrs. W. placated her with pacifier or bottle. Her mouth gaped like a big, dark hole, her grief never more than temporarily assuaged.

Mrs. W. explained, as she gave the screaming child her pacifier, that Brooke had been born addicted to codeine and had had to go through withdrawal. "I was up every hour with that fretful baby the first few months," she told us. "Even now," she added, "if I leave the room, Brooke cries." As if to prove her mother wrong, Brooke calmly walked away and handed a doll baby to D. S. and engaged him in a game of handing the doll back and forth. Surprised, Mrs. W. cried, "She's not clinging to me here!" *I thought there was a trace of unconscious outrage and disappointment in her tone.*

Mr. W. said, "I just leave Brooke to cry. Why can't my wife do that?"

Mrs. W. complained, "It's not possible. She cries more for me than for you." *I noted some pride in Mrs. W.'s remark. I had a sense of parental competition, the mother claiming ownership of the cry as a proof of love and the father achieving extinction of the cry as a proof of competence.*

Right on cue, Brooke began to cry and was settled with a bottle while Terri, playing with puppets, had the horse and rabbit fight about which of them had the crayon first. Meanwhile the parents were talking about Mr. W.'s need for a well-balanced checkbook and a tidy house and Mrs. W.'s inability to maintain the house or the checkbook because of all the errands to do and messes to clean up. Terri then tried to draw a picture for D. S. but could not complete it because Brooke scribbled on it. *Here the play reflected the theme, as the sibling play picked up mother's complaint of mess and interruption.*

Mrs. W. continued, "I can't get everything done. I'm exhausted because Brooke gets me up five times a night." Brooke had found a toy garbage can with a pop-up Oscar the Grouch inside. She was playing at opening and shutting the lid. Then she took it to her father.

I was thinking of referring to Brooke's portrayal of her mother as a grouch, but I thought that this might be too hurtful to Mrs. W. More important to me was the "now-you-see-him-now-you-don't" quality of the play, which I thought was a re-creation of Brooke's nighttime separations from and reunions with her mother. Her playful repetition indicated an attempt to work in the displacement on the conflict over separation. In handing her father the pop-up toy, Brooke was looking to him to validate her struggle. I was thinking that Brooke was indicating her readiness to be more separate if and when her parents would forego the gratification to their guilt that her clinging afforded.

I said, "It's hard for you to see Brooke through her period of frustration because you cannot bear the guilty feelings of seeing her suffer any more than she already did. I also think it's hard for you to admit how angry you are at her for all the suffering she has caused you."

"Well, I know I'm angry. That's why I put her in her room—otherwise I'd hit her," said Mr. W., while Mrs. W. looked disapprovingly at him.

The parents continued to discuss their complaints against each other and noted how they arose from the conflict between his mid-West German immigrant ethic and her laid-back New Mexico style. Mr. W. became very critical of his wife, and Brooke climbed on Mrs. W.'s lap and looked concerned while Mr. W. laughed and Mrs. W. jokingly patted his arm. I said, "You feel you have to laugh off angry feelings, but Brooke is aware of Mom's upset and her need for comfort." The parents responded by getting angrier. Terri created a diversion by painting all her toenails with purple marker. Brooke started to cry to get someone to take off her shoes, too.

I have not reported in full the number of times Brooke began to cry. But in the session, when I found myself counting them, I knew I was defending against the pain by quantifying it. When she cried, her mouth took over her face like a gaping black hole, and her shriek cut through me, tearing at my chest. The cries of children other than my own do not usually affect me intensely, but this cry had enormous power to evoke pain and helplessness. Then I realized that this was true for me only at the beginning of the cry, which began petering out even before the bottle was offered. And many times Brooke merely played with the bottle, pushing the nipple in and out. My countertransference response gelled with my detection of the game of peek-a-boo with the nipple as well as with the pop-up Oscar-the-Grouch garbage can.

This analysis enabled me to question the parents with empathy and yet distance about their experience of the cry. They too had wondered if Brooke would keep it up if not gratified by her mother. After we worked through their defenses against guilt and anger at Brooke, and after I showed them the evidence of her readiness, they agreed to try to let her cry it out.

The family was unable merely to hold the baby and allow her to quiet herself. It was painful to listen to her scream and watch her being fed when not hungry or see her aching mouth plugged with a pacifier. Because of guilt and anger, this family had a deficient holding capacity for a family member who needed to express helplessness, rage, and fear at separation. The family was afraid that the therapist would be similarly deficient. This has been referred to as the family's transference to our holding capacity (Scharff and Scharff 1987), and it emerged in their calling us before and after the session, checking the arrangements, and worrying that videotape might be used in a way that would harm them.

A week later, in the second diagnostic session, the parents returned to the theme of their discord over Mrs. W.'s failure to run a perfect house. Mrs. W. spoke of missing her mother, to whom she used to turn for advice and help. Meanwhile, Brooke was sitting on her mother's lap sucking on her pacifier while Terri built a low, enclosed building with two sheep inside and Oscar the Grouch coming outside. *I noticed that, as usual, Terri played contentedly and unobtrusively. She made the sort of low, enclosed building typical of 4-year-old girls, and her use of animals was also age-appropriate. I was wondering if the two sheep represented the parents from whom the Grouch — representingTerri or Brooke — was separating, or if the two sheep represented the identification between mother and baby and Oscar represented the growing child that differentiates from the symbiosis. There was not enough evidence to be sure.*
    As the parents spoke more heatedly about their differences, Brooke messed up Terri's game. Terri punched her. Brooke started to cry and returned to her mother's lap. D. S. noted that when the parents were talking about their difficulties, Brooke and Terri fought to draw anger onto themselves. "I think it's their way of trying to bust up the fight," he added, "Because it happens when you are talking about your anger at each other."
    "No! It's *any* time we talk, they fight," Mrs. W. corrected him.
    Mr. W. went on to describe Terri's insistence on being heard and on interrupting her parents' conversations. I said, "So Terri wants to bust up Mother's and Father's being together, as well as Mother's and Brooke's closeness." Terri responded in play: She had Oscar the Grouch peek out at some cows who wanted to play with him. "He's wondering what they're doing," she explained.
    At the surface level, this play mirrored Terri's distrust of her

parents' interest in her. It also suggested her oedipal concerns about dealing with exclusion by curiosity and the desire to watch. Now that these two levels of play had become apparent, I could see the fighting as having to do with a struggle about which developmental level would dominate. Would Terri regress to Brooke's level, or could Brooke advance to Terri's?

At this point, the girls began to play in parallel with no conflict, Brooke putting dolls in cars and saying bye-bye to them and Terri developing her animal play to include their getting on each other's backs. *Here the family was able to allow differentiation of individual needs for expression: Brooke was able to express preoedipal separation themes while Terri explored oedipal concerns about exclusion, inclusion, and, now more obviously, sexuality.*

Momentarily, we were able to talk of the children's envy of the parents' time together. But as we did, Terri again pushed Brooke off the game and again Brooke cried. Mrs. W. took Brooke on her lap and told Terri that she knew it was upsetting to have Brooke spoiling things but that she must not punch her. She said that she and her husband had read that a 4-year-old could be expected to be angry at a new baby. "So," she went on, "we were both very sensitive to Brooke's anger and did lots of special things for her, but she did not respond."

Obviously, Mrs. W. had meant to say that they had been sensitive to *Terri's* anger. I said that Mrs. W.'s slip suggested that she is preoccupied with Brooke—which Terri has picked up. Mrs. W. took my comment as a correction rather than an interpretation and went on describing, now using the correct name, how much Mr. W. still does with Terri, who is nonetheless jealous and says, "All you care about is Brooke."

Meanwhile, Terri had Oscar let the sheep out because he was lonely and wanted to play with them. *Here the play seemed to be focused at the preoedipal level of wanting to be part of the mother–infant couple.* So I said, "You can do so much for Terri as a 4-year-old now. But you can never make her your baby again. That's what she's jealous about."

"Well, yes," Mrs. W. said thoughtfully. "She will come to me and say 'Wa-wa, hold me.' Maybe she wants to be a baby again."

"Not a baby," I retorted, "*the* baby."

Now Terri was offensively guarding her play, fearing that Brooke would try to knock it down; Brooke, crying, went back to her mother. I commented on how Brooke's piercing cry was used to cement herself to her mother. "Exactly!" said Mrs. W. "I can't even take a shower in peace. As soon as I get out of the shower, I hear her crying." Immediately Brooke cried for no apparent reason and clung to her mother, who had to interrupt her example to talk soothingly to Brooke and then returned to her story to add that Terri didn't ever cry like that.

This was a reenactment in the session of a typical frustration sequence at home. Of course, this is a common complaint by the mother of a toddler, but two items distinguish it from the norm: (1) The mother continues to take a shower when no one else is there to mind the toddler, and (2) this toddler's cry is more wrenching than most.

Mrs. W. went on to describe that she gets mad at Terri, too. "Still," she said, "I don't yell. I just explain that I don't like what Terri did and then I give her a hug. Then Terri says, 'I'm bad. You think I'm bad and I hate you.' And at this," Mrs. W. added, "I get even more mad. I don't know where she learned it. We never say she is bad. We never say, 'I hate you.' We say, 'I don't like what you did, but I love you.' "

"That is the sort of advice to teachers and parents that sounds good," I agreed, "But surely only teachers can follow it all the time." Mrs. W. replied, "Yes, I'm a teacher, and it works well in the classroom." D. S. pointed out that Terri was nonetheless registering her mother's disapproval. Mrs. W. anxiously interrupted, "But we always follow criticism with affection so she won't feel bad."

D. S. asked, "So *who* won't feel bad?" Mrs. W. looked shocked, Mr. W. nodded gravely, and D. S. asked about how the parents had felt when criticized as children.

Here D. S. was taking an object relations history at a moment of affect. No formal history was taken, no genogram done, because these yield facts without linkage to the present interaction. He asked the question at a point when the history was alive in the session, recreated in the present relationships.

Mr. W. gave many graphic examples of not being good enough for his mother, who held grudges against him for every misdemeanor. I could see how he had become openly critical, blunt, and forthright so as not to be a pent-up, resentful person like his mother, but I could also see how he projected onto his wife an aspect of himself that his mother had felt to be not good enough. His wife, in contrast, did not want to hurt people by direct criticism and went to such lengths to be tactful and positive that she was left, not unlike her husband's mother, with a store of resentment.

Now near the end of the second session, Mrs. W. told of her childhood. Her sister, who had been blunt like her husband, had become manic-depressive. Any small comment could set her off, so Mrs. W. learned to tiptoe around her feelings. She tended to do the same with her children and her husband, a courtesy he, at least, did not require. As Mrs. W. related this, Terri and Brooke began to fight again and their father said, "Is your sister pickin' on you again?" *This was an example of sibling strain being discussed among one generation, being described as it recurs in the marital relationship through projective identification, and being enacted in the next generation through play in the session.*

Brooke was comforted and then went off to lie in the doll bed, very still. Mrs. W. talked of her own mother as her best chum. They would go out and do things as girls together while her father stayed to work in the yard. I could not make sense of Brooke's corpselike play until Mrs. W. said that her father had died working in his yard when she was 19. She was angry at him for allowing his perfectionism to drive him to an early death. Meanwhile, Terri was playing with the animals, telling D. S., "The horse is lonely, but the two sheep are not lonely 'cause they got each other." Here the same play that was earlier understood to be only about the child's exclusion from the parents now has the additional meaning of Mrs. W. and her sister missing their dead father or of Mrs. W. and her mother missing the father who stayed in the yard while they went out.

D. S. interpreted that it seemed important to Mrs. W. to not do things perfectly because her father's perfectionism had taken him away from her and her mother, intensifying their need for each other and ultimately killing him. He went on, "Now Mother worries that being compulsive will take her away from the children, and Father worries that not being compulsive will take her away from him. Instead, Mother is compulsive about never getting angry at her naughty and messy children just as she tried not to be mad at her father for dying."

That the information about Mrs. W.'s father's death came up near the end of the session was unconsciously determined by their problems with separation and loss, which were probably aggravated by the family's reaction to completing the diagnostic phase and not knowing whether they would be taken on in therapy or would be referred and thus lose one or both of the co-therapy team. It is also often found that affect-laden material comes up at the end of the session because of the protection afforded by there being too little time to explore it thoroughly.

TRANSFERENCE AND COUNTERTRANSFERENCE IN CO-THERAPY

The therapist becomes aware of feelings and reactions to the family group. These constitute the countertransference. Once the therapist separates responses unique to her own personality, the persisting feelings specific to this family then offer evidence about the family's inner relationships and fantasies that determine how it relates to others. In co-therapy, the reception of the family's inner object relations occurs mainly within the co-therapy relationship. Family qualities will often be split and experienced as residing in one or the other therapist. This gives a further example, usefully displaced away from the primary family relationships, which reflects the family's assignment of attributes to its various members, who then embody and enact the basic family conflict. The co-therapy relationship provides an exceptionally useful medium because it is open to process and review by both therapists. Their relationship becomes a subject for study by family and therapists in order to shed light on the family patterns of relating.

In the situation just described, I was experiencing some tension between D. S. and myself. I felt he was taking control and talking too much, oblivious to my contributions. But when I reviewed his actual behavior, I could not justify my feeling. It was time to scrutinize my countertransference.

I was feeling put down by my more talkative co-therapist husband. I felt he had more authority than I had, and I felt ignored by the family except when Mrs. W. caught my eye in a meaningful female-to-female glance as she described her awful man or child. I concluded that I was experiencing in the transference some of the denigration of the woman's role that Mrs. W. felt. I found myself envying my co-therapist's ease with play, yet I was becoming more and more dissatisfied with my work and his. We did not seem to be a cooperative team. And I could not find a way to say any of this. I examined this feeling, reviewed the reality bases for it, and concluded that I was receiving in the co-therapy relationship the couple's projection of a transference to us from their relationship that derived from the previous generation. I, as Mrs. W.'s father, felt remote, and then in danger of being killed off if I did not fight. As her mother, I felt pulled into being a buddy with her. As Mr. W.'s mother criticizing him, I was feeling that my co-therapist was not good enough. As Mr. W. himself, I was feeling that my spouse's work was not good enough. Like Terri, I was feeling interrupted, and like Brooke, I could not find words for my discomfort.

Without more information about Mr. W.'s father, I could not quite complete this preliminary object relations history as experienced in the countertransference. Nonetheless, by this point in the assessment, this countertransference analysis helped me to appreciate the transgenerational transmission of the object relations onto the marriage and then beyond into Terri, who felt so bad, and into Brooke, whose scream had to be suppressed. These projections from the parents seemed to represent the blackness, emptiness, and agony of the combined families of origin experienced in separation from the attentive mother and from the withdrawn and ultimately dead father.

After the diagnostic session, D. S. and I reviewed our countertransference, which had been experienced most acutely in me, just as in the couple Mrs. W. felt the most pain. After metabolizing our reactions, he and I would be free to work with these projections onto our relationship during on-going therapy. In this case, however, as in so many others, the family could not afford two therapists. Thus on-going co-therapy analysis was not possible, but the experience was registered and used to understand future responses of the therapist working alone.

This family accepted a recommendation for conjoint couple and family therapy with me, but not until it was reestablished that I, too, was a trained child and family psychiatrist. Throughout the interview, it emerged, the family had thought that I was there "as his wife." My countertransference response of denigration was now clarified and provided a basis for my future work with the family.

Summary

Comfort with play is an extension of the therapist's holding capacity. The therapist who can respond to play as communication facilitates the re-creation of the child's view of family life. The attitude of providing for, encouraging, and valuing play communicates interest in the children and in the forgotten childhood of the parents and sets the stage for creative, playful, yet serious work on family issues.

References

Adler, G. (1973). Hospital treatment of borderline patients. *American Journal of Psychiatry* 130:32–36.

Balint, M. (1959). *Thrills and Regressions.* New York: International Universities Press.

Benedek, T. (1959). Parenthood as a developmental phase. *Journal of the American Psychoanalytic Association* 7:389–417.

_____ (1970). The family as a psychologic field. In *Parenthood,* ed. E. J. Anthony and T. Benedek, pp. 109–136. Boston: Little, Brown.

Berkowitz, D. A., Shapiro, R. L., Zinner, J., and Shapiro, E. R. (1974a). Concurrent family treatment of narcissistic disorders. *International Journal of Psychoanalytic Psychotherapy* 3(4):379–396.

_____ (1974b). Family contributions to narcissistic disturbances in adolescents. *International Review of Psycho–Analysis* 1:353–362.

Bion, W. R. (1961). *Experiences in Groups and Other Papers.* London: Tavistock.

_____ (1967). *Second Thoughts.* London: Heinemann.

Blos, P. (1962). *On Adolescence: A Psychoanalytic Interpretation.* New York: The Free Press.

_____ (1967). The second individuation process of adolescence. *Psychoanalytic Study of the Child* 22:162–186.

Boszormenyi-Nagy, I. (1966). From family therapy to a psychology of relationships: fictions of the individual and fictions of the family. *Comprehensive Psychiatry* 7:408–423.

_____ (1967). Relational modes and meaning. In *Family Therapy and Disturbed Families*, ed. G. H. Zuk and I. Boszormenyi-Nagy, pp. 58–73. Palo Alto: Science and Behavior Books.

Bowen, M. (1965). Family psychotherapy with schizophrenia in the hospital and in private practice. In *Intensive Family Therapy*, ed. I. Boszormenyi-Nagy and J. L. Framo, pp. 213–243. New York: Hoeber Medical Division, Harper & Row.

Bowlby, J. (1969). *Attachment and Loss.* Vol. 1. *Attachment.* New York: Basic Books.

Box, S. (1981). Introduction: space for thinking in families. In *Psychotherapy with Families: An Analytic Approach*, ed. S. Box, B. Copley, J. Magagna, and E. Moustaki, pp. 1–8. London: Routledge and Kegan Paul.

_____ (1984). Containment and countertransference. Paper presented at the Washington School of Psychiatry, Fifth Annual Symposium on Psychoanalytic Family Therapy, Bethesda, MD, April.

Box, S., Copley, B., Magagna, J., and Moustaki, E., eds. (1981). *Psychotherapy with Families: An Analytic Approach.* London: Routledge and Kegan Paul.

Brodey, W. M. (1965). On the dynamics of narcissism: I. externalization and early ego development. *Psychoanalytic Study of the Child* 20:165–193.

Buber, M. (1957). Distance and relation. The William Alanson White memorial lecture, fourth series. *Psychiatry* 20:97–104.

Burlingham, D. (1955). Simultaneous analysis of mother and child. *Psychoanalytic Study of the Child* 10:165–186.

Dicks, H. V. (1963). Object relations theory and marital studies. *British Journal of Medical Psychology* 36:125–129.

_____ (1967). *Marital Tensions: Clinical Studies Towards a Psychoanalytic Theory of Interaction.* London: Routledge and Kegan Paul.

Edelson, M. (1970). *Sociotherapy and Psychotherapy.* Chicago: University of Chicago Press.

Edgcumbe, R., and Burgner, M. (1975). The phallic-narcissistic phase: a differentiation between preoedipal and oedipal aspects of phallic development. *Psychoanalytic Study of the Child* 30:160–180.

Eissler, K. R. (1950). Ego-psychological implications of the psychoanalytic treatment of delinquents. *Psychoanalytic Study of the Child* 5:97–121.

_____ (1953). The effect of the structure of the ego on psychoanalytic technique. *Journal of the American Psychoanalytic Association* 1:104–143.

Erikson, E. H. (1950). *Childhood and Society.* New York: W. W. Norton.

_____ (1956). The problem of ego identity. *Journal of the American Psychoanalytic Association* 4:56–121.

_____ (1958). *Young Man Luther: A Study in Psychoanalysis and History.* New York: W. W. Norton.

_____ (1959). *Identity and the Life Cycle.* New York: International Universities Press.

_____ (1965). Reality and actuality. *Journal of the American Psychoanalytic Association* 10:451–474.

Escalona, S. K. (1963). Patterns of infantile experience and the developmental process. *Psychoanalytic Study of the Child* 18:197–244.

Ezriel, H. (1952). Notes on psychoanalytic group therapy: II. interpretation and research. *Psychiatry* 15:119–126.

Fairbairn, W. R. D. (1952). *Psychoanalytic Studies of the Personality*. London: Routledge and Kegan Paul. Also published as *An Object Relations Theory of the Personality*. New York: Basic Books, 1954.

_____ (1954). Observations on the nature of hysterical states. *British Journal of Medical Psychology* 27(3):105–125.

_____ (1963). Synopsis of an object-relations theory of the personality. *International Journal of Psycho–Analysis* 44:224–225.

Framo, J. (1965). Rationale and techniques of intensive family therapy. In *Intensive Family Therapy: Theoretical and Practical Aspects*, ed. I. Boszormenyi-Nagy and J. Framo, pp. 143–212. New York: Harper & Row.

_____ (1970). Symptoms from a family transactional viewpoint. In *Family Therapy in Transition*, ed. N. Ackerman, pp. 125–171. Boston: Little, Brown.

Freud, A. (1936). *The Ego and Mechanisms of Defence*. New York: International Universities Press, 1946.

_____ (1958). Adolescence. *Psychoanalytic Study of the Child* 13:255–279.

_____ (1960). Introduction to Kata Levy: simultaneous analysis of a mother and her adolescent daughter. *Psychoanalytic Study of the Child* 15:378–380.

Freud, S. (1905). Three essays on the theory of sexuality. *Standard Edition* 7:135–245.

_____ (1912). Recommendations to physicians practicing psychoanalysis. *Standard Edition* 12:111–120.

_____ (1914). On narcissism: an introduction. *Standard Edition* 14:67–102.

_____ (1917). Introductory lectures on psychoanalysis. *Standard Edition* 16:448–463.

_____ (1921). Group psychology and the analysis of the ego. *Standard Edition* 18:69–143.

_____ (1923). The ego and the id. *Standard Edition* 19:12–66.

Frosch, J. (1971). Technique in regard to some specific ego defects in the treatment of borderline patients. *Psychiatric Quarterly* 45:216–220.

Giffin, M. E., Johnson, A. M., and Litin, E. M. (1960). The transmission of superego defects in the family. In *A Modern Introduction to the Family*, ed. N. W. Bell and E. F. Vogel, pp. 623–635. Riverside, NJ: Free Press.

Gosse, E. (1963). *Father and Son: A Study of Two Temperaments.* New York: W. W. Norton.

Greenacre, P. (1960). Considerations regarding the parent–infant relationship. *International Journal of Psycho-Analysis* 41:571–584.

Greenson, R. R. (1965). The working alliance and the transference neurosis. *Psychoanalytic Quarterly* 34:155–181.

Greenson, R. R., and Wexler, M. (1969). The nontransference relationship in the psychoanalytic situation. *International Journal of Psycho-Analysis* 50:27–39.

Hartmann, H. (1939). *Ego Psychology and the Problem of Adaptation.* New York: International Universities Press, 1958.

_____ (1950). Comments on the psychoanalytic theory of the ego. *Psychoanalytic Study of the Child* 5:74–95. Reprinted in *Essays on Ego Psychology.* New York: International Universities Press, 1964.

Hatfield, A. (1987). *Families of the Mentally Ill.* New York: Guilford Press.

Hellman, I. (1960). Simultaneous analysis of mother and child. *Psychoanalytic Study of the Child* 15:359–377.

Inhelder, B., and Piaget, J. (1958). *The Growth of Logical Thinking from Childhood to Adolescence.* New York: Basic Books.

Jacobson, E. (1954). The self and the object world: vicissitudes of their infantile cathexes and their influence on ideational and affective development. *Psychoanalytic Study of the Child* 9:75–127.

_____ (1961). Adolescent moods and the remodeling of psychic structures in adolescence. *Psychoanalytic Study of the Child* 16:164–183.

_____ (1964). *The Self and the Object World*. New York: International Universities Press.

Jaffe, D. S. (1968). The mechanism of projection: its dual role in object relations. *International Journal of Psycho-Analysis* 49:662–677.

Johnson, A. M. (1949). Sanctions for superego lacunae of adolescents. In *Searchlights on Delinquency*, ed. K. R. Eissler, pp. 225–245. New York: International Universities Press.

Johnson, A. M., and Szurek, S. A. (1952). The genesis of anti-social acting out in children and adults. *Psychoanalytic Quarterly* 21:313–343.

Kernberg, O. (1965). Notes on countertransference. *Journal of the American Psychoanalytic Association* 35:38–56.

_____ (1966). Structural derivatives of object relationships. *International Journal of Psycho–Analysis* 47:236–253.

_____ (1967). Borderline personality organization. *Journal of the American Psychoanalytic Association* 15:641–685.

_____ (1968). The treatment of patients with borderline personality organization. *International Journal of Psycho–Analysis* 49:600–619.

_____ (1970). Factors in the psychoanalytic treatment of narcissistic personalities. *Journal of the American Psychoanalytic Association* 15:51–85.

_____ (1972). Early ego integration and object relations. *Annals of the New York Academy of Science* 193:233–247.

_____ (1975). *Borderline Conditions and Pathological Narcissism*. New York: Jason Aronson.

_____ (1976). *Object Relations Theory and Pathological Narcissism*. New York: Jason Aronson.

Kleeman, J. (1966). Genital self-discovery during a boy's second year. *Psychoanalytic Study of the Child* 21:358–392.

_____ (1967). Genital self-stimulation in infant and toddler girls. In *Masturbation: From Infancy to Senescence*, ed. I. Marcus and J. Francis, pp. 77–106. New York: International Universities Press.

Klein, M. (1935). A contribution to the psychogenesis of manic-depressive states. *International Journal of Psycho-Analysis*, 16:145–174.

_____ (1946). Notes on some schizoid mechanisms. *International Journal of Psycho-Analysis* 27(3):99–110. Also published in *Envy and Gratitude and Other Works, 1946–1963*. New York: Delacorte Press, 1975.

_____ (1955). On identification. In *New Directions in Psychoanalysis*, ed. M. Klein, P. Heimann, and R. E. Money-Kyrle, pp. 309–345. New York: Basic Books.

_____ (1975a). *Love, Guilt and Reparation and Other Works, 1921–1945*. London: Hogarth Press and the Institute of Psycho-Analysis.

_____ (1975b). *Envy and Gratitude and Other Works, 1946–1963*. London: Hogarth Press and the Institute of Psycho-Analysis.

Kohut, H. (1968). The psychoanalytic treatment of narcissistic personality disorders. *Psychoanalytic Study of the Child* 23:86–113.

_____ (1971). *The Analysis of the Self*. New York: International Universities Press.

_____ (1972). Thoughts on narcissism and narcissistic rage. *Psychoanalytic Study of the Child* 27:360–400.

_____ (1977). *The Restoration of the Self*. New York: International Universities Press.

Laing, R. D. (1962). *The Self and Others: Further Studies in Sanity and Madness*. Chicago: Quadrangle.

Laing, R. D., Phillipson, H., and Lee, A. R. (1966). *Interpersonal Perception*. London: Tavistock.

Landis, B. (1970). Ego boundaries. *Psychological Issues Mono-*

graph No. 24, vol. 6. New York: International Universities Press.

Langs, R. (1976). *The Therapeutic Interaction.* Vol. 2. *A Critical Overview and Synthesis.* New York: Jason Aronson.

Laufer, M. (1965). Assessment of adolescent disturbances: the application of Anna Freud's diagnostic profile. *Psychoanalytic Study of the Child* 20:99–123.

_____ (1976). The central masturbation fantasy, the final sexual organization, and adolescence. *Psychoanalytic Study of the Child* 31:297–316.

Levy, K. (1960). Simultaneous analysis of a mother and her adolescent daughter: the mother's contribution to the loosening of the infantile object tie. *Psychoanalytic Study of the Child* 15:378–391.

Lichtenstein, H. (1961). Identity and sexuality: a study of their interrelationship in man. *Journal of the American Psychoanalytic Association* 9:179–260.

Lidz, T., Cornelison, A. R., Fleck, S., and Terry, D. (1957). The intrafamilial environment of schizophrenic patients: II. marital schism and marital skew. *American Journal of Psychiatry* 114:241–248.

Little, M. (1966). Transference in borderline states. *International Journal of Psycho–Analysis* 47:476–485.

Loewald, H. (1960). On the therapeutic action of psychoanalysis. *International Journal of Psycho–Analysis* 41:16–33.

_____ (1962). Internalization, separation, mourning, and the superego. *Psychoanalytic Quarterly* 31:483–504.

_____ (1966). Review of psychoanalytic concepts and the structural theory by J. Arlow and C. Brenner. *Psychoanalytic Quarterly* 35:430–436.

_____ (1979). The waning of the Oedipus Complex. In *Papers on Psychoanalysis*, pp. 384–404. New Haven: Yale University Press.

Mahler, M. S. (1952). On child psychosis and schizophrenia:

autistic and symbiotic infantile psychoses. *Psychoanalytic Study of the Child* 7:286–305.

_____ (1968). *On Human Symbiosis and the Vicissitudes of Individuation*. New York: International Universities Press.

_____ (1971). A study of the separation–individuation process and its possible application to borderline phenomena in the psychoanalytic situation. *Psychoanalytic Study of the Child* 26:403–424.

Mahler, M., Pine, F., and Bergman, A. (1975). *The Psychological Birth of the Human Infant: Symbiosis and Individuation*. New York: Basic Books.

Malin, A., and Grotstein, J. D. (1966). Projective identification in the therapeutic process. *International Journal of Psycho-Analysis* 47:26–31.

Masters, W. H., and Johnson, V. E. (1966). *Human Sexual Response*. Boston: Little, Brown.

_____ (1970). *Human Sexual Inadequacy*. Boston: Little, Brown.

Masterson, J. F. (1972). *Treatment of the Borderline Adolescent: A Developmental Approach*. New York: Wiley.

McDougall, J. (1978). Countertransference and primitive communication. In *Plea for a Measure of Abnormality*. New York: International Universities Press, 1980.

Mill, John Stuart (1969). *John Stuart Mill: Autobiography*. Ed. J. Stillinger. Boston: Houghton Mifflin.

Miller, E. J., and Rice, A. K. (1963). *Systems of Organization*. London: Tavistock.

Murphy, E., Silber, E., Coelho, G., Hamburg, D., and Greenburg, I. (1963). Development of autonomy and parent-child interaction in late adolescence. *American Journal of Orthopsychiatry* 33:643–652.

Ogden, T. (1982). *Projective Identification and Psychotherapeutic Technique*. New York: Jason Aronson.

_____ (1986). *The Matrix of the Mind: Object Relations and the Psychoanalytic Dialogue*. Northvale, NJ: Jason Aronson.

Olden, C. (1953). On adult empathy with children. *Psychoanalytic Study of the Child* 8:111–125.

Racker, H. (1957). The meanings and uses of countertransference. *Psychoanalytic Quarterly* 26:303–357.

Rangell, L. (1955). The return of the repressed "Oedipus." *Bulletin of the Menninger Clinic* 19:9–15. Also published in *Parenthood: Its Psychology and Psychopathology*, ed. E. J. Anthony and T. Benedek, pp. 325–334. Boston: Little, Brown, 1970.

Rapaport, D. (1958). The theory of ego autonomy: a generalization. *Bulletin of the Menninger Clinic* 22:13–35.

_____ (1959). *A Historical Survey of Psychoanalytic Ego Psychology.* New York: International Universities Press.

Reich, A. (1960). Pathological forms of self-esteem regulation. *Psychoanalytic Study of the Child* 15:215–232.

Rice, A. K. (1967). *Learning for Leadership: Interpersonal and Intergroup Relations.* London: Tavistock.

_____ (1969). Individual, group and intergroup processes. *Human Relations* 22:565–584.

Rioch, M. J. (1971). "All we like sheep . . ." (Isaiah 53:6): followers and leaders. *Psychiatry* 34:258–273.

Ritvo, S., and Solnit, A. J. (1958). Influences of early mother–child interaction on identification processes. *Psychoanalytic Study of the Child* 13:64–85.

Roland, A. (1967). The reality of the psychoanalytic relationship and situation in the handling of the transference resistance. *International Journal of Psycho–Analysis* 48:504–510.

Ryckoff, I., Day, J., and Wynne, L. (1959). Maintenance of stereotyped roles in the families of schizophrenics. *AMA Archives of Psychiatry* (July)1:93–98.

Schafer, R. (1968). *Aspects of Internalization.* New York: International Universities Press.

Scharff, D. (1982). *The Sexual Relationship: An Object Relations*

View of Sex and the Family. London: Routledge and Kegan Paul.

Scharff, D. E., and Scharff, J. S. (1987). *Object Relations Family Therapy*. Northvale, NJ: Jason Aronson.

Searles, H. (1959). Oedipal love in the countertransference. *International Journal of Psycho-Analysis* 40:180–190.

_____ (1963). Transference psychosis in the psychotherapy of schizophrenia. *International Journal of Psycho-Analysis* 44:249–281.

Segal, H. (1957). Notes on symbol formation. In *The Work of Hanna Segal: A Kleinian Approach to Clinical Practice*, pp. 49–65. New York: Jason Aronson, 1981.

_____ (1964). *Introduction to the Work of Melanie Klein*. London: Heinemann. Also published in enlarged edition, London: Hogarth Press, 1973.

Settlage, C. (1974). The technique of defense analysis in the psychoanalysis of an early adolescent. In *The Analyst and the Adolescent at Work*, ed. M. Harley, pp. 3–39. New York: Quadrangle.

Shapiro, E., Zinner, J., Shapiro, R., and Berkowitz, D. (1975). The influence of family experience on borderline personality development. *International Review of Psycho-Analysis* 2(4):399–411.

Shapiro, E., Shapiro, R., Zinner, J., and Berkowitz, D. (1977). The borderline ego and the working alliance: indications for family and individual treatment in adolescence. *International Journal of Psycho-Analysis* 58(1):77–89.

Shapiro, R. L. (1963). Adolescence and the psychology of the ego. *Psychiatry Journal for the Study of Interpersonal Process* 26:77–87.

_____ (1966). Identity and ego autonomy in adolescence. In *Science and Psychoanalysis*, ed. J. H. Masserman, pp. 16–24. New York: Grune & Stratton.

_____ (1967). The origin of adolescent disturbances in the

family: some considerations in theory and implications for therapy. In *Family Therapy and Disturbed Families,* ed. G. H. Zuk and I. Boszormenyi-Nagy, pp. 221–238. Palo Alto: Science and Behavior Books.

———— (1968). Action and family interaction in adolescence. In *Modern Psychoanalysis,* ed. J. Marmor, pp. 454–475. New York: Basic Books.

———— (1969). Adolescent ego autonomy and the family. In *Adolescence: Psychosocial Perspectives,* ed. G. Caplan and S. Lebovici, pp. 113–121. New York: Basic Books.

———— (1978). Ego psychology: its relation to Sullivan, Erikson, and object relations theory. In *American Psychoanalysis,* ed. J. Quen and E. Carlson, pp. 162–179. New York: Brunner/ Mazel.

———— (1979). Family dynamics and object-relations theory: an analytic, group-interpretive approach to family therapy. In *Adolescent Psychiatry: Developmental and Clinical Studies,* ed. S. C. Feinstein and P. L. Giovacchini, pp. 118–135. Chicago: University of Chicago Press.

———— (1989). The facilitating function of the family and the adolescent individuation process. In *Psychoanalysis and Psychosis,* ed. A. Silver, in press. New York: International Universities Press.

Shapiro, R. L., and Zinner, J. (1971). Family organization and adolescent development. In *Task and Organization,* ed. E. Miller, pp. 289–308. London: Wiley, 1976.

———— (1979). The adolescent, the family, and the group: boundary considerations. In *Exploring Individual and Organizational Boundaries,* ed. G. Lawrence, pp. 153–168. New York: Wiley.

Shapiro, R., Zinner, J., Berkowitz, D., and Shapiro, E. (1975). The impact of group experiences on adolescent development. In *The Adolescent in Group and Family Therapy,* ed. M. Sugar, pp. 87–104. New York: Brunner/Mazel.

Singer, M. T., and Wynne, L. C. (1965). Thought disorder and family relations of schizophrenics: III. methodology using projective techniques. IV. results and implications. *Archives of General Psychiatry* 12:187–212.

Sperling, M. (1950). Children's interpretation and reaction to the unconscious of their mothers. *International Journal of Psycho–Analysis* 31:36–41.

Stanton, A. H., and Schwartz, M. S. (1954). *The Mental Hospital: A Study of Institutional Participation in Psychiatric Illness and Treatment.* New York: Basic Books.

Sterba, R. (1934). The fate of the ego in analytic therapy. *International Journal of Psycho–Analysis* 15:117–126.

Stern, D. N. (1985). *The Interpersonal World of the Infant: A View from Psychoanalysis and Developmental Psychology.* New York: Basic Books.

Stone, L. (1961). *The Psychoanalytic Situation.* New York: International Universities Press.

Strachey, J. (1934). The nature of the therapeutic action of psychoanalysis. *International Journal of Psycho–Analysis* 15:127–159.

Sullivan, H. S. (1953). *The Collected Works of Harry Stack Sullivan.* New York: W. W. Norton.

Sutherland, J. (1963). Object relations theory and the conceptual model of psychoanalysis. *British Journal of Medical Psychology* 36:109–124.

Szurek, S. (1942). Genesis of psychopathic personality trends. *Psychiatry* 5:1–16.

_____ (1974). Concerning the sexual disorders of parents and their children. *Journal of Nervous and Mental Disease* 120:369–378.

Szurek, S., Johnson, A., and Falstein, E. (1942). Collaborative psychiatric therapy of parent–child problems. *American Journal of Orthopsychiatry* 12:511–516.

Tolpin, M. (1971). On the beginnings of a cohesive self. *Psychoanalytic Study of the Child* 26:316–352.

Turquet, P. M. (1971). Four lectures. The Bion hypothesis: the work group and the basic assumption group. Presented at the NIMH, Bethesda, Maryland. May 26, May 28, June 2, June 6.

—— (1974). Leadership, the individual and the group. In *Analysis of Groups*, ed. G. S. Gibbard, J. J. Hartman, and R. D. Mann, pp. 337–371. San Francisco: Jossey-Bass.

Vogel, E. F., and Bell, N. W. (1960). The emotionally disturbed child as the family scapegoat. In *A Modern Introduction to the Family*, ed. N. W. Bell and E. F. Vogel, pp. 382–397. Riverside, NJ: Free Press.

Wangh, M. (1962). The evocation of a proxy: a psychological manoeuvre, its use as a defence, its purposes and genesis. *Psychoanalytic Study of the Child* 17:451–469.

Williams, A. H. (1981). The micro-environment. In *Psychotherapy with Families: An Analytic Approach*, ed. S. Box, B. Copley, J. Magagna, and E. Moustaki, pp. 105–119. London: Routledge and Kegan Paul.

Williams, F. S. (1973). Family therapy: its role in adolescent psychiatry. In *Adolescent Psychiatry*, vol. 2, *Developmental and Clinical Studies*, ed. S. C. Feinstein and P. Giovacchini, pp. 324–339. New York: Basic Books.

Winnicott, D. W. (1951). Transitional objects and transitional phenomena. In *Collected Papers: Through Paediatrics to Psycho-Analysis*, pp. 229–242. London: Hogarth Press, 1975.

—— (1954). The depressive position in normal emotional development. In *Collected Papers: Through Paediatrics to Psycho-Analysis*, pp. 262–277. London: Hogarth Press, 1975.

—— (1956). Primary maternal preoccupation. In *Collected Papers: Through Paediatrics to Psycho-Analysis*, pp. 37–55. London: Hogarth Press, 1975.

—— (1960). The theory of the parent–infant relationship. *International Journal of Psycho-Analysis* 41:585–595. Also in

The Maturational Processes and the Facilitating Environment, pp. 37–55. London: Hogarth Press, 1972.

_____ (1969). The use of an object. *International Journal of Psycho–Analysis* 50:711–716.

_____ (1970). The mother–infant experience of mutuality. In *Parenthood*, ed. E. J. Anthony and T. Benedek, pp. 245–256. Boston: Little, Brown.

_____ (1971). *Playing and Reality*. London: Tavistock.

Wynne, L. C. (1965). Some indications and contraindications for exploratory family therapy. In *Intensive Family Therapy*, ed. I. Boszormenyi-Nagy and J. Framo, pp. 289–322. New York: Hoeber Medical Division, Harper & Row (1965), and New York: Brunner/Mazel, 1985.

Wynne, L. C., Ryckoff, I. M., Day, J., and Hirsch, S. I. (1958). Pseudo-mutuality in the family relations of schizophrenics. *Psychiatry* 21:205–220.

Wynne, L. C., and Singer, M. T. (1963). Thought disorder and family relations of schizophrenics: I. a research strategy. II. classification of forms of thinking. *Archives of General Psychiatry* 9:191–206.

Zetzel, E. R. (1958). Therapeutic alliance in the analysis of hysteria. In *The Capacity for Emotional Growth*, pp. 182–196. New York: International Universities Press, 1970.

_____ (1968). The so-called good hysteric. In *The Capacity for Emotional Growth*, pp. 229–245. New York: International Universities Press, 1970.

_____ (1970). *The Capacity for Emotional Growth*. New York: International Universities Press.

_____ (1971). A developmental approach to the borderline patient. *American Journal of Psychiatry* 127:867–871.

Zilbach, J. J. (1986). *Young Children in Family Therapy*. New York: Brunner/Mazel.

Zinner, J. (1976). The implications of projective identification for marital interaction. In *Contemporary Marriage: Structure*,

Dynamics, and Therapy, ed. H. Grunebaum and J. Christ, pp. 293–308. Boston: Little, Brown.

Zinner, J., and Shapiro, E. R. (1975). Splitting in families of borderline adolescents. In *Borderline States in Psychiatry,* ed. J. Mack, pp. 103–122. New York: Grune & Stratton.

Zinner, J., and Shapiro, R. L. (1972). Projective identification as a mode of perception and behaviour in families of adolescents. *International Journal of Psycho–Analysis* 53:523–530.

_____ (1974). The family group as a single psychic entity: implications for acting out in adolescence. *International Review of Psycho–Analysis* 1(1):179–186.

Index

479